A COLLEGE BOOK

OF

MODERN VERSE

A COLLEGE BOOK
OF
MODERN VERSE

Edited by

JAMES K. ROBINSON

and

WALTER B. RIDEOUT

HARPER & ROW, PUBLISHERS

New York

Acknowledgments

Grateful acknowledgment is made to the publishers and authors who granted permission to reprint the following poems and notes.

"Petition," "Which Side Am I Supposed To Be On?" and "Something Is Bound To Happen" from *The Collected Poetry of W. H. Auden*. Copyright 1934 by The Modern Library, Inc. Reprinted by permission of Random House, Inc.

"Look, Stranger, on This Island Now," "Now the Leaves Are Falling Fast," and "O for Doors To Be Open" from *The Collected Poetry of W. H. Auden*. Copyright 1937 by Random House, Inc. Reprinted by permission of Random House, Inc.

"Night Falls on China" from *The Collected Poetry of W. H. Auden*. Copyright 1939 by W. H. Auden and Christopher Isherwood. Reprinted by permission of Random House, Inc.

"Lay Your Sleeping Head, My Love," "Musée des Beaux Arts," "In Memory of W. B. Yeats," and "September 1, 1939" from *The Collected Poetry of W. H. Auden*. Copyright 1940 by W. H. Auden. Reprinted by permission of Random House, Inc.

"Who's Who," "Law Like Love," and "In Memory of Sigmund Freud" from *The Collected Poetry of W. H. Auden*. Copyright 1945 by W. H. Auden. Reprinted by permission of Random House, Inc.

"In Praise of Limestone" and "Nones" from *Nones,* by W. H. Auden. Copyright 1951 by W. H. Auden. Reprinted by permission of Random House, Inc.

"I Will Not Let Thee Go," "Elegy," "A Passer-by," "London Snow," "Nightingales," and "Low Barometer" from *Shorter Poems of Robert Bridges,* published by the Clarendon Press. By permission of the publisher.

"Black Tambourine," "Praise for an Urn," "Repose of Rivers," "At Melville's Tomb," "Voyages II," "To Brooklyn Bridge," "The River," "The Hurricane," and "The Broken Tower" from *Collected Poems of Hart Crane*. Black and Gold Library. Copyright 1933, Liveright Publishing Corp. By permission of the publisher.

"a man who had fallen among thieves," "somewhere i have never travelled,gladly beyond," "anyone lived in a pretty how town," "my father moved through dooms of love," and "pity this busy monster,manunkind" from *Poems 1934–1954,* by E. E. Cummings. Harcourt, Brace and Company. Copyright 1926, 1935, 1940, 1944, 1954 by E. E. Cummings. Reprinted by permission.

"The Listeners," "An Epitaph," "Fare Well," "Maerchen," and "Sunk Lyonesse," by Walter de la Mare. Permission granted by the Literary Trustees of Walter de la Mare and The Society of Authors as their Representative.

"Nostalgia" and "The Chart" from *The Burning Glass,* by Walter de la Mare. Copyright 1945 by Walter de la Mare. Reprinted by permission of The Viking Press, Inc.

"Go Far, Come Near" from *Winged Chariot and Other New Poems,* by Walter de la Mare. Copyright 1950, 1951 by Walter de la Mare. Reprinted by permission of The Viking Press, Inc.

"The Love Song of J. Alfred Prufrock," "Sweeney Among the Nightingales," "Gerontion," *The Waste Land,* "The Hollow Men," and *Ash-Wednesday* from *Collected Poems 1909–1935,* by T. S. Eliot. Copyright 1936, by Harcourt, Brace and Company, Inc. Reprinted by permission of the publishers.

"The World's End," "To an Old Lady," "This Last Pain," "Ignorance of Death," "Missing Dates," and "Manchouli" from *Collected Poems of William Empson.* Copyright 1935, 1940, 1949 by William Empson. Reprinted by permission of Harcourt, Brace and Company, Inc.

"The Vantage Point," "The Tuft of Flowers," "Mending Wall," "Home Burial," "After Apple-Picking," "The Wood-Pile," "The Road Not Taken," "The Oven Bird," "The Witch of Coös," "Fire and Ice," "Stopping by Woods on a Snowy Evening," "The Onset," "To Earthward," "Two Look at Two," "Once by the Pacific," "Acquainted with the Night," "The Lovely Shall Be Choosers," "Two Tramps in Mud Time," "Desert Places," "Neither Out Far Nor In Deep," "Design," "The Gift Outright," and "Directive" from *Complete Poems of Robert Frost.* Copyright 1930, 1939, 1943, 1947, 1949 by Henry Holt and Company, Inc. Copyright 1936, 1942, 1945, 1948 by Robert Frost. By permission of the publishers.

"The Pier-Glass," "Pure Death," "Recalling War," "Certain Mercies," "To Juan at the Winter Solstice," and "Cry Faugh" from *Collected Poems 1955,* by Robert Graves. Reprinted by permission of Doubleday & Company, Inc.

"Hap," "Neutral Tones," "Friends Beyond," "Nature's Questioning," "Drummer Hodge," "Shelley's Skylark," "To an Unborn Pauper Child," "The Darkling Thrush," "The Curate's Kindness," "The Man He Killed," "Channel Firing," "The Convergence of the Twain," "Rain on a Grave," "The Satin Shoes," "The Oxen," "In Time of 'The Breaking of Nations,'" "The Pedigree," "Midnight on the Great Western," and "An Ancient to Ancients" from Thomas Hardy, *Collected Poems of Thomas Hardy.* Copyright 1925 by the Macmillan Company, and used with permission.

"The Wreck of the Deutschland," "The Windhover," "Pied Beauty," "Binsey Poplars," "The Leaden Echo and the Golden Echo," "Spelt from Sibyl's Leaves," "I Wake and Feel the Fell of Dark," "Patience, Hard Thing!" "My Own Heart Let Me More Have Pity On," and "That Nature Is a Heraclitean Fire" from *Poems of Gerard Manley Hopkins,* Oxford University Press, London. Reprinted by permission of the publisher.

"1887," "Loveliest of Trees," "The Lads in Their Hundreds," "Is My Team Ploughing?" "On Wenlock Edge," "The Carpenter's Son," "Terence, This Is Stupid Stuff," "Epitaph on an Army of Mercenaries," and "Tell Me Not Here" from *The Collected Poems of A. E. Housman.* Copyright 1922, 1940 by Henry Holt and Company, Inc. Copyright 1936 by Barclays Bank, Ltd. By permission of Henry Holt and Company, Inc., New York, N.Y.

"90 North" from *Blood for a Stranger,* by Randall Jarrell, copyright 1942 by Harcourt, Brace and Company, Inc., and reprinted with their permission.

"Second Air Force," "Losses," and "The Death of the Ball Turret Gunner" from *Little Friend, Little Friend,* by Randall Jarrell. Copyright 1945 by Randall Jarrell. Dial Press. Reprinted by permission.

"The Orient Express" and "Seele im Raum" from *The Seven-League Crutches,* by Randall Jarrell. Copyright 1951 by Randall Jarrell. Reprinted by permission of Harcourt, Brace and Company, Inc.

Randall Jarrell's notes on "Second Air Force," "The Death of the Ball Turret Gunner," and "Seele im Raum" from the Introduction to *Selected Poetry,* by Randall Jarrell. Alfred A. Knopf, Inc., 1955, by permission of the publisher.

"Night," "Birds," "Apology for Bad Dreams," and "Promise of Peace" from *Roan Stallion, Tamar and Other Poems,* by Robinson Jeffers. Copyright 1925 and renewed 1953 by Robinson Jeffers. Reprinted by permission of Random House, Inc.

"Hurt Hawks" from *The Selected Poetry of Robinson Jeffers.* Copyright 1928 and renewed 1956 by Robinson Jeffers. Reprinted by permission of Random House, Inc.

"The Eye" from *The Double Axe and Other Poems,* by Robinson Jeffers. Copyright 1948 by Robinson Jeffers. Reprinted by permission of Random House, Inc.

"Ocean" from *Hungerfield and Other Poems,* by Robinson Jeffers. Copyright 1954 by Robinson Jeffers. Reprinted by permission of Random House, Inc.

"The Wild Common," "Last Words to Miriam," "Ballad of Another Ophelia," "Hymn to Priapus," "Song of a Man Who Has Come Through," and "Snake" from *Collected Poems,* by D. H. Lawrence. Copyright 1929 by Jonathan Cape and Harrison Smith, Inc.; 1957 by Frieda Lawrence Ravagli. Reprinted by permission of The Viking Press, Inc., N.Y.

"Rest from Loving," "Nearing Again the Legendary Isle," and "Come, Live with Me" from *Collected Poems 1954,* by C. Day Lewis. Hogarth Press, Ltd., reprinted by permission of the publisher.

"Maple and Sumach" and "Departure in the Dark" from *Short Is the Time,* by C. Day Lewis. Copyright 1940, 1943 by Oxford University Press, Inc. Reprinted by permission.

"Birthday Poem for Thomas Hardy" from *Poems 1943–1947,* by C. Day Lewis. Copyright 1948 by Oxford University Press, Inc. Reprinted by permission.

"Colloquy in Black Rock," "The Quaker Graveyard in Nantucket," "As a Plane Tree by the Water," "After the Surprising Conversions," and "Where the Rainbow Ends" from *Lord Weary's Castle,* by Robert Lowell. Copyright 1944, 1946 by Robert Lowell. Reprinted by permission of Harcourt, Brace and Company, Inc.

"Falling Asleep over the Aeneid" from *The Mills of the Kavanaughs,* by Robert Lowell. Copyright 1946, 1947, 1948, 1950, 1951 by Robert Lowell. Reprinted by permission of Harcourt, Brace and Company, Inc.

"The Silent Slain," "Ars poetica," and "The End of the World" from *Streets in the Moon,* by Archibald MacLeish. Houghton Mifflin Company, by permission of the publisher.

"You, Andrew Marvell," "Immortal Autumn," and " 'Not Marble Nor the Gilded Monuments' " from *New Found Land,* by Archibald MacLeish. Houghton Mifflin Company, by permission of the publisher.

"Pole Star" from *Public Speech,* by Archibald MacLeish. Copyright 1936 by

Archibald MacLeish. Reprinted by permission of Rinehart & Company, Inc., New York, publishers.

"Perseus" and "Sunday Morning" from *Poems 1925–1940,* by Louis MacNeice. Copyright 1937 by Louis MacNeice. Reprinted by permission of Random House, Inc.

"The Sunlight on the Garden" from *Poems 1925–1940,* by Louis MacNeice. Copyright 1937, 1939 by Louis MacNeice. Reprinted by permission of Random House, Inc.

"Les Sylphides" from *Poems 1925–1940,* by Louis MacNeice. Copyright 1940 by Louis MacNeice. Reprinted by permission of Random House, Inc.

"Explorations" and "Neutrality" from *Springboard 1941–1944,* by Louis MacNeice. Copyright 1945 by Random House, Inc. Reprinted by permission of Random House, Inc.

"Poetry," "The Steeple-Jack," "No Swan So Fine," "The Pangolin," "What are Years?" "The Mind is an Enchanting Thing," "In Distrust of Merits," and "Armour's Undermining Modesty" from Marianne Moore, *Collected Poems.* Copyright 1951 by Marianne Moore and used with permission of The Macmillan Company.

"From My Diary, July 1914," "Dulce et Decorum Est," "Futility," "Anthem for Doomed Youth," "Apologia pro Poemate Meo," and "Strange Meeting" from *Poems,* by Wilfred Owen. All rights reserved; reprinted by permission of New Directions.

"Sestina: Altaforte," "A Virginal," "The Return," "Lament of the Frontier Guard," and *Hugh Selwyn Mauberley* from *Personae,* by Ezra Pound. Copyright 1926 by Ezra Pound. Reprinted by permission of New Directions.

"Canto I" and "Canto II" from *The Cantos of Ezra Pound.* All rights reserved. Copyright 1948 by Ezra Pound. Reprinted by permission of New Directions.

"Bells for John Whiteside's Daughter," "Here Lies a Lady," and "Captain Carpenter," copyright 1924, 1945 by Alfred A. Knopf, Inc. Reprinted from *Selected Poems by John Crowe Ransom,* by permission of Alfred A. Knopf, Inc.

"Vision by Sweetwater," copyright 1927 by Alfred A. Knopf, Inc. Reprinted from *Two Gentlemen in Bonds,* by John Crowe Ransom, by permission of Alfred A. Knopf, Inc.

"Piazza Piece," "Antique Harvesters," and "The Equilibrists," copyright 1927, 1945 by Alfred A. Knopf, Inc. Reprinted from *Selected Poems by John Crowe Ransom,* by permission of Alfred A. Knopf, Inc.

"Prelude to an Evening" and "Painted Head," copyright 1945 by Alfred A. Knopf, Inc. Reprinted from *Selected Poems by John Crowe Ransom,* by permission of Alfred A. Knopf, Inc.

"George Crabbe," "Luke Havergal," and "Cliff Klingenhagen" from *Children of the Night,* by Edwin Arlington Robinson. Reprinted by permission of Charles Scribner's Sons.

"How Annandale Went Out," "Miniver Cheevy," and "For a Dead Lady" from *The Town Down the River,* by Edwin Arlington Robinson. Copyright 1910 by Charles Scribner's Sons; 1938 by Ruth Nivison. Reprinted by permission of the publishers.

"The Gift of God," "Hillcrest," "Eros Turannos," "Bewick Finzer," "The Man Against the Sky," "The Dark Hills," "Mr. Flood's Party," "The Sheaves," and "Karma" from Edwin Arlington Robinson, *Collected Poems of Edwin Arlington*

Robinson. Copyright 1937 by The Macmillan Company and used with permission.

"Open House," copyright 1941 by Theodore Roethke; "Four for Sir John Davies," copyright 1952 by The Atlantic Monthly Company; "The Waking," copyright 1953 by Theodore Roethke. From *The Waking: Poems, 1933–1953,* by Theodore Roethke, reprinted by permission of Doubleday & Company, Inc.

"Moss-Gathering," copyright 1946 by Editorial Publications, Inc.; "Dolor," copyright 1947 by Theodore Roethke; "The Lost Son," copyright 1947 by the University of the South. From *The Lost Son and Other Poems,* by Theodore Roethke, reprinted by permission of Doubleday and Company, Inc.

"The Dome of Sunday" from *Poems 1940–1953,* by Karl Shapiro. Copyright 1941 by Karl Jay Shapiro. Reprinted by permission of Random House, Inc.

"The Potomac" from *Poems 1940–1953,* by Karl Shapiro. Copyright 1941 by Karl Shapiro. Reprinted by permission of Random House, Inc.

"Nostalgia," from *Poems 1940–1953,* by Karl Shapiro. Copyright 1942 by Karl Jay Shapiro. Reprinted by permission of Random House, Inc.

"V-Letter" from *Poems 1940–1953,* by Karl Shapiro. Copyright 1943 by Karl Shapiro. Reprinted by permission of Random House, Inc.

"Elegy for a Dead Soldier" from *Poems 1940–1953,* by Karl Shapiro. Copyright 1944 by Karl Shapiro. Reprinted by permission of Random House, Inc.

"The Sickness of Adam" from "Adam and Eve" in *Poems 1940–1953,* by Karl Shapiro. Copyright 1951 by Karl Shapiro. Reprinted by permission of Random House, Inc.

"An Old Woman," copyright 1946, 1949, 1954 by Edith Sitwell; "Still Falls the Rain," copyright 1948, 1954 by Edith Sitwell; "The Shadow of Cain," copyright 1948, 1949, 1954 by Edith Sitwell; "Sir Beelzebub," copyright 1949, 1954 by Edith Sitwell; "Street Song," copyright 1949, 1954 by Edith Sitwell. Reprinted by permission of the publishers, Vanguard Press, Inc., from *The Collected Poems of Edith Sitwell.*

The notes on "An Old Woman" and "The Shadow of Cain" from *The Collected Poems of Edith Sitwell,* by Dame Edith Sitwell. Copyright 1954 by Dame Edith Sitwell. Published by Vanguard Press, Inc.

"What I Expected" and "The Landscape Near an Aerodrome" from *Collected Poems 1928–1953,* by Stephen Spender. Copyright 1934 by The Modern Library, Inc. Reprinted by permission of Random House, Inc.

"An Elementary School Classroom" and "Two Armies" from *Collected Poems 1928–1953,* by Stephen Spender. Copyright 1942 by Stephen Spender. Reprinted by permission of Random House, Inc.

"The Trance" and "Seascape" from *Collected Poems 1928–1953,* by Stephen Spender. Copyright 1947 by Stephen Spender. Reprinted by permission of Random House, Inc.

"Anecdote of the Jar," "To the One of Fictive Music," and "Sea Surface Full of Clouds," copyright 1923, 1931, 1954 by Wallace Stevens. Reprinted from *The Collected Poems of Wallace Stevens,* by permission of Alfred A. Knopf, Inc.

"Domination of Black," "The Snow Man," "Le Monocle de Mon Oncle," "A High-Toned Old Christian Woman," "The Emperor of Ice-Cream," "Sunday Morning," "Peter Quince at the Clavier," and "Thirteen Ways of Looking at a Blackbird," copyright 1931, 1954 by Wallace Stevens. Reprinted from *The Collected Poems of Wallace Stevens,* by permission of Alfred A. Knopf, Inc.

"The Idea of Order at Key West," copyright 1935, 1936, 1954 by Wallace

Stevens. Reprinted from *The Collected Poems of Wallace Stevens*, by permission of Alfred A. Knopf, Inc.

"The Glass of Water" and "The Sense of the Sleight-of-Hand Man," copyright 1942, 1954 by Wallace Stevens. Reprinted from *The Collected Poems of Wallace Stevens*, by permission of Alfred A. Knopf, Inc.

"Credences of Summer," copyright 1947, 1954 by Wallace Stevens. Reprinted from *The Collected Poems of Wallace Stevens*, by permission of Alfred A. Knopf, Inc.

"The Force That Through the Green Fuse Drives the Flower," "Altarwise by Owl-Light," "After the Funeral," "Ballad of the Long-Legged Bait," "A Refusal To Mourn," "Poem in October," "Ceremony after a Fire Raid," "Fern Hill," and "Do Not Go Gentle into That Good Night" from *Collected Poems*, by Dylan Thomas. Copyright 1953 by Dylan Thomas. Reprinted by permission of New Directions.

"Tract," "The Widow's Lament in Springtime," "Spring and All," "To Elsie," "Rain," "The Yachts," and "These" from *Collected Earlier Poems* by William Carlos Williams. Copyright 1950, 1951 by William Carlos Williams. Reprinted by permission of New Directions Books.

"Burning the Christmas Greens" from *Collected Later Poems*, by William Carlos Williams. Copyright 1950, 1951 by William Carlos Williams. Reprinted by permission of New Directions Books.

"Preface" to *Paterson*, Book I, by William Carlos Williams. Copyright 1950 by William Carlos Williams. Reprinted by permission of New Directions Books.

"The Lake Isle of Innisfree," "Adam's Curse," "That the Night Come," "September 1913," "The Magi," "The Fisherman," "An Irish Airman Foresees His Death," "Easter 1916," "The Second Coming," "A Prayer for My Daughter," "Leda and the Swan," "Sailing to Byzantium," "The Tower," "Two Songs from a Play," "Among School Children," "Byzantium," "Crazy Jane Talks with the Bishop," "Lapis Lazuli," "Under Ben Bulben," and "News for the Delphic Oracle" from W. B. Yeats, *The Collected Poems of W. B. Yeats*, copyright 1950 by The Macmillan Company and used with permission.

Preface

We have prepared *A College Book of Modern Verse* because there is no single collection of modern poetry that we as teachers have found satisfactory for use in upper-class courses in modern poetry or in modern British or American literature. Although existing collections have their excellences, no important one is organized with classroom use as its primary objective.

Bearing in mind the practices in the teaching of poetry that have developed in recent years, we have rejected the "shotgun" method of including a few poems by each of a hundred or so poets of markedly varied abilities. Instead, we recognize the need for concentration on several poems by a few authors. Consequently we have limited the number of poets represented to thirty-two—sixteen British and sixteen American—whose reputations seem to us most firmly established. In choosing our poets and their poems we have been governed by no conscious critical bias; they belong to many schools and to no school at all. At least two-thirds of the sixteen names from either country would probably appear on any list of sixteen prepared by any teacher of modern literature.

Of our thirty-two poets, ten are outstanding, and so we have weighted our offerings in their favor. We include the most poems and the most lines by Hardy, Hopkins, Yeats, Auden, and Thomas; Robinson, Frost, Stevens, Pound, and Eliot. No poem is presented in abridged form, yet we have included not only those long poems one would expect, such as Eliot's *The Waste Land* and Robinson's "The Man Against the Sky," but also Hopkins' "The Wreck of the Deutschland," Yeats's "The Tower," Thomas' "The Ballad of the Long-Legged Bait," and Pound's *Hugh Selwyn Mauberley*.

As teachers of poetry, we know that every selection must be reliable as to text, and that each poet's work should be presented in some intelligible sequence. For each poem we have tried to reproduce the most recent text presumably authorized by the poet himself. Titles, punctuation, spelling, capitalization, and stanzaic divisions have been respected. The arrangement of poems is chronological in each section, and we have dated the selections according to their first appearance in an original collection.

Believing that our editorial function is to be both helpful and unobtrusive, we have placed at the end of our book a considerable body of notes. For each poet we give a biographical sketch, a list of his important writings, a selective

xii PREFACE

list of biographical and critical studies of him, and comments on the poems designed to illuminate words or phrases not readily to be found in standard reference works. We do not feel it to be our function to impose on the reader our interpretations of individual poems. Instead, we have made available a selective list of analyses and explications by well-known critics of modern poetry.

For various kinds of assistance in preparing this book, we wish to thank Richard Ellmann, John J. Espey, Bergen Evans, Thomas M. Folds, Robert Mayo, Edmund B. Perry, Felix Pollak, Jeanette Rideout, Carl Roebuck, Stuart Small, Norman Spector, and Hugh B. Staples.

Although the planning and preparation of *A College Book of Modern Verse* has been a joint undertaking, Robinson has been primarily responsible for the British poets, Rideout for the American.

WALTER B. RIDEOUT
JAMES K. ROBINSON

Northwestern University
May, 1958

Table of Contents

MODERN AMERICAN POETS

COMMENTARY

INDEXES

MODERN BRITISH POETS

Thomas Hardy

1840-1928

HAP

(1898)

[handwritten: sonnet 14 line poem]

If but some vengeful god would call to me
From up the sky, and laugh: "Thou suffering thing,
Know that thy sorrow is my ecstasy,
That thy love's loss is my hate's profiting!"

Then would I bear it, clench myself, and die,
Steeled by the sense of ire unmerited;
Half-eased in that a Powerfuller than I
Had willed and meted me the tears I shed.

But not so. How arrives it joy lies slain,
And why unblooms the best hope ever sown?   10
—Crass Casualty obstructs the sun and rain,
And dicing Time for gladness casts a moan. . . .
These purblind Doomsters had as readily strown
Blisses about my pilgrimage as pain.

[handwritten margin notes: then he would know there was someone; but life is chance; philosophic meditation]

NEUTRAL TONES

(1898)

We stood by a pond that winter day,
And the sun was white, as though chidden of God,
And a few leaves lay on the starving sod;
  —They had fallen from an ash, and were gray.

3

Your eyes on me were as eyes that rove
Over tedious riddles of years ago;
And some words played between us to and fro
 On which lost the more by our love.

The smile on your mouth was the deadest thing
Alive enough to have strength to die;   10
And a grin of bitterness swept thereby
 Like an ominous bird a-wing. . . .

Since then, keen lessons that love deceives,
And wrings with wrong, have shaped to me
Your face, and the God-curst sun, and a tree,
 And a pond edged with grayish leaves.

FRIENDS BEYOND
(1898)

William Dewy, Tranter Reuben, Farmer Ledlow late at plough,
 Robert's kin, and John's, and Ned's,
And the Squire, and Lady Susan, lie in Mellstock churchyard now!

"Gone," I call them, gone for good, that group of local hearts and heads;
 Yet at mothy curfew-tide,
And at midnight when the noon-heat breathes it back from walls and leads,

They've a way of whispering to me—fellow-wight who yet abide—
 In the muted, measured note
Of a ripple under archways, or a lone cave's stillicide:

"We have triumphed: this achievement turns the bane to antidote, 10
 Unsuccesses to success,
Many thought-worn eves and morrows to a morrow free of thought.

"No more need we corn and clothing, feel of old terrestial stress;
 Chill detraction stirs no sigh;
Fear of death has even bygone us: death gave all that we possess."

W. D.—"Ye mid burn the old bass-viol that I set such value by."
Squire.—"You may hold the manse in fee,
 You may wed my spouse, may let my children's memory of me die."

Lady S.—"You may have my rich brocades, my laces; take each household
    key;
    Ransack coffer, desk, bureau;   20
  Quiz the few poor treasures hid there, con the letters kept by me."

Far.—"Ye mid zell my favourite heifer, ye mid let the charlock grow,
    Foul the grinterns, give up thrift."
Far. Wife.—"If ye break my best blue china, children, I shan't care or ho."

All.—"We've no wish to hear the tidings, how the people's fortunes shift;
    What your daily doings are;
  Who are wedded, born, divided; if your lives beat slow or swift.

"Curious not the least are we if our intents you make or mar,
    If you quire to our old tune,
If the City stage still passes, if the weirs still roar afar."   30

—Thus, with very gods' composure, freed those crosses late and soon,
    Which, in life, the Trine allow
(Why, none witteth), and ignoring all that haps beneath the moon.

William Dewy, Tranter Reuben, Farmer Ledlow late at plough,
    Robert's kin, and John's, and Ned's,
And the Squire, and Lady Susan, murmur mildly to me now.

NATURE'S QUESTIONING
(1898)

    When I look forth at dawning, pool,
      Field, flock, and lonely tree,
      All seem to gaze at me
Like chastened children sitting silent in a school;

    Their faces dulled, constrained, and worn,
      As though the master's ways
      Through the long teaching days
Had cowed them till their early zest was overborne.

    Upon them stirs in lippings mere
      (As if once clear in call,   10
      But now scarce breathed at all)—
"We wonder, ever wonder, why we find us here!

"Has some Vast Imbecility,
   Mighty to build and blend,
   But impotent to tend,
Framed us in jest, and left us now to hazardry?

"Or come we of an Automaton
   Unconscious of our pains? . . .
   Or are we live remains
Of Godhead dying downwards, brain and eye now gone?   20

"Or is it that some high Plan betides,
   As yet not understood,
   Of Evil stormed by Good,
We the Forlorn Hope over which Achievement strides?"

Thus things around. No answerer I . . .
   Meanwhile the winds, and rains,
   And Earth's old glooms and pains
Are still the same, and Life and Death are neighbours nigh.

DRUMMER HODGE

(1902)

I

They throw in Drummer Hodge, to rest
   Uncoffined—just as found:
His landmark is a kopje-crest
   That breaks the veldt around;
And foreign constellations west
   Each night above his mound.

II

Young Hodge the Drummer never knew—
   Fresh from his Wessex home—
The meaning of the broad Karoo,
   The Bush, the dusty loam,   10
And why uprose to nightly view
   Strange stars amid the gloam.

III

Yet portion of that unknown plain
    Will Hodge for ever be;
His homely Northern breast and brain
    Grow to some Southern tree,
And strange-eyed constellations reign
    His stars eternally.

SHELLEY'S SKYLARK
The Neighbourhood of Leghorn: March 1887

(1902)

Somewhere afield here something lies
In Earth's oblivious eyeless trust
That moved a poet to prophecies—
A pinch of unseen, unguarded dust:

The dust of the lark that Shelley heard,
And made immortal through times to be;—
Though it only lived like another bird,
And knew not its immortality:

Lived its meek life; then, one day, fell—
A little ball of feather and bone;   10
And how it perished, when piped farewell,
And where it wastes, are alike unknown.

Maybe it rests in the loam I view,
Maybe it throbs in a myrtle's green,
Maybe it sleeps in the coming hue
Of a grape on the slopes of yon inland scene.

Go find it, faeries, go and find
That tiny pinch of priceless dust,
And bring a casket silver-lined,
And framed of gold that gems encrust;   20

And we will lay it safe therein,
And consecrate it to endless time;
For it inspired a bard to win
Ecstatic heights in thought and rhyme.

TO AN UNBORN PAUPER CHILD
(1902)

I

Breathe not, hid Heart: cease silently,
And though thy birth-hour beckons thee,
    Sleep the long sleep:
    The Doomsters heap
Travails and teens around us here,
And Time-wraiths turn our songsingings to fear.

II

Hark, how the peoples surge and sigh,
And laughters fail, and greetings die:
    Hopes dwindle; yea,
    Faiths waste away,   10
Affections and enthusiasms numb;
Thou canst not mend these things if thou dost come.

III

Had I the ear of wombèd souls
Ere their terrestrial chart unrolls,
    And thou wert free
    To cease, or be,
Then would I tell thee all I know,
And put it to thee: Wilt thou take Life so?

IV

Vain vow! No hint of mine may hence
To theeward fly: to thy locked sense   20
    Explain none can
    Life's pending plan:
Thou wilt thy ignorant entry make
Though skies spout fire and blood and nations quake.

V

Fain would I, dear, find some shut plot
Of earth's wide wold for thee, where not
    One tear, one qualm,
    Should break the calm.
But I am weak as thou and bare;
No man can change the common lot to rare.   30

VI

Must come and bide. And such are we—
Unreasoning, sanguine, visionary—
    That I can hope
    Health, love, friends, scope
In full for thee; can dream thou wilt find
Joys seldom yet attained by humankind!

THE DARKLING THRUSH

(1902)

I leaned upon a coppice gate
    When Frost was spectre-gray,
And Winter's dregs made desolate
    The weakening eye of day.
The tangled bine-stems scored the sky
    Like strings from broken lyres,
And all mankind that haunted nigh
    Had sought their household fires.

The land's sharp features seemed to be
    The Century's corpse outleant;   10
His crypt the cloudy canopy,
    The wind his death-lament.
The ancient pulse of germ and birth
    Was shrunken hard and dry,
And every spirit upon earth
    Seemed fervourless as I.

At once a voice burst forth among
    The bleak twigs overhead
In a full-hearted evensong
    Of joy illimited;   2c
An aged thrush, frail, gaunt and small,
    In blast-beruffled plume,
Had chosen thus to fling his soul
    Upon the growing gloom.

[handwritten annotation in left margin: nature is dismal / symbolically dismal / means life]

but old bird
may see hope

So little cause for carolings
   Of such ecstatic sound
Was written on terrestrial things
   Afar or nigh around,
That I could think there trembled through
   His happy good-night air   30
Some blessed hope, whereof he knew
   And I was unaware.

THE CURATE'S KINDNESS
A Workhouse Irony

(1909)

I

traditional stanza

I thought they'd be strangers aroun' me,
   But she's to be there!
Let me jump out o' waggon and go back and drown me
   At Pummery or Ten-Hatches Weir.

II

I thought: "Well, I've come to the Union—
   The workhouse at last—
After honest hard work all the week, and Communion
   O' Zundays, these fifty years past.

III

" 'Tis hard; but," I thought, "never mind it:
   There's gain in the end: 10
And when I get used to the place I shall find it
   A home, and may find there a friend.

IV

"Life there will be better than t'other,
   For peace is assured.
The men in one wing and their wives in another
   Is strictly the rule of the Board."

V

Just then one young Pa'son arriving
   Steps up out of breath
To the side o' the waggon wherein we were driving
   To Union; and calls out and saith: 20

VI

"Old folks, that harsh order is altered,
    Be not sick of heart!
The Guardians they poohed and they pished and they paltered
    When urged not to keep you apart.

VII

" 'It is wrong,' I maintained, 'to divide them,
    Near forty years wed.'
'Very well, sir. We promise, then, they shall abide them
    In one wing together,' they said."

VIII

Then I sank—knew 'twas quite a foredone thing
    That misery should be   30
To the end! . . . To get freed of her there was the one thing
    Had made the change welcome to me.

IX

To go there was ending but badly;
    'Twas shame and 'twas pain;
"But anyhow," thought I, "thereby I shall gladly
    Get free of this forty years' chain."

X

I thought they'd be strangers aroun' me,
    But she's to be there!
Let me jump out o' waggon and go back and drown me
    At Pummery or Ten-Hatches Weir.   40

THE MAN HE KILLED
(1909)

"Had he and I but met
    By some old ancient inn,
We should have sat us down to wet
    Right many a nipperkin!

"But ranged as infantry,
    And staring face to face,
I shot at him as he at me,
    And killed him in his place.

"I shot him dead because—
  Because he was my foe,
Just so: my foe of course he was;
  That's clear enough; although   10

"He thought he'd 'list, perhaps,
  Off-hand-like—just as I—
Was out of work—had sold his traps—
  No other reason why.

"Yes; quaint and curious war is!
  You shoot a fellow down
You'd treat if met where any bar is,
  Or help to half-a-crown."   20

CHANNEL FIRING
(1914)

That night your great guns, unawares,
Shook all our coffins as we lay,
And broke the chancel window-squares,
We thought it was the Judgment-day

And sat upright. While drearisome
Arose the howl of wakened hounds:
The mouse let fall the altar-crumb,
The worms drew back into the mounds,

The glebe cow drooled. Till God called, "No;
It's gunnery practice out at sea   10
Just as before you went below;
The world is as it used to be:

"All nations striving strong to make
Red war yet redder. Mad as hatters
They do no more for Christés sake
Than you who are helpless in such matters.

"That this is not the judgment-hour
For some of them's a blessed thing,
For if it were they'd have to scour
Hell's floor for so much threatening. . . .   20

"Ha, ha. It will be warmer when
I blow the trumpet (if indeed
I ever do; for you are men,
And rest eternal sorely need)."

So down we lay again. "I wonder,
Will the world ever saner be,"
Said one, "than when He sent us under
In our indifferent century!"

And many a skeleton shook his head.
"Instead of preaching forty 'year,"   30
My neighbour Parson Thirdly said,
"I wish I had stuck to pipes and beer."

Again the guns disturbed the hour,
Roaring their readiness to avenge,
As far inland as Stourton Tower,
And Camelot, and starlit Stonehenge.

THE CONVERGENCE OF THE TWAIN
Lines on the Loss of the "Titanic"

(1914)

I
In a solitude of the sea
Deep from human vanity,
And the Pride of Life that planned her, stilly couches she.

II
Steel chambers, late the pyres
Of her salamandrine fires,
Cold currents thrid, and turn to rhythmic tidal lyres.

III

Over the mirrors meant
  To glass the opulent
The sea-worm crawls—grotesque, slimed, dumb, indifferent.

IV

Jewels in joy designed   10
  To ravish the sensuous mind
Lie lightless, all their sparkles bleared and black and blind.

V

Dim moon-eyed fishes near
  Gaze at the gilded gear
And query: "What does this vaingloriousness down here?"

VI

Well: while was fashioning
  This creature of cleaving wing,
The Immanent Will that stirs and urges everything

VII

Prepared a sinister mate
  For her—so gaily great   20
A Shape of Ice, for the time far and dissociate.

VIII

And as the smart ship grew
  In stature, grace, and hue,
In shadowy silent distance grew the Iceberg too.

IX

Alien they seemed to be;
  No mortal eye could see
The intimate welding of their later history,

X

Or sign that they were bent
  By paths coincident
On being anon twin halves of one august event,   30

XI

Till the Spinner of the Years
  Said "Now!" And each one hears,
And consummation comes, and jars two hemispheres.

RAIN ON A GRAVE

(1914)

Clouds spout upon her
   Their waters amain
   In ruthless disdain,—
Her who but lately
   Had shivered with pain
As at touch of dishonour
If there had lit on her
So coldly, so straightly
   Such arrows of rain:

One who to shelter   10
   Her delicate head
Would quicken and quicken
   Each tentative tread
If drops chanced to pelt her
   That summertime spills
   In dust-paven rills
When thunder-clouds thicken
   And birds close their bills.

Would that I lay there
   And she were housed here!   20
Or better, together
Were folded away there
Exposed to one weather
We both,—who would stray there
When sunny the day there,
   Or evening was clear
   At the prime of the year.

Soon will be growing
   Green blades from her mound,
And daisies be showing   30
   Like stars on the ground,
Till she form part of them—
Ay—the sweet heart of them,
Loved beyond measure
With a child's pleasure
   All her life's round.

THE SATIN SHOES

(1914)

"If ever I walk to church to wed,
　　As other maidens use,
And face the gathered eyes," she said,
　　"I'll go in satin shoes!"

She was as fair as early day
　　Shining on meads unmown,
And her sweet syllables seemed to play
　　Like flute-notes softly blown.

The time arrived when it was meet
　　That she should be a bride;　　　　　　　10
The satin shoes were on her feet,
　　Her father was at her side.

They stood within the dairy door,
　　And gazed across the green;
The church loomed on the distant moor,
　　But rain was thick between.

"The grass-path hardly can be stepped.
　　The lane is like a pool!"—
Her dream is shown to be inept,
　　Her wish they overrule.　　　　　　　　20

"To go forth shod in satin soft
　　A coach would be required!"
For thickest boots the shoes were doffed—
　　Those shoes her soul desired. . . .

All day the bride, as overborne,
　　Was seen to brood apart,
And that the shoes had not been worn
　　Sat heavy on her heart.

From her wrecked dream, as months flew on,
    Her thought seemed not to range.   30
"What ails the wife," they said anon,
    "That she should be so strange?" . . .

Ah—what coach comes with furtive glide—
    A coach of closed-up kind?
It comes to fetch the last year's bride,
    Who wanders in her mind.

She strove with them, and fearfully ran
    Stairward with one low scream:
"Nay—coax her," said the madhouse man,
    "With some old household theme."   40

"If you will go, dear, you must fain
    Put on those shoes—the pair
Meant for your marriage, which the rain
    Forbade you then to wear."

She clapped her hands, flushed joyous hues:
    "O yes—I'll up and ride
If I am to wear my satin shoes
    And be a proper bride!"

Out then her little foot held she,
    As to depart with speed;   50
The madhouse man smiled pleasantly
    To see the wile succeed.

She turned to him when all was done,
    And gave him her thin hand,
Exclaiming like an enraptured one,
    "This time it will be grand!"

She mounted with a face elate,
    Shut was the carriage door;
They drove her to the madhouse gate,
    And she was seen no more. . . .   60

Yet she was fair as early day
  Shining on meads unmown,
And her sweet syllables seemed to play
  Like flute-notes softly blown.

THE OXEN
(1916)

Christmas Eve, and twelve of the clock,
  "Now they are all on their knees,"
An elder said as we sat in a flock
  By the embers in hearthside ease.

We pictured the meek mild creatures where
  They dwelt in their strawy pen,
Nor did it occur to one of us there
  To doubt they were kneeling then.

So fair a fancy few would weave
  In these years! Yet, I feel,   10
If someone said on Christmas Eve,
  "Come; see the oxen kneel

"In the lonely barton by yonder coomb
  Our childhood used to know,"
I should go with him in the gloom,
  Hoping it might be so.

IN TIME OF "THE BREAKING OF NATIONS"
(1916)

Only a man harrowing clods
  In a slow silent walk
With an old horse that stumbles and nods
  Half asleep as they stalk.

Only thin smoke without flame
  From the heaps of couch grass:
Yet this will go onward the same
  Though Dynasties pass.

Yonder a maid and her wight
   Come whispering by;   10
War's annals will fade into night
   Ere their story die.

THE PEDIGREE

(1917)

I

   I bent in the deep of night
Over a pedigree the chronicler gave
As mine; and as I bent there, half-unrobed,
The uncurtained panes of my window-square let in the wa-
     tery light
   Of the moon in its old age:
And green-rheumed clouds were hurrying past where mute
     and cold it globed
Like a drifting dolphin's eye seen through a lapping wave.

II

   So, scanning my sire-sown tree,
And the hieroglyphs of this spouse tied to that,
   With offspring mapped below in lineage,   10
   Till the tangles troubled me,
The branches seemed to twist into a seared and cynic face
  Which winked and tokened towards the window like a
     Mage
   Enchanting me to gaze again thereat.

III

   It was a mirror now,
  And in it a long perspective I could trace
Of my begetters, dwindling backward each past each
   All with the kindred look,
  Whose names had since been inked down in their place
   On the recorder's book,   20
Generation and generation of my mien, and build, and brow.

IV

And then did I divine
That every heave and coil and move I made
Within my brain, and in my mood and speech,
    Was in the glass portrayed
As long forestalled by their so making it;
The first of them, the primest fuglemen of my line,
Being fogged in far antiqueness past surmise and reason's
        reach.

V

    Said I then, sunk in tone,
"I am merest mimicker and counterfeit!—   30
    Though thinking, *I am I,
And what I do I do myself alone.*"
—The cynic twist of the page thereat unknit
Back to its normal figure, having wrought its purport wry,
    The Mage's mirror left the window-square,
And the stained moon and drift retook their places there.

MIDNIGHT ON THE GREAT WESTERN
(1917)

In the third-class seat sat the journeying boy,
    And the roof-lamp's oily flame
Played down on his listless form and face,
Bewrapt past knowing to what he was going,
    Or whence he came.

In the band of his hat the journeying boy
    Had a ticket stuck; and a string
Around his neck bore the key of his box,
That twinkled gleams of the lamp's sad beams
    Like a living thing.   10

What past can be yours, O journeying boy
    Towards a world unknown,
Who calmly, as if incurious quite
On all at stake, can undertake
    This plunge alone?

Knows your soul a sphere, O journeying boy,
    Our rude realms far above,
Whence with spacious vision you mark and mete
This region of sin that you find you in,
      But are not of?   20

AN ANCIENT TO ANCIENTS

(1922)

Where once we danced, where once we sang,
    Gentlemen,
The floors are sunken, cobwebs hang,
And cracks creep; worms have fed upon
The doors. Yea, sprightlier times were then
Than now, with harps and tabrets gone,
    Gentlemen!

Where once we rowed, where once we sailed,
    Gentlemen,
And damsels took the tiller, veiled   10
Against too strong a stare (God wot
Their fancy, then or anywhen!)
Upon that shore we are clean forgot,
    Gentlemen!

We have lost somewhat, afar and near,
    Gentlemen,
The thinning of our ranks each year
Affords a hint we are nigh undone,
That we shall not be ever again
The marked of many, loved of one,   20
    Gentlemen.

In dance the polka hit our wish,
    Gentlemen,
The paced quadrille, the spry schottische,
"Sir Roger."—And in opera spheres
The "Girl" (the famed "Bohemian"),
And "Trovatore," held the ears,
    Gentlemen.

This season's paintings do not please,
   Gentlemen,   30
Like Etty, Mulready, Maclise;
Throbbing romance has waned and wanned;
No wizard wields the witching pen
Of Bulwer, Scott, Dumas, and Sand,
   Gentlemen.

The bower we shrined to Tennyson,
   Gentlemen,
Is roof-wrecked; damps there drip upon
Sagged seats, the creeper-nails are rust,
The spider is sole denizen;   40
Even she who voiced those rhymes is dust,
   Gentlemen!

We who met sunrise sanguine-souled,
   Gentlemen,
Are wearing weary. We are old;
These younger press; we feel our rout
Is imminent to Aïdes' den,—
That evening shades are stretching out,
   Gentlemen!

And yet, though ours be failing frames, 50
   Gentlemen,
So were some others' history names,
Who rode their track light-limbed and fast
As these youth, and not alien
From enterprise, to their long last,
   Gentlemen.

Sophocles, Plato, Socrates,
   Gentlemen,
Pythagoras, Thucydides,
Herodotus, and Homer,—yea,   60
Clement, Augustin, Origen,
Burnt brightlier towards their setting-day,
   Gentlemen.

And ye, red-lipped and smooth-browed; list,
      Gentlemen;
Much is there waits you we have missed;
Much lore we leave you worth the knowing,
Much, much has lain outside our ken:
Nay, rush not: time serves: we are going,
      Gentlemen.   70

Gerard Manley Hopkins
1844-1889

THE HABIT OF PERFECTION
(1918)

Elected Silence, sing to me
And beat upon my whorlèd ear,
Pipe me to pastures still and be
The music that I care to hear.

Shape nothing, lips; be lovely-dumb:
It is the shut, the curfew sent
From there where all surrenders come
Which only makes you eloquent.

Be shellèd, eyes, with double dark
And find the uncreated light: 10
This ruck and reel which you remark
Coils, keeps, and teases simple sight.

Palate, the hutch of tasty lust,
Desire not to be rinsed with wine:
The can must be so sweet, the crust
So fresh that come in fasts divine!

Nostrils, your careless breath that spend
Upon the stir and keep of pride,
What relish shall the censers send
Along the sanctuary side!   20

O feel-of-primrose hands, O feet
That want the yield of plushy sward,
But you shall walk the golden street
And you unhouse and house the Lord.

And, Poverty, be thou the bride
And now the marriage feast begun,
And lily-coloured clothes provide
Your spouse not laboured-at nor spun.

THE WRECK OF THE DEUTSCHLAND
(1918)

To the
happy memory of five Franciscan Nuns
exiles by the Falk Laws
drowned between midnight and morning of
Dec. 7th, 1875

PART THE FIRST

1

Thou mastering me
God! giver of breath and bread;
World's strand, sway of the sea;
Lord of living and dead;
Thou hast bound bones and veins in me, fastened me flesh,
And after it almost unmade, what with dread,
Thy doing: and dost thou touch me afresh?
Over again I feel thy finger and find thee.

2

I did say yes
O at lightning and lashed rod;   10
Thou heardst me truer than tongue confess
Thy terror, O Christ, O God;
Thou knowest the walls, altar and hour and night:
The swoon of a heart that the sweep and the hurl of thee
trod
Hard down with a horror of height:
And the midriff astrain with leaning of, laced with fire of stress.

3

The frown of his face

Before me, the hurtle of hell

Behind, where, where was a, where was a place?

I whirled out wings that spell   20

And fled with a fling of the heart to the heart of the Host.

My heart, but you were dovewinged, I can tell,

Carrier-witted, I am bold to boast,

To flash from the flame to the flame then, tower from the grace to
the grace.

4

I am soft sift

In an hourglass—at the wall

Fast, but mined with a motion, a drift,

And it crowds and it combs to the fall;

I steady as a water in a well, to a poise, to a pane,

But roped with, always, all the way down from the tall

Fells or flanks of the voel, a vein   31

Of the gospel proffer, a pressure, a principle, Christ's gift.

5

I kiss my hand

To the stars, lovely-asunder

Starlight, wafting him out of it; and

Glow, glory in thunder;

Kiss my hand to the dappled-with-damson west:

Since, tho' he is under the world's splendour and wonder,

His mystery must be instressed, stressed;

For I greet him the days I meet him, and bless when I under-
stand.   40

6

Not out of his bliss

Springs the stress felt

Nor first from heaven (and few know this)

Swings the stroke dealt—

Stroke and a stress that stars and storms deliver,

That guilt is hushed by, hearts are flushed by and melt—

But it rides time like riding a river

(And here the faithful waver, the faithless fable and miss).

7

It dates from day
Of his going in Galilee;   50
Warm-laid grave of a womb-life grey;
Manger, maiden's knee;
The dense and the driven Passion, and frightful sweat;
Thence the discharge of it, there its swelling to be,
Though felt before, though in high flood yet—
What none would have known of it, only the heart, being hard at
bay,

8

Is out with it! Oh,
We lash with the best or worst
Word last! How a lush-kept plush-capped sloe
Will, mouthed to flesh-burst,   60
Gush!—flush the man, the being with it, sour or sweet,
Brim, in a flash, full!—Hither then, last or first,
To hero of Calvary, Christ,'s feet—
Never ask if meaning it, wanting it, warned of it—men go.

9

Be adored among men,
God, three-numberèd form;
Wring thy rebel, dogged in den,
Man's malice, with wrecking and storm.
Beyond saying sweet, past telling of tongue,
Thou art lightning and love, I found it, a winter and warm;   70
Father and fondler of heart thou hast wrung:
Hast thy dark descending and most art merciful then.

10

With an anvil-ding
And with fire in him forge thy will
Or rather, rather then, stealing as Spring
Through him, melt him but master him still:
Whether at once, as once at a crash Paul,
Or as Austin, a lingering-out swéet skíll,
Make mercy in all of us, out of us all
Mastery, but be adored, but be adored King.   80

PART THE SECOND

11

"Some find me a sword; some
The flange and the rail; flame,
Fang, or flood" goes Death on drum,
And storms bugle his fame.
But wé dream we are rooted in earth—Dust!
Flesh falls within sight of us, we, though our flower the same,
Wave with the meadow, forget that there must
The sour scythe cringe, and the blear share come.

12

On Saturday sailed from Bremen,
American-outward-bound,   90
Take settler and seamen, tell men with women,
Two hundred souls in the round—
O Father, not under thy feathers nor ever as guessing
The goal was a shoal, of a fourth the doom to be drowned;
Yet did the dark side of the bay of thy blessing
Not vault them, the millions of rounds of thy mercy not reeve even
    them in?

13

Into the snows she sweeps,
Hurling the haven behind,
The Deutschland, on Sunday; and so the sky keeps,
For the infinite air is unkind,   100
And the sea flint-flake, black-backed in the regular blow,
Sitting Eastnortheast, in cursed quarter, the wind;
Wiry and white-fiery and whirlwind-swivellèd snow
Spins to the widow-making unchilding unfathering deeps.

14

She drove in the dark to leeward,
She struck—not a reef or a rock
But the combs of a smother of sand: night drew her
Dead to the Kentish Knock;
And she beat the bank down with her bows and the ride of her keel:
The breakers rolled on her beam with ruinous shock;   110
And canvas and compass, the whorl and the wheel
Idle for ever to waft her or wind her with, these she endured.

15

Hope had grown grey hairs,
Hope had mourning on,
Trenched with tears, carved with cares,
Hope was twelve hours gone;
And frightful a nightfall folded rueful a day
Nor rescue, only rocket and lightship, shone,
And lives at last were washing away:
To the shrouds they took,—they shook in the hurling and horrible airs.

16

One stirred from the rigging to save   121
The wild woman-kind below,
With a rope's end round the man, handy and brave—
He was pitched to his death at a blow,
For all his dreadnought breast and braids of thew:
They could tell him for hours, dandled the to and fro
Through the cobbled foam-fleece, what could he do
With the burl of the fountains of air, buck and the flood of the wave?

17

They fought with God's cold—
And they could not and fell to the deck   130
(Crushed them) or water (and drowned them) or rolled
With the sea-romp over the wreck.
Night roared, with the heart-break hearing a heart-broke rabble,
The woman's wailing, the crying of child without check—
Till a lioness arose breasting the babble,
A prophetess towered in the tumult, a virginal tongue told.

18

Ah, touched in your bower of bone
Are you! turned for an exquisite smart,
Have you! make words break from me here all alone,
Do you!—mother of being in me, heart.   140
O unteachably after evil, but uttering truth,
Why, tears! is it? tears; such a melting, a madrigal start!
Never-eldering revel and river of youth,
What can it be, this glee? the good you have there of your own?

19

Sister, a sister calling
A master, her master and mine!—
And the inboard seas run swirling and hawling;
The rash smart sloggering brine

Blinds her; but she that weather sees one thing, one;
Has one fetch in her: she rears herself to divine   150
Ears, and the call of the tall nun
To the men in the tops and the tackle rode over the storm's brawling.

20

She was first of a five and came
Of a coifèd sisterhood.
(O Deutschland, double a desperate name!
O world wide of its good!
But Gertrude, lily, and Luther, are two of a town,
Christ's lily and beast of the waste wood:
From life's dawn it is drawn down,
Abel is Cain's brother and breasts they have sucked the same.)   160

21

Loathed for a love men knew in them,
Banned by the land of their birth,
Rhine refused them. Thames would ruin them;
Surf, snow, river and earth
Gnashed: but thou art above, thou Orion of light;
Thy unchancelling poising palms were weighing the worth,
Thou martyr-master: in thy sight
Storm flakes were scroll-leaved flowers, lily showers—sweet heaven was
astrew in them.

22

Five! the finding and sake
And cipher of suffering Christ.   170
Mark, the mark is of man's make
And the word of it Sacrificed.
But he scores it in scarlet himself on his own bespoken,
Before-time-taken, dearest prizèd and priced—
Stigma, signal, cinquefoil token
For lettering of the lamb's fleece, ruddying of the rose-flake.

23

Joy fall to thee, father Francis,
Drawn to the Life that died;
With the gnarls of the nails in thee, niche of the lance, his
Lovescape crucified   180
And seal of his seraph-arrival! and these thy daughters
And five-livèd and leavèd favour and pride,
Are sisterly sealed in wild waters,
To bathe in his fall-gold mercies, to breathe in his all-fire glances.

24

Away in the loveable west,
On a pastoral forehead of Wales,
I was under a roof here, I was at rest,
And they the prey of the gales;
She to the black-about air, to the breaker, the thickly
Falling flakes, to the throng that catches and quails   190
Was calling "O Christ, Christ, come quickly":
The cross to her she calls Christ to her, christens her wild-worst Best.

25

The majesty! what did she mean?
Breathe, arch and original Breath.
Is it love in her of the being as her lover had been?
Breathe, body of lovely Death.
They were else-minded then, altogether, the men
Woke thee with a *we are perishing* in the weather of Gennesareth.
Or is it that she cried for the crown then,
The keener to come at the comfort for feeling the combating keen?   200

26

For how to the heart's cheering
The down-dugged ground-hugged grey
Hovers off, the jay-blue heavens appearing
Of pied and peeled May!
Blue-beating and hoary-glow height; or night, still higher,
With belled fire and the moth-soft Milky Way,
What by your measure is the heaven of desire,
The treasure never eyesight got, nor was ever guessed what for the hearing?

27

No, but it was not these.
The jading and jar of the cart,   210
Time's tasking, it is fathers that asking for case
Of the sodden-with-its-sorrowing heart,
Not danger, electrical horror; then further it finds
The appealing of the Passion is tenderer in prayer apart:
Other, I gather, in measure her mind's
Burden, in wind's burly and beat of endragonèd seas.

28

But how shall I . . . make me room there:
Reach me a . . . Fancy, come faster—
Strike you the sight of it? look at it loom there,
Thing that she . . . there then! the Master,   220

Ipse, the only one, Christ, King, Head:
He was to cure the extremity where he had cast her;
    Do, deal, lord it with living and dead;
Let him ride, her pride, in his triumph, despatch and have done with his
    doom there.

29

Ah! there was a heart right!
There was single eye!
Read the unshapeable shock night
And knew the who and the why;
Wording it how but by him that present and past,
Heaven and earth are word of, worded by?—   230
    The Simon Peter of a soul! to the blast
Tarpeian-fast, but a blown beacon of light.

30

Jesu, heart's light,
Jesu, maid's son,
What was the feast followed the night
Thou hadst glory of this nun?—
Feast of the one woman without stain.
For so conceivèd, so to conceive thee is done;
    But here was heart-throe, birth of a brain,
Word, that heard and kept thee and uttered thee outright.   240

31

Well, she has thee for the pain, for the
Patience; but pity of the rest of them!
Heart, go and bleed at a bitterer vein for the
Comfortless unconfessed of them—
No not uncomforted: lovely-felicitous Providence
Finger of a tender of, O of a feathery delicacy, the breast of the
    Maiden could obey so, be a bell to, ring of it, and
Startle the poor sheep back! is the shipwrack then a harvest, does tempest
    carry the grain for thee?

32

I admire thee, master of the tides
Of the Yore-flood, of the year's fall;   250
The recurb and the recovery of the gulf's sides,
The girth of it and the wharf of it and the wall;

Stanching, quenching ocean of a motionable mind;
    Ground of being, and granite of it: past all
      Grasp God, throned behind
Death with a sovereignty that heeds but hides, bodes but abides;

33

    With a mercy that outrides
      The all of water, an ark
    For the listener; for the lingerer with a love glides
      Lower than death and the dark;   260
A vein for the visiting of the past-prayer, pent in prison,
  The-last-breath penitent spirits—the uttermost mark
    Our passion-plungèd giant risen,
The Christ of the Father compassionate, fetched in the storm of his
  strides.

34

    Now burn, new born to the world,
      Double-naturèd name,
    The heaven-flung, heart-fleshed, maiden-furled
      Miracle-in-Mary-of-flame,
Mid-numbered He in three of the thunder-throne!
Not a dooms-day dazzle in his coming nor dark as he came;   270
    Kind, but royally reclaiming his own;
A released shower, let flash to the shire, not a lightning of fire hard-hurled.

35

    Dame, at our door
      Drowned, and among our shoals,
    Remember us in the roads, the heaven-haven of the Reward:
      Our King back, oh, upon English souls!
Let him easter in us, be a dayspring to the dimness of us, be a
  crimson-cresseted east,
More brightening her, rare-dear Britain, as his reign rolls,
    Pride, rose, prince, hero of us, high-priest,
Our hearts' charity's hearth's fire, our thoughts' chivalry's throng's Lord. 280

THE WINDHOVER
To Christ our Lord

sonnet

(1918)

I caught this morning morning's minion, king-
    dom of daylight's dauphin, dapple-dawn-drawn Falcon, in his riding
      Of the rolling level underneath him steady air, and striding
High there, how he rung upon the rein of a wimpling wing
In his ecstasy! then off, off forth on swing,
    As a skate's heel sweeps smooth on a bow-bend: the hurl and gliding
      Rebuffed the big wind. My heart in hiding
Stirred for a bird,—the achieve of, the mastery of the thing!

Brute beauty and valour and act, oh, air, pride, plume, here
    Buckle! AND the fire that breaks from thee then, a billion   10
Times told lovelier, more dangerous, O my chevalier!

    No wonder of it: shéer plód makes plough down sillion
Shine, and blue-bleak embers, ah my dear,
    Fall, gall themselves, and gash gold-vermilion.

PIED BEAUTY
(1918)

abb. sonnet 6 lines, 5½

Glory be to God for dappled things—
    For skies of couple-colour as a brinded cow;
      For rose-moles all in stipple upon trout that swim;
Fresh-firecoal chestnut-falls; finches' wings;
    Landscape plotted and pieced—fold, fallow, and plough;
      And áll trádes, their gear and tackle and trim.

All things counter, original, spare, strange;
    Whatever is fickle, freckled (who knows how?)
      With swift, slow; sweet, sour; adazzle, dim;
He fathers-forth whose beauty is past change: 10
    Praise him.

BINSEY POPLARS
Felled 1879

(1918)

My aspens dear, whose airy cages quelled,
Quelled or quenched in leaves the leaping sun,
All felled, felled, are all felled;
    Of a fresh and following folded rank
        Not spared, not one
        That dandled a sandalled
      Shadow that swam or sank
On meadow and river and wind-wandering weed-winding bank.

    O if we but knew what we do
        When we delve or hew—   10
    Hack and rack the growing green!
        Since country is so tender
    To touch, her being só slender,
    That, like this sleek and seeing ball
    But a prick will make no eye at all,
    Where we, even where we mean
        To mend her we end her,
      When we hew or delve:
After-comers cannot guess the beauty been.
    Ten or twelve, only ten or twelve   20
      Strokes of havoc únselve
      The sweet especial scene,
    Rural scene, a rural scene,
    Sweet especial rural scene.

THE LEADEN ECHO AND THE GOLDEN ECHO
Maidens' Song from St. Winefred's Well

(1918)

THE LEADEN ECHO

How to kéep—is there ány any, is there none such, nowhere known some,
    bow or brooch or braid or brace, láce, latch or catch or key to keep
Back beauty, keep it, beauty, beauty, beauty, . . . from vanishing away?
Ó is there no frowning of these wrinkles, rankèd wrinkles deep,

Down? no waving off of these most mournful messengers, still messengers,
 sad and stealing messengers of grey?
No there's none, there's none, O no there's none,
Nor can you long be, what you now are, called fair,
Do what you may do, what, do what you may,
And wisdom is early to despair:
Be beginning; since, no, nothing can be done
To keep at bay   10
Age and age's evils, hoar hair,
Ruck and wrinkle, drooping, dying, death's worst, winding sheets, tombs
 and worms and tumbling to decay;
So be beginning, be beginning to despair.
O there's none; no no no there's none:
Be beginning to despair, to despair,
Despair, despair, despair, despair.

THE GOLDEN ECHO

     Spare!
There ís one, yes I have one (Hush there!);
Only not within seeing of the sun,
Not within the singeing of the strong sun,   20
Tall sun's tingeing, or treacherous the tainting of the earth's air,
Somewhere elsewhere there is ah well where! one,
Óne. Yes I can tell such a key, I do know such a place,
Where whatever's prized and passes of us, everything that's fresh and fast
 flying of us, seems to us sweet of us and swiftly away with, done
 away with, undone,
Úndone, done with, soon done with, and yet dearly and dangerously sweet
Of us, the wimpled-water-dimpled, not-by-morning-matchèd face,
The flower of beauty, fleece of beauty, too too apt to, ah! to fleet,
Never fleets móre, fastened with the tenderest truth
To its own best being and its loveliness of youth: it is an everlastingness of,
 O it is an all youth!
Come then, your ways and airs and looks, locks, maiden gear, gallantry and
 gaiety and grace,   30
Winning ways, airs innocent, maiden manners, sweet looks, loose locks, long
 locks, lovelocks, gaygear, going gallant, girlgrace—
Resign them, sign them, seal them, send them, motion them with breath,
And with sighs soaring, soaring síghs deliver
Them; beauty-in-the-ghost, deliver it, early now, long before death
Give beauty back, beauty, beauty, beauty, back to God, beauty's self and
 beauty's giver.

See; not a hair is, not an eyelash, not the least lash lost; every hair
Is, hair of the head, numbered.
Nay, what we had lighthanded left in surly the mere mould
Will have waked and have waxed and have walked with the wind what
    while we slept,
This side, that side hurling a heavyheaded hundredfold   40
That while we, while we slumbered.
O then, weary then whý should we tread? O why are we so haggard at the
    heart, so care-coiled, care-killed, so fagged, so fashed, so cogged, so
    cumbered,
When the thing we freely fórfeit is kept with fonder a care,
Fonder a care kept than we could have kept it, kept
Far with fonder a care (and we, we should have lost it) finer, fonder
A care kept.—Where kept? Do but tell us where kept, where.—
Yonder.—What high as that! We follow, now we follow.—
    Yonder, yes yonder, yonder,
Yonder.

SPELT FROM SIBYL'S LEAVES
(1918)

Earnest, earthless, equal, attuneable, | vaulty, voluminous, . . stupendous
Evening strains to be tíme's vást, | womb-of-all, home-of-all, hearse-of-all
    night.
Her fond yellow hornlight wound to the west, | her wild hollow hoarlight
    hung to the height
Waste; her earliest stars, earl-stars, | stárs principal, overbend us,
Fíre-féaturing heaven. For earth | her being has unbound, her dapple is at
    an end, as-
tray or aswarm, all throughther, in throngs; | self ín self steepèd and pashed
    —qúite
Disremembering, dísmémbering | áll now. Heart, you round me right
With: Óur évening is over us; óur night | whélms, whélms, and will end us.
Only the beak-leaved boughs dragonish | damask the tool-smooth bleak light;
    black,
Ever so black on it. Óur tale, O óur oracle! | Lét life, wáned, ah lét life
    wind   10
Off hér once skéined stained véined varíety | upon, áll on twó spools; párt,
    pen, páck

Now her áll in twó flocks, twó folds—black, white; | right, wrong; reckon
    but, reck but, mind
But thése two; wáre of a wórld where bút these | twó tell, each off the
    óther; of a rack
Where, selfwrung, selfstrung, sheathe- and shelterless, | thóughts agáinst
    thoughts ín groans grínd.

TO SEEM THE STRANGER LIES MY LOT
(1918)

To seem the stranger lies my lot, my life
Among strangers. Father and mother dear,
Brothers and sisters are in Christ not near
And he my peace my parting, sword and strife.
    England, whose honour O all my heart woos, wife
To my creating thought, would neither hear
Me, were I pleading, plead nor do I: I weary of idle a being but by where wars are rife.

    I am in Ireland now; now I am at a thírd
Remove. Not but in all removes I can   10
Kind love both give and get. Only what word
Wisest my heart breeds dark heaven's baffling ban
Bars or hell's spell thwarts. This to hoard unheard,
Heard unheeded, leaves me a lonely began.

I WAKE AND FEEL THE FELL OF DARK
(1918)

I wake and feel the fell of dark, not day.
What hours, O what black hoürs we have spent
This night! what sights you, heart, saw; ways you went!
And more must, in yet longer light's delay.
    With witness I speak this. But where I say
Hours I mean years, mean life. And my lament
Is cries countless, cries like dead letters sent
To dearest him that lives alas! away.

I am gall, I am heartburn. God's most deep decree
Bitter would have me taste: my taste was me;   10
Bones built in me, flesh filled, blood brimmed the curse.
   Selfyeast of spirit a dull dough sours. I see
The lost are like this, and their scourge to be
As I am mine, their sweating selves; but worse.

PATIENCE, HARD THING!
(1918)

Patience, hard thing! the hard thing but to pray,
But bid for, Patience is! Patience who asks
Wants war, wants wounds; weary his times, his tasks;
To do without, take tosses, and obey.
   Rare patience roots in these, and, these away,
Nowhere. Natural heart's ivy, Patience masks
Our ruins of wrecked past purpose. There she basks
Purple eyes and seas of liquid leaves all day.

   We hear our hearts grate on themselves: it kills
To bruise them dearer. Yet the rebellious wills
Of us we do bid God bend to him even so.   10
   And where is he who more and more distils
Delicious kindness?—He is patient. Patience fills
His crisp combs, and that comes those ways we know.

MY OWN HEART LET ME MORE HAVE PITY ON
(1918)

My own heart let me more have pity on; let
Me live to my sad self hereafter kind,
Charitable; not live this tormented mind
With this tormented mind tormenting yet.
   I cast for comfort I can no more get
By groping round my comfortless, than blind
Eyes in their dark can day or thirst can find
Thirst's all-in-all in all a world of wet.

Soul, self; come, poor Jackself, I do advise
You, jaded, let be; call off thoughts awhile   10
Elsewhere; leave comfort root-room; let joy size
At God knows when to God knows what; whose smile
's not wrung, see you; unforeseen times rather—as skies
Betweenpie mountains—lights a lovely mile.

THAT NATURE IS A HERACLITEAN FIRE AND OF THE COMFORT OF THE RESURRECTION
(1918)

Cloud-puffball, torn tufts, tossed pillows | flaunt forth, then chevy on an air-
built thoroughfare: heaven-roysterers, in gay-gangs | they throng; they glitter
    in marches.
Down roughcast, down dazzling whitewash, | wherever an elm arches,
Shivelights and shadowtackle in long | lashes lace, lance, and pair.
Delightfully the bright wind boisterous | ropes, wrestles, beats earth bare
Of yestertempest's creases; in pool and rut peel parches
Squandering ooze to squeezed | dough, crust, dust; stanches, starches
Squadroned masks and manmarks | treadmire toil there
Footfretted in it. Million-fuelèd, | nature's bonfire burns on.
But quench her bonniest, dearest | to her, her clearest-selvèd spark   10
Man, how fast his firedint, | his mark on mind, is gone!
Both are in an unfathomable, all is in an enormous dark
Drowned. O pity and indig | nation! Manshape, that shone
Sheer off, disseveral, a star, | death blots black out; nor mark
    Is any of him at all so stark
But vastness blurs and time | beats level. Enough! the Resurrection,
A heart's-clarion! Away grief's gasping, | joyless days, dejection.
    Across my foundering deck shone
A beacon, an eternal beam. | Flesh fade, and mortal trash
Fall to the residuary worm; | world's wildfire, leave but ash: 20
    In a flash, at a trumpet crash,
1 am all at once what Christ is, | since he was what I am, and
This Jack, joke, poor potsherd, | patch, matchwood, immortal diamond,
    Is immortal diamond.

THOU ART INDEED JUST, LORD
(1918)

Justus quidem tu es, Domine, si disputem tecum: verum-
tamen justa loquar ad te: Quare via impiorum prosperatur? &c.

Thou art indeed just, Lord, if I contend
With thee; but, sir, so what I plead is just.
Why do sinners' ways prosper? and why must
Disappointment all I endeavour end?
   Wert thou my enemy, O thou my friend,
How wouldst thou worse, I wonder, than thou dost
Defeat, thwart me? Oh, the sots and thralls of lust
Do in spare hours more thrive than I that spend,
Sir, life upon thy cause. See, banks and brakes
Now, leavèd how thick! lacèd they are again   10
With fretty chervil, look, and fresh wind shakes
Them; birds build—but not I build; no, but strain,
Time's eunuch, and not breed one work that wakes.
Mine, O thou lord of life, send my roots rain.

TO R. B.
(1918)

The fine delight that fathers thought; the strong
Spur, live and lancing like the blowpipe flame,
Breathes once and, quenchèd faster than it came,
Leaves yet the mind a mother of immortal song.
Nine months she then, nay years, nine years she long
Within her wears, bears, cares and combs the same:
The widow of an insight lost she lives, with aim
Not known and hand at work now never wrong.
   Sweet fire the sire of muse, my soul needs this;
I want the one rapture of an inspiration.   10
O then if in my lagging lines you miss
The roll, the rise, the carol, the creation,
My winter world, that scarcely breathes that bliss
Now, yields you, with some sighs, our explanation.

Robert Bridges
1844-1930

I WILL NOT LET THEE GO
(1873)

I will not let thee go.
Ends all our month-long love in this?
    Can it be summed up so,
    Quit in a single kiss?
I will not let thee go.

I will not let thee go.
If thy words' breath could scare thy deeds,
    As the soft south can blow
    And toss the feathered seeds,
Then might I let thee go.   10

I will not let thee go.
Had not the great sun seen, I might;
    Or were he reckoned slow
    To bring the false to light,
Then might I let thee go.

I will not let thee go.
The stars that crowd the summer skies
    Have watched us so below
    With all their million eyes,
I dare not let thee go.   20

I will not let thee go.
Have we not chid the changeful moon,
　　Now rising late, and now
　　Because she set too soon,
　　And shall I let thee go?

I will not let thee go.
Have not the young flowers been content,
Plucked ere their buds could blow,
　　To seal our sacrament?
　　I cannot let thee go.　　　　　　　　　　　30

I will not let thee go.
I hold thee by too many bands:
　　Thou sayest farewell, and lo!
　　I have thee by the hands,
　　And will not let thee go.

ELEGY

On a Lady, Whom Grief for the Death of Her Betrothed Killed

(1873)

Assemble, all ye maidens, at the door,
And all ye loves, assemble; far and wide
Proclaim the bridal, that proclaimed before
Has been deferred to this late eventide:
　　For on this night the bride,
　　The days of her betrothal over,
　　Leaves the parental hearth for evermore;
To-night the bride goes forth to meet her lover.

Reach down the wedding vesture, that has lain
Yet all unvisited, the silken gown:　　　　　　　　10
Bring out the bracelets, and the golden chain
Her dearer friends provided: sere and brown
　　Bring out the festal crown,
　　And set it on her forehead lightly:
　　Though it be withered, twine no wreath again;
This only is the crown she can wear rightly.

Cloke her in ermine, for the night is cold,
And wrap her warmly, for the night is long,
In pious hands the flaming torches hold,
While her attendants, chosen from among   20
   Her faithful virgin throng,
   May lay her in her cedar litter,
  Decking her coverlet with sprigs of gold,
Roses, and lilies white that best befit her.

Sound flute and tabor, that the bridal be
Not without music, nor with these alone;
But let the viol lead the melody,
With lesser intervals, and plaintive moan
   Of sinking semitone;
   And, all in choir, the virgin voices   30
  Rest not from singing in skilled harmony
The song that aye the bridegroom's ear rejoices.

Let the priests go before, arrayed in white,
And let the dark-stoled minstrels follow slow,
Next they that bear her, honoured on this night,
And then the maidens, in a double row,
   Each singing soft and low,
   And each on high a torch upstaying:
  Unto her lover lead her forth with light,
With music, and with singing, and with praying.   40

'Twas at this sheltering hour he nightly came,
And found her trusty window open wide,
And knew the signal of the timorous flame,
That long the restless curtain would not hide
   Her form that stood beside;
   As scarce she dared to be delighted,
  Listening to that sweet tale, that is no shame
To faithful lovers, that their hearts have plighted.

But now for many days the dewy grass
Has shown no markings of his feet at morn: 50
And watching she has seen no shadow pass
The moonlit walk, and heard no music borne

Upon her ear forlorn.
In vain has she looked out to greet him;
He has not come, he will not come, alas!
So let us bear her out where she must meet him.

Now to the river bank the priests are come:
The bark is ready to receive its freight:
Let some prepare her place therein, and some
Embark the litter with its slender weight: 60
The rest stand by in state,
And sing her a safe passage over;
While she is oared across to her new home,
Into the arms of her expectant lover.

And thou, O lover, that art on the watch,
Where, on the banks of the forgetful streams,
The pale indifferent ghosts wander, and snatch
The sweeter moments of their broken dreams,—
Thou, when the torchlight gleams,
When thou shalt see the slow procession,   70
And when thine ears the fitful music catch,
Rejoice, for thou art near to thy possession.

A PASSER–BY

(1879)

*victorian, romantic
+ traditional – sprung
rhythm*

Whither, O splendid ship, thy white sails crowding,
Leaning across the bosom of the urgent West,
That fearest nor sea rising, nor sky clouding,
Whither away, fair rover, and what thy quest?
Ah! soon, when Winter has all our vales opprest,
When skies are cold and misty, and hail is hurling,
Wilt thóu glíde on the blue Pacific, or rest
In a summer haven asleep, thy white sails furling.

I there before thee, in the country that well thou knowest,
Already arrived am inhaling the odorous air: 10
I watch thee enter unerringly where thou goest,
And anchor queen of the strange shipping there,

Thy sails for awnings spread, thy masts bare;
Nor is aught from the foaming reef to the snow-capp'd, grandest
  Peak, that is over the feathery palms, more fair
Than thou, so upright, so stately, and still thou standest.

And yet, O splendid ship, unhail'd and nameless,
  I know not if, aiming a fancy, I rightly divine
That thou hast a purpose joyful, a courage blameless,
  Thy port assured in a happier land than mine.   20
  But for all I have given thee, beauty enough is thine,
As thou, aslant with trim tackle and shrouding,
  From the proud nostril curve of a prow's line
In the offing scatterest foam, thy white sails crowding.

LONDON SNOW
(1880)

terza rima

imitate style of topic

When men were all asleep the snow came flying,   A
  In large white flakes falling on the city brown,   B
Stealthily and perpetually settling and loosely lying,   A
  Hushing the latest traffic of the drowsy town;
Deadening, muffling, stifling its murmurs failing;
Lazily and incessantly floating down and down;
  contrast dirtiness of the city   Silently sifting and veiling road, roof and railing;
Hiding difference, making unevenness even,
Into angles and crevices softly drifting and sailing.
  All night it fell, and when full inches seven   10
It lay in the depth of its uncompacted lightness,
The clouds blew off from a high and frosty heaven;
  And all woke earlier for the unaccustomed brightness
Of the winter dawning, the strange unheavenly glare:
The eye marvelled—marvelled at the dazzling whiteness;
  The ear hearkened to the stillness of the solemn air;
No sound of wheel rumbling nor of foot falling,
And the busy morning cries came thin and spare.
  Then boys I heard, as they went to school, calling;
They gathered up the crystal manna to freeze   20
Their tongues with tasting, their hands with snow-balling;
  Or rioted in a drift, plunging up to the knees;
Or peering up from under the white-mossed wonder,

"O look at the trees!" they cried. "O look at the trees!"
   With lessened load, a few carts creak and blunder,
Following along the white deserted way,
A country company long dispersed asunder:
   When now already the sun, in pale display
Standing by Paul's high dome, spread forth below
His sparkling beams, and awoke the stir of the day.   30
   For now doors open, and war is waged with the snow;
And trains of somber men, past tale of number,
Tread long brown paths, as toward their toil they go:
   But even for them awhile no cares encumber
Their minds diverted; the daily word is unspoken,
The daily thoughts of labour and sorrow slumber
At the sight of the beauty that greets them, for the charm they
   have broken.

NIGHTINGALES

(1893)

Beautiful must be the mountains whence ye come,
And bright in the fruitful valleys the streams wherefrom
         Ye learn your song:
Where are those starry woods? O might I wander there,
   Among the flowers, which in that heavenly air
         Bloom the year long!

Nay, barren are those mountains and spent the streams:
Our song is the voice of desire, that haunts our dreams,
         A throe of the heart,
Whose pining visions dim, forbidden hopes profound,   10
   No dying cadence nor long sigh can sound,
         For all our art.

Alone, aloud in the raptured ear of men
We pour our dark nocturnal secret; and then,
         As night is withdrawn
From these sweet-springing meads and bursting boughs of May,
   Dream, while the innumerable choir of day
         Welcome the dawn.

LOW BAROMETER
(1925)

The south-wind strengthens to a gale,
Across the moon the clouds fly fast,
The house is smitten as with a flail,
The chimney shudders to the blast.

On such a night, when Air has loosed
Its guardian grasp on blood and brain,
Old terrors then of god or ghost
Creep from their caves to life again;

And Reason kens he herits in
A haunted house. Tenants unknown   10
Assert their squalid lease of sin
With earlier title than his own.

Unbodied presences, the pack'd
Pollution and remorse of Time,
Slipp'd from oblivion reënact
The horrors of unhouseld crime.

Some men would quell the thing with prayer
Whose sightless footsteps pad the floor,
Whose fearful trespass mounts the stair
Or bursts the lock'd forbidden door.   20

Some have seen corpses long interr'd
Escape from hallowing control,
Pale charnel forms—nay ev'n have heard
The shrilling of a troubled soul,

That wanders till the dawn hath cross'd
The dolorous dark, or Earth hath wound
Closer her storm-spredd cloke, and thrust
The baleful phantoms underground.

A. E. Housman

1859-1936

1887

(1896)

From Clee to heaven the beacon burns,
    The shires have seen it plain,
From north and south the sign returns
    And beacons burn again.

Look left, look right, the hills are bright,
    The dales are light between,
Because 'tis fifty years to-night
    That God has saved the Queen.

Now, when the flame they watch not towers
    About the soil they trod,   10
Lads, we'll remember friends of ours
    Who shared the work with God.

To skies that knit their heartstrings right,
    To fields that bred them brave,
The saviours come not home to-night:
    Themselves they could not save.

It dawns in Asia, tombstones show
    And Shropshire names are read;
And the Nile spills his overflow
    Beside the Severn's dead.   20

We pledge in peace by farm and town
  The Queen they served in war,
And fire the beacons up and down
  The land they perished for.

"God save the Queen" we living sing,
  From height to height 'tis heard;
And with the rest your voices ring,
  Lads of the Fifty-third.

Oh, God will save her, fear you not:
  Be you the men you've been,
Get you the sons your fathers got,   30
  And God will save the Queen.

LOVELIEST OF TREES
(1896)

Loveliest of trees, the cherry now
Is hung with bloom along the bough,
And stands about the woodland ride
Wearing white for Eastertide.

Now, of my threescore years and ten,
Twenty will not come again,
And take from seventy springs a score,
It only leaves me fifty more.

And since to look at things in bloom
Fifty springs are little room,   10
About the woodlands I will go
To see the cherry hung with snow.

THE LADS IN THEIR HUNDREDS
(1896)

The lads in their hundreds to Ludlow come in for the fair,
  There's men from the barn and the forge and the mill and the fold,
The lads for the girls and the lads for the liquor are there,
  And there with the rest are the lads that will never be old.

There's chaps from the town and the field and the till and the cart,
  And many to count are the stalwart, and many the brave,
And many the handsome of face and the handsome of heart,
  And few that will carry their looks or their truth to the grave.

I wish one could know them, I wish there were tokens to tell
  The fortunate fellows that now you can never discern;   10
And then one could talk with them friendly and wish them farewell
  And watch them depart on the way that they will not return.

But now you may stare as you like and there's nothing to scan;
  And brushing your elbow unguessed-at and not to be told
They carry back bright to the coiner the mintage of man,
  The lads that will die in their glory and never be old.

IS MY TEAM PLOUGHING?
(1896)

"Is my team ploughing,
    That I was used to drive
  And hear the harness jingle
    When I was man alive?"

Ay, the horses trample,
    The harness jingles now;
  No change though you lie under
    The land you used to plough.

"Is football playing
    Along the river shore,   10
  With lads to chase the leather,
    Now I stand up no more?"

Ay, the ball is flying,
    The lads play heart and soul;
  The goal stands up, the keeper
    Stands up to keep the goal.

"Is my girl happy,
    That I thought hard to leave,
  And has she tired of weeping
    As she lies down at eve?"   20

*put she
in not
anymore*

Ay, she lies down lightly,
 She lies not down to weep:
Your girl is well contented.
 Be still, my lad, and sleep.

"Is my friend hearty,
 Now I am thin and pine,
And has he found to sleep in
 A better bed than mine?"

Yes, lad, I lie easy,
 I lie as lads would choose;   30
I cheer a dead man's sweetheart,
 Never ask me whose.

ON WENLOCK EDGE

(1896)

On Wenlock Edge the wood's in trouble;
 His forest fleece the Wrekin heaves;
The gale, it plies the saplings double,
 And thick on Severn snow the leaves.

'Twould blow like this through holt and hanger
 When Uricon the city stood:
'Tis the old wind in the old anger,
 But then it threshed another wood.

Then, 'twas before my time, the Roman
 At yonder heaving hill would stare: 10
The blood that warms an English yeoman,
 The thoughts that hurt him, they were there.

There, like the wind through woods in riot,
 Through him the gale of life blew high;
The tree of man was never quiet:
 Then 'twas the Roman, now 'tis I.

The gale, it plies the sapling double,
 It blows so hard, 'twill soon be gone:
To-day the Roman and his trouble
 Are ashes under Uricon.   20

THE CARPENTER'S SON
(1896)

chvist

"Here the hangman stops his cart:
Now the best of friends must part.
Fare you well, for ill fare I:
Live, lads, and I will die.

"Oh, at home had I but stayed
'Prenticed to my father's trade,
Had I stuck to plane and adze,
I had not been lost, my lads.

"Then I might have built perhaps
Gallows-trees for other chaps,   10
Never dangled on my own,
Had I left but ill alone.

"Now, you see, they hang me high,
And the people passing by
Stop to shake their fists and curse;
So 'tis come from ill to worse.

"Here hang I, and right and left
Two poor fellows hang for theft:
All the same's the luck we prove,
Though the midmost hangs for love.   20

"Comrades all, that stand and gaze,
Walk henceforth in other ways;
See my neck and save your own:
Comrades all, leave ill alone.

"Make some day a decent end,
Shrewder fellows than your friend.
Fare you well, for ill fare I:
Live, lads, and I will die."

TERENCE, THIS IS STUPID STUFF
(1896)

"Terence, this is stupid stuff:
You eat your victuals fast enough;
There can't be much amiss, 'tis clear,
To see the rate you drink your beer.
But oh, good Lord, the verse you make,
It gives a chap the belly-ache.
The cow, the old cow, she is dead;
It sleeps well, the horned head:
We poor lads, 'tis our turn now
To hear such tunes as killed the cow.   10
Pretty friendship 'tis to rhyme
Your friends to death before their time
Moping melancholy mad:
Come, pipe a tune to dance to, lad."

Why, if 'tis dancing you would be,
There's brisker pipes than poetry.
Say, for what were hop-yards meant,
Or why was Burton built on Trent?
Oh many a peer of England brews
Livelier liquor than the Muse,   20
And malt does more than Milton can
To justify God's ways to man.
Ale, man, ale's the stuff to drink
For fellows whom it hurts to think:
Look into the pewter pot
To see the world as the world's not.
And faith, 'tis pleasant till 'tis past:
The mischief is that 'twill not last.
Oh I have been to Ludlow fair
And left my necktie God knows where,   30
And carried half-way home, or near,
Pints and quarts of Ludlow beer:
Then the world seemed none so bad,
And I myself a sterling lad;
And down in lovely muck I've lain,
Happy till I woke again.

Then I saw the morning sky:
Heigho, the tale was all a lie;
The world, it was the old world yet,
I was I, my things were wet, 40
And nothing now remained to do
But begin the game anew.

Therefore, since the world has still
Much good, but much less good than ill,
And while the sun and moon endure
Luck's a chance, but trouble's sure,
I'd face it as a wise man would,
And train for ill and not for good.
'Tis true, the stuff I bring for sale
Is not so brisk a brew as ale: 50
Out of a stem that scored the hand
I wrung it in a weary land.
But take it: if the smack is sour,
The better for the embittered hour;
It should do good to heart and head
When your soul is in my soul's stead;
And I will friend you, if I may,
In the dark and cloudy day.

There was a king reigned in the East:
There, when kings will sit to feast, 60
They get their fill before they think
With poisoned meat and poisoned drink.
He gathered all that springs to birth
From the many-venomed earth;
First a little, thence to more,
He sampled all her killing store;
And easy, smiling, seasoned sound,
Sate the king when healths went round.
They put arsenic in his meat
And stared aghast to watch him eat; 70
They poured strychnine in his cup
And shook to see him drink it up:
They shook, they stared as white's their shirt:
Them it was their poison hurt.
—I tell the tale that I heard told.
Mithridates, he died old.

EPITAPH ON AN ARMY OF MERCENARIES
(1922)

These, in the day when heaven was falling,
  The hour when earth's foundations fled,
Followed their mercenary calling
  And took their wages and are dead.

Their shoulders held the sky suspended;
  They stood, and earth's foundations stay;
What God abandoned, these defended,
  And saved the sum of things for pay.

TELL ME NOT HERE
(1922)

Tell me not here, it needs not saying,
  What tune the enchantress plays
In aftermaths of soft September
  Or under blanching mays,
For she and I were long acquainted
  And I knew all her ways.

On russet floors, by waters idle,
  The pine lets fall its cone;
The cuckoo shouts all day at nothing
  In leafy dells alone;
And traveller's joy beguiles in autumn
  Hearts that have lost their own.

10

On acres of the seeded grasses
  The changing burnish heaves;
Or marshalled under moons of harvest
  Stand still all night the sheaves;
Or beeches strip in storms for winter
  And stain the wind with leaves.

Possess, as I possessed a season,
    The countries I resign,   20
Where over elmy plains the highway
    Would mount the hills and shine,
And full of shade the pillared forest
    Would murmur and be mine.

For nature, heartless, witless nature,
    Will neither care nor know
What stranger's feet may find the meadow
    And trespass there and go,
Nor ask amid the dews of morning
    If they are mine or no.   30

William Butler Yeats
1865-1939

1st period
romantic *contrast*

heart realism
(changes the Eng.)
then actual world
last - turns to his own symbolic

THE LAKE ISLE OF INNISFREE
(1892)

I will arise and go now, and go to Innisfree,
And a small cabin build there, of clay and wattles made:
Nine bean rows will I have there, a hive for the honey bee,
  And live alone in the bee-loud glade.

And I shall have some peace there, for peace comes dropping slow,
Dropping from the veils of the morning to where the cricket sings;
There midnight's all a glimmer, and noon a purple glow,
  And evening full of the linnet's wings.

I will arise and go now, for always night and day
I hear lake water lapping with low sounds by the shore;   10
While I stand on the roadway, or on the pavements gray,
  I hear it in the deep heart's core.

ADAM'S CURSE
(1903)

We sat together at one summer's end,
That beautiful mild woman, your close friend,
And you and I, and talked of poetry.
I said, "A line will take us hours maybe;
Yet if it does not seem a moment's thought,
Our stitching and unstitching has been naught.

Better go down upon your marrow-bones
And scrub a kitchen pavement, or break stones
Like an old pauper, in all kinds of weather;
For to articulate sweet sounds together   10
Is to work harder than all these, and yet
Be thought an idler by the noisy set
Of bankers, schoolmasters, and clergymen
The martyrs call the world."

                    And thereupon
That beautiful mild woman for whose sake
There's many a one shall find out all heartache
On finding that her voice is sweet and low
Replied, "To be born woman is to know—
Although they do not talk of it at school—
That we must labour to be beautiful."   20

I said, "It's certain there is no fine thing
Since Adam's fall but needs much labouring.
There have been lovers who thought love should be
So much compounded of high courtesy
That they would sigh and quote with learned looks
Precedents out of beautiful old books;
Yet now it seems an idle trade enough."

We sat grown quiet at the name of love;
We saw the last embers of daylight die,
And in the trembling blue-green of the sky   30
A moon, worn as if it had been a shell
Washed by time's waters as they rose and fell
About the stars and broke in days and years.

I had a thought for no one's but your ears:
That you were beautiful, and that I strove
To love you in the old high way of love;
That it had all seemed happy, and yet we'd grown
As weary-hearted as that hollow moon.

THAT THE NIGHT COME
(1912)

She lived in storm and strife,
Her soul had such desire
For what proud death may bring
That it could not endure
The common good of life,
But lived as 'twere a king
That packed his marriage day
With banneret and pennon,
Trumpet and kettledrum,
And the outrageous cannon,   10
To bundle time away
That the night come.

SEPTEMBER 1913
(1914)

What need you, being come to sense,
But fumble in a greasy till
And add the halfpence to the pence
And prayer to shivering prayer, until
You have dried the marrow from the bone?
For men were born to pray and save:
Romantic Ireland's dead and gone,
It's with O'Leary in the grave.

Yet they were of a different kind,
The names that stilled your childish play,   10
They have gone about the world like wind,
But little time had they to pray
For whom the hangman's rope was spun,
And what, God help us, could they save?
Romantic Ireland's dead and gone,
It's with O'Leary in the grave.

Was it for this the wild geese spread
The grey wing upon every tide;
For this that all that blood was shed,
For this Edward Fitzgerald died,   20

And Robert Emmet and Wolfe Tone,
All that delirium of the brave?
Romantic Ireland's dead and gone,
It's with O'Leary in the grave.

Yet could we turn the years again,
And call those exiles as they were
In all their loneliness and pain,
You'd cry, "Some woman's yellow hair
Has maddened every mother's son":
They weighed so lightly what they gave.   30
But let them be, they're dead and gone,
They're with O'Leary in the grave.

THE MAGI
(1914)

Now as at all times I can see in the mind's eye,
In their stiff, painted clothes, the pale unsatisfied ones
Appear and disappear in the blue depth of the sky
With all their ancient faces like rain-beaten stones,
And all their helms of silver hovering side by side,
And all their eyes still fixed, hoping to find once more,
Being by Calvary's turbulence unsatisfied,
The uncontrollable mystery on the bestial floor.

THE FISHERMAN
(1916)

Although I can see him still,
The freckled man who goes
To a grey place on a hill
In grey Connemara clothes
At dawn to cast his flies,
It's long since I began
To call up to the eyes
This wise and simple man.
All day I'd looked in the face
What I had hoped 'twould be   10

To write for my own race
And the reality;
The living men that I hate,
The dead man that I loved,
The craven man in his seat,
The insolent unreproved,
And no knave brought to book
Who has won a drunken cheer,
The witty man and his joke
Aimed at the commonest ear,   20
The clever man who cries
The catch-cries of the clown,
The beating down of the wise
And great Art beaten down.

Maybe a twelvemonth since
Suddenly I began,
In scorn of this audience,
Imagining a man,
And his sun-freckled face,
And grey Connemara cloth,   30
Climbing up to a place
Where stone is dark under froth,
And the down-turn of his wrist
When the flies drop in the stream;
A man who does not exist,
A man who is but a dream;
And cried, "Before I am old
I shall have written him one
Poem maybe as cold
And passionate as the dawn."   40

AN IRISH AIRMAN FORESEES HIS DEATH
(1919)

I know that I shall meet my fate
Somewhere among the clouds above;
Those that I fight I do not hate,
Those that I guard I do not love;

My country is Kiltartan Cross,
My countrymen Kiltartan's poor,
No likely end could bring them loss
Or leave them happier than before.
Nor law, nor duty bade me fight,
Nor public men, nor cheering crowds,   10
A lonely impulse of delight
Drove to this tumult in the clouds;
I balanced all, brought all to mind,
The years to come seemed waste of breath,
A waste of breath the years behind
In balance with this life, this death.

EASTER 1916

(1920)

I have met them at close of day
Coming with vivid faces
From counter or desk among grey
Eighteenth-century houses.
I have passed with a nod of the head
Or polite meaningless words,
Or have lingered awhile and said
Polite meaningless words,
And thought before I had done
Of a mocking tale or a gibe   10
To please a companion
Around the fire at the club,
Being certain that they and I
But lived where motley is worn:
All changed, changed utterly:
A terrible beauty is born.

That woman's days were spent
In ignorant good-will,
Her nights in argument
Until her voice grew shrill.   20
What voice more sweet than hers
When, young and beautiful,
She rode to harriers?
This man had kept a school

And rode our wingèd horse;
This other his helper and friend
Was coming into his force;
He might have won fame in the end,
So sensitive his nature seemed,
So daring and sweet his thought.   30
This other man I had dreamed
A drunken, vainglorious lout.
He had done most bitter wrong
To some who are near my heart,
Yet I number him in the song;
He, too, has resigned his part
In the casual comedy;
He, too, has been changed in his turn,
Transformed utterly:
A terrible beauty is born.   40

Hearts with one purpose alone
Through summer and winter seem
Enchanted to a stone
To trouble the living stream.
The horse that comes from the road,
The rider, the birds that range
From cloud to tumbling cloud,
Minute by minute they change;
A shadow of cloud on the stream
Changes minute by minute;   50
A horse-hoof slides on the brim,
And a horse plashes within it;
The long-legged moor-hens dive,
And hens to moor-cocks call;
Minute by minute they live:
The stone's in the midst of all.

Too long a sacrifice
Can make a stone of the heart.
O when may it suffice?
That is Heaven's part, our part   60
To murmur name upon name,
As a mother names her child
When sleep at last has come

On limbs that had run wild.
What is it but nightfall?
No, no, not night but death;
Was it needless death after all?
For England may keep faith
For all that is done and said.
We know their dream; enough   70
To know they dreamed and are dead;
And what if excess of love
Bewildered them till they died?
I write it out in a verse—
MacDonagh and MacBride
And Connolly and Pearse
Now and in time to be,
Wherever green is worn,
Are changed, changed utterly:
A terrible beauty is born.   80

THE SECOND COMING

(1920)

Turning and turning in the widening gyre
The falcon cannot hear the falconer;
Things fall apart; the centre cannot hold;
Mere anarchy is loosed upon the world,
The blood-dimmed tide is loosed, and everywhere
The ceremony of innocence is drowned;
The best lack all conviction, while the worst
Are full of passionate intensity.

Surely some revelation is at hand;
Surely the Second Coming is at hand.   10
The Second Coming! Hardly are those words out
When a vast image out of *Spiritus Mundi*
Troubles my sight: somewhere in sands of the desert
A shape with lion body and the head of a man,
A gaze blank and pitiless as the sun,
Is moving its slow thighs, while all about it
Reel shadows of the indignant desert birds.
The darkness drops again; but now I know

That twenty centuries of stony sleep
Were vexed to nightmare by a rocking cradle,   20
And what rough beast, its hour come round at last,
Slouches towards Bethlehem to be born?

A PRAYER FOR MY DAUGHTER
(1920)

Once more the storm is howling, and half hid
Under this cradle-hood and coverlid
My child sleeps on. There is no obstacle
But Gregory's wood and one bare hill
Whereby the haystack- and roof-levelling wind,
Bred on the Atlantic, can be stayed;
And for an hour I have walked and prayed
Because of the great gloom that is in my mind.

I have walked and prayed for this young child an hour
And heard the sea-wind scream upon the tower,   10
And under the arches of the bridge, and scream
In the elms above the flooded stream;
Imagining in excited reverie
That the future years had come,
Dancing to a frenzied drum,
Out of the murderous innocence of the sea.

May she be granted beauty and yet not
Beauty to make a stranger's eye distraught,
Or hers before a looking-glass, for such,
Being made beautiful overmuch,   20
Consider beauty a sufficient end,
Lose natural kindness and maybe
The heart-revealing intimacy
That chooses right, and never find a friend.

Helen being chosen found life flat and dull
And later had much trouble from a fool,
While that great Queen, that rose out of the spray,
Being fatherless could have her way

Yet chose a bandy-leggèd smith for man.
It's certain that fine women eat
A crazy salad with their meat
Whereby the Horn of Plenty is undone.

In courtesy I'd have her chiefly learned;
Hearts are not had as a gift but hearts are earned
By those that are not entirely beautiful;
Yet many, that have played the fool
For beauty's very self, has charm made wise,
And many a poor man that has roved,
Loved and thought himself beloved,
From a glad kindness cannot take his eyes.

May she become a flourishing hidden tree
That all her thoughts may like the linnet be,
And have no business but dispensing round
Their magnanimities of sound,
Nor but in merriment begin a chase,
Nor but in merriment a quarrel.
O may she live like some green laurel
Rooted in one dear perpetual place.

My mind, because the minds that I have loved,
The sort of beauty that I have approved,
Prosper but little, has dried up of late,
Yet knows that to be choked with hate
May well be of all evil chances chief.
If there's no hatred in a mind
Assault and battery of the wind
Can never tear the linnet from the leaf.

An intellectual hatred is the worst,
So let her think opinions are accursed.
Have I not seen the loveliest woman born
Out of the mouth of Plenty's horn,
Because of her opinionated mind
Barter that horn and every good
By quiet natures understood
For an old bellows full of angry wind?

Considering that, all hatred driven hence,
The soul recovers radical innocence
And learns at last that it is self-delighting,
Self-appeasing, self-affrighting,
And that its own sweet will is Heaven's will;
She can, though every face should scowl   70
And every windy quarter howl
Or every bellows burst, be happy still.

And may her bridegroom bring her to a house
Where all's accustomed, ceremonious;
For arrogance and hatred are the wares
Peddled in the thoroughfares.
How but in custom and in ceremony
Are innocence and beauty born?
Ceremony's a name for the rich horn,
And custom for the spreading laurel tree.   80

LEDA AND THE SWAN
(1924)

A sudden blow: the great wings beating still
Above the staggering girl, her thighs caressed
By the dark webs, her nape caught in his bill,
He holds her helpless breast upon his breast.

How can those terrified vague fingers push
The feathered glory from her loosening thighs?
And how can body, laid in that white rush,
But feel the strange heart beating where it lies?

A shudder in the loins engenders there
The broken wall, the burning roof and tower   10
And Agamemnon dead.
                        Being so caught up,
So mastered by the brute blood of the air,
Did she put on his knowledge with his power
Before the indifferent beak could let her drop?

SAILING TO BYZANTIUM
(1928)

I

That is no country for old men. The young
In one another's arms, birds in the trees
—Those dying generations—at their song,
The salmon-falls, the mackerel-crowded seas,
Fish, flesh, or fowl, commend all summer long
Whatever is begotten, born, and dies.
Caught in that sensual music all neglect
Monuments of unageing intellect.

II

An aged man is but a paltry thing,
A tattered coat upon a stick, unless   10
Soul clap its hands and sing, and louder sing
For every tatter in its mortal dress,
Nor is there singing school but studying
Monuments of its own magnificence;
And therefore I have sailed the seas and come
To the holy city of Byzantium.

III

O sages standing in God's holy fire
As in the gold mosaic of a wall,
Come from the holy fire, perne in a gyre,
And be the singing-masters of my soul.   20
Consume my heart away; sick with desire
And fastened to a dying animal
It knows not what it is; and gather me
Into the artifice of eternity.

IV

Once out of nature I shall never take
My bodily form from any natural thing,
But such a form as Grecian goldsmiths make
Of hammered gold and gold enamelling
To keep a drowsy Emperor awake;
Or set upon a golden bough to sing   30
To lords and ladies of Byzantium
Of what is past, or passing, or to come.

THE TOWER
(1928)

I

What shall I do with this absurdity—
O heart, O troubled heart—this caricature,
Decrepit age that has been tied to me
As to a dog's tail?
              Never had I more
Excited, passionate, fantastical
Imagination, nor an ear and eye
That more expected the impossible—
No, not in boyhood when with rod and fly,
Or the humbler worm, I climbed Ben Bulben's back
And had the livelong summer day to spend.   10
It seems that I must bid the Muse go pack,
Choose Plato and Plotinus for a friend
Until imagination, ear and eye,
Can be content with argument and deal
In abstract things; or be derided by
A sort of battered kettle at the heel.

II

I pace upon the battlements and stare
On the foundations of a house, or where
Tree, like a sooty finger, starts from the earth;
And send imagination forth   20
Under the day's declining beam, and call
Images and memories
From ruin or from ancient trees,
For I would ask a question of them all.

Beyond that ridge lived Mrs. French, and once
When every silver candlestick or sconce
Lit up the dark mahogany and the wine,
A serving-man, that could divine
That most respected lady's every wish,
Ran and with the garden shears   30
Clipped an insolent farmer's ears
And brought them in a little covered dish.

Some few remembered still when I was young
A peasant girl commended by a song,
Who'd lived somewhere upon that rocky place,
And praised the colour of her face,
And had the greater joy in praising her,
Remembering that, if walked she there,
Farmers jostled at the fair
So great a glory did the song confer.   40

And certain men, being maddened by those rhymes,
Or else by toasting her a score of times,
Rose from the table and declared it right
To test their fancy by their sight;
But they mistook the brightness of the moon
For the prosaic light of day—
Music had driven their wits astray—
And one was drowned in the great bog of Cloone.

Strange, but the man who made the song was blind;
Yet, now I have considered it, I find   50
That nothing strange; the tragedy began
With Homer that was a blind man,
And Helen has all living hearts betrayed.
O may the moon and sunlight seem
One inextricable beam,
For if I triumph I must make men mad.

And I myself created Hanrahan
And drove him drunk or sober through the dawn
From somewhere in the neighbouring cottages.
Caught by an old man's juggleries   60
He stumbled, tumbled, fumbled to and fro
And had but broken knees for hire
And horrible splendour of desire;
I thought it all out twenty years ago:

Good fellows shuffled cards in an old bawn;
And when that ancient ruffian's turn was on
He so bewitched the cards under his thumb
That all but the one card became
A pack of hounds and not a pack of cards,

And that he changed into a hare.   70
Hanrahan rose in frenzy there
And followed up those baying creatures towards—

O towards I have forgotten what—enough!
I must recall a man that neither love
Nor music nor an enemy's clipped ear
Could, he was so harried, cheer;
A figure that has grown so fabulous
There's not a neighbour left to say
When he finished his dog's day:
An ancient bankrupt master of this house.   80

Before that ruin came, for centuries,
Rough men-at-arms, cross-gartered to the knees
Or shod in iron, climbed the narrow stair,
And certain men-at-arms there were
Whose images, in the Great Memory stored,
Come with loud cry and panting breast
To break upon a sleeper's rest
While their great wooden dice beat on the board.

As I would question all, come all who can;
Come old, necessitous, half-mounted man;   90
And bring beauty's blind rambling celebrant;
The red man the juggler sent
Through God-forsaken meadows; Mrs. French,
Gifted with so fine an ear;
The man drowned in a bog's mire,
When mocking Muses chose the country wench.

Did all old men and women, rich and poor,
Who trod upon these rocks or passed this door,
Whether in public or in secret rage
As I do now against old age?   100
But I have found an answer in those eyes
That are impatient to be gone;
Go therefore; but leave Hanrahan,
For I need all his mighty memories.

Old lecher with a love on every wind,
Bring up out of that deep considering mind

All that you have discovered in the grave,
For it is certain that you have
Reckoned up every unforeknown, unseeing
Plunge, lured by a softening eye,   110
Or by a touch or a sigh,
Into the labyrinth of another's being;

Does the imagination dwell the most
Upon a woman won or a woman lost?
If on the lost, admit you turned aside
From a great labyrinth out of pride,
Cowardice, some silly over-subtle thought
Or anything called conscience once;
And that if memory recur, the sun's
Under eclipse and the day blotted out.   120

III

It is time that I wrote my will;
I choose upstanding men
That climb the streams until
The fountain leap, and at dawn
Drop their cast at the side
Of dripping stone; I declare
They shall inherit my pride,
The pride of people that were
Bound neither to Cause nor to State,
Neither to slaves that were spat on,   130
Nor to the tyrants that spat,
The people of Burke and of Grattan
That gave, though free to refuse—
Pride, like that of the morn,
When the headlong light is loose,
Or that of the fabulous horn,
Or that of the sudden shower
When all streams are dry,
Or that of the hour
When the swan must fix his eye   140
Upon a fading gleam,
Float out upon a long
Last reach of glittering stream
And there sing his last song.
And I declare my faith:

I mock Plotinus' thought
And cry in Plato's teeth,
Death and life were not
Till man made up the whole,
Made lock, stock and barrel   150
Out of his bitter soul,
Aye, sun and moon and star, all.
And further add to that
That, being dead, we rise,
Dream and so create
Translunar Paradise.
I have prepared my peace
With learned Italian things
And the proud stones of Greece,
Poet's imaginings   160
And memories of love,
Memories of the words of women,
All those things whereof
Man makes a superhuman
Mirror-resembling dream.

As at the loophole there
The daws chatter and scream,
And drop twigs layer upon layer.
When they have mounted up,
The mother bird will rest   170
On their hollow top,
And so warm her wild nest.

I leave both faith and pride
To young upstanding men
Climbing the mountain-side,
That under bursting dawn
They may drop a fly;
Being of that metal made
Till it was broken by
This sedentary trade.   180

Now shall I make my soul,
Compelling it to study
In a learned school

Till the wreck of body,
Slow decay of blood,
Testy delirium
Or dull decrepitude,
Or what worse evil come—
The death of friends, or death
Of every brilliant eye   190
That made a catch in the breath—
Seem but the clouds of the sky
When the horizon fades;
Or a bird's sleepy cry
Among the deepening shades.

TWO SONGS FROM A PLAY
(1928)

I

I saw a staring virgin stand
Where holy Dionysus died,
And tear the heart out of his side,
And lay the heart upon her hand
And bear that beating heart away;
And then did all the Muses sing
Of Magnus Annus at the spring,
As though God's death were but a play.

Another Troy must rise and set,
Another lineage feed the crow,   10
Another Argo's painted prow
Drive to a flashier bauble yet.
The Roman Empire stood appalled:
It dropped the reigns of peace and war
When that fierce virgin and her Star
Out of the fabulous darkness called.

II

In pity for man's darkening thought
He walked that room and issued thence
In Galilean turbulence;
The Babylonian starlight brought   20
A fabulous, formless darkness in;

Odour of blood when Christ was slain
Made all Platonic tolerance vain
And vain all Doric discipline.

Everything that man esteems
Endures a moment or a day.
Love's pleasure drives his love away,
The painter's brush consumes his dreams;
The herald's cry, the soldier's tread
Exhaust his glory and his might: 30
Whatever flames upon the night
Man's own resinous heart has fed.

AMONG SCHOOL CHILDREN
(1928)

I
I walk through the long schoolroom questioning;
A kind old nun in a white hood replies;
The children learn to cipher and to sing,
To study reading-books and history,
To cut and sew, be neat in everything
In the best modern way—the children's eyes
In momentary wonder stare upon
A sixty-year-old smiling public man.

II
I dream of a Ledaean body, bent
Above a sinking fire, a tale that she   10
Told of a harsh reproof, or trivial event
That changed some childish day to tragedy—
Told, and it seemed that our two natures blent
Into a sphere from youthful sympathy,
Or else, to alter Plato's parable,
Into the yolk and white of the one shell.

III
And thinking of that fit of grief or rage
I look upon one child or t'other there
And wonder if she stood so at that age—
For even daughters of the swan can share   20

Something of every paddler's heritage—
And had that colour upon cheek or hair,
And thereupon my heart is driven wild:
She stands before me as a living child.

IV

Her present image floats into the mind—
Did Quattrocento finger fashion it
Hollow of cheek as though it drank the wind
And took a mess of shadows for its meat?
And I though never of Ledaean kind
Had pretty plumage once—enough of that,   30
Better to smile on all that smile, and show
There is a comfortable kind of old scarecrow.

V

What youthful mother, a shape upon her lap
Honey of generation had betrayed,
And that must sleep, shriek, struggle to escape
As recollection or the drug decide,
Would think her son, did she but see that shape
With sixty or more winters on its head,
A compensation for the pang of his birth,
Or the uncertainty of his setting forth?   40

VI

Plato thought nature but a spume that plays
Upon a ghostly paradigm of things;
Solider Aristotle played the taws
Upon the bottom of a king of kings;
World-famous golden-thighed Pythagoras
Fingered upon a fiddle-stick or strings
What a star sang and careless Muses heard:
Old clothes upon old sticks to scare a bird.

VII

Both nuns and mothers worship images,
But those the candles light are not as those   50
That animate a mother's reveries,
But keep a marble or a bronze repose.
And yet they too break hearts—O Presences
That passion, piety or affection knows,
And that all heavenly glory symbolize—
O self-born mockers of man's enterprise;

VIII

Labour is blossoming or dancing where
The body is not bruised to pleasure soul,
Nor beauty born out of its own despair,
Nor blear-eyed wisdom out of midnight oil.   60
O chestnut tree, great rooted blossomer,
Are you the leaf, the blossom or the bole?
O body swayed to music, O brightening glance,
How can we know the dancer from the dance?

BYZANTIUM

(1932)

The unpurged images of day recede;
The Emperor's drunken soldiery are abed;
Night resonance recedes, night-walkers' song
After great cathedral gong;
A starlit or a moonlit dome disdains
All that man is,
All mere complexities,
The fury and the mire of human veins.

Before me floats an image, man or shade,
Shade more than man, more image than a shade;   10
For Hades' bobbin bound in mummy-cloth
May unwind the winding path;
A mouth that has no moisture and no breath
Breathless mouths may summon;
I hail the superhuman;
I call it death-in-life and life-in-death.

Miracle, bird or golden handiwork,
More miracle than bird or handiwork,
Planted on the star-lit golden bough,
Can like the cocks of Hades crow,   20
Or, by the moon embittered, scorn aloud
In glory of changeless metal
Common bird or petal
And all complexities of mire or blood.

At midnight on the Emperor's pavement flit
Flames that no faggot feeds, nor steel has lit,
Nor storm disturbs, flames begotten of flame,
Where blood-begotten spirits come
And all complexities of fury leave,
Dying into a dance,   30
An agony of trance,
An agony of flame that cannot singe a sleeve.

Astraddle on the dolphin's mire and blood,
Spirit after spirit! The smithies break the flood,
The golden smithies of the Emperor!
Marbles of the dancing floor
Break bitter furies of complexity,
Those images that yet
Fresh images beget,
That dolphin-torn, that gong-tormented sea.   40

CRAZY JANE TALKS WITH THE BISHOP
(1933)

I met the Bishop on the road
And much said he and I.
"Those breasts are flat and fallen now,
Those veins must soon be dry;
Live in a heavenly mansion,
Not in some foul sty."

"Fair and foul are near of kin,
And fair needs foul," I cried.
"My friends are gone, but that's a truth
Nor grave nor bed denied,   10
Learned in bodily lowliness
And in the heart's pride.

"A woman can be proud and stiff
When on love intent;
But Love has pitched his mansion in
The place of excrement;
For nothing can be sole or whole
That has not been rent."

LAPIS LAZULI
For Harry Clifton

(1938)

I have heard the hysterical women say
They are sick of the palette and fiddle-bow,
Of poets that are always gay,
For everybody knows or else should know
That if nothing drastic is done
Aeroplane and Zeppelin will come out,
Pitch like King Billy bomb-balls in
Until the town lie beaten flat.

All perform their tragic play,
There struts Hamlet, there is Lear,   10
That's Ophelia, that Cordelia;
Yet they, should the last scene be there,
The great stage curtain about to drop,
If worthy their prominent part in the play,
Do not break up their lines to weep.
They know that Hamlet and Lear are gay;
Gaiety transfiguring all that dread.
All men have aimed at, found and lost;
Black out; Heaven blazing into the head:
Tragedy wrought to its uttermost.   20
Though Hamlet rambles and Lear rages,
And all the drop-scenes drop at once
Upon a hundred thousand stages,
It cannot grow by an inch or an ounce.

On their own feet they came, or on shipboard,
Camel-back, horse-back, ass-back, mule-back,
Old civilisations put to the sword.
Then they and their wisdom went to rack:
No handiwork of Callimachus,
Who handled marble as if it were bronze,   30
Made draperies that seemed to rise
When sea-wind swept the corner, stands;
His long lamp-chimney shaped like the stem

Of a slender palm, stood but a day;
All things fall and are built again,
And those that build them again are gay.

Two Chinamen, behind them a third,
Are carved in lapis lazuli,
Over them flies a long-legged bird,
A symbol of longevity;   40
The third, doubtless a serving-man,
Carries a musical instrument.

Every discoloration of the stone,
Every accidental crack or dent,
Seems a water-course or an avalanche,
Or lofty slope where it still snows
Though doubtless plum or cherry-branch
Sweetens the little half-way house
Those Chinamen climb towards, and I
Delight to imagine them seated there;   50
There, on the mountain and the sky,
On all the tragic scene they stare.
One asks for mournful melodies;
Accomplished fingers begin to play.
Their eyes mid many wrinkles, their eyes,
Their ancient, glittering eyes, are gay.

UNDER BEN BULBEN
(1939)

I

Swear by what the sages spoke
Round the Mareotic Lake
That the Witch of Atlas knew,
Spoke and set the cocks a-crow.

Swear by those horsemen, by those women
Complexion and form prove superhuman,
That pale, long-visaged company
That air in immortality

Completeness of their passions won;
Now they ride the wintry dawn   10
Where Ben Bulben sets the scene.

Here's the gist of what they mean.

II
Many times man lives and dies
Between his two eternities,
That of race and that of soul,
And ancient Ireland knew it all.
Whether man die in his bed
Or the rifle knock him dead,
A brief parting from those dear
Is the worst man has to fear.   20
Though grave-diggers' toil is long,
Sharp their spades, their muscles strong,
They but thrust their buried men
Back in the human mind again.

III
You that Mitchel's prayer have heard,
"Send war in our time, O Lord!"
Know that when all words are said
And a man is fighting mad,
Something drops from eyes long blind,
He completes his partial mind,   30
For an instant stands at ease,
Laughs aloud, his heart at peace.
Even the wisest man grows tense
With some sort of violence
Before he can accomplish fate,
Know his work or choose his mate.

IV
Poet and sculptor, do the work,
Nor let the modish painter shirk
What his great forefathers did,
Bring the soul of man to God,   40
Make him fill the cradles right.

Measurement began our might:
Forms a stark Egyptian thought,

Forms that gentler Phidias wrought.
Michael Angelo left a proof
On the Sistine Chapel roof,
Where but half-awakened Adam
Can disturb globe-trotting Madam
Till her bowels are in heat,
Proof that there's a purpose set   50
Before the secret working mind:
Profane perfection of mankind.

Quattrocento put in paint
On backgrounds for a God or Saint
Gardens where a soul's at ease;
Where everything that meets the eye,
Flowers and grass and cloudless sky,
Resemble forms that are or seem
When sleepers wake and yet still dream,
And when it's vanished still declare,   60
With only bed and bedstead there,
That heavens had opened.
                              Gyres run on;
When that greater dream had gone
Calvert and Wilson, Blake and Claude,
Prepared a rest for the people of God,
Palmer's phrase, but after that
Confusion fell upon our thought.

                    v
Irish poets, learn your trade,
Sing whatever is well made,
Scorn the sort now growing up   70
All out of shape from toe to top,
Their unremembering hearts and heads
Base-born products of base beds.
Sing the peasantry, and then
Hard-riding country gentlemen,
The holiness of monks, and after
Porter-drinkers' randy laughter;
Sing the lords and ladies gay
That were beaten into the clay
Through seven heroic centuries;   80
Cast your mind on other days

That we in coming days may be
Still the indomitable Irishry.

VI

Under bare Ben Bulben's head
In Drumcliff churchyard Yeats is laid.
An ancestor was rector there
Long years ago, a church stands near,
By the road an ancient cross.
No marble, no conventional phrase;
On limestone quarried near the spot   90
By his command these words are cut:
> *Cast a cold eye*
> *On life, on death.*
> *Horseman, pass by!*

NEWS FOR THE DELPHIC ORACLE

(1939)

I

There all the golden codgers lay,
There all the silver dew,
And the great water sighed for love,
And the wind sighed too.
Man-picker Niamh leant and sighed
By Oisin on the grass;
There sighed amid his choir of love
Tall Pythagoras.
Plotinus came and looked about,
The salt-flakes on his breast,   10
And having stretched and yawned awhile
Lay sighing like the rest.

II

Straddling each a dolphin's back
And steadied by a fin,
Those Innocents re-live their death,
Their wounds open again.
The ecstatic waters laugh because
Their cries are sweet and strange,
Through their ancestral patterns dance,

And the brute dolphins plunge   20
Until, in some cliff-sheltered bay
Where wades the choir of love
Proffering its sacred laurel crowns,
They pitch their burdens off.

III

Slim adolescence that a nymph has stripped,
Peleus on Thetis stares.
Her limbs are delicate as an eyelid,
Love has blinded him with tears;
But Thetis' belly listens.
Down the mountain walls   30
From where Pan's cavern is
Intolerable music falls.
Foul goat-head, brutal arm appear,
Belly, shoulder, bum,
Flash fishlike; nymphs and satyrs
Copulate in the foam.

Walter de la Mare
1873-1956

THE LISTENERS
(1912)

"Is there anybody there?" said the Traveller, *4 stresses*
    Knocking on the moonlit door; *3 unaccent irregular*
And his horse in the silence champed the grasses
    Of the forest's ferny floor.
And a bird flew up out of the turret,
    Above the Traveller's head;
And he smote upon the door again a second time;
    "Is there anybody there?" he said.
But no one descended to the Traveller;
    No head from the leaf-fringed sill   10
Leaned over and looked into his grey eyes,
    Where he stood perplexed and still.
But only a host of phantom listeners
    That dwelt in the lone house then
Stood listening in the quiet of the moonlight
    To that voice from the world of men:
Stood thronging the faint moonbeams on the dark stair
    That goes down to the empty hall,
Hearkening in an air stirred and shaken
    By the lonely Traveller's call.   20
And he felt in his heart their strangeness,
    Their stillness answering his cry,
While his horse moved, cropping the dark turf,
    'Neath the starred and leafy sky;
For he suddenly smote on the door, even

beginning of the 20th cent. undeterminite ending

86

Louder, and lifted his head:—
"Tell them I came, and no one answered,
  That I kept my word," he said.
Never the least stir made the listeners,
  Though every word he spake   30
Fell echoing through the shadowiness of the still house
  From the one man left awake:
Aye, they heard his foot upon the stirrup,
  And the sound of iron on stone,
And how the silence surged softly backward,
  When the plunging hoofs were gone.

AN EPITAPH

(1912)

Here lies a most beautiful lady,
Light of step and heart was she;
I think she was the most beautiful lady
That ever was in the West Country.
But beauty vanishes; beauty passes;
However rare—rare it be;
And when I crumble, who will remember
This lady of the West Country?

FARE WELL

(1918)

When I lie where shades of darkness
Shall no more assail mine eyes,
Nor the rain make lamentation
    When the wind sighs;
How will fare the world whose wonder
Was the very proof of me?
Memory fades, must the remembered
    Perishing be?

Oh, when this my dust surrenders
Hand, foot, lip, to dust again,   10
May these loved and loving faces
    Please other men!

May the rustling harvest hedgerow
Still the Traveller's Joy entwine,
And as happy children gather
    Posies once mine.

Look thy last on all things lovely,
Every hour. Let no night
Seal thy sense in deathly slumber
    Till to delight   20
Thou have paid thy utmost blessing;
Since that all things thou wouldst praise
Beauty took from those who loved them
    In other days.

MAERCHEN

(1921)

Soundless the moth-flit, crisp the death-watch tick;
Crazed in her shaken arbour bird did sing;
Slow wreathed the grease adown from soot-clogged wick:
    The Cat looked long and softly at the King.

Mouse frisked and scampered, leapt, gnawed, squeaked;
Small at the window looped cowled bat a-wing;
The dim-lit rafters with the night-mist reeked:
    The Cat looked long and softly at the King.

O wondrous robe enstarred, in night dyed deep:
O air scarce-stirred with the Court's far junketing: 10
O stagnant Royalty—A-swoon? Asleep?
    The Cat looked long and softly at the King.

SUNK LYONESSE

(1921)

In sea-cold Lyonesse,
When the Sabbath eve shafts down
On the roofs, walls, belfries
Of the foundered town,

The Nereids pluck their lyres
Where the green translucency beats,
And with motionless eyes at gaze
Make minstrelsy in the streets.

And the ocean water stirs
In salt-worn casemate and porch.   10
Plies the blunt-snouted fish
With fire in his skull for torch.
And the ringing wires resound;
And the unearthly lovely weep,
In lament of the music they make
In the sullen courts of sleep:

Whose marble flowers bloom for aye:
And—lapped by the moon-guiled tide—
Mock their carver with heart of stone,
Caged in his stone-ribbed side.   20

NOSTALGIA

(1945)

In the strange city of life
A house I know full well—
That wherein Silence a refuge has,
Where Dark doth dwell.

Gable and roof it stands,
Fronting the dizzied street,
Where Vanity flaunts her gilded booths
In the noontide glare and heat.

Green-graped upon its walls
Earth's ancient hoary vine   10
Clusters the carven lichenous stone
With tendril serpentine.

Deafened, incensed, dismayed,
Dazed in the clamorous throng,
I thirst for the soundless fount that rills
As if from my inmost heart, and fills
The stillness with its song.

As yet I knock in vain:
Nor yet what is hidden can tell;
Where Silence perpetual vigil keeps,   20
Where Dark doth dwell.

THE CHART

(1945)

That grave small face, but twelve hours here,
Maps secrets stranger than the seas',
In hieroglyphics more austere,
And older far than Rameses'.

GO FAR; COME NEAR

(1950)

free verse

the self becomes important

Go far; come near;
You still must be
The centre of your own small mystery.
Range body and soul—
Goal on to further goal,
Still shall you find
At end, nought else but *thee*.
Oh, in what straitened bounds
Of thought and aim—
And even sights and sounds—   10
Your earthly lot is doomed to stay!

And yet, your smallest whim
By secret grace
To look the simplest flower in the face
Gives an inevitable reflection back,
Not of your own self only,
But of one
Who, having achieved its miracle,
Rests there, and is not gone;
Who still o'er your own darker deeps holds sway   20
Into whatever shallows you may stray.

Whatever quicksands loom before you yet,—
Indifference, the endeavour to forget,
Whatever truce for which your soul may yearn,
Gives you but smaller room
In which to turn,
Until you reach the haven
Of the tomb.

"The haven?" Count the chances. . . . Is that so?
You are your Universe. Could death's quick dart   30
Be aimed at aught less mortal than the heart?
Could body's end,
Whereto it soon shall go,
Be end of all you mean, and are, my friend?

Ah, when clocks stop, and no-more-time begins,
May he who gave the flower
Its matchless hour,
And you the power
To win the love that only loving wins,
Have mercy on your miseries and your sins.

D. H. Lawrence
1885-1930

English

Optimist
love of nature
praise god

THE WILD COMMON
(1916)

The quick sparks on the gorse-bushes are leaping
Little jets of sunlight texture imitating flame;
Above them, exultant, the peewits are sweeping:
They have triumphed again o'er the ages, their screamings proclaim.

Rabbits, handfuls of brown earth, lie
Low-rounded on the mournful turf they have bitten down to the quick.
Are they asleep?—are they living?—Now see, when I
Lift my arms, the hill bursts and heaves under their spurting kick!

The common flaunts bravely; but below, from the rushes
Crowds of glittering king-cups surge to challenge the blossoming bushes;
There the lazy streamlet pushes   11
His bent course mildly; here wakes again, leaps, laughs, and gushes

Into a deep pond, an old sheep-dip,
Dark, overgrown with willows, cool, with the brook ebbing through so slow;
Naked on the steep, soft lip
Of the turf I stand watching my own white shadow quivering to and fro.

What if the gorse-flowers shrivelled, and I were gone?
What if the waters ceased, where were the marigolds then, and the gudgeon?
What is this thing that I look down upon?
White on the water wimples my shadow, strains like a dog on a string, to
    run on.   20

How it looks back, like a white dog to its master!
I on the bank all substance, my shadow all shadow looking up to me, looking
      back!
And the water runs, and runs faster, runs faster,
And the white dog dances and quivers, I am holding his cord quite slack.

But how splendid it is to be substance, here!
My shadow is neither here nor there; but I, I am royally here!
I am here! I am here! screams the peewit; the may-blobs burst out in a laugh
      as they hear!
Here! flick the rabbits. Here! pants the gorse. Here! say the insects far and
      near.

Over my skin in the sunshine, the warm, clinging air
Flushed with the songs of seven larks singing at once, goes kissing me glad.
You are here! You are here! We have found you! Everywhere   31
We sought you substantial, you touchstone of caresses, you naked lad!

Oh but the water loves me and folds me,
Plays with me, sways me, lifts me and sinks me, murmurs: Oh marvellous
      stuff!
No longer shadow!—and it holds me
Close, and it rolls me, enfolds me, touches me, as if never it could touch me
      enough.

Sun, but in substance, yellow water-blobs!
Wings and feathers on the crying, mysterious ages, peewits wheeling!
All that is right, all that is good, all that is God takes substance! a rabbit lobs
In confirmation, I hear sevenfold lark-songs pealing.   40

LAST WORDS TO MIRIAM
(1916)

Yours is the sullen sorrow,
    The disgrace is also mine;
Your love was intense and thorough,
Mine was the love of a growing flower
    For the sunshine.

You had the power to explore me,
    Blossom me stalk by stalk;

You woke my spirit, you bore me
To consciousness, you gave me the dour
    Awareness—then I suffered a balk.   10

Body to body I could not
    Love you, although I would.
We kissed, we kissed though we should not.
You yielded, we threw the last cast,
    And it was no good.

You only endured, and it broke
    My craftsman's nerve.
No flesh responded to my stroke;
So I failed to give you the last
    Fine torture you did deserve.   20

You are shapely, you are adorned
    But opaque and null in the flesh;
Who, had I but pierced with the thorned
Full anguish, perhaps had been cast
    In a lovely illumined mesh

Like a painted window; the best
    Fire passed through your flesh,
Undrossed it, and left it blest
In clean new awareness. But now
    Who shall take you afresh?   30

Now who will burn you free
    From your body's deadness and dross?
Since the fire has failed in me,
What man will stoop in your flesh to plough
    The shrieking cross?

A mute, nearly beautiful thing
    Is your face, that fills me with shame
As I see it hardening;
I should have been cruel enough to bring
    You through the flame.   40

BALLAD OF ANOTHER OPHELIA
(1916)

O the green glimmer of apples in the orchard,
Lamps in a wash of rain!
O the wet walk of my brown hen through the stackyard!
O tears on the window-pane!

Nothing now will ripen the bright green apples
Full of disappointment and of rain;
Blackish they will taste, of tears, when the yellow dapples
Of autumn tell the withered tale again.

All round the yard it is cluck! my brown hen.
Cluck! and the rain-wet wings;   10
Cluck! my marigold bird, and again
Cluck! for your yellow darlings.

For a grey rat found the gold thirteen
Huddled away in the dark.
Flutter for a moment, oh, the beast is quick and keen,
Extinct one yellow-fluffy spark!

Once I had a lover bright like running water,
Once his face was open like the sky,
Open like the sky looking down in all its laughter
On the buttercups, and the buttercups was I.   20

What then is there hidden in the skirts of all the blossom?
What is peeping from your skirts, O mother hen?
'Tis the sun that asks the question, in a lovely haste for wisdom;
What a lovely haste for wisdom is in men!

Yea, but it is cruel when undressed is all the blossom
And her shift is lying white upon the floor,
That a grey one, like a shadow, like a rat, a thief, a rainstorm
Creeps upon her then and ravishes her store!

O the grey garner that is full of half-grown apples!
O the golden sparkles laid extinct!   30
And O, behind the cloud-leaves, like yellow autumn dapples,
Did you see the wicked sun that winked?

HYMN TO PRIAPUS
(1917)

My love lies underground
With her face upturned to mine,
And her mouth unclosed in a last long kiss
That ended her life and mine.

I dance at the Christmas party
Under the mistletoe
Along with a ripe, slack country lass
Jostling to and fro.

The big, soft country lass,
Like a loose sheaf of wheat   10
Slipped through my arms on the threshing floor
At my feet.

The warm, soft country lass,
Sweet as an armful of wheat
At threshing-time broken, was broken
For me, and ah, it was sweet!

Now I am going home
Fulfilled and alone,
I see the great Orion standing
Looking down.   20

He's the star of my first beloved
Love-making.
The witness of all that bitter-sweet
Heart-aching.

Now he sees this as well,
This last commission.
Nor do I get any look
Of admonition.

He can add the reckoning up
I suppose, between now and then,   30
Having walked himself in the thorny, difficult
Ways of men.

He has done as I have done
No doubt:
Remembered and forgotten
Turn and about.

My love lies underground
With her face upturned to mine,
And her mouth unclosed in the last long kiss
That ended her life and mine.   40

She fares in the stark immortal
Fields of death;
I in these goodly, frozen
Fields beneath.

Something in me remembers
And will not forget.
The stream of my life in the darkness
Deathward set!

And something in me has forgotten,
Has ceased to care.   50
Desire comes up, and contentment
Is debonair.

I, who am worn and careful,
How much do I care?
How is it I grin then, and chuckle
Over despair?

Grief, grief, I suppose and sufficient
Grief makes us free
To be faithless and faithful together
As we have to be.   60

SONG OF A MAN WHO HAS COME THROUGH
(1917)

Not I, not I, but the wind that blows through me!
A fine wind is blowing the new direction of Time.

If only I let it bear me, carry me, if only it carry me!
If only I am sensitive, subtle, oh, delicate, a winged gift!
If only, most lovely of all, I yield myself and am borrowed
By the fine, fine wind that takes its course through the chaos of the world
Like a fine, an exquisite chisel, a wedge-blade inserted;
If only I am keen and hard like the sheer tip of a wedge
Driven by invisible blows,
The rock will split, we shall come at the wonder, we shall find the
    Hesperides.

O, for the wonder that bubbles into my soul,   11
I would be a good fountain, a good well-head,
Would blur no whisper, spoil no expression.

What is the knocking?
What is the knocking at the door in the night?
It is somebody wants to do us harm.

No, no, it is the three strange angels.
Admit them, admit them.

SNAKE

(1923)

A snake came to my water-trough
On a hot, hot day, and I in pyjamas for the heat,
To drink there.

In the deep, strange-scented shade of the great dark carob-tree
I came down the steps with my pitcher — biblical
And must wait, must stand and wait, for there he was at the trough before me.

He reached down from a fissure in the earth-wall in the gloom
And trailed his yellow-brown slackness soft-bellied down, over the edge of the
    stone trough
And rested his throat upon the stone bottom,
And where the water had dripped from the tap, in a small clearness,   10
He sipped with his straight mouth,
Softly drank through his straight gums, into his slack long body,
Silently.

snake
supreme
in
nature

beauty
of
snake

Someone was before me at my water-trough,
And I, like a second comer, waiting.

He lifted his head from his drinking, as cattle do,
And looked at me vaguely, as drinking cattle do,
And flickered his two-forked tongue from his lips, and mused a moment,
And stooped and drank a little more,
Being earth-brown, earth-golden from the burning bowels of the earth   20
On the day of Sicilian July, with Etna smoking.

The voice of my education said to me
He must be killed,
For in Sicily the black, black snakes are innocent, the gold are venomous.

And voices in me said, If you were a man
You would take a stick and break him now, and finish him off.

But must I confess how I liked him,
How glad I was he had come like a guest in quiet, to drink at my water-trough
And depart peaceful, pacified, and thankless,
Into the burning bowels of this earth?   30

Was it cowardice, that I dared not kill him?
Was it perversity, that I longed to talk to him?
Was it humility, to feel so honoured?
I felt so honoured.

And yet those voices:
If you were not afraid, you would kill him!

And truly I was afraid, I was most afraid,
But even so, honoured still more
That he should seek my hospitality
From out the dark door of the secret earth.   40

He drank enough
And lifted his head, dreamily, as one who has drunken,
And flickered his tongue like a forked night on the air, so black,
Seeming to lick his lips,
And looked around like a god, unseeing, into the air,
And slowly turned his head,

And slowly, very slowly, as if thrice adream,
Proceeded to draw his slow length curving round
And climb again the broken bank of my wall-face.

And as he put his head into that dreadful hole,   50
And as he slowly drew up, snake-easing his shoulders, and entered farther,
A sort of horror, a sort of protest against his withdrawing into that horrid
    black hole,
Deliberately going into the blackness, and slowly drawing himself after,
Overcame me now his back was turned.

I looked round, I put down my pitcher,
I picked up a clumsy log
And threw it at the water-trough with a clatter.

I think it did not hit him,
But suddenly that part of him that was left behind convulsed in undignified
    haste,
Writhed like lightning, and was gone   60
Into the black hole, the earth-lipped fissure in the wall-front,
At which, in the intense still noon, I stared with fascination.

And immediately I regretted it.
I thought how paltry, how vulgar, what a mean act!
I despised myself and the voices of my accursed human education.

And I thought of the albatross,
And I wished he would come back, my snake.

For he seemed to me again like a king,
Like a king in exile, uncrowned in the underworld,
Now due to be crowned again.   70

And so, I missed my chance with one of the lords
Of life.
And I have something to expiate;
A pettiness.

Edith Sitwell

1887–1965

SIR BEELZEBUB

(1922)

When
Sir
Beelzebub called for his syllabub in the hotel in Hell
    Where Proserpine first fell,
Blue as the gendarmerie were the waves of the sea,

    (Rocking and shocking the bar-maid).

Nobody comes to give him his rum but the
Rim of the sky hippopotamus-glum
Enhances the chances to bless with a benison
Alfred Lord Tennyson crossing the bar laid   10
With cold vegetation from pale deputations
Of temperance workers (all signed In Memoriam)
Hoping with glory to trip up the Laureate's feet

    (Moving in classical meters) . . .

Like Balaclava, the lava came down from the
Roof, and the sea's blue wooden gendarmerie
Took them in charge while Beelzebub roared for his rum.

    . . . None of them come!

AN OLD WOMAN

I

(1942)

I, an old woman in the light of the sun,
Wait for my Wanderer, and my upturned face
Has all the glory of the remembering Day,
The hallowed grandeur of the primeval clay
That knew the Flood and suffered all the dryness
Of the uncaring heaven, the sun its lover.

For the sun is the first lover of the world,
Blessing all humble creatures, all life-giving,
Blessing the end of life and the work done,
The clean and the unclean, ores in earth, and splendors   10
Within the heart of man, that second sun.

For when the first founts and deep waterways
Of the young light flow down and lie like peace
Upon the upturned faces of the blind
From life, it comes to bless
Eternity in its poor mortal dress—
Shining upon young lovers and old lechers
Rising from their beds, and laying gold
Alike in the unhopeful path of beggars
And in the darkness of the miser's heart.   20
The crooked has a shadow light made straight,
The shallow places gain their strength again—
And desert hearts, waste heavens, the barren height
Forget that they are cold.
The man-made chasms between man and man
Of creeds and tongues are filled, the guiltless light
Remakes all men and things in holiness.

And he who blessed the fox with a golden fleece,
And covered earth with ears of corn like the planets
Bearded with thick ripe gold,   30
For the holy bread of mankind, blessed my clay:
For the sun cares not that I am a simple woman;
To him, laughing, the veins in my arms and the wrinkles

From work on my nursing hands are sacred as branches
And furrows of harvest . . . to him, the heat of the earth
And beat of the heart are one—
Born from the energy of the world, the love
That keeps the Golden Ones in their place above,
And hearts and blood of beasts ever in motion—
Without which comets, sun, plants, and all living beings   40
And warmth in the inward parts of the earth would freeze.
And the sun does not care if I live in holiness:
To him, my mortal dress
Is sacred, part of the earth, a lump of the world
With my splendors, ores, impurities, and harvest,
Over which shines my heart, that ripening sun.

Though the dust, the shining racer, overtake me,
I, too, was a golden woman like those that walk
In the fields of the heavens:—but am now grown old
And must sit by the fire and watch the fire grow cold—   50
A country Fate whose spool is the household task.
Yet still I am loved by the sun, and still am part
Of earth. In the evenings bringing home the workers,
Bringing the Wanderer home and the dead child,
The child unborn and never to be conceived,
Home to the mother's breast, I sit by the fire
Where the seed of gold drops dead and the kettle simmers
With a sweet sound like that of a hive of bees;
And I wait for my Wanderer to come home to rest—
Covered with earth as if he had been working   60
Among the happy gardens, the holy fields
Where the bread of mankind ripens in the stillness.
Unchanged to me by death, I shall hold to my breast
My little child in his sleep, I shall seem the consoling
Earth, the mother of corn, nurse of the unreturning.

Wise is the earth, consoling grief and glory,
The golden heroes proud as pomp of waves—
Great is the earth embracing them, their graves;
And great is the earth's story.
For though the soundless wrinkles fall like snow   70
On many a golden cheek, and creeds grow old
And change—man's heart, that sun,

Outlives all terrors shaking the old night:
The world's huge fevers burn and shine, turn cold,
Yet the heavenly bodies and young lovers burn and shine,
The golden lovers walk in the holy fields
Where the Abraham-bearded sun, the father of all things,
Is shouting of ripeness, and the whole world of dews and
    splendors are singing
To the cradles of earth, of men, beasts, harvests, swinging
In the peace of God's heart. And I, the primeval clay   80
That has known earth's grief and harvest's happiness,
Seeing mankind's dark seed-time, come to bless,
Forgive and bless all men like the holy light.

II

HARVEST
To Stephen Spender

(1944)

I, an old woman whose heart is like the Sun
That has seen too much, looked on too many sorrows,
Yet is not weary of shining, fulfilment, and harvest,
Heard the priests that howled for rain and the universal darkness,
Saw the golden princes sacrificed to the Rain-god,
The cloud that came and was small as the hand of Man.   89
And now in the time of the swallow, the bright one, the chatterer,
The young women wait like the mother of corn for the lost one—
Their golden eyelids are darkened like the great rain-clouds.
But in bud and branch the nature of Fate begins
—And love with the Lion's claws and the Lion's hunger
Hides in the brakes in the nihilistic Spring.
Old men feel their scolding heart
Reproach the veins that for fire have only anger.
And Christ has forgiven all men—the thunder-browed Caesar,
That stone-veined Tantalus howling with thirst in the plain
Where for innocent water flows only the blood of the slain,   100
Falling forever from veins that held in their noonday
The foolish companion of summer, the weeping rose.
We asked for a sign that we have not been forsaken—
And for answer the Abraham-bearded Sun, the father of all things,

Is shouting of ripeness over our harvest forever.
And with the sound of growth, lion-strong, and the laughing Sun,
Whose great flames stretch like branches in the heat
Across the firmament, we almost see
The great gold planets spangling the wide air
And earth—
             O sons of men, the firmament's belovèd,   110
The Golden Ones of heaven have us in care—
With planetary wisdom, changeless laws,
Ripening our lives and ruling hearts and rhythms,
Immortal hungers in the veins and heart
Born from the primal Cause
That keeps the hearts and blood of men and beasts ever in motion,
The amber blood of the smooth-weeping tree
Rising towards the life-giving heat of the Sun. . . .
For is not the blood—the divine, the animal heat
That is not fire—derived from the solar ray?   120
And does not the Beast surpass all elements
In power, through the heat and wisdom of the blood
Creating other Beasts—the Lion a Lion, the Bull a Bull,
The Bear a Bear—some like great stars in the rough
And uncreated dark—or unshaped universes
With manes of fire and a raging sun for heart?
Gestation, generation, and duration—
The cycles of all lives upon the earth—
Plants, beasts, and men, must follow those of heaven;
The rhythms of our lives   130
Are those of the ripening, dying of the seasons,
Our sowing and reaping in the holy fields,
Our love and giving birth—then growing old
And sinking into sleep in the maternal
Earth, mother of corn, the wrinkled darkness.
So we, ruled by those laws, see their fulfilment.
And I who stood in the grave-clothes of my flesh
Unutterably spotted with the world's woes
Cry, "I am Fire. See, I am the bright gold
That shines like a flaming fire in the night—the gold-trained
        planet,   140
The laughing heat of the Sun that was born from darkness—
Returning to darkness—I am fecundity, harvest."
For on each country road,

Grown from the needs of men as boughs from trees,
The reapers walk like the harvesters of heaven—
Jupiter and his great train, and the corn-goddess,
And Saturn marching in the Dorian mode.
We heard in the dawn the first ripe-bearded fire
Of wheat (so flames that are men's spirits break from their thick
    earth),
Then came the Pentecostal Rushing of Flames, God in the wind
    that comes to the wheat,   .   150
Returned from the Dead for the guilty hands of Caesar
Like the rose at morning shouting of red joys
And redder sorrows fallen from young veins and heart-springs,
Come back for the wrong and the right, the wise and the
    foolish,
Who like the rose care not for our philosophies
Of life and death, knowing the earth's forgiveness
And the great dews that comes to the sick rose:
For those who build great mornings for the world
From Edens of lost light seen in each other's eyes,
Yet soon must wear no more the light of the Sun   160
But say farewell among the morning sorrows.
The universal language of the Bread—
(O Thou who are not broken, or divided—
Thou who art eaten, but like the Burning Bush
Art not consumed—Thou Bread of Men and Angels)—
The Seraphim rank on rank of the ripe wheat—
Gold-bearded thunders and hierarchies of heaven
Roar from the earth: "Our Christ is arisen, He comes to give a
    sign from the Dead."

STILL FALLS THE RAIN— Bombs
The Raids, 1940. Night and Dawn

(1942)

Still falls the Rain—
Dark as the world of man, black as our loss—
Blind as the nineteen hundred and forty nails
Upon the Cross.

Still falls the Rain
With a sound like the pulse of the heart that is changed to the
      hammer-beat
In the Potter's Field, and the sound of the impious feet

On the Tomb:
           Still falls the Rain
In the Field of Blood where the small hopes breed and the human
      brain
Nurtures its greed, that worm with the brow of Cain.   10

Still falls the Rain
At the feet of the Starved Man hung upon the Cross.
Christ that each day, each night, nails there, have mercy on us—
On Dives and on Lazarus:
Under the Rain the sore and the gold are as one.

Still falls the Rain—
Still falls the Blood from the Starved Man's wounded Side:
He bears in His Heart all wounds,—those of the light that died,
The last faint spark
In the self-murdered heart, the wounds of the sad uncomprehend-
      ing dark,   20
The wounds of the baited bear—
The blind and weeping bear whom the keepers beat
On his helpless flesh . . . the tears of the hunted hare.

Still falls the Rain—
Then—O Ile leape up to my God: who pulles me doune—
See, see where Christ's blood streames in the firmament:
It flows from the Brow we nailed upon the tree
Deep to the dying, to the thirsting heart
That holds the fires of the world,—dark-smirched with pain
As Caesar's laurel crown.   30

Then sounds the voice of One who like the heart of man
Was once a child who among beasts has lain—
"Still do I love, still shed my innocent light, my Blood, for thee."

STREET SONG
(1942)

"Love my heart for an hour, but my bone for a day—
At least the skeleton smiles, for it has a morrow:
But the hearts of the young are now the dark treasure of Death,
And summer is lonely.

Comfort the lonely light and the sun in its sorrow,
Come like the night, for terrible is the sun
As truth, and the dying light shows only the skeleton's hunger
For peace, under the flesh like the summer rose.

Come through the darkness of death, as once through the branches
Of youth you came, through the shade like the flowering door   10
That leads into Paradise, far from the street—you, the unborn
City seen by the homeless, the night of the poor.

You walk in the city ways, where Man's threatening shadow,
Red-edged by the sun like Cain, has a changing shape—
Elegant like the Skeleton, crouched like the Tiger,
With the age-old wisdom and aptness of the Ape.

The pulse that beats in the heart is changed to the hammer
That sounds in the Potter's Field where they build a new world
From our Bone, and the carrion-bird days' foul droppings and clamor—
But you are my night, and my peace—   20

The holy night of conception, of rest, the consoling
Darkness when all men are equal—the wrong and the right,
And the rich and the poor are no longer separate nations—
They are brothers in night."

This was the song I heard; but the Bone is silent!
Who knows if the sound was that of the dead light calling—
Of Caesar rolling onward his heart, that stone,
Or the burden of Atlas falling.

THE SHADOW OF CAIN
To C. M. Bowra

(1949)

Under great yellow flags and banners of the ancient Cold
Began the huge migrations
From some primeval disaster in the heart of Man.

There were great oscillations
Of temperature. . . . You knew there had once been warmth;

But the Cold is the highest mathematical Idea . . . the Cold is
      Zero—
The Nothing from which arose
All Being and all variation. . . . It is the sound too high for our
      hearing, the Point that flows

Till it becomes the line of Time . . . an endless positing
Of Nothing, or the Ideal that tries to burgeon   10
Into Reality through multiplying. . . . Then Time froze

To immobility and changed to Space.
Black flags among the ice, blue rays
And the purple perfumes of the polar Sun
Freezing the bone to sapphire and to zircon—
Those were our days.

And now, in memory of great oscillations
Of temperature in that epoch of the Cold,
We found a continent of turquoise, vast as Asia
In the yellowing airs of the Cold: the tooth of a mammoth;   20
And there, in a gulf, a dark pine-sword

To show there had once been warmth and the gulf stream in our
      veins
Where only the Chaos of the Antarctic Pole
Or the peace of its atonic coldness reigns.

And sometimes we found the trace
Of a bird's claw in the immensity of the Cold:
The trace of the first letters we could not read:
Some message of Man's need

And of the slow subsidence of a Race;
And of great heats in which the Pampean mud was formed,   30
In which the Megatherium Mylodon
Lies buried under Mastodon-trumpetings of leprous Suns.

The Earth had cloven in two in that primal disaster.
But when the glacial period began
There was still some method of communication
Between Man and his brother Man—
Although their speech
Was alien, each from each,
As the Bird's from the Tiger's, born from the needs of their oppos-
        ing famines.
Each said, "This is the Race of the dead . . . their blood is
        cold. . . .   40
For the heat of those more recent on the Earth
Is higher . . . the blood-beat of the Bird more high
Than that of the ancient race of the primeval Tiger:—
The Earth had lived without the Bird

In that Spring when there were no flowers like thunders in the air.
And now the Earth lies flat beneath the shade of an iron wing.
And of what does the Pterodactyl sing—
Of what red buds in what tremendous Spring?"

The thunders of the Spring began. . . . We came again
After that long migration   50
To the city built before the Flood by our brother Cain.

And when we reached an open door
The Fate said, "My feet ache."
The Wanderers said, "Our hearts ache."

There was great lightning
In flashes coming to us over the floor:
The Whiteness of the Bread

The Whiteness of the Dead
The Whiteness of the Claw—
All this coming to us in flashes through the open door.   60

There were great emerald thunders in the air
In the violent Spring, the thunders of the sap and the blood in the
            heart—
The Spiritual Light, the physical Revelation.

In the streets of the City of Cain there were great Rainbows
Of emeralds: the young people, crossing and meeting.

And everywhere
The great voice of the Sun in sap and bud
Fed from the heart of Being, the panic Power,
The sacred Fury, shouts of Eternity
To the blind eyes, the heat in the wingèd seed, the fire in the blood,

And through the works of Death,   71
The dust's aridity, is heard the sound
Of mounting saps like monstrous bull-voices of unseen fearful mimes:
And the great rolling world-wide thunders of that drumming under-
            ground

Proclaim our Christ, and roar, "Let there be harvest!
Let there be no more Poor—
For the Son of God is sowed in every furrow!"

We did not heed the Cloud in the Heavens shaped like the hand
Of Man . . . But there came a roar as if the Sun and Earth had
            come together—
The Sun descending and the Earth ascending   80
To take its place above . . . the Primal Matter
Was broken, the womb from which all life began,
Then to the murdered Sun a totem pole of dust arose in memory of
            Man.

The cataclysm of the Sun down-pouring
Seemed the roar
Of those vermilion Suns, the drops of the blood
That, bellowing like Mastodons at war,
Rush down the length of the world—away—away—

The violence of torrents, cataracts, maelstroms, rains
That went before the Flood—   90
These covered the earth from the freshets of our brothers' veins.

And with them, the forked lightnings of the gold
From the split mountains,
Blasting their rivals, the young foolish wheat-ears
Amid those terrible rains.

The gulf that was torn across the world seemed as if the beds of
         all the Oceans
Were emptied. . . . Naked, and gaping at what once had been the
         Sun,
Like the mouth of the Universal Famine,
It stretched its jaws from one end of the Earth to the other.

And in that hollow lay the body of our brother   100
Lazarus, upheaved from the world's tomb.
He lay in that great Death like the gold in the husk
Of the world . . . And round him, like spent lightnings, lay the
         Ore—
The balm for the world's sore.

And the gold lay in its husk of rough earth like the core
In the furred almond, the chestnut in its prickly
Bark, the walnut in a husk green and bitter.

Then to that hollow sea
The civilization of the Maimed, and, too, Life's lepers, came
As once to Christ near the Sea of Galilee.   110

They brought the Aeons of Blindness and the Night
Of the World, crying to him, "Lazarus, give us sight!
O you whose sores are of gold, who are the new Light
Of the World!"

                                        They brought to the Tomb
The Condemned of Man, who wear as stigmata from the womb
The depression of the skull as in the lesser
Beasts of Prey, the marks of Ape and Dog,
The canine and lemurine muscle . . . the pitiable, the terrible,

The loveless, whose deformities arose
Before their birth, or from a betrayal by the gold wheat-ear.   120
"Lazarus, for all love we knew the great Sun's kiss

On the loveless cheek. He came to the dog-fang and the lion-claw
That Famine gave the empty mouth, the workless hands.
He came to the inner leaf of the forsaken heart—
He spoke of our Christ and of a golden love. . . .
But our Sun is gone. . . . Will your gold bring warmth to the
        loveless lips and harvest to barren lands?"

Then Dives was brought. . . . He lay like a leprous Sun
That is covered with the sores of the world . . . the leprosy
Of gold encrusts the world that was his heart.

Like a great ear of wheat that is swoln with grain,   130
Then ruined by white rain,
He lay. . . . His hollow face, dust white, was cowled with a hood
        of gold;
But you saw there was no beat or pulse of blood—
You would not know him now from Lazarus!

He did not look at us.
He said. "What was spilt still surges like the Flood.
But Gold shall be the Blood
Of the world. . . . Brute gold condemned to the primal essence
Has the texture, smell, warmth, color of Blood. We must take

A quintessence of the disease for remedy. Once hold   140
The primal matter of all gold—
From which it grows
(That Rose of the World) as the sharp clear tree from the seed of
        the great rose—

Then give of this, condensed to the transparency
Of the beryl, the weight of twenty barley grains:
And the leper's face will be full as the rose's face
After great rains.

It will shape again the Shadow of Man. Or at least will take
From all roots of life the symptoms of the leper—

And make the body sharp as the honeycomb,   150
And the roots of life that are left like the red roots of the rose-
    branches."

But near him a gold sound—
The voice of an unborn wheat-ear accusing Dives—
Said, "Soon I shall be more rare, more precious than gold."

There are no thunders, there are no fires, no suns, no earthquakes
Left in our blood. . . . But yet, like the rolling thunders of all the
    fires in the world, we cry
To Dives: "You are the shadow of Cain. Your shade is the primal
    Hunger."
"I lie under what condemnation?"
"The same as Adam, the same as Cain, the same as Sodom, the same
    as Judas.

And the fires of your Hell shall not be quenched by the rain   160
From those torn and parti-colored garments of Christ, those rags
That once were Men. Each wound, each stripe,
Cries out more loudly than the voice of Cain—
Saying, 'Am I my brother's keeper?'" Think! When the last clamor
    of the Bought and Sold,
The agony of Gold,
Is hushed. . . . When the last Judas-kiss
Has died upon the cheek of the Starved Man Christ, those ashes
    that were men
Will rise again
To be our Fires upon the Judgment Day!
And yet—who dreamed that Christ has died in vain?   170
He walks again on the Seas of Blood, He comes in the terrible Rain.

Wilfred Owen
1893-1918

FROM MY DIARY, JULY 1914
(1931)

Leaves
  Murmuring by myriads in the shimmering trees.
Lives
  Wakening with wonder in the Pyrenees.
Birds
  Cheerily chirping in the early day.
Bards
  Singing of summer scything thro' the hay.
Bees
  Shaking the heavy dews from bloom and frond.   10
Boys
  Bursting the surface of the ebony pond.
Flashes
  Of swimmers carving thro' the sparkling cold.
Fleshes
  Gleaming with wetness to the morning gold.
A mead
  Bordered about with warbling water brooks.
A maid
  Laughing the love-laugh with me; proud of looks.   20
The heat
  Throbbing between the upland and the peak.
Her heart
  Quivering with passion to my pressed cheek.
Braiding

Of floating flames across the mountain brow.
Brooding
Of stillness; and a sighing of the bough.
Stirs
Of leaflets in the gloom; soft petal-showers;   30
Stars
Expanding with the starr'd nocturnal flowers.

DULCE ET DECORUM EST
(1921)

Bent double, like old beggars under sacks,
Knock-kneed, coughing like hags, we cursed through sludge,
Till on the haunting flares we turned our backs,
And towards our distant rest began to trudge.
Men marched asleep. Many had lost their boots,
But limped on, blood-shod. All went lame, all blind;
Drunk with fatigue; deaf even to the hoots
Of gas-shells dropping softly behind.

Gas! GAS! Quick, boys!—An ecstasy of fumbling,
Fitting the clumsy helmets just in time,   10
But someone still was yelling out and stumbling
And flound'ring like a man in fire or lime.—
Dim through the misty panes and thick green light,
As under a green sea, I saw him drowning.

In all my dreams before my helpless sight
He plunges at me, guttering, choking, drowning.

If in some smothering dreams, you too could pace
Behind the wagon that we flung him in,
And watch the white eyes wilting in his face,
His hanging face, like a devil's sick of sin,   20
If you could hear, at every jolt, the blood
Come gargling from the froth-corrupted lungs
Bitten as the cud
Of vile, incurable sores on innocent tongues,—
My friend, you would not tell with such high zest
To children ardent for some desperate glory,

The old Lie: *Dulce et decorum est*
Pro patria mori.

FUTILITY
(1921)

Move him into the sun—
Gently its touch awoke him once,
At home, whispering of fields unsown.
Always it woke him, even in France,
Until this morning and this snow.
If anything might rouse him now
The kind old sun will know.

Think how it wakes the seeds—
Woke, once, the clay of a cold star.
Are limbs so dear-achieved, are sides   10
Full-nerved,—still warm,—too hard to stir?
Was it for this the clay grew tall?
—Oh, what made fatuous sunbeams toil
To break earth's sleep at all?

ANTHEM FOR DOOMED YOUTH
(1921)

What passing-bells for these who die as cattle?
Only the monstrous anger of the guns.
Only the stuttering rifles' rapid rattle
Can patter out their hasty orisons.
No mockeries for them from prayers or bells,
Nor any voice of mourning save the choirs,—
The shrill, demented choirs of wailing shells;
And bugles calling for them from sad shires.

What candles may be held to speed them all?
Not in the hands of boys, but in their eyes   10
Shall shine the holy glimmers of good-byes.
The pallor of girls' brows shall be their pall;
Their flowers the tenderness of patient minds,
And each slow dusk a drawing-down of blinds.

APOLOGIA PRO POEMATE MEO

(1921)

I, too, saw God through mud—
    The mud that cracked on cheeks when wretches smiled.
    War brought more glory to their eyes than blood,
    And gave their laughs more glee than shakes a child.

Merry it was to laugh there—
    Where death becomes absurd and life absurder.
    For power was on us as we slashed bones bare
    Not to feel sickness or remorse of murder.

I, too, have dropped off fear—
    Behind the barrage, dead as my platoon,   10
    And sailed my spirit surging, light and clear
    Past the entanglement where hopes lay strewn;

And witnessed exultation—
    Faces that used to curse me, scowl for scowl,
    Shine and lift up with passion of oblation,
    Seraphic for an hour, though they were foul.

I have made fellowships—
    Untold of happy lovers in old song.
    For love is not the binding of fair lips
    With the soft silk of eyes that look and long,   20

By Joy, whose ribbon slips,—
    But wound with war's hard wire whose stakes are strong;
    Bound with the bandage of the arm that drips;
    Knit in the welding of the rifle-thong.

I have perceived much beauty
    In the hoarse oaths that kept our courage straight;
    Heard music in the silentness of duty;
    Found peace where shell-storms spouted reddest spate.

Nevertheless, except you share
    With them in hell the sorrowful dark of hell,   30
    Whose world is but the trembling of a flare,
    And heaven but as the highway for a shell,

You shall not hear their mirth:
    You shall not come to think them well content
    By any jest of mine. These men are worth
    Your tears. You are not worth their merriment.

STRANGE MEETING

(1921)

It seemed that out of the battle I escaped
Down some profound dull tunnel, long since scooped
Through granites which titanic wars had groined.
Yet also there encumbered sleepers groaned,
Too fast in thought or death to be bestirred.
Then, as I probed them, one sprang up, and stared
With piteous recognition in fixed eyes,
Lifting distressful hands as if to bless.
And by his smile, I knew that sullen hall;
By his dead smile I knew I stood in Hell.   10
With a thousand fears that vision's face was grained;
Yet no blood reached there from the upper ground,
And no guns thumped, or down the flues made moan.
"Strange, friend," I said, "here is no cause to mourn."
"None," said the other, "save the undone years,
The hopelessness. Whatever hope is yours,
Was my life also; I went hunting wild
After the wildest beauty in the world,
Which lies not calm in eyes, or braided hair,
But mocks the steady running of the hour,   20
And if it grieves, grieves richlier than here.
For by my glee might many men have laughed,
And of my weeping something had been left,
Which must die now. I mean the truth untold,
The pity of war, the pity war distilled.
Now men will go content with what we spoiled.
Or, discontent, boil bloody, and be spilled.
They will be swift with swiftness of the tigress,
None will break ranks, though nations trek from progress.
Courage was mine, and I had mystery,   30
Wisdom was mine, and I had mastery;
To miss the march of this retreating world

Into vain citadels that are not walled.
Then when much blood had clogged their chariot-wheels
I would go up and wash them from sweet wells,
Even with truths that lie too deep for taint.
I would have poured my spirit without stint
But not through wounds; not on the cess of war.
Foreheads of men have bled where no wounds were.
I am the enemy you killed, my friend.   40
I knew you in this death; for so you frowned
Yesterday through me as you jabbed and killed.
I parried; but my hands were loath and cold.
Let us sleep now. . . ."

Robert Graves

1895-

THE PIER–GLASS

(1921)

Lost manor where I walk continually
A ghost, though yet in woman's flesh and blood.
Up your broad stairs mounting with outspread fingers
And gliding steadfast down your corridors
I come by nightly custom to this room,
And even on sultry afternoons I come
Drawn by a thread of time-sunk memory.

Empty, unless for a huge bed of state
Shrouded with rusty curtains drooped awry
(A puppet theatre where malignant fancy   10
Peoples the wings with fear). At my right hand
A ravelled bell-pull hangs in readiness
To summon me from attic glooms above
Service of elder ghosts; here, at my left,
A sullen pier-glass, cracked from side to side,
Scorns to present the face (as do new mirrors)
With a lying flush, but shows it melancholy
And pale, as faces grow that look in mirrors.

Is there no life, nothing but the thin shadow
And blank foreboding, never a wainscot rat   20
Rasping a crust? Or at the window-pane
No fly, no bluebottle, no starveling spider?
The windows frame a prospect of cold skies
Half-merged with sea, as at the first creation—

Abstract, confusing welter. Face about,
Peer in the glass once more, take note
Of self, the grey lips and long hair dishevelled,
Sleep-staring eyes. Ah, mirror, for Christ's love
Give me one token that there still abides
Remote—beyond this island mystery,   30
So be it only this side Hope, somewhere,
In streams, on sun-warm mountain pasturage—
True life, natural breath; not this phantasma.

PURE DEATH

(1927)

We looked, we loved, and therewith instantly
Death became terrible to you and me.
By love we disenthralled our natural terror
From every comfortable philosopher
Or tall, grey doctor of divinity:
Death stood at last in his true rank and order.

It happened soon, so wild of heart were we,
Exchange of gifts grew to a malady:
Their worth rose always higher on each side
Till there seemed nothing but ungivable pride   10
That yet remained ungiven, and this degree
Called a conclusion not to be denied.

Then we at last bethought ourselves, made shift
And simultaneously this final gift
Gave: each with shaking hands unlocks
The sinister, long, brass-bound coffin-box,
Unwraps pure death, with such bewilderment
As greeted our love's first accomplishment.

RECALLING WAR

(1938)

Entrance and exit wounds are silvered clean,
The track aches only when the rain reminds.

The one-legged man forgets his leg of wood,
The one-armed man his jointed wooden arm.
The blinded man sees with his ears and hands
As much or more than once with both his eyes.
Their war was fought these twenty years ago
And now assumes the nature-look of time,
As when the morning traveller turns and views
His wild night-stumbling carved into a hill.   10

What, then, was war? No mere discord of flags
But an infection of the common sky
That sagged ominously upon the earth
Even when the season was the airiest May.
Down pressed the sky, and we, oppressed, thrust out
Boastful tongue, clenched fist and valiant yard.
Natural infirmities were out of mode,
For Death was young again: patron alone
Of healthy dying, premature fate-spasm.

Fear made fine bed-fellows. Sick with delight   20
At life's discovered transitoriness,
Our youth became all-flesh and waived the mind.
Never was such antiqueness of romance,
Such tasty honey oozing from the heart.
And old importances came swimming back—
Wine, meat, log-fires, a roof over the head,
A weapon at the thigh, surgeons at call.
Even there was a use again for God—
A word of rage in lack of meat, wine, fire,
In ache of wounds beyond all surgeoning.   30

War was return of earth to ugly earth,
War was foundering of sublimities,
Extinction of each happy art and faith
By which the world had still kept head in air.
Protesting logic or protesting love,
Until the unendurable moment struck—
The inward scream, the duty to run mad.

And we recall the merry ways of guns—
Nibbling the walls of factory and church

Like a child, piecrust; felling groves of trees   40
Like a child, dandelions with a switch!
Machine-guns rattle toy-like from a hill,
Down in a row the brave tin-soldiers fall:
A sight to be recalled in elder days
When learnedly the future we devote
To yet more boastful visions of despair.

CERTAIN MERCIES
(1938)

Now must all satisfaction
Appear mere mitigation
Of an accepted curse?

Must we henceforth be grateful
That the guards, though spiteful,
Are slow of foot and wit?

That by night we may spread
Over the plank bed
A thin coverlet?

That the rusty water   10
In the unclean pitcher
Our thirst quenches?

That the rotten, detestable
Food is yet eatable
By us ravenous?

That the prison censor
Permits a weekly letter?
(We may write: "we are well.")

That, with patience and deference,
We do not experience   20
The punishment cell?

That each new indignity
Defeats only the body,
Pampering the spirit
With obscure, proud merit?

TO JUAN AT THE WINTER SOLSTICE
(1946)

praise of fertility

There is one story and one story only
That will prove worth your telling, *— love*
Whether as learned bard or gifted child;
To it all lines or lesser gauds belong
That startle with their shining
Such common stories as they stray into.

Is it of trees you tell, their months and virtues,
Or strange beasts that beset you,
Of birds that croak at you the Triple will? *mother lover bearer — woman*
Or of the Zodiac and how slow it turns   10
Below the Boreal Crown,
Prison of all true kings that ever reigned?

Water to water, ark again to ark,
From woman back to woman:
So each new victim treads unfalteringly
The never altered circuit of his fate,
Bringing twelve peers as witness
Both to his starry rise and starry fall.

Aphrodite
Or is it of the Virgin's silver beauty,
All fish below the thighs?   20
She in her left hand bears a leafy quince;
When, with her right she crooks a finger smiling,
How may the King hold back?
Royally then he barters life for love.

Or of the undying snake from chaos hatched,
Whose coils contain the ocean,
Jason → Into whose chops with naked sword he springs,
Then in black water, tangled by the reeds,
death

trinity

Battles three days and nights,
To be spewed up beside her scalloped shore?　　30

Much snow is falling, winds roar hollowly,
death The owl hoots from the elder,
man *woman*
Fear in your heart cries to the loving-cup:
Sorrow to sorrow as the sparks fly upward.
The log groans and confesses
There is one story and one story only.

dedication to woman and love — you will be ok.
Dwell on her graciousness, dwell on her smiling,
Do not forget what flowers
The great boar trampled down in ivy time.
Her brow was creamy as the crested wave,　　40
Her sea-blue eyes were wild
But nothing promised that is not performed.

CRY FAUGH!

(1953)

Caria and Philistia considered
Only pre-marital adventures wise;
The bourgeois French argue contrariwise.

Socrates and Plato burked the issue
(Namely, how man-and-woman love should be)
With homosexual ideology.

Apocalyptic Israelites, foretelling
The Imminent End, called only for a chaste
Sodality: all dead below the waist.

Curious, various, amoral, moral—　　10
Confess, what elegant square or lumpish hamlet
Lives free from nymphological disquiet?

"Yet males and females of the lower species
Contrive to eliminate the sexual problem,"
Scientists ponder: "Why not learn from them?"

Cry faugh! on science, ethics, metaphysics,
On antonyms of sacred and profane—
Come walk with me, love, in a golden rain

Past toppling colonnades of glory,
The moon alive on each uptilted face: 20
Proud remnants of a visionary race.

C. Day Lewis

1904-

REST FROM LOVING AND BE LIVING

(1931)

Rest from loving and be living.
Fallen is fallen past retrieving
The unique flyer dawn's dove
Arrowing down feathered with fire.

sunrise on realistic level

scial statmant get out to real world

Cease denying, begin knowing.   *Froend*
Comes peace this way here comes renewing
With dower of bird and bud knocks
Loud on winter wall on death's door.

move to affermative action

Here's no meaning but of morning.
Naught soon of night but stars remaining,   10
Sink lower, fade, as dark womb
Recedes creation will step clear.

NEARING AGAIN THE LEGENDARY ISLE

(1933)

n·

Nearing again the legendary isle
Where sirens sang and mariners were skinned,
We wonder now what was there to beguile
That such stout fellows left their bones behind.

128

Those chorus-girls are surely past their prime,
Voices grow shrill and paint is wearing thin,
Lips that sealed up the sense from gnawing time
Now beg the favour with a graveyard grin.

We have no flesh to spare and they can't bite,
Hunger and sweat have stripped us to the bone;   10
A skeleton crew we toil upon the tide
And mock the theme-song meant to lure us on:

No need to stop the ears, avert the eyes   *no such mythicle*
From purple rhetoric of evening skies.   *world*

COME, LIVE WITH ME AND BE MY LOVE
(1935)

Come, live with me and be my love,
And we will all the pleasures prove   *Sarcasm*
Of peace and plenty, bed and board,
That chance employment may afford.

I'll handle dainties on the docks
And thou shalt read of summer frocks:
At evening by the sour canals
We'll hope to hear some madrigals.

Care on thy maiden brow shall put
A wreath of wrinkles, and thy foot   10
Be shod with pain: not silken dress
But toil shall tire thy loveliness.

Hunger shall make thy modest zone
And cheat fond death of all but bone—
If these delights thy mind may move,
Then live with me and be my love.

MAPLE AND SUMACH
(1938)

Maple and sumach down this autumn ride—
Look, in what scarlet character they speak!

For this their russet and rejoicing week
Trees spend a year of sunsets on their pride.
You leaves drenched with the lifeblood of the year—
What flamingo dawns have wavered from the east,
What eves have crimsoned to their toppling crest
To give the fame and transience that you wear!
Leaf-low he shall lie soon: but no such blaze
Briefly can cheer man's ashen, harsh decline;   10
His fall is short of pride, he bleeds within
And paler creeps to the dead end of his days.
O light's abandon and the fire-crest sky
Speak in me now for all who are to die!

DEPARTURE IN THE DARK
(1943)

Nothing so sharply reminds a man he is mortal
As leaving a place
In a winter morning's dark, the air on his face
Unkind as the touch of sweating metal:
Simple goodbyes to children or friends become
A felon's numb
Farewell, and love that was a warm, a meeting place—
Love is the suicide's grave under the nettles.

Gloomed and clemmed as if by an imminent ice-age
Lies the dear world   10
Of your street-strolling, field-faring. The senses, curled
At the dead end of a shrinking passage,
Care not if close the inveterate hunters creep,
And memories sleep
Like mammoths in lost caves. Drear, extinct is the world,
And has no voice for consolation or presage.

There is always something at such times of the passover,
When the dazed heart
Beats for it knows not what, whether you part
From home or prison, acquaintance or lover—   20
Something wrong with the time-table, something unreal
In the scrambled meal

And the bag ready packed by the door, as though the heart
Has gone ahead, or is staying here for ever.

No doubt for the Israelites that early morning
It was hard to be sure
If home were prison or prison home: the desire
Going forth meets the desire returning.
This land, that had cut their pride down to the bone
Was now their own   30
By ancient deeds of sorrow. Beyond, there was nothing sure
But a desert of freedom to quench their fugitive yearnings.

At this blind hour the heart is informed of nature's
Ruling that man
Should be nowhere a more tenacious settler than
Among wry thorns and ruins, yet nurture
A seed of discontent in his ripest ease.
There's a kind of release
And a kind of torment in every goodbye for every man
And will be, even to the last of his dark departures.   40

BIRTHDAY POEM FOR THOMAS HARDY
(1948)

Is it birthday weather for you, dear soul?
Is it fine your way,
With tall moon-daisies alight, and the mole
Busy, and elegant hares at play
By meadow paths where once you would stroll
In the flush of day?

I fancy the beasts and flowers there beguiled
By a visitation
That casts no shadow, a friend whose mild
Inquisitive glance lights with compassion,   10
Beyond the tomb, on all of this wild
And humbled creation.

It's hard to believe a spirit could die
Of such generous glow,
Or to doubt that somewhere a bird-sharp eye

Still broods on the capers of men below,
A stern voice asks the Immortals why
They should plague us so.

Dear poet, wherever you are, I greet you.
Much irony, wrong,   20
Innocence you'd find here to tease or entreat you,
And many the fate-fires have tempered strong,
But none that in ripeness of soul could meet you
Or magic of song.

Great brow, frail frame—gone. Yet you abide
In the shadow and sheen,
All the mellowing traits of a countryside
That nursed your tragi-comical scene;
And in us, warmer-hearted and brisker-eyed
Since you have been.   30

William Empson
1906-

THE WORLD'S END
(1935)

"Fly with me then to all's and the world's end
And plumb for safety down the gaps of stars;
Let the last gulf or topless cliff befriend,
What tyrant there our variance debars?"

Alas, how hope for freedom, no bars bind;
Space is like earth, rounded, a padded cell;
Plumb the stars' depth, your lead bumps you behind;
Blind Satan's voice rattled the whole of Hell.

On cushioned air what is such metal worth
To pierce to the gulf that lies so snugly curled?   10
Each tangent plain touches one top of earth,
Each point in one direction ends the world.

Apple of knowledge and forgetful mere
From Tantalus too differential bend.
The shadow clings. The world's end is here.
This place's curvature precludes its end.

TO AN OLD LADY

(1935)

readiness   *dying—old age*

Ripeness is all; her in her cooling planet
Revere; do not presume to think her wasted.
no false pity — Project her no projectile, plan nor man it;
Gods cool in turn, by the sun long outlasted.

all die   only life lasts — nature

Our earth alone given no name of god
Gives, too, no hold for such a leap to aid her;   *sensibility*
sympathy — Landing, you break some palace and seem odd;
Bees sting their need, the keeper's queen invader.

No, to your telescope; spy out the land; *Stay at a proper distant*
ritual + tradition — Watch while her ritual is still to see,
Still stand her temples emptying in the sand *time*   10
Whose waves o'erthrew their crumbled tracery;

Still stand uncalled-on her soul's appanage;
Much social detail whose successor fades,   *— what she*
Wit used to run a house and to play Bridge,   *has left*
And tragic fervour, to dismiss her maids.

Years her precession do not throw from gear.   *ritual*
She reads a compass certain of her pole;
Confident, finds no confines on her sphere,   *knows she is*
Whose failing crops are in her sole control.   *dying*   20

Stars how much further from me fill my night.
Strange that she too should be inaccessible, —   *conflict between old*
life itself — Who shares my sun. He curtains her from sight,   *& young*
And but in darkness is she visible.
death

THIS LAST PAIN

(1935)

secularism This last pain for the damned the Fathers found:
"They knew the bliss with which they were not crowned."
Such, but on earth, let me foretell,
Is all, of heaven or of hell.

Man, as the prying housemaid of the soul,   *all we have is*
May know her happiness by eye to hole: *occasional glimpses*
   He's safe; the key is lost; he knows   *of the holy*
   Door will not open, nor hole close.

"What is conceivable can happen too,"
Said Wittgenstein, who had not dreamt of you;   *– leaves* *out spirit* 10
   But wisely; if we worked it long
   We should forget where it was wrong. *-- wrong theory* ✱

     sorrows   *win*
Those thorns are crowns which, woven into knots,
Crackle under and soon boil fool's pots; *man*
   And no man's watching, wise and long,
   Would ever stare them into song.   *Knowledge does not become joy*
       educative but leads to
   time caves   *all suffering one*   *nothing*
Thorns burn to a consistent ash, like man;
A splendid cleanser for the frying-pan: *time is*   *life*
   And those who leap from pan to fire
   Should this brave opposite admire.   20
     of thorn to ash

All those large dreams by which men long live well
    dreams
Are magic-lanterned on the smoke of hell; *- life itself*
   This then is real, I have implied,
   A painted, small, transparent slide.
    /artificial   *'suspect*
  fictions
These the inventive can hand-paint at leisure,   *make up own dreams*
Or most emporia would stock our measure;
   And feasting in their dappled shade
   We should forget how they were made. *- by men*

Feign then what's by a decent tact believed   *stoicism*
And act that state is only so conceived,   30
   And build an edifice of form *- custom, ritual*
   For house where phantoms may keep warm.

Imagine, then, by miracle, with me,
(Ambiguous gifts, as what gods give must be)
   What could not possibly be there,
   And learn a style from a despair.
    joy living

IGNORANCE OF DEATH
(1940)

Then there is this civilising love of death, by which
Even music and painting tell you what else to love.
Buddhists and Christians contrive to agree about death

Making death their ideal basis for different ideals.
The Communists however disapprove of death
Except when practical. The people who dig up

Corpses and rape them are I understand not reported.
The Freudians regard the death-wish as fundamental,
Though "the clamour of life" proceeds from its rival "Eros."

Whether you are to admire a given case for making less clamour   10
Is not their story. Liberal hopefulness
Regards death as a mere border to an improving picture.

Because we have neither hereditary nor direct knowledge of death
It is the trigger of the literary man's biggest gun
And we are happy to equate it to any conceived calm.

Heaven me, when a man is ready to die about something
Other than himself, and is in fact ready because of that,
Not because of himself, that is something clear about himself.

Otherwise I feel very blank upon this topic,
And think that though important, and proper for anyone to bring up,
It is one that most people should be prepared to be blank upon.   21

MISSING DATES
(1940)

Slowly the poison the whole blood stream fills.
It is not the effort nor the failure tires.
The waste remains, the waste remains and kills.

It is not your system or clear sight that mills
Down small to the consequence a life requires;
Slowly the poison the whole blood stream fills.

They bled an old dog dry yet the exchange rills
Of young dog blood gave but a month's desires;
The waste remains, the waste remains and kills.

It is the Chinese tombs and the slag hills   10
Usurp the soil, and not the soil retires.
Slowly the poison the whole blood stream fills.

Not to have fire is to be a skin that shrills.
The complete fire is death. From partial fires
The waste remains, the waste remains and kills.

It is the poems you have lost, the ills
From missing dates, at which the heart expires.
Slowly the poison the whole blood stream fills.
The waste remains, the waste remains and kills.

MANCHOULI

(1940)

I find it normal, passing these great frontiers,
That you scan the crowds in rags eagerly each side
With awe; that the nations seem real; that their ambitions
Having such achieved variety within one type, seem sane;
I find it normal;
So too to extract false comfort from that word.

W. H. Auden
1907-

PETITION
(1930)

[handwritten: prayer]

[handwritten: , God]

Sir, no man's enemy, forgiving all
But will its negative inversion, be prodigal: *[handwritten: generous]*
Send to us power and light, a sovereign touch
[handwritten: free] Curing the intolerable neural itch, *[handwritten: renaissance kings]*
The exhaustion of weaning, the liar's quinsy,
And the distortions of ingrown virginity. *[handwritten: - guilt]*
Prohibit sharply the rehearsed response
And gradually correct the coward's stance;
Cover in time with beams those in retreat
That, spotted, they turn though the reverse were great;   10
Publish each healer that in city lives
Or country houses at the end of drives;
Harrow the house of the dead; look shining at
New styles of architecture, a change of heart.
[handwritten: living]

WHICH SIDE AM I SUPPOSED TO BE ON?
(1932)

Though aware of our rank and alert to obey orders,
Watching with binoculars the movement of the grass for an ambush,
The pistol cocked, the code-word committed to memory;
          The youngest drummer
Knows all the peace-time stories like the oldest soldier,
          Though frontier-conscious.

About the tall white gods who landed from their open boat,
Skilled in the working of copper, appointing our feast-days,
Before the islands were submerged, when the weather was calm,
      The maned lion common,   10
An open wishing-well in every garden;
        When love came easy.

Perfectly certain, all of us, but not from the records,
Not from the unshaven agent who returned to the camp;
The pillar dug from the desert recorded only
      The sack of a city,
The agent clutching his side collapsed at our feet,
      "Sorry! They got me!"

Yes, they were living here once but do not now,
Yes, they are living still but do not here;   20
Lying awake after Lights Out a recruit may speak up:
      "Who told you all this?"
The tent-talk pauses a little till a veteran answers
      "Go to sleep, Sonny!"

Turning over he closes his eyes, and then in a moment
Sees the sun at midnight bright over cornfield and pasture,
Our hope. . . . Someone jostles him, fumbling for boots,
      Time to change guard:
Boy, the quarrel was before your time, the aggressor
      No one you know.   30

Your childish moments of awareness were all of our world,
At five you sprang, already a tiger in the garden,
At night your mother taught you to pray for our Daddy
      Far away fighting,
One morning you fell off a horse and your brother mocked you:
      "Just like a girl!"

You've got their names to live up to and questions won't help,
You've a very full programme, first aid, gunnery, tactics,
The technique to master of raids and hand-to-hand fighting;
      Are you in training?   40
Are you taking care of yourself? are you sure of passing
      The endurance test?

Now we're due to parade on the square in front of the Cathedral,
When the bishop has blessed us, to file in after the choirboys,
To stand with the wine-dark conquerors in the roped-off pews,
   Shout ourselves hoarse:
"They ran like hares; we have broken them up like firewood;
   They fought against God."

While in a great rift in the limestone miles away
At the same hour they gather, tethering their horses beside them; 50
A scarecrow prophet from a boulder foresees our judgment,
   Their oppressors howling;
And the bitter psalm is caught by the gale from the rocks:
   "How long shall they flourish?"

What have we all been doing to have made from Fear
That laconic war-bitten captain addressing them now?
"Heart and head shall be keener, mood the more
   As our might lessens":
To have caused their shout "We will fight till we lie down beside
   The Lord we have loved." 60

There's Wrath who has learnt every trick of guerrilla warfare,
The shamming dead, the night-raid, the feinted retreat;
Envy their brilliant pamphleteer, to lying
   As husband true,
Expert impersonator and linguist, proud of his power
   To hoodwink sentries.

Gluttony living alone, austerer than us,
Big simple Greed, Acedia famed with them all
For her stamina, keeping the outposts, and somewhere Lust
   With his sapper's skill, 70
Muttering to his fuses in a tunnel "Could I meet here with Love,
   I would hug her to death."

There are faces there for which for a very long time
We've been on the look-out, though often at home we imagined,
Catching sight of a back or hearing a voice through a doorway,
   We had found them at last;
Put our arms round their necks and looked in their eyes and discovered
   We were unlucky.

And some of them, surely, we seem to have seen before:
Why, that girl who rode off on her bicycle one fine summer evening
And never returned, she's there; and the banker we'd noticed   81
    Worried for weeks;
Till he failed to arrive one morning and his room was empty,
    Gone with a suitcase.

They speak of things done on the frontier we were never told,
The hidden path to their squat Pictish tower
They will never reveal though kept without sleep, for their code is
    "Death to the squealer":
They are brave, yes, though our newspapers mention their bravery
    In inverted commas.   90

But careful; back to our lines; it is unsafe there,
Passports are issued no longer; that area is closed;
There's no fire in the waiting-room now at the climbers' Junction,
    And all this year
Work has been stopped on the power-house; the wind whistles under
    The half-built culverts.

Do you think that because you have heard that on Christmas Eve
In a quiet sector they walked about on the skyline,
Exchanged cigarettes, both learning the words for "I love you"
    In either language: 100
You can stroll across for a smoke and a chat any evening?
    Try it and see.

That rifle-sight you're designing; is it ready yet?
You're holding us up; the office is getting impatient;
The square munition works out on the old allotments
    Needs stricter watching;
If you see any loiterers there you may shoot without warning,
    We must stop that leakage.

All leave is cancelled tonight; we must say good-bye.
We entrain at once for the North; we shall see in the morning   110
The headlands we're doomed to attack; snow down to the tide-line:
    Though the bunting signals
"Indoors before it's too late; cut peat for your fires,"
    We shall lie out there.

SOMETHING IS BOUND TO HAPPEN
(1933)

Doom is dark and deeper than any sea-dingle:
Upon what man it fall
In spring, day-wishing flowers appearing,
Avalanche sliding, white snow from rock-face,
That he should leave his house,
No cloud-soft hands can hold him, restraint by women,
But ever that man goes
Through place-keepers, through forest trees,
A stranger to strangers over undried sea,
Houses for fishes, suffocating water;   10
Or lonely on fell as chat,
By pot-holed becks
A bird stone-haunting, an unquiet bird.

There head falls forward, fatigued at evening,
And dreams of home,
Waving from window, spread of welcome,
Kissing of wife under single sheet;
But waking sees
Bird-flocks nameless to him, through doorway voices
Of new men making another love.   20

Save him from hostile capture,
From sudden tiger's spring at corner:
Protect his house,
His anxious house where days are counted
From thunderbolt protect,
From gradual ruin spreading like a stain;
Converting number from vague to certain,
Bring joy, bring day of his returning,
Lucky with day approaching, with leaning dawn.

LOOK, STRANGER, ON THIS ISLAND NOW
(1936)

Look, stranger, on this island now
The leaping light for your delight discovers,
Stand stable here

And silent be,
That through the channels of the ear
May wander like a river
The swaying sound of the sea.

Here at the small field's ending pause
Where the chalk wall falls to the foam and its tall ledges
Oppose the pluck   10
And knock of the tide,
And the shingle scrambles after the suck-
ing surf,
And the gull lodges
A moment on its sheer side.

Far off like floating seeds the ships
Diverge on urgent voluntary errands;
And the full view
Indeed may enter
And move in memory as now these clouds do,   20
That pass the harbour mirror
And all the summer through the water saunter.

NOW THE LEAVES ARE FALLING FAST
(1936)

Now the leaves are falling fast,
Nurse's flowers will not last;
Nurses to the graves are gone,
And the prams go rolling on.

Whispering neighbours, left and right,
Pluck us from the real delight;
And the active hands must freeze
Lonely on the separate knees.

Dead in hundreds at the back
Follow wooden in our track,   10
Arms raised stiffly to reprove
In false attitudes of love.

Starving through the leafless wood
Trolls run scolding for their food;
And the nightingale is dumb,
And the angel will not come.

Cold, impossible, ahead
Lifts the mountain's lovely head
Whose white waterfall could bless
Travellers in their last distress.   20

WHO'S WHO
(1936)

A shilling life will give you all the facts:
How Father beat him, how he ran away,
What were the struggles of his youth, what acts
Made him the greatest figure of his day:
Of how he fought, fished, hunted, worked all night,
Though giddy, climbed new mountains; named a sea:
Some of the last researchers even write
Love made him weep his pints like you and me.

With all his honours on, he sighed for one
Who, say astonished critics, lived at home;   10
Did little jobs about the house with skill
And nothing else; could whistle; would sit still
Or potter round the garden; answered some
Of his long marvellous letters but kept none.

O FOR DOORS TO BE OPEN
(1936)

—"O for doors to be open and an invite with gilded edges
  To dine with Lord Lobcock and Count Asthma on the platinum benches,
  With the somersaults and fireworks, the roast and the smacking kisses"—
      Cried the cripples to the silent statue,
      The six beggared cripples.

—"And Garbo's and Cleopatra's wits to go astraying,
  In a feather ocean with me to go fishing and playing,
  Still jolly when the cock has burst himself with crowing"—
      Cried the cripples to the silent statue,
      The six beggared cripples.   10

—"And to stand on green turf among the craning yellow faces
  Dependent on the chestnut, the sable, and Arabian horses,
  And me with a magic crystal to foresee their places"—
      Cried the cripples to the silent statue,
      The six beggared cripples.

—"And this square to be deck and these pigeons sails to rig,
  And to follow the delicious breeze like a tantony pig
  To the shaded feverless islands where the melons are big"—
      Cried the cripples to the silent statue,
      The six beggared cripples.   20

—"And these shops to be turned to tulips in a garden bed,
  And me with my crutch to thrash each merchant dead
  As he pokes from a flower his bald and wicked head"—
      Cried the cripples to the silent statue,
      The six beggared cripples.

—"And a hole in the bottom of heaven, and Peter and Paul
  And each smug surprised saint like parachutes to fall,
  And every one-legged beggar to have no legs at all"—
      Cried the cripples to the silent statue,
      The six beggared cripples.   30

NIGHT FALLS ON CHINA
(1939)

Night falls on China; the great arc of travelling shadow
Moves over land and ocean, altering life:
Thibet already silent, the packed Indias cooling,

Inert in the paralysis of caste. And though in Africa
The vegetation still grows fiercely like the young,
And in the cities that receive the slanting radiations

The lucky are at work, and most still know they suffer.
The dark will touch them soon: night's tiny noises
Will echo vivid in the owl's developed ear,

Vague in the anxious sentry's; and the moon look down   10
On battlefields and dead men lying, heaped like treasure,
On lovers ruined in a brief embrace, on ships

Where exiles watch the sea: and in the silence
The cry that streams out into the indifferent spaces,
And never stops or slackens, may be heard more clearly,

Above the everlasting murmur of the woods and rivers,
And more insistent than the lulling answer of the waltzes,
Or hum of printing-presses turning forests into lies;

As now I hear it, rising round me from Shanghai,
And mingling with the distant mutter of guerrilla fighting,   20
The voice of Man: "O teach us to outgrow our madness.

Ruffle the perfect manners of the frozen heart,
And once again compel it to be awkward and alive,
To all it suffered once a weeping witness.

Clear from the head the masses of impressive rubbish;
Rally the lost and trembling forces of the will,
Gather them up and let them loose upon the earth,

Till, as the contribution of our star, we follow
The clear instructions of that Justice, in the shadow
Of Whose uplifting, loving, and constraining power   30
All human reasons do rejoice and operate."

LAW LIKE LOVE

(1940)

Law, say the gardeners, is the sun,
Law is the one
All gardeners obey
Tomorrow, yesterday, today.

Law is the wisdom of the old
The impotent grandfathers shrilly scold;
The grandchildren put out a treble tongue,
Law is the senses of the young.

Law, says the priest with a priestly look,
Expounding to an unpriestly people,   10
Law is the words in my priestly book,
Law is my pulpit and my steeple.

Law, says the judge as he looks down his nose,
Speaking clearly and most severely,
Law is as I've told you before,
Law is as you know I suppose,
Law is but let me explain it once more,
Law is The Law.

Yet law-abiding scholars write;
Law is neither wrong nor right,   20
Law is only crimes
Punished by places and by times,
Law is the clothes men wear
Anytime, anywhere,
Law is Good-morning and Good-night.

Others say, Law is our Fate;
Others say, Law is our State;
Others say, others say
Law is no more,
Law is gone away.   30

And always the loud angry crowd
Very angry and very loud
Law is We,
And always the soft idiot softly Me.

If we, dear, know we know no more
Than they about the law,
If I no more than you
Know what we should and should not do
Except that all agree

Gladly or miserably   40
That the law is
And that all know this,
If therefore thinking it absurd
To identify Law with some other word,
Unlike so many men
I cannot say Law is again,
No more than they can we suppress
The universal wish to guess
Or slip out of our own position
Into an unconcerned condition.   50
Although I can at least confine
Your vanity and mine
To stating timidly
A timid similarity,
We shall boast anyway:
Like love I say.

Like love we don't know where or why
Like love we can't compel or fly
Like love we often weep
Like love we seldom keep.   60

LAY YOUR SLEEPING HEAD, MY LOVE
(1940)

Lay your sleeping head, my love,
Human on my faithless arm;
Time and fevers burn away
Individual beauty from
Thoughtful children, and the grave
Proves the child ephemeral:
But in my arms till break of day
Let the living creature lie,
Mortal, guilty, but to me   moral attributes
The entirely beautiful.   10

Soul and body have no bounds:
To lovers as they lie upon
Her tolerant enchanted slope
Venus

In their ordinary swoon,
Grave the vision Venus sends
Of supernatural sympathy,
Universal love and hope;
While an abstract insight wakes
Among the glaciers and the rocks
The hermit's sensual ecstasy.   20

Certainty, fidelity
On the stroke of midnight pass
Like vibrations of a bell,
And fashionable madmen raise
Their pedantic boring cry:
Every farthing of the cost,
All the dreaded cards foretell,
Shall be paid, but from this night
Not a whisper, not a thought,
Not a kiss nor look be lost.   30

Beauty, midnight, vision dies:
Let the winds of dawn that blow
Softly round your dreaming head
Such a day of sweetness show
Eye and knocking heart may bless,
Find the mortal world enough;
Noons of dryness see you fed
By the involuntary powers,
Nights of insult let you pass
Watched by every human love.   40

MUSÉE DES BEAUX ARTS
(1940)

About suffering they were never wrong,
The Old Masters: how well they understood
Its human position; how it takes place
While someone else is eating or opening a window or just walking dully along;
How, when the aged are reverently, passionately waiting
For the miraculous birth, there always must be

Children who did not specially want it to happen, skating
On a pond at the edge of the wood:
They never forgot
That even the dreadful martyrdom must run its course   10
Anyhow in a corner, some untidy spot
Where the dogs go on with their doggy life and the torturer's horse
Scratches its innocent behind on a tree.

In Brueghel's *Icarus*, for instance: how everything turns away
Quite leisurely from the disaster; the ploughman may
Have heard the splash, the forsaken cry,
But for him it was not an important failure; the sun shone
As it had to on the white legs disappearing into the green
Water; and the expensive delicate ship that must have seen
Something amazing, a boy falling out of the sky,   20
Had somewhere to get to and sailed calmly on.

IN MEMORY OF W. B. YEATS
(d. Jan. 1939)
(1940)

I

He disappeared in the dead of winter:
The brooks were frozen, the airports almost deserted,
And snow disfigured the public statues;
The mercury sank in the mouth of the dying day.
O all the instruments agree ·social idifference
The day of his death was a dark cold day.

Far from his illness
The wolves ran on through the evergreen forests,
The peasant river was untempted by the fashionable quays;
By mourning tongues   10
The death of the poet was kept from his poems· immortality in his
                                                                    art

But for him it was his last afternoon as himself,
An afternoon of nurses and rumours;
The provinces of his body revolted,

The squares of his mind were empty,
Silence invaded the suburbs,   — *city imagery*
The current of his feeling failed: he became his admirers.

Now he is scattered among a hundred cities
And wholly given over to unfamiliar affections;
To find his happiness in another kind of wood   20
And be punished under a foreign code of conscience.
The words of a dead man   *works modified by each reader*
Are modified in the guts of the living.

But in the importance and noise of tomorrow
When the brokers are roaring like beasts on the floor of the Bourse,
And the poor have the sufferings to which they are fairly accustomed,
And each in the cell of himself is almost convinced of his freedom;   *—capitalism*
A few thousand will think of this day
As one thinks of a day when one did something slightly unusual.
O all the instruments agree   30
The day of his death was a dark cold day.

                    II
You were silly like us: your gift survived it all;
The parish of rich women, physical decay,   *not idealist*
Yourself; mad Ireland hurt you into poetry.   *realistic*
Now Ireland has her madness and her weather still,
For poetry makes nothing happen: it survives
In the valley of its saying where executives   *— anti system*
Would never want to tamper; it flows south
From ranches of isolation and the busy griefs,
Raw towns that we believe and die in; it survives,   40
A way of happening, a mouth.

                    III
Earth, receive an honoured guest;   *incantation like*
William Yeats is laid to rest:
Let the Irish vessel lie
Emptied of its poetry.

Time that is intolerant   —
Of the brave and innocent,
And indifferent in a week
To a beautiful physique,   *always changing*

Worships language and forgives   50
Everyone by whom it lives;
Pardons cowardice, conceit,
Lays its honours at their feet.

Time that with this strange excuse
Pardoned Kipling and his views,
And will pardon Paul Claudel,
Pardons him for writing well.

In the nightmare of the dark
All the dogs of Europe bark,
And the living nations wait,   60
Each sequestered in its hate;

Intellectual disgrace
Stares from every human face,
And the seas of pity lie
Locked and frozen in each eye.

Follow, poet, follow right
To the bottom of the night,
With your unconstraining voice
Still persuade us to rejoice;

With the farming of a verse   70
Make a vineyard of the curse,
Sing of human unsuccess
In a rapture of distress;

In the deserts of the heart
Let the healing fountain start,
In the prison of his days
Teach the free man how to praise.

SEPTEMBER 1, 1939
(1940)

I sit in one of the dives
On Fifty-Second Street
Uncertain and afraid
As the clever hopes expire

Of a low dishonest decade:
Waves of anger and fear
Circulate over the bright
And darkened lands of the earth,
Obsessing our private lives;
The unmentionable odour of death   10
Offends the September night.

Accurate scholarship can
Unearth the whole offence
From Luther until now
That has driven a culture mad,
Find what occurred at Linz,
What huge imago made
A psychopathic god:
I and the public know
What all schoolchildren learn,   20
Those to whom evil is done
Do evil in return.

Exiled Thucydides knew
All that a speech can say
About Democracy,
And what dictators do,
The elderly rubbish they talk
To an apathetic grave;
Analysed all in his book,
The enlightenment driven away,   30
The habit-forming pain,
Mismanagement and grief:
We must suffer them all again.

Into this neutral air
Where blind skyscrapers use
Their full height to proclaim
The strength of Collective Man,
Each language pours its vain
Competitive excuse:
But who can live for long   40
In an euphoric dream;

Out of the mirror they stare,
Imperialism's face
And the international wrong.

Faces along the bar
Cling to their average day:
The lights must never go out,
The music must always play,
All the conventions conspire
To make this fort assume   50
The furniture of home;
Lest we should see where we are,
Lost in a haunted wood,
Children afraid of the night
Who have never been happy or good.

The windiest militant trash
Important Persons shout
Is not so crude as our wish:
What mad Nijinsky wrote
About Diaghilev   60
Is true of the normal heart;
For the error bred in the bone
Of each woman and each man
Craves what it cannot have,
Not universal love
But to be loved alone.

From the conservative dark
Into the ethical life
The dense commuters come,
Repeating their morning vow;   70
"I *will* be true to the wife,
I'll concentrate more on my work,"
And helpless governors wake
To resume their compulsory game:
Who can release them now,
Who can reach the deaf,
Who can speak for the dumb?

Defenceless under the night
Our world in stupor lies;

Yet, dotted everywhere,   80
Ironic points of light
Flash out wherever the Just
Exchange their messages:
May I, composed like them
Of Eros and of dust,
Beleaguered by the same
Negation and despair,
Show an affirming flame.

IN MEMORY OF SIGMUND FREUD
(d. Sept. 1939)
(1940)

When there are so many we shall have to mourn,
When grief has been made so public, and exposed
            To the critique of a whole epoch
            The frailty of our conscience and anguish,

Of whom shall we speak? For every day they die
Among us, those who were doing us some good,
            And knew it was never enough but
            Hoped to improve a little by living.

Such was this doctor: still at eighty he wished
To think of our life, from whose unruliness   10
            So many plausible young futures
            With threats or flattery ask obedience.

But his wish was denied him; he closed his eyes
Upon that last picture common to us all,
            Of problems like relatives standing
            Puzzled and jealous about our dying.

For about him at the very end were still
Those he had studied, the nervous and the nights,
            And shades that still waited to enter
            The bright circle of his recognition   20

Turned elsewhere with their disappointment as he
Was taken away from his old interest
        To go back to the earth in London,
        An important Jew who died in exile.

Only Hate was happy, hoping to augment
His practice now, and his shabby clientèle
        Who think they can be cured by killing
        And covering the gardens with ashes.

They are still alive but in a world he changed
Simply by looking back with no false regrets;   30
        All that he did was to remember
        Like the old and be honest like children.

He wasn't clever at all: he merely told
The unhappy Present to recite the Past
        Like a poetry lesson till sooner
        Or later it faltered at the line where

Long ago the accusations had begun,
And suddenly knew by whom it had been judged,
        How rich life had been and how silly,
        And was life-forgiven and more humble.   40

Able to approach the Future as a friend
Without a wardrobe of excuses, without
        A set mask of rectitude or an
        Embarrassing over-familiar gesture.

No wonder the ancient cultures of conceit
In his technique of unsettlement foresaw
        The fall of princes, the collapse of
        Their lucrative patterns of frustration.

If he succeeded, why, the Generalised Life
Would become impossible, the monolith   50
        Of State be broken and prevented
        The co-operation of avengers.

Of course they called on God: but he went his way,
Down among the Lost People like Dante, down
    To the stinking fosse where the injured
    Lead the ugly life of the rejected.

And showed us what evil is: not as we thought
Deeds that must be punished, but our lack of faith,
    Our dishonest mood of denial,
    The concupiscence of the oppressor. 60

And if something of the autocratic pose,
The paternal strictness he distrusted, still
    Clung to his utterance and features,
    It was a protective imitation

For one who lived among enemies so long;
If often he was wrong and at times absurd,
    To us he is no more a person
    Now but a whole climate of opinion,

Under whom we conduct our differing lives:
Like weather he can only hinder or help, 70
    The proud can still be proud but find it
    A little harder, and the tyrant tries

To make him do but doesn't care for him much.
He quietly surrounds all our habits of growth;
    He extends, till the tired in even
    The remotest most miserable duchy

Have felt the change in their bones and are cheered,
And the child unlucky in his little State,
    Some hearth where freedom is excluded,
    A hive whose honey is fear and worry, 80

Feels calmer now and somehow assured of escape;
While as they lie in the grass of our neglect,
    So many long-forgotten objects
    Revealed by his undiscouraged shining

Are returned to us and made precious again;
Games we had thought we must drop as we grew up,
    Little noises we dared not laugh at,
    Faces we made when no one was looking.

But he wishes us more than this: to be free
Is often to be lonely; he would unite   90
    The unequal moieties fractured
    By our own well-meaning sense of justice.

Would restore to the larger the wit and will
The smaller possesses but can only use
    For arid disputes, would give back to
    The son the mother's richness of feeling.

But he would have us remember most of all
To be enthusiastic over the night
    Not only for the sense of wonder
    It alone has to offer, but also   100

Because it needs our love: for with sad eyes
Its delectable creatures look up and beg
    Us dumbly to ask them to follow;
    They are exiles who long for the future

That lies in our power. They too would rejoice
If allowed to serve enlightenment like him,
    Even to bear our cry of "Judas,"
    As he did and all must bear who serve it.

One rational voice is dumb: over a grave
The household of Impulse mourns one dearly loved.   110
    Sad is Eros, builder of cities,
    And weeping anarchic Aphrodite.

IN PRAISE OF LIMESTONE
(1951)

If it form the one landscape that we the inconstant ones
    Are consistently homesick for, this is chiefly
Because it dissolves in water. Mark these rounded slopes

With their surface fragrance of thyme and beneath
A secret system of caves and conduits; hear these springs
    That spurt out everywhere with a chuckle
Each filling a private pool for its fish and carving
    Its own little ravine whose cliffs entertain
The butterfly and the lizard; examine this region
    Of short distances and definite places: 10
What could be more like Mother or a fitter background
    For her son, for the nude young male who lounges
Against a rock displaying his dildo, never doubting
    That for all his faults he is loved, whose works are but
Extensions of his power to charm? From weathered outcrop
    To hill-top temple, from appearing waters to
Conspicuous fountains, from a wild to a formal vineyard,
    Are ingenious but short steps that a child's wish
To receive more attention than his brothers, whether
    By pleasing or teasing, can easily take.   20

Watch, then, the band of rivals as they climb up and down
    Their steep stone gennels in twos and threes, sometimes
Arm in arm, but never, thank God, in step; or engaged
    On the shady side of a square at midday in
Voluble discourse, knowing each other too well to think
    There are any important secrets, unable
To conceive a god whose temper-tantrums are moral
    And not to be pacified by a clever line
Or a good lay: for, accustomed to a stone that responds,
    They have never had to veil their faces in awe   30
Of a crater whose blazing fury could not be fixed;
    Adjusted to the local needs of valleys
Where everything can be touched or reached by walking,
    Their eyes have never looked into infinite space
Through the lattice-work of a nomad's comb; born lucky,
    Their legs have never encountered the fungi
And insects of the jungle, the monstrous forms and lives
    With which we have nothing, we like to hope, in common.
So, when one of them goes to the bad, the way his mind works
    Remains comprehensible: to become a pimp   40
Or deal in fake jewelry or ruin a fine tenor voice
    For effects that bring down the house could happen to all
But the best and the worst of us. . . .
                That is why, I suppose,

The best and worst never stayed here long but sought
Immoderate soils where the beauty was not so external,
    The light less public and the meaning of life
Something more than a mad camp. "Come!" cried the granite
        wastes,
    "How evasive is your humor, how accidental
Your kindest kiss, how permanent is death." (Saints-to-be
    Slipped away sighing.) "Come!" purred the clays and gravels.
"On our plains there is room for armies to drill; rivers   51
    Wait to be tamed and slaves to construct you a tomb
In the grand manner: soft as the earth is mankind and both
    Need to be altered." (Intendant Caesars rose and
Left, slamming the door.) But the really reckless were fetched
    By an older colder voice, the oceanic whisper:
"I am the solitude that asks and promises nothing;
    That is how I shall set you free. There is no love;
There are only the various envies, all of them sad."

    They were right, my dear, all those voices were right   60
And still are; this land is not the sweet home that it looks,
    Nor its peace the historical calm of a site
Where something was settled once and for all: A backward
    And dilapidated province, connected
To the big busy world by a tunnel, with a certain
    Seedy appeal, is that all it is now? Not quite:
It has a worldly duty which in spite of itself
    It does not neglect, but calls into question
All the Great Powers assume; it disturbs our rights. The poet,
    Admired for his earnest habit of calling   70
The sun the sun, his mind Puzzle, is made uneasy
    By these solid statues which so obviously doubt
His antimythological myth; and these gamins,
    Pursuing the scientist down the tiled colonnade
With such lively offers, rebuke his concern for Nature's
    Remotest aspects: I, too, am reproached, for what
And how much you know. Not to lose time, not to get caught,
    Not to be left behind, not, please! to resemble
The beasts who repeat themselves, or a thing like water
    Or stone whose conduct can be predicted, these   80
Are our Common Prayer, whose greatest comfort is music
    Which can be made anywhere, is invisible,

And does not smell. In so far as we have to look forward
    To death as a fact, not doubt we are right: But if
Sins can be forgiven, if bodies rise from the dead,
    These modifications of matter into
Innocent athletes and gesticulating fountains,
    Made solely for pleasure, make a further point:
The blessed will not care what angle they are regarded from,
    Having nothing to hide. Dear, I know nothing of   90
Either, but when I try to imagine a faultless love
    Or the life to come, what I hear is the murmur
Of underground streams, what I see is a limestone landscape.

NONES

(1951)

What we know to be not possible
    Though time after time foretold
By wild hermits, by shaman and sybil
    Gibbering in their trances,
Or revealed to a child in some chance rhyme
    Like *will* and *kill*, comes to pass
Before we realise it: we are surprised
    At the ease and speed of our deed
And uneasy: it is barely three,
    Mid afternoon, yet the blood   10
Of our sacrifice is already
    Dry on the grass; we are not prepared
For silence so sudden and so soon;
    The day is too hot, too bright, too still,
Too ever, the dead remains too nothing.
    What shall we do till nightfall?

The wind has dropped and we have lost our public.
    The faceless many who always
Collect when any world is to be wrecked,
    Blown up, burnt down, cracked open,   20
Felled, sawn in two, hacked through, torn apart,
    Have all melted away: not one
Of these who in the shade of walls and trees
    Lie sprawled now, calmly sleeping,

Harmless as sheep, can remember why
   He shouted or what about
So loudly in the sunlight this morning;
   All, if challenged, would reply
—"It was a monster with one red eye,
   A crowd that saw him die, not I—."   30
The hangman has gone to wash, the soldiers to eat:
   We are left alone with our feat.

The Madonna with the green woodpecker,
   The Madonna of the fig tree,
The Madonna beside the yellow dam,
   Turn their kind faces from us
And our projects under construction,
   Look only in one direction,
Fix their gaze on our completed work.
   Pile-driver, concrete-mixer,   40
Crane and pickaxe wait to be used again,
   But how can we repeat this?
Outliving our act we stand where we are
   As disregarded as some
Discarded artifact of our own,
   Like torn gloves, rusted kettles,
Abandoned branchlines, worn lop-sided
   Grindstones buried in nettles.

This mutilated flesh, our victim,
   Explains too nakedly, too well,   50
The spell of the asparagus garden,
   The aim of our chalk-pit game: stamps,
Bird's eggs are not the same: behind the wonder
   Of tow-paths and sunken lanes,
Behind the rapture on the spiral stair,
   We shall always now be aware
Of the deed into which they lead, under
   The mock chase and mock capture,
The racing and tussling and splashing,
   The panting and the laughter,   60
Be listening for the cry and stillness
   To follow after. Wherever
The sun shines, brooks run, books are written,
   There will also be this death.

Soon cool tramontana will stir the leaves,
  The shops will re-open at four,
The empty blue bus in the empty pink square
  Fill up and drive off: we have time
To misrepresent, excuse, deny,
  Mythify, use this event   70
While, under a hotel bed, in prison,
  Down wrong turnings, its meaning
Waits for our lives. Sooner than we would choose
  Bread will melt, water will burn,
And the great quell begin; Abaddon
  Set up his triple gallows
At our seven gates, fat Belial make
  Our wives waltz naked: meanwhile
It would be best to go home, if we have a home,
  In any case good to rest.   80

That our dreaming wills may seem to escape
  This dead calm, wander instead
On knife edges, on black and white squares,
  Across moss, baize, velvet, boards,
Over cracks and hillocks, in mazes
  Of string and penitent cones,
Down granite ramps and damp passages,
  Through gates that will not relatch
And doors marked Private, pursued by Moors
  And watched by latent robbers,   90
To hostile villages at the heads of fjords,
  To dark châteaux where wind sobs
In the pine-trees and telephones ring
  Inviting trouble, to a room
Lit by one weak bulb where our double sits
  Writing and does not look up.

That while we are thus away our own wronged flesh
  May work undisturbed, restoring
The order we try to destroy, the rhythm
  We spoil out of spite: valves close   100
And open exactly, glands secrete,
  Vessels contract and expand
At the right moment, essential fluids
  Flow to renew exhausted cells,

Not knowing quite what has happened but awed
  By death like all the creatures
Now watching this spot, like the hawk looking down
  Without blinking, the smug hens
Passing close by in their pecking order,
  The bug whose view is baulked by grass,   110
Or the deer who shyly from afar
  Peer through chinks in the forest.

Louis MacNeice
1907-1963

PERSEUS
(1935)

Borrowed wings on his ankles,
Carrying a stone death,
The hero entered the hall,
All in the hall looked up,
Their breath frozen on them,
And there was no more shuffle or clatter in the hall at all.

So a friend of a man comes in
And leaves a book he is lending or flowers
And goes again, alive but as good as dead,
And you are left alive, no better than dead,   10
And you dare not turn the leaden pages of the book or touch the flowers,
      the hooded and arrested hours.

Close your eyes,
There are suns beneath your lids,
Or look in the looking-glass in the end room—
You will find it full of eyes,
The ancient smiles of men cut out with scissors and kept in mirrors.

Ever to meet me comes, in sun or dull,
The gay hero swinging the Gorgon's head
And I am left, with the dull drumming of the sun, suspended and dead,
Or the dumb grey-brown of the day is a leper's cloth,   20
And one feels the earth going round and round the globe of the blackening
      mantle, a mad moth.

SUNDAY MORNING

(1935)

Down the road someone is practising scales,
The notes like little fishes vanish with a wink of tails,
Man's heart expands to tinker with his car
For this is Sunday morning, Fate's great bazaar;
Regard these means as ends, concentrate on this Now,
And you may grow to music or drive beyond Hindhead anyhow,
Take corners on two wheels until you go so fast
That you can clutch a fringe or two of the windy past,
That you can abstract this day and make it to the week of time
A small eternity, a sonnet self-contained in rhyme.   10

But listen, up the road, something gulps, the church spire
Opens its eight bells out, skulls' mouths which will not tire
To tell how there is no music or movement which secures
Escape from the weekday time. Which deadens and endures.

THE SUNLIGHT ON THE GARDEN

(1938)

The sunlight on the garden
Hardens and grows cold,
We cannot cage the minute
Within its nets of gold,
When all is told
We cannot beg for pardon.

Our freedom as free lances
Advances towards its end;
The earth compels, upon it
Sonnets and birds descend;   10
And soon, my friend,
We shall have no time for dances.

The sky was good for flying
Defying the church bells
And every evil iron
Siren and what it tells:

The earth compels,
We are dying, Egypt, dying

And not expecting pardon,
Hardened in heart anew,   20
But glad to have sat under
Thunder and rain with you,
And grateful too
For sunlight on the garden.

LES SYLPHIDES
(1941)

Life in a day: he took his girl to the ballet;
Being shortsighted himself could hardly see it—
 The white skirts in the grey
 Glade and the swell of the music
 Lifting the white sails.

Calyx upon calyx, canterbury bells in the breeze
The flowers on the left mirror to the flowers on the right
 And the naked arms above
 The powdered faces moving
 Like seaweed in a pool.   10

Now, he thought, we are floating—ageless, oarless—
Now there is no separation, from now on
 You will be wearing white
 Satin and a red sash
 Under the waltzing trees.

But the music stopped, the dancers took their curtain,
The river had come to a lock—a shuffle of programmes—
 And we cannot continue down
 Stream unless we are ready
 To enter the lock and drop.   20

So they were married—to be the more together—
And found they were never again so much together,
 Divided by the morning tea,
 By the evening paper,
 By children and tradesmen's bills.

Waking at times in the night she found assurance
In his regular breathing but wondered whether
 It was really worth it and where
 The river had flowed away
And where were the white flowers.   30

EXPLORATIONS

(1944)

The whale butting through scarps of moving marble,
The tapeworm probing the intestinal darkness,
The swallows drawn collectively to their magnet,
 These are our prototypes and yet,
Though we may envy them still, they are merely patterns
 To wonder at—and forget.

For the ocean-carver, cumbrous but unencumbered,
Who tired of land looked for his freedom and frolic in water,
Though he succeeded, has failed; it is only instinct
 That plots his graph and he,   10
Though appearing to us a free and a happy monster, is merely
 An appanage of the sea.

And the colourless blind worm, triumphantly self-degraded,
Who serves as an image to men of the worst adjustment—
Oxymoron of parasitical glory—
 Cannot even be cursed,
Lacking the only pride of his way of life, not knowing
 That he has chosen the worst.

So even that legion of birds who appear so gladly
Purposeful, with air in their bones, enfranchised   20
Citizens of the sky and never at odds with
 The season or out of line,
Can be no model to us; their imputed purpose
 Is a foregone design—

And ours is not. For we are unique, a conscious
Hoping and therefore despairing creature, the final
Anomaly of the world, we can learn no method

From whales or birds or worms;
Our end is our own to be won by our own endeavour
And held on our own terms.   30

NEUTRALITY

(1944)

The neutral island facing the Atlantic,
The neutral island in the heart of man,
Are bitterly soft reminders of the beginnings
That ended before the end began.

Look into your heart, you will find a County Sligo,
A Knocknarea with for navel a cairn of stones,
You will find the shadow and sheen of a moleskin mountain
And a litter of chronicles and bones.

Look into your heart, you will find fermenting rivers,
Intricacies of gloom and glint,   10
You will find such ducats of dream and great doubloons
      of ceremony
As nobody today would mint.

But then look eastward from your heart, there bulks
A continent, close, dark, as archetypal sin,
While to the west off your own shores the mackerel
Are fat—on the flesh of your kin.

Stephen Spender
1909-

WHAT I EXPECTED
(1933)

What I expected, was
Thunder, fighting,
Long struggles with men
And climbing.
After continual straining
I should grow strong;
Then the rocks would shake,   *personal victory*
And I rest long.   *resolution*

What I had not foreseen   *when not able to*
Was the gradual day   *carry through*   10
Weakening the will
Leaking the brightness away,
The lack of good to touch,
The fading of body and soul
—Smoke before wind,
Corrupt, unsubstantial.

                            social results
The wearing of Time,
And the watching of cripples pass
With limbs shaped like questions
In their odd twist,   20
The pulverous grief
Melting the bones with pity,
The sick falling from earth—
These, I could not foresee.

Expecting always
Some brightness to hold in trust,
Some final innocence
Exempt from dust,
That, hanging solid,
Would dangle through all,   30
Like the created poem,
Or faceted crystal.

THE LANDSCAPE NEAR AN AERODROME
(1933)

More beautiful and soft than any moth
With burring furred antennae feeling its huge path
Through dusk, the air liner with shut-off engines
Glides over suburbs and the sleeves set trailing tall
To point the wind. Gently, broadly, she falls,
Scarcely disturbing charted currents of air.

Lulled by descent, the travellers across sea
And across feminine land indulging its easy limbs
In miles of softness, now let their eyes trained by watching
Penetrate through dusk the outskirts of this town   10
Here where industry shows a fraying edge.
Here they may see what is being done.

Beyond the winking masthead light
And the landing ground, they observe the outposts
Of work: chimneys like lank black fingers
Or figures, frightening and mad: and squat buildings
With their strange air behind trees, like women's faces
Shattered by grief. Here where few houses
Moan with faint light behind their blinds,
They remark the unhomely sense of complaint, like a dog   20
Shut out, and shivering at the foreign moon.

In the last sweep of love, they pass over fields
Behind the aerodrome, where boys play all day
Hacking dead grass: whose cries, like wild birds,
Settle upon the nearest roofs
But soon are hid under the loud city.

Then, as they land, they hear the tolling bell
Reaching across the landscape of hysteria,
To where, louder than all those batteries
And charcoaled towers against that dying sky,⁣ 30
Religion stands, the Church blocking the sun.

AN ELEMENTARY SCHOOL CLASSROOM IN A SLUM
(1939)

Far far from gusty waves these children's faces.
Like rootless weeds, the hair torn round their pallor.
The tall girl with her weighed-down head. The paper-
seeming boy, with rat's eyes. The stunted, unlucky heir
Of twisted bones, reciting a father's gnarled disease,
His lesson from his desk. At back of the dim class
One unnoted, sweet and young. His eyes live in a dream
Of squirrel's game, in tree room, other than this.

On sour cream walls, donations. Shakespeare's head,
Cloudless at dawn, civilized dome riding all cities.⁣ 10
Belled, flowery, Tyrolese valley. Open-handed map
Awarding the world its world. And yet, for these
Children, these windows, not this world, are world,
Where all their future's painted with a fog,
A narrow street sealed in with a lead sky,
Far far from rivers, capes, and stars of words.

Surely, Shakespeare is wicked, the map a bad example
With ships and sun and love tempting them to steal—
For lives that slyly turn in their cramped holes
From fog to endless night? On their slag heap, these children⁣ 20
Wear skins peeped through by bones and spectacles of steel
With mended glass, like bottle bits on stones.
All of their time and space are foggy slum.
So blot their maps with slums as big as doom.

Unless, governor, teacher, inspector, visitor,
This map becomes their window and these windows
That shut upon their lives like catacombs,
Break O break open till they break the town

And show the children to green fields, and make their world
Run azure on gold sands, and let their tongues   30
Run naked into books, the white and green leaves open
History theirs whose language is the sun.

TWO ARMIES
(1939)

Deep in the winter plain, two armies
Dig their machinery, to destroy each other.
Men freeze and hunger. No one is given leave
On either side, except the dead, and wounded.
These have their leave; while new battalions wait
On time at last to bring them violent peace.

All have become so nervous and so cold
That each man hates the cause and distant words
That brought him here, more terribly than bullets.
Once a boy hummed a popular marching song,   10
Once a novice hand flapped their salute;
The voice was choked, the lifted hand fell,
Shot through the wrist by those of his own side.

From their numb harvest, all would flee, except
For discipline drilled once in an iron school
Which holds them at the point of the revolver.
Yet when they sleep, the images of home
Ride wishing horses of escape
Which herd the plain in a mass unspoken poem.

Finally, they cease to hate: for although hate   20
Bursts from the air and whips the earth with hail
Or shoots it up in fountains to marvel at,
And although hundreds fall, who can connect
The inexhaustible anger of the guns
With the dumb patience of those tormented animals?

Clean silence drops at night, when a little walk
Divides the sleeping armies, each
Huddled in linen woven by remote hands.

When the machines are stilled, a common suffering
Whitens the air with breath and makes both one   30
As though these enemies slept in each other's arms.

Only the lucid friend to aerial raiders
The brilliant pilot moon, stares down
Upon this plain she makes a shining bone
Cut by the shadows of many thousand bones.
Where amber clouds scatter on No-Man's-Land
She regards death and time throw up
The furious words and minerals which destroy.

THE TRANCE
(1946)

Sometimes, apart in sleep, by chance,
You fall out of my arms, alone,
Into the chaos of your separate trance.
My eyes gaze through your forehead, through the bone,
And see where in your sleep distress has torn
Its violent path, which on your lips is shown
And on your hands and in your dream forlorn.

Restless, you turn to me, and press
Those timid words against my ear
Which thunder at my heart like stones.   10
"Mercy," you plead, Then "Who can bless?"
You ask. "I am pursued by Time," you moan.
I watch that precipice of fear
You tread, naked in naked distress.

To that deep care we are committed
Beneath the wildness of our flesh
And shuddering horror of our dream,
Where unmasked agony is permitted.
Our bodies, stripped of clothes that seem,
And our souls, stripped of beauty's mesh,   20
Meet their true selves, their charms outwitted.

This pure trance is the oracle
That speaks no language but the heart,

Our angel with our devil meets
In the atrocious dark nor do they part
But each each forgives and greets,
And their mutual terrors heal
Within our married miracle.

SEASCAPE
In Memoriam, M. A. S.
(1946)

There are some days the happy ocean lies
Like an unfingered harp, below the land.
Afternoon gilds all the silent wires
Into a burning music for the eyes.
On mirrors flashing between fine-strung fires
The shore, heaped up with roses, horses, spires,
Wanders on water, walking above ribbed sand.

The motionlessness of the hot sky tires
And a sigh, like a woman's, from inland
Brushes the instrument with shadowing hand   10
Drawing across its wires some gull's sharp cries
Or bell, or shout, from distant, hedged-in shires;
These, deep as anchors, the hushing wave buries.

Then from the shore, two zig-zag butterflies,
Like errant dog-roses, cross the bright strand
Spiralling over sea in foolish gyres
Until they fall into reflected skies.
They drown. Fishermen understand
Such wings sunk in such ritual sacrifice,

Recalling legends of undersea, drowned cities.   20
What voyagers, oh what heroes, flamed like pyres
With helmets plumed, have set forth from some island
And them the sea engulfed. Their eyes,
Contorted by the cruel waves' desires
Glitter with coins through the tide scarcely scanned,
While, above them, that harp assumes their sighs.

Dylan Thomas
1914-1953

THE FORCE THAT THROUGH THE GREEN FUSE DRIVES THE FLOWER

(1934)

The force that through the green fuse drives the flower
Drives my green age; that blasts the roots of trees
Is my destroyer.
And I am dumb to tell the crooked rose
My youth is bent by the same wintry fever.

The force that drives the water through the rocks
Drives my red blood; that dries the mouthing streams
Turns mine to wax.
And I am dumb to mouth unto my veins
How at the mountain spring the same mouth sucks.   10

The hand that whirls the water in the pool
Stirs the quicksand; that ropes the blowing wind
Hauls my shroud sail.
And I am dumb to tell the hanging man
How of my clay is made the hangman's lime.

The lips of time leech to the fountain head;
Love drips and gathers, but the fallen blood
Shall calm her sores.
And I am dumb to tell a weather's wind
How time has ticked a heaven round the stars.   20

And I am dumb to tell the lover's tomb
How at my sheet goes the same crooked worm.

176

ALTARWISE BY OWL–LIGHT
(1936)

I

Altarwise by owl-light in the halfway-house
The gentleman lay graveward with his furies;
Abaddon in the hang-nail cracked from Adam,
And, from his fork, a dog among the fairies,
The atlas-eater with a jaw for news,
Bit out the mandrake with to-morrow's scream.
Then, penny-eyed, that gentleman of wounds,
Old cock from nowheres and the heaven's egg,
With bones unbuttoned to the halfway winds,
Hatched from the windy salvage on one leg,   10
Scraped at my cradle in a walking word
That night of time under the Christward shelter:
I am the long world's gentleman, he said,
And share my bed with Capricorn and Cancer.

II

Death is all metaphors, shape in one history;
The child that sucketh long is shooting up,
The planet-ducted pelican of circles
Weans on an artery the gender's strip;
Child of the short spark in a shapeless country
Soon sets alight a long stick from the cradle;   20
The horizontal cross-bones of Abaddon,
You by the cavern over the black stairs,
Rung bone and blade, the verticals of Adam,
And, manned by midnight, Jacob to the stars.
Hairs of your head, then said the hollow agent,
Are but the roots of nettles and of feathers
Over these groundworks thrusting through a pavement
And hemlock-headed in the wood of weathers.

III

First there was the lamb on knocking knees
And three dead seasons on a climbing grave   30
That Adam's wether in the flock of horns,
Butt of the tree-tailed worm that mounted Eve,

Horned down with skullfoot and the skull of toes
Of thunderous pavements in the garden time;
Rip of the vaults, I took my marrow-ladle
Out of the wrinkled undertaker's van,
And, Rip Van Winkle from a timeless cradle,
Dipped me breast-deep in the descended bone;
The black ram, shuffling of the year, old winter,
Alone alive among his mutton fold,   40
We rung our weathering changes on the ladder,
Said the antipodes, and twice spring chimed.

IV

What is the metre of the dictionary?
The size of genesis? the short spark's gender?
Shade without shape? the shape of Pharaoh's echo?
(My shape of age nagging the wounded whisper).
Which sixth of wind blew out the burning gentry?
(Questions are hunchbacks to the poker marrow).
What of a bamboo man among your acres?
Corset the boneyards for a crooked boy?   50
Button your bodice on a hump of splinters,
My camel's eyes will needle through the shrowd.
Love's reflection of the mushroom features,
Stills snapped by night in the bread-sided field,
Once close-up smiling in the wall of pictures,
Arc-lamped thrown back upon the cutting flood.

V

And from the windy West came two-gunned Gabriel,
From Jesu's sleeve trumped up the king of spots,
The sheath-decked jacks, queen with a shuffled heart;
Said the fake gentleman in suit of spades,   60
Black-tongued and tipsy from salvation's bottle.
Rose my Byzantine Adam in the night.
For loss of blood I fell on Ishmael's plain,
Under the milky mushrooms slew my hunger,
A climbing sea from Asia had me down
And Jonah's Moby snatched me by the hair,
Cross-stroked salt Adam to the frozen angel
Pin-legged on pole-hills with a black medusa
By waste seas where the white bear quoted Virgil
And sirens singing from our lady's sea-straw.   70

VI

Cartoon of slashes on the tide-traced crater,
He in a book of water tallow-eyed
By lava's light split through the oyster vowels
And burned sea silence on a wick of words.
Pluck, cock, my sea eye, said medusa's scripture,
Lop, love, my fork tongue, said the pin-hilled nettle;
And love plucked out the stinging siren's eye,
Old cock from nowheres lopped the minstrel tongue
Till tallow I blew from the wax's tower
The fats of midnight when the salt was singing;   80
Adam, time's joker, on a witch of cardboard
Spelt out the seven seas, an evil index,
The bagpipe-breasted ladies in the deadweed
Blew out the blood gauze through the wound of manwax.

VII

Now stamp the Lord's Prayer on a grain of rice,
A Bible-leaved of all the written woods
Strip to this tree: a rocking alphabet,
Genesis in the root, the scarecrow word,
And one light's language in the book of trees.
Doom on deniers at the wind-turned statement.   90
Time's tune my ladies with the teats of music,
The scaled sea-sawers, fix in a naked sponge
Who sucks the bell-voiced Adam out of magic,
Time, milk, and magic, from the world beginning.
Time is the tune my ladies lend their heartbreak,
From bald pavilions and the house of bread
Time tracks the sound of shape on man and cloud,
On rose and icicle the ringing handprint.

VIII

This was the crucifixion on the mountain,
Time's nerve in vinegar, the gallow grave   100
As tarred with blood as the bright thorns I wept;
The world's my wound, God's Mary in her grief,
Bent like three trees and bird-papped through her shift,
With pins for teardrops is the long wound's woman.
This was the sky, Jack Christ, each minstrel angle
Drove in the heaven-driven of the nails
Till the three-coloured rainbow from my nipples

From pole to pole leapt round the snail-waked world.
I by the tree of thieves, all glory's sawbones,
Unsex the skeleton this mountain minute,   110
And by this blowclock witness of the sun
Suffer the heaven's children through my heartbeat.

IX

From the oracular archives and the parchment,
Prophets and fibre kings in oil and letter,
The lamped calligrapher, the queen in splints,
Buckle to lint and cloth their natron footsteps,
Draw on the glove of prints, dead Cairo's henna
Pour like a halo on the caps and serpents.
This was the resurrection in the desert,
Death from a bandage, rants the mask of scholars   120
Gold on such features, and the linen spirit
Weds my long gentleman to dusts and furies;
With priest and pharaoh bed my gentle wound,
World in the sand, on the triangle landscape,
With stones of odyssey for ash and garland
And rivers of the dead around my neck.

X

Let the tale's sailor from a Christian voyage
Atlaswise hold half-way off the dummy bay
Time's ship-racked gospel on the globe I balance:
So shall winged harbours through the rockbirds' eyes   130
Spot the blown word, and on the seas I image
December's thorn screwed in a brow of holly.
Let the first Peter from a rainbow's quayrail
Ask the tall fish swept from the bible east,
What rhubarb man peeled in her foam-blue channel
Has sown a flying garden round that sea-ghost?
Green as beginning, let the garden diving
Soar, with its two bark towers, to that Day
When the worm builds with the gold straws of venom
My nest of mercies in the rude, red tree.   140

AFTER THE FUNERAL
In Memory of Ann Jones

(1939)

After the funeral, mule praises, brays,   *not genuine in grief*
Windshake of sailshaped ears, muffle-toed tap
Tap happily of one peg in the thick
Grave's foot, blinds down the lids, the teeth in black,   *impressionistic*
The spittled eyes, the salt ponds in the sleeves,
Morning smack of the spade that wakes up sleep,
Shakes a desolate boy who slits his throat -   *suicide, or opening life blood of poem*
In the dark of the coffin and sheds dry leaves,
That breaks one bone to light with a judgment clout,   *death / poem*
After the feast of tear-stuffed time and thistles   *hard to take*   10
In a room with a stuffed fox and a stale fern,   *deadness of aunt + poets feeling*
I stand, for this memorial's sake, alone
In the snivelling hours with dead, humped Ann
Whose hooded, fountain heart once fell in puddles   *life*
Round the parched worlds of Wales and drowned each sun
(Though this for her is a monstrous image blindly
Magnified out of praise; her death was a still drop;
She would not have me sinking in the holy   *wanting*
Flood of her heart's fame; she would lie dumb and deep
And need no druid of her broken body).   *poem*   20
But I, Ann's bard on a raised hearth, call all
The seas to service that her wood-tongued virtue
Babble like a bellbuoy over the hymning heads,
Bow down the walls of the ferned and foxy woods   *symbols*
That her love sing and swing through a brown chapel,
Bless her bent spirit with four, crossing birds.   *compass   spiritual lift.*
Her flesh was meek as milk, but this skyward statue
With the wild breast and blessed and giant skull
Is carved from her in a room with a wet window   *ressurection*
In a fiercely mourning house in a crooked year.   30
I know her scrubbed and sour humble hands
Lie with religion in their cramp, her threadbare
Whisper in a damp word, her wits drilled hollow,
Her fist of a face died clenched on a round pain;
And sculptured Ann is seventy years of stone.
These cloud-sopped, marble hands, this monumental

dead

Argument of the hewn voice, gesture and psalm
Storm me forever over her grave until
The stuffed lung of the fox twitch and cry Love   *immortalian*
And the strutting fern lay seeds on the black sill.   40
regrowth

BALLAD OF THE LONG–LEGGED BAIT
(1943)

The bows glided down, and the coast
Blackened with birds took a last look
At his thrashing hair and whale-blue eye;
The trodden town rang its cobbles for luck.

Then good-bye to the fishermanned
Boat with its anchor free and fast
As a bird hooking over the sea,
High and dry by the top of the mast,

Whispered the affectionate sand
And the bulwarks of the dazzled quay.   10
For my sake sail, and never look back,
Said the looking land.

Sails drank the wind, and white as milk
He sped into the drinking dark;
The sun shipwrecked west on a pearl
And the moon swam out of its hulk.

Funnels and masts went by in a whirl.
Good-bye to the man on the sea-legged deck
To the gold gut that sings on his reel
To the bait that stalked out of the sack,   20

For we saw him throw to the swift flood
A girl alive with his hooks through her lips;
All the fishes were rayed in blood,
Said the dwindling ships.

Good-bye to chimneys and funnels,
Old wives that spin in the smoke,
He was blind to the eyes of candles
In the praying windows of waves

But heard his bait buck in the wake
And tussle in a shoal of loves.　　　　　　　　　　30
Now cast down your rod, for the whole
Of the sea is hilly with whales,

She longs among horses and angels,
The rainbow-fish bend in her joys,
Floated the lost cathedral
Chimes of the rocked buoys.

Where the anchor rode like a gull
Miles over the moonstruck boat
A squall of birds bellowed and fell,
A cloud blew the rain from its throat;　　　　　40

He saw the storm smoke out to kill
With fuming bows and ram of ice,
Fire on starlight, rake Jesu's stream;
And nothing shone on the water's face

But the oil and bubble of the moon,
Plunging and piercing in his course
The lured fish under the foam
Witnessed with a kiss.

Whales in the wake like capes and Alps
Quaked the sick sea and snouted deep,　　　50
Deep the great bushed bait with raining lips
Slipped the fins of those humpbacked tons

And fled their love in a weaving dip.
Oh, Jericho was falling in their lungs!
She nipped and dived in the nick of love,
Spun on a spout like a long-legged ball

Till every beast blared down in a swerve
Till every turtle crushed from his shell
Till every bone in the rushing grave
Rose and crowed and fell!　　　　　　　　60

Good luck to the hand on the rod,
There is thunder under its thumbs;
Gold gut is a lightning thread,
His fiery reel sings off its flames,

The whirled boat in the burn of his blood
Is crying from nets to knives,
Oh the shearwater birds and their boatsized brood
Oh the bulls of Biscay and their calves

Are making under the green, laid veil
The long-legged beautiful bait their wives.   70
Break the black news and paint on a sail
Huge weddings in the waves,

Over the wakeward-flashing spray
Over the gardens of the floor
Clash out the mounting dolphin's day,
My mast is a bell-spire,

Strike and smoothe, for my decks are drums,
Sing through the water-spoken prow
The octopus walking into her limbs
The polar eagle with his tread of snow.   80

From salt-lipped beak to the kick of the stern
Sing how the seal has kissed her dead!
The long, laid minute's bride drifts on
Old in her cruel bed.

Over the graveyard in the water
Mountains and galleries beneath
Nightingale and hyena
Rejoicing for that drifting death

Sing and howl through sand and anemone
Valley and sahara in a shell,   90
Oh all the wanting flesh his enemy
Thrown to the sea in the shell of a girl

Is old as water and plain as an eel;
Always good-bye to the long-legged bread
Scattered in the paths of his heels
For the salty birds fluttered and fed

And the tall grains foamed in their bills;
Always good-bye to the fires of the face,
For the crab-backed dead on the sea-bed rose
And scuttled over her eyes,   100

The blind, clawed stare is cold as sleet.
The tempter under the eyelid
Who shows to the selves asleep
Mast-high moon-white women naked

Walking in wishes and lovely for shame
Is dumb and gone with his flame of brides.
Sussanah's drowned in the bearded stream
And no-one stirs at Sheba's side

But the hungry kings of the tides;
Sin who had a woman's shape   110
Sleeps till Silence blows on a cloud
And all the lifted waters walk and leap.

Lucifer that bird's dropping
Out of the sides of the north
Has melted away and is lost
Is always lost in her vaulted breath,

Venus lies star-struck in her wound
And the sensual ruins make
Seasons over the liquid world,
White springs in the dark.   120

Always good-bye, cried the voices through the shell,
Good-bye always for the flesh is cast
And the fisherman winds his reel
With no more desire than a ghost.

Always good luck, praised the finned in the feather
Bird after dark and the laughing fish
As the sails drank up the hail of thunder
And the long-tailed lightning lit his catch.

The boat swims into the six-year weather,
A wind throws a shadow and it freezes fast.   130
See what the gold gut drags from under
Mountains and galleries to the crest!

See what clings to hair and skull
As the boat skims on with drinking wings!
The statues of great rain stand still,
And the flakes fall like hills.

Sing and strike his heavy haul
Toppling up the boatside in a snow of light!
His decks are drenched with miracles.
Oh miracle of fishes! The long dead bite!   140

Out of the urn the size of a man
Out of the room the weight of his trouble
Out of the house that holds a town
In the continent of a fossil

One by one in dust and shawl,
Dry as echoes and insect-faced,
His fathers cling to the hand of the girl
And the dead hand leads the past,

Leads them as children and as air
On to the blindly tossing tops;   150
The centuries throw back their hair
And the old men sing from newborn lips:

Time is bearing another son.
Kill Time! She turns in her pain!
The oak is felled in the acorn
And the hawk in the egg kills the wren.

He who blew the great fire in
And died on a hiss of flames
Or walked on the earth in the evening
Counting the denials of the grains   160

Clings to her drifting hair, and climbs;
And he who taught their lips to sing
Weeps like the risen sun among
The liquid choirs of his tribes.

The rod bends low, divining land,
And through the sundered water crawls
A garden holding to her hand
With birds and animals

With men and women and waterfalls
Trees cool and dry in the whirlpool of ships   170
And stunned and still on the green, laid veil
Sand with legends in its virgin laps

And prophets loud on the burned dunes;
Insects and valleys hold her thighs hard,
Time and places grip her breast bone,
She is breaking with seasons and clouds;

Round her trailed wrist fresh water weaves,
With moving fish and rounded stones
Up and down the greater waves
A separate river breathes and runs;   180

Strike and sing his catch of fields
For the surge is sown with barley,
The cattle graze on the covered foam,
The hills have footed the waves away,

With wild sea fillies and soaking bridles
With salty colts and gales in their limbs
All the horses of his haul of miracles
Gallop through the arched, green farms.

Trot and gallop with gulls upon them
And thunderbolts in their manes.   190
O Rome and Sodom To-morrow and London
The country tide is cobbled with towns,

And steeples pierce the cloud on her shoulder
And the streets that the fisherman combed
When his long-legged flesh was a wind on fire
And his loin was a hunting flame

Coil from the thoroughfares of her hair
And terribly lead him home alive
Lead her prodigal home to his terror,
And furious ox-killing house of love.   200

Down, down, down, under the ground,
Under the floating villages,
Turns the moon-chained and water-wound
Metropolis of fishes,

There is nothing left of the sea but its sound,
Under the earth the loud sea walks,
In deathbeds of orchards the boat dies down
And the bait is drowned among hayricks,

Land, land, land, nothing remains
Of the pacing, famous sea but its speech,   210
And into its talkative seven tombs
The anchor dives through the floors of a church.

Good-bye, good luck, struck the sun and the moon,
To the fisherman lost on the land.
He stands alone at the door of his home,
With his long-legged heart in his hand.

A REFUSAL TO MOURN THE DEATH, BY FIRE, OF A CHILD IN LONDON

(1946)

Never until the mankind making
Bird beast and flower
Fathering and all humbling darkness
Tells with silence the last light breaking
And the still hour
Is come of the sea tumbling in harness

And I must enter again the round
Zion of the water bead
And the synagogue of the ear of corn
Shall I let pray the shadow of a sound   10
Or sow my salt seed
In the least valley of sackcloth to mourn

The majesty and burning of the child's death.
I shall not murder
The mankind of her going with a grave truth
Nor blaspheme down the stations of the breath
With any further
Elegy of innocence and youth.

Deep with the first dead lies London's daughter,
Robed in the long friends,   20
The grains beyond age, the dark veins of her mother,
Secret by the unmourning water
Of the riding Thames.
After the first death, there is no other.

POEM IN OCTOBER

(1946)

It was my thirtieth year to heaven
Woke to my hearing from harbour and neighbour wood
And the mussel pooled and the heron religious symbol
Priested shore

> The morning beckon
> With water praying and call of seagull and rook [rel.] [bird symbol] [death]
> And the knock of sailing boats on the net webbed wall
> Myself to set foot
> That second
> In the still sleeping town and set forth.   10
>
> My birthday began with the water-
> Birds and the birds of the winged trees flying my name   [nature holy]
> Above the farms and the white horses
> And I rose
> In rainy autumn
> And walked abroad in a shower of all my days.
> High tide and the heron dived when I took the road
> Over the border   [life vs. death]
> And the gates
> Of the town closed as the town awoke.   20
>
> A springful of larks in a rolling
> Cloud and the roadside bushes brimming with whistling
> Blackbirds and the sun of October
> Summery   [vs. town]
> On the hill's shoulder,
> Here were fond climates and sweet singers suddenly
> Come in the morning where I wandered and listened
> To the rain wringing
> Wind blow cold
> In the wood faraway under me.   30
>
> Pale rain over the dwindling harbour
> And over the sea wet church the size of a snail   [town]
> With its horns through mist and the castle
> Brown as owls
> But all the gardens
> Of spring and summer were blooming in the tall tales   [hill]
> Beyond the border and under the lark full cloud.
> There could I marvel
> My birthday
> Away but the weather turned around. [memory of past]   40
>
> It turned away from the blithe country
> And down the other air and the blue altered sky

Streamed again a wonder of summer
    With apples
    Pears and red currants
And I saw in the turning so clearly a child's
Forgotten mornings when he walked with his mother
    Through the parables -
    Of sun light --
And the legends of the green chapels _   50

And the twice told fields of infancy
That his tears burned my cheeks and his heart moved in mine.
    These were the woods the river and sea
    Where a boy
    In the listening
Summertime of the dead whispered the truth of his joy
To the trees and the stones and the fish in the tide.
    And the mystery
    Sang alive
Still in the water and singingbirds.   60

And there could I marvel my birthday
Away but the weather turned around. And the true
    Joy of the long dead child sang burning
    In the sun.
    It was my thirtieth
Year to heaven stood there then in the summer noon
Though the town below lay leaved with October blood.
    O may my heart's truth
    Still be sung
On this high hill in a year's turning.   70

CEREMONY AFTER A FIRE RAID
(1946)

I

Myselves
The grievers
Grieve
Among the street burned to tireless death
A child of a few hours

With its kneading mouth
Charred on the black breast of the grave
The mother dug, and its arms full of fires.

Begin
With singing   10
Sing
Darkness kindled back into beginning
When the caught tongue nodded blind,
A star was broken
Into the centuries of the child
Myselves grieve now, and miracles cannot atone.

Forgive
Us forgive
Us your death that myselves the believers
May hold it in a great flood   20
Till the blood shall spurt,
And the dust shall sing like a bird
As the grains blow, as your death grows, through our heart.

Crying
Your dying
Cry,
Child beyond cockcrow, by the fire-dwarfed
Street we chant the flying sea
In the body bereft.
Love is the last light spoken. Oh   30
Seed of sons in the loin of the black husk left.

II

I know not whether
Adam or Eve, the adorned holy bullock
Or the white ewe lamb
Or the chosen virgin
Laid in her snow
On the altar of London,
Was the first to die
In the cinder of the little skull,
O bride and bride groom   40
O Adam and Eve together

Lying in the lull
Under the sad breast of the head stone
White as the skeleton
Of the garden of Eden.

I know the legend
Of Adam and Eve is never for a second
Silent in my service
Over the dead infants
Over the one   50
Child who was priest and servants,
Word, singers, and tongue
In the cinder of the little skull,
Who was the serpent's
Night fall and the fruit like a sun,
Man and woman undone,
Beginning crumbled back to darkness
Bare as the nurseries
Of the garden of wilderness.

III

Into the organpipes and steeples   60
Of the luminous cathedrals,
Into the weathercocks' molten mouths
Rippling in twelve-winded circles,
Into the dead clock burning the hour
Over the urn of sabbaths
Over the whirling ditch of daybreak
Over the sun's hovel and the slum of fire
And the golden pavements laid in requiems,
Into the bread in a wheatfield of flames,
Into the wine burning like brandy,   70
The masses of the sea
The masses of the sea under
The masses of the infant-bearing sea
Erupt, fountain, and enter to utter for ever
Glory glory glory
The sundering ultimate kingdom of genesis' thunder.

FERN HILL
(1946)

Now as I was young and easy under the apple boughs
About the lilting house and happy as the grass was green,
    The night above the dingle starry,
      Time let me hail and climb
     Golden in the heydays of his eyes,
And honoured among wagons I was prince of the apple towns
And once below a time I lordly had the trees and leaves
      Trail with daisies and barley
     Down the rivers of the windfall light.

And as I was green and carefree, famous among the barns   10
About the happy yard and singing as the farm was home,
    In the sun that is young once only,
      Time let me play and be
     Golden in the mercy of his means,
And green and golden I was huntsman and herdsman, the calves
Sang to my horn, the foxes on the hills barked clear and cold,
      And the sabbath rang slowly
     In the pebbles of the holy streams.

All the sun long it was running, it was lovely, the hay
Fields high as the house, the tunes from the chimneys, it was air
    And playing, lovely and watery   21
      And fire green as grass.
     And nightly under the simple stars
As I rode to sleep the owls were bearing the farm away,
All the moon long I heard, blessed among stables, the nightjars
      Flying with the ricks, and horses
     Flashing into the dark.

And then to awake, and the farm, like a wanderer white
With the dew, come back, the cock on his shoulder: it was all
    Shining, it was Adam and maiden,   30
      The sky gathered again
     And the sun grew round that very day.
So it must have been after the birth of the simple light

In the first, spinning place, the spellbound horses walking warm
  Out of the whinnying green stable
    On to the fields of praise.

And honoured among foxes and pheasants by the gay house
Under the new made clouds and happy as the heart was long
  In the sun born over and over,
    I ran my heedless ways,   40
  My wishes raced through the house high hay
And nothing I cared, at my sky blue trades, that time allows
In all his tuneful turning so few and such morning songs
  Before the children green and golden
    Follow him out of grace.

Nothing I cared, in the lamb white days, that time would take me
Up to the swallow thronged loft by the shadow of my hand,
  In the moon that is always rising,
    Nor that riding to sleep
  I should hear him fly with the high fields   50
And wake to the farm forever fled from the childless land.
Oh as I was young and easy in the mercy of his means,
    Time held me green and dying
  Though I sang in my chains like the sea.

DO NOT GO GENTLE INTO THAT GOOD NIGHT
(1952)

    Do not go gentle into that good night,
    Old age should burn and rave at close of day;
    Rage, rage against the dying of the light.

    Though wise men at their end know dark is right,
    Because their words had forked no lightning they
    Do not go gentle into that good night.

    Good men, the last wave by, crying how bright
    Their frail deeds might have danced in a green bay,
    Rage, rage against the dying of the light.

Wild men who caught and sang the sun in flight,   10
And learn, too late, they grieved it on its way,
Do not go gentle into that good night.

Grave men, near death, who see with blinding sight
Blind eyes could blaze like meteors and be gay,
Rage, rage against the dying of the light.

And you, my father, there on the sad height,
Curse, bless, me now with your fierce tears, I pray.
Do not go gentle into that good night.
Rage, rage against the dying of the light.

MODERN AMERICAN POETS

Edwin Arlington Robinson
1869-1935

GEORGE CRABBE
(1896)

Give him the darkest inch your shelf allows,
Hide him in lonely garrets, if you will,—
But his hard, human pulse is throbbing still
With the sure strength that fearless truth endows.
In spite of all fine science disavows,
Of his plain excellence and stubborn skill
There yet remains what fashion cannot kill,
Though years have thinned the laurel from his brows.

Whether or not we read him, we can feel
From time to time the vigor of his name   10
Against us like a finger for the shame
And emptiness of what our souls reveal
In books that are as altars where we kneel
To consecrate the flicker, not the flame.

LUKE HAVERGAL
(1896)

Go to the western gate, Luke Havergal,
There where the vines cling crimson on the wall,
And in the twilight wait for what will come.
The leaves will whisper there of her, and some,
Like flying words, will strike you as they fall;

But go, and if you listen she will call.
Go to the western gate, Luke Havergal—
Luke Havergal.

No, there is not a dawn in eastern skies
To rift the fiery night that's in your eyes;
But there, where western glooms are gathering,
The dark will end the dark, if anything:
God slays Himself with every leaf that flies,
And hell is more than half of paradise.
No, there is not a dawn in eastern skies—
In eastern skies.

Out of a grave I come to tell you this,
Out of a grave I come to quench the kiss
That flames upon your forehead with a glow
That blinds you to the way that you must go.
Yes, there is yet one way to where she is,
Bitter, but one that faith may never miss.
Out of a grave I come to tell you this—
To tell you this.

There is the western gate, Luke Havergal,
There are the crimson leaves upon the wall.
Go, for the winds are tearing them away,—
Nor think to riddle the dead words they say,
Nor any more to feel them as they fall;
But go, and if you trust her she will call.
There is the western gate, Luke Havergal—
Luke Havergal.

CLIFF KLINGENHAGEN
(1897)

Cliff Klingenhagen had me in to dine
With him one day; and after soup and meat,
And all the other things there were to eat,
Cliff took two glasses and filled one with wine
And one with wormwood. Then, without a sign
For me to choose at all, he took the draught

Of bitterness himself, and lightly quaffed
It off, and said the other one was mine.

And when I asked him what the deuce he meant
By doing that, he only looked at me   10
And smiled, and said it was a way of his.
And though I know the fellow, I have spent
Long time a-wondering when I shall be
As happy as Cliff Klingenhagen is.

HOW ANNANDALE WENT OUT

(1910)

"They called it Annandale—and I was there
To flourish, to find words, and to attend:
Liar, physician, hypocrite, and friend,
I watched him; and the sight was not so fair
As one or two that I have seen elsewhere:
An apparatus not for me to mend—
A wreck, with hell between him and the end,
Remained of Annandale; and I was there.

"I knew the ruin as I knew the man;
So put the two together, if you can,
Remembering the worst you know of me.   10
Now view yourself as I was, on the spot—
With a slight kind of engine. Do you see?
Like this . . . You wouldn't hang me? I thought not."

MINIVER CHEEVY

(1910)

Miniver Cheevy, child of scorn,
    Grew lean while he assailed the seasons;
He wept that he was ever born,
    And he had reasons.

Miniver loved the days of old
    When swords were bright and steeds were prancing;
The vision of a warrior bold
    Would set him dancing.

Miniver sighed for what was not,
   And dreamed, and rested from his labors;   10
He dreamed of Thebes and Camelot,
   And Priam's neighbors.

Miniver mourned the ripe renown
   That made so many a name so fragrant;
He mourned Romance, now on the town,
   And Art, a vagrant.

Miniver loved the Medici,
   Albeit he had never seen one;
He would have sinned incessantly
   Could he have been one.   20

Miniver cursed the commonplace
   And eyed a khaki suit with loathing;
He missed the mediæval grace
   Of iron clothing.

Miniver scorned the gold he sought,
   But sore annoyed was he without it;
Miniver thought, and thought, and thought,
   And thought about it.

Miniver Cheevy, born too late,
   Scratched his head and kept on thinking;   30
Miniver coughed, and called it fate,
   And kept on drinking.

FOR A DEAD LADY

(1910)

No more with overflowing light
Shall fill the eyes that now are faded,
Nor shall another's fringe with night
Their woman-hidden world as they did.
No more shall quiver down the days
The flowing wonder of her ways,
Whereof no language may requite
The shifting and the many-shaded.

The grace, divine, definitive,
Clings only as a faint forestalling;   10
The laugh that love could not forgive
Is hushed, and answers to no calling;
The forehead and the little ears
Have gone where Saturn keeps the years;
The breast where roses could not live
Has done with rising and with falling.

The beauty, shattered by the laws
That have creation in their keeping,
No longer trembles at applause,
Or over children that are sleeping;   20
And we who delve in beauty's lore
Know all that we have known before
Of what inexorable cause
Makes Time so vicious in his reaping.

THE GIFT OF GOD
(1916)

Blessed with a joy that only she
Of all alive shall ever know,
She wears a proud humility
For what it was that willed it so,—
That her degree should be so great
Among the favored of the Lord
That she may scarcely bear the weight
Of her bewildering reward.

As one apart, immune, alone,
Or featured for the shining ones,   10
And like to none that she has known
Of other women's other sons,—
The firm fruition of her need,
He shines anointed; and he blurs
Her vision, till it seems indeed
A sacrilege to call him hers.

She fears a little for so much
Of what is best, and hardly dares
To think of him as one to touch
With aches, indignities, and cares;   20
She sees him rather at the goal,
Still shining; and her dream foretells
The proper shining of a soul
Where nothing ordinary dwells.

Perchance a canvass of the town
Would find him far from flags and shouts, ·
And leave him only the renown
Of many smiles and many doubts;
Perchance the crude and common tongue
Would havoc strangely with his worth;   30
But she, with innocence unwrung,
Would read his name around the earth.

And others, knowing how this youth
Would shine, if love could make him great,
When caught and tortured for the truth
Would only writhe and hesitate;
While she, arranging for his days
What centuries could not fulfill,
Transmutes him with her faith and praise,
And has him shining where she will.   40

She crowns him with her gratefulness,
And says again that life is good;
And should the gift of God be less
In him than in her motherhood,
His fame, though vague, will not be small,
As upward through her dream he fares,
Half clouded with a crimson fall
Of roses thrown on marble stairs.

HILLCREST

To Mrs. Edward MacDowell

(1916)

No sound of any storm that shakes
Old island walls with older seas
Comes here where now September makes
An island in a sea of trees.

Between the sunlight and the shade
A man may learn till he forgets
The roaring of a world remade,
And all his ruins and regrets;

And if he still remembers here
Poor fights he may have won or lost,—   10
If he be ridden with the fear
Of what some other fight may cost,—

If, eager to confuse too soon,
What he has known with what may be,
He reads a planet out of tune
For cause of his jarred harmony,—

If here he venture to unroll
His index of adagios,
And he be given to console
Humanity with what he knows,—   20

He may by contemplation learn
A little more than what he knew,
And even see great oaks return
To acorns out of which they grew.

He may, if he but listen well,
Through twilight and the silence here,
Be told what there are none may tell
To vanity's impatient ear;

And he may never dare again
Say what awaits him, or be sure   30
What sunlit labyrinth of pain
He may not enter and endure.

Who knows to-day from yesterday
May learn to count no thing too strange:
Love builds of what Time takes away,
Till Death itself is less than Change.

Who sees enough in his duress
May go as far as dreams have gone;
Who sees a little may do less
Than many who are blind have done;   40

Who sees unchastened here the soul
Triumphant has no other sight
Than has a child who sees the whole
World radiant with his own delight.

Far journeys and hard wandering
Await him in whose crude surmise
Peace, like a mask, hides everything
That is and has been from his eyes;

And all his wisdom is unfound,
Or like a web that error weaves   50
On airy looms that have a sound
No louder now than falling leaves.

EROS TURRANOS
(1916)

She fears him, and will always ask
    What fated her to choose him;
She meets in his engaging mask
    All reasons to refuse him;
But what she meets and what she fears
Are less than are the downward years,
Drawn slowly to the foamless weirs
    Of age, were she to lose him.

Between a blurred sagacity
   That once had power to sound him,   10
And Love, that will not let him be
   The Judas that she found him,
Her pride assuages her almost,
As if it were alone the cost.—
He sees that he will not be lost,
   And waits and looks around him.

A sense of ocean and old trees
   Envelops and allures him;
Tradition, touching all he sees,
   Beguiles and reassures him;   20
And all her doubts of what he says
Are dimmed with what she knows of days—
Till even prejudice delays
   And fades, and she secures him.

The falling leaf inaugurates
   The reign of her confusion;
The pounding wave reverberates
   The dirge of her illusion;
And home, where passion lived and died,
Becomes a place where she can hide,   30
While all the town and harbor side
   Vibrate with her seclusion.

We tell you, tapping on our brows,
   The story as it should be,—
As if the story of a house
   Were told, or ever could be;
We'll have no kindly veil between
Her visions and those we have seen,—
As if we guessed what hers have been,
   Or what they are or would be.   40

Meanwhile we do no harm; for they
   That with a god have striven,
Not hearing much of what we say,
   Take what the god has given;
Though like waves breaking it may be,

Or like a changed familiar tree,
Or like a stairway to the sea
  Where down the blind are driven.

BEWICK FINZER
(1916)

Time was when his half million drew
  The breath of six per cent;
But soon the worm of what-was-not
  Fed hard on his content;
And something crumbled in his brain
  When his half million went.

Time passed, and filled along with his
  The place of many more;
Time came, and hardly one of us
  Had credence to restore,   10
From what appeared one day, the man
  Whom we had known before.

The broken voice, the withered neck,
  The coat worn out with care,
The cleanliness of indigence,
  The brilliance of despair,
The fond imponderable dreams
  Of affluence,—all were there.

Poor Finzer, with his dreams and schemes,
  Fares hard now in the race,   20
With heart and eye that have a task
  When he looks in the face
Of one who might so easily
  Have been in Finzer's place.

He comes unfailing for the loan
  We give and then forget;
He comes, and probably for years
  Will he be coming yet,—
Familiar as an old mistake,
  And futile as regret.   30

THE MAN AGAINST THE SKY
(1916)

Between me and the sunset, like a dome
Against the glory of a world on fire,
Now burned a sudden hill,
Bleak, round, and high, by flame-lit height made higher,
With nothing on it for the flame to kill
Save one who moved and was alone up there
To loom before the chaos and the glare
As if he were the last god going home
Unto his last desire.

Dark, marvelous, and inscrutable he moved on   10
Till down the fiery distance he was gone,
Like one of those eternal, remote things
That range across a man's imaginings
When a sure music fills him and he knows
What he may say thereafter to few men,—
The touch of ages having wrought
An echo and a glimpse of what he thought
A phantom or a legend until then;
For whether lighted over ways that save,
Or lured from all repose,   20
If he go on too far to find a grave,
Mostly alone he goes.

Even he, who stood where I had found him,
On high with fire all round him,
Who moved along the molten west,
And over the round hill's crest
That seemed half ready with him to go down,
Flame-bitten and flame-cleft,
As if there were to be no last thing left
Of a nameless unimaginable town,—   30
Even he who climbed and vanished may have taken
Down to the perils of a depth not known,
From death defended though by men forsaken,
The bread that every man must eat alone;
He may have walked while others hardly dared

Look on to see him stand where many fell;
And upward out of that, as out of hell,
He may have sung and striven
To mount where more of him shall yet be given,
Bereft of all retreat,   40
To sevenfold heat,—
As on a day when three in Dura shared
The furnace, and were spared
For glory by that king of Babylon
Who made himself so great that God, who heard,
Covered him with long feathers, like a bird.

Again, he may have gone down easily,
By comfortable altitudes, and found,
As always, underneath him solid ground
Whereon to be sufficient and to stand   50
Possessed already of the promised land,
Far stretched and fair to see:
A good sight, verily,
And one to make the eyes of her who bore him
Shine glad with hidden tears.
Why question of his ease of who before him,
In one place or another where they left
Their names as far behind them as their bones,
And yet by dint of slaughter toil and theft,
And shrewdly sharpened stones,   60
Carved hard the way for his ascendency
Through deserts of lost years?
Why trouble him now who sees and hears
No more than what his innocence requires,
And therefore to no other height aspires
Than one at which he neither quails nor tires?
He may do more by seeing what he sees
Than others eager for iniquities;
He may, by seeing all things for the best,
Incite futurity to do the rest.   70

Or with an even likelihood,
He may have met with atrabilious eyes
The fires of time on equal terms and passed
Indifferently down, until at last

His only kind of grandeur would have been,
Apparently, in being seen.
He may have had for evil or for good
No argument; he may have had no care
For what without himself went anywhere
To failure or to glory, and least of all   80
For such a stale, flamboyant miracle;
He may have been the prophet of an art
Immovable to old idolatries;
He may have been a player without a part,
Annoyed that even the sun should have the skies
For such a flaming way to advertise;
He may have been a painter sick at heart
With Nature's toiling for a new surprise;
He may have been a cynic, who now, for all
Of anything divine that his effete   90
Negation may have tasted,
Saw truth in his own image, rather small,
Forebore to fever the ephemeral,
Found any barren height a good retreat
From any swarming street,
And in the sun saw power superbly wasted:
And when the primitive old-fashioned stars
Came out again to shine on joys and wars
More primitive, and all arrayed for doom,
He may have proved a world a sorry thing   100
In his imagining,
And life a lighted highway to the tomb.

Or, mounting with infirm unsearching tread,
His hopes to chaos led,
He may have stumbled up there from the past,
And with an aching strangeness viewed the last
Abysmal conflagration of his dreams,—
A flame where nothing seems
To burn but flame itself, by nothing fed;
And while it all went out,   110
Not even the faint anodyne of doubt
May then have eased a painful going down
From pictured heights of power and lost renown,
Revealed at length to his outlived endeavor

Remote and unapproachable forever;
And at his heart there may have gnawed
Sick memories of a dead faith foiled and flawed
And long dishonored by the living death
Assigned alike by chance
To brutes and hierophants;   120
And anguish fallen on those he loved around him
May once have dealt the last blow to confound him,
And so have left him as death leaves a child,
Who sees it all too near;
And he who knows no young way to forget
May struggle to the tomb unreconciled.
Whatever suns may rise or set
There may be nothing kinder for him here
Than shafts and agonies;
And under these   130
He may cry out and stay on horribly;
Or, seeing in death too small a thing to fear,
He may go forward like a stoic Roman
Where pangs and terrors in his pathway lie,—
Or, seizing the swift logic of a woman,
Curse God and die.

Or maybe there, like many another one
Who might have stood aloft and looked ahead,
Black-drawn against wild red,
He may have built, unawed by fiery gules   140
That in him no commotion stirred,
A living reason out of molecules
Why molecules occurred,
And one for smiling when he might have sighed
Had he seen far enough,
And in the same inevitable stuff
Discovered an odd reason too for pride
In being what he must have been by laws
Infrangible and for no kind of cause.
Deterred by no confusion or surprise   150
He may have seen with his mechanic eyes
A world without a meaning, and had room,
Alone amid magnificence and doom,
To build himself an airy monument

That should, or fail him in his vague intent,
Outlast an accidental universe—
To call it nothing worse—
Or, by the burrowing guile
Of Time disintegrated and effaced,
Like once-remembered mighty trees go down   160
To ruin, of which by man may now be traced
No part sufficient even to be rotten,
And in the book of things that are forgotten
Is entered as a thing not quite worth while.
He may have been so great
That satraps would have shivered at his frown,
And all he prized alive may rule a state
No larger than a grave that holds a clown;
He may have been a master of his fate,
And of his atoms,—ready as another   170
In his emergence to exonerate
His father and his mother;
He may have been a captain of a host,
Self-eloquent and ripe for prodigies,
Doomed here to swell by dangerous degrees,
And then give up the ghost.
Nahum's great grasshoppers were such as these,
Sun-scattered and soon lost.

Whatever the dark road he may have taken,
This man who stood on high   180
And faced alone the sky,
Whatever drove or lured or guided him,—
A vision answering a faith unshaken,
An easy trust assumed of easy trials,
A sick negation born of weak denials,
A crazed abhorrence of an old condition,
A blind attendance on a brief ambition,—
Whatever stayed him or derided him,
His way was even as ours;
And we, with all our wounds and all our powers,   190
Must each await alone at his own height
Another darkness or another light;
And there, of our poor self dominion reft,
If inference and reason shun

Hell, Heaven, and Oblivion,
May thwarted will (perforce precarious,
But for our conservation better thus)
Have no misgiving left
Of doing yet what here we leave undone?
Or if unto the last of these we cleave,   200
Believing or protesting we believe
In such an idle and ephemeral
Florescence of the diabolical,—
If, robbed of two fond old enormities,
Our being had no onward auguries,
What then were this great love of ours to say
For launching other lives to voyage again
A little farther into time and pain,
A little faster in a futile chase
For a kingdom and a power and a Race   210
That would have still in sight
A manifest end of ashes and eternal night?
Is this the music of the toys we shake
So loud,—as if there might be no mistake
Somewhere in our indomitable will?
Are we no greater than the noise we make
Along one blind atomic pilgrimage
Whereon by crass chance billeted we go
Because our brains and bones and cartilage
Will have it so?   220
If this we say, then let us all be still
About our share in it, and live and die
More quietly thereby.

Where was he going, this man against the sky?
You know not, nor do I.
But this we know, if we know anything:
That we may laugh and fight and sing
And of our transcience here make offering
To an orient Word that will not be erased,
Or, save in incommunicable gleams   230
Too permanent for dreams,
Be found or known.
No tonic and ambitious irritant
Of increase or of want

Has made an otherwise insensate waste
Of ages overthrown
A ruthless, veiled, implacable foretaste
Of other ages that are still to be
Depleted and rewarded variously
Because a few, by fate's economy,   240
Shall seem to move the world the way it goes;
No soft evangel of equality,
Safe-cradled in a communal repose
That huddles into death and may at last
Be covered well with equatorial snows—
And all for what, the devil only knows—
Will aggregate an inkling to confirm
The credit of a sage or of a worm,
Or tell us why one man in five
Should have a care to stay alive   250
While in his heart he feels no violence
Laid on his humor and intelligence
When infant Science makes a pleasant face
And waves again that hollow toy, the Race;
No planetary trap where souls are wrought
For nothing but the sake of being caught
And sent again to nothing will attune
Itself to any key of any reason
Why man should hunger through another season
To find out why 'twere better late than soon   260
To go away and let the sun and moon
And all the silly stars illuminate
A place for creeping things,
And those that root and trumpet and have wings,
And herd and ruminate,
Or dive and flash and poise in rivers and seas,
Or by their loyal tails in lofty trees
Hang screeching lewd victorious derision
Of man's immortal vision.

Shall we, because Eternity records   270
Too vast an answer for the time-born words
We spell, whereof so many are dead that once
In our capricious lexicons
Were so alive and final, hear no more

The Word itself, the living word
That none alive has ever heard
Or ever spelt,
And few have ever felt
Without the fears and old surrenderings
And terrors that began   280
When Death let fall a feather from his wings
And humbled the first man?
Because the weight of our humility,
Wherefrom we gain
A little wisdom and much pain,
Falls here too sore and there too tedious,
Are we in anguish or complacency,
Not looking far enough ahead
To see by what mad couriers we are led
Along the roads of the ridiculous,   290
To pity ourselves and laugh at faith
And while we curse life bear it?
And if we see the soul's dead end in death,
Are we to fear it?
What folly is here that has not yet a name
Unless we say outright that we are liars?
What have we seen beyond our sunset fires
That lights again the way by which we came?
Why pay we such a price, and one we give
So clamoringly, for each racked empty day   300
That leads one more last human hope away,
As quiet fiends would lead past our crazed eyes
Our children to an unseen sacrifice?
If after all that we have lived and thought,
All comes to Nought,—
If there be nothing after Now,
And we be nothing anyhow,
And we know that,—why live?
'Twere sure but weaklings' vain distress
To suffer dungeons where so many doors   310
Will open on the cold eternal shores
That look sheer down
To the dark tideless floods of Nothingness
Where all who know may drown.

THE DARK HILLS

(1920)

Dark hills at evening in the west,
Where sunset hovers like a sound
Of golden horns that sang to rest
Old bones of warriors under ground,
Far now from all the bannered ways
Where flash the legions of the sun,
You fade—as if the last of days
Were fading, and all wars were done.

MR. FLOOD'S PARTY

(1921)

Old Eben Flood, climbing alone one night
Over the hill between the town below
And the forsaken upland hermitage
That held as much as he should ever know
On earth again of home, paused warily.
The road was his with not a native near;
And Eben, having leisure, said aloud,
For no man else in Tilbury Town to hear:

"Well, Mr. Flood, we have the harvest moon
Again, and we may not have many more;   10
The bird is on the wing, the poet says,
And you and I have said it here before.
Drink to the bird." He raised up to the light
The jug that he had gone so far to fill,
And answered huskily: "Well, Mr. Flood,
Since you propose it, I believe I will."

Alone, as if enduring to the end
A valiant armor of scarred hopes outworn,
He stood there in the middle of the road
Like Roland's ghost winding a silent horn.   20
Below him, in the town among the trees,

Where friends of other days had honored him,
A phantom salutation of the dead
Rang thinly till old Eben's eyes were dim.

Then, as a mother lays her sleeping child
Down tenderly, fearing it may awake,
He set the jug down slowly at his feet
With trembling care, knowing that most things break;
And only when assured that on firm earth
It stood, as the uncertain lives of men   30
Assuredly did not, he paced away,
And with his hand extended paused again:

"Well, Mr. Flood, we have not met like this
In a long time; and many a change has come
To both of us, I fear, since last it was
We had a drop together. Welcome home!"
Convivially returning with himself,
Again he raised the jug up to the light;
And with an acquiescent quaver said:
"Well, Mr. Flood, if you insist, I might.   40

"Only a very little, Mr. Flood—
For auld lang syne. No more, sir; that will do."
So, for the time, apparently it did,
And Eben evidently thought so too;
For soon amid the silver loneliness
Of night he lifted up his voice and sang,
Secure, with only two moons listening,
Until the whole harmonious landscape rang—

"For auld lang syne." The weary throat gave out,
The last word wavered, and the song was done.   50
He raised again the jug regretfully
And shook his head, and was again alone.
There was not much that was ahead of him,
And there was nothing in the town below—
Where strangers would have shut the many doors
That many friends had opened long ago.

THE SHEAVES
(1925)

Where long the shadows of the wind had rolled,
Green wheat was yielding to the change assigned;
And as by some vast magic undivined
The world was turning slowly into gold.
Like nothing that was ever bought or sold
It waited there, the body and the mind;
And with a mighty meaning of a kind
That tells the more the more it is not told.

So in a land where all days are not fair,
Fair days went on till on another day   10
A thousand golden sheaves were lying there,
Shining and still, but not for long to stay—
As if a thousand girls with golden hair
Might rise from where they slept and go away.

KARMA
(1925)

Christmas was in the air and all was well
With him, but for a few confusing flaws
In divers of God's images. Because
A friend of his would neither buy nor sell,
Was he to answer for the axe that fell?
He pondered; and the reason for it was,
Partly, a slowly freezing Santa Claus
Upon the corner, with his beard and bell.

Acknowledging an improvident surprise,
He magnified a fancy that he wished   10
The friend whom he had wrecked were here again.
Not sure of that, he found a compromise;
And from the fulness of his heart he fished
A dime for Jesus who had died for men.

Robert Frost
1874-1963

THE VANTAGE POINT
(1913)

If tired of trees I seek again mankind,
   Well I know where to hie me—in the dawn,
   To a slope where the cattle keep the lawn.
There amid lolling juniper reclined,
Myself unseen, I see in white defined
   Far off the homes of men, and farther still,
   The graves of men on an opposing hill,
Living or dead, whichever are to mind.

And if by noon I have too much of these,
   I have but to turn on my arm, and lo,
   The sun-burned hillside sets my face aglow,   10
My breathing shakes the bluet like a breeze,
   I smell the earth, I smell the bruisèd plant,
   I look into the crater of the ant.

THE TUFT OF FLOWERS
(1913)

I went to turn the grass once after one
Who mowed it in the dew before the sun.

The dew was gone that made his blade so keen
Before I came to view the leveled scene.

I looked for him behind an isle of trees;
I listened for his whetstone on the breeze.

But he had gone his way, the grass all mown,
And I must be, as he had been,—alone,

"As all must be," I said within my heart,
"Whether they work together or apart."   10

But as I said it, swift there passed me by
On noiseless wing a bewildered butterfly,

Seeking with memories grown dim o'er night
Some resting flower of yesterday's delight.

And once I marked his flight go round and round,
As where some flower lay withering on the ground.

And then he flew as far as eye could see,
And then on tremulous wing came back to me.

I thought of questions that have no reply,
And would have turned to toss the grass to dry;   20

But he turned first, and led my eye to look
At a tall tuft of flowers beside a brook,

A leaping tongue of bloom the scythe had spared
Beside a reedy brook the scythe had bared.

The mower in the dew had loved them thus,
By leaving them to flourish, not for us,

Nor yet to draw one thought of ours to him,
But from sheer morning gladness at the brim.

The butterfly and I had lit upon,
Nevertheless, a message from the dawn,   30

That made me hear the wakening birds around,
And hear his long scythe whispering to the ground,

And feel a spirit kindred to my own;
So that henceforth I worked no more alone;

But glad with him, I worked as with his aid,
And weary, sought at noon with him the shade;

And dreaming, as it were, held brotherly speech
With one whose thought I had not hoped to reach.

"Men work together," I told him from the heart,
"Whether they work together or apart."   40

MENDING WALL
(1914)

Something there is that doesn't love a wall,
That sends the frozen-ground-swell under it,
And spills the upper boulders in the sun;
And makes gaps even two can pass abreast.
The work of hunters is another thing:
I have come after them and made repair
Where they have left not one stone on a stone,
But they would have the rabbit out of hiding,
To please the yelping dogs. The gaps I mean,
No one has seen them made or heard them made,   10
But at spring mending-time we find them there.
I let my neighbor know beyond the hill;
And on a day we meet to walk the line
And set the wall between us once again.
We keep the wall between us as we go.
To each the boulders that have fallen to each.
And some are loaves and some so nearly balls
We have to use a spell to make them balance:
"Stay where you are until our backs are turned!"
We wear our fingers rough with handling them.   20
Oh, just another kind of outdoor game,
One on a side. It comes to little more:
There where it is we do not need the wall:
He is all pine and I am apple orchard.
My apple trees will never get across

And eat the cones under his pines, I tell him.
He only says, "Good fences make good neighbors."
Spring is the mischief in me, and I wonder
If I could put a notion in his head:
"*Why* do they make good neighbors? Isn't it   30
Where there are cows? But here there are no cows.
Before I built a wall I'd ask to know
What I was walling in or walling out,
And to whom I was like to give offense.
Something there is that doesn't love a wall,
That wants it down." I could say "Elves" to him,
But it's not elves exactly, and I'd rather
He said it for himself. I see him there
Bringing a stone grasped firmly by the top
In each hand, like an old-stone savage armed.   40
He moves in darkness as it seems to me,
Not of woods only and the shade of trees.
He will not go behind his father's saying,
And he likes having thought of it so well
He says again, "Good fences make good neighbors."

HOME BURIAL

(1914)

He saw her from the bottom of the stairs
Before she saw him. She was starting down,
Looking back over her shoulder at some fear.
She took a doubtful step and then undid it
To raise herself and look again. He spoke
Advancing toward her: "What is it you see
From up there always—for I want to know."
She turned and sank upon her skirts at that,
And her face changed from terrified to dull.
He said to gain time: "What is it you see,"   10
Mounting until she cowered under him.
"I will find out now—you must tell me, dear."
She, in her place, refused him any help
With the least stiffening of her neck and silence.
She let him look, sure that he wouldn't see,

Blind creature; and awhile he didn't see.
But at last he murmured, "Oh," and again, "Oh."

"What is it—what?" she said.

                    "Just that I see."

"You don't," she challenged. "Tell me what it is."

"The wonder is I didn't see at once.   20
I never noticed it from here before.
I must be wonted to it—that's the reason.
The little graveyard where my people are!
So small the window frames the whole of it.
Not so much larger than a bedroom, is it?
There are three stones of slate and one of marble,
Broad-shouldered little slabs there in the sunlight
On the sidehill. We haven't to mind *those*.
But I understand: it is not the stones,
But the child's mound—"

                    "Don't, don't, don't, don't," she cried.

She withdrew shrinking from beneath his arm   31
That rested on the bannister, and slid downstairs;
And turned on him with such a daunting look,
He said twice over before he knew himself:
"Can't a man speak of his own child he's lost?"

"Not you! Oh, where's my hat? Oh, I don't need it!
I must get out of here. I must get air.
I don't know rightly whether any man can."

"Amy! Don't go to someone else this time.
Listen to me. I won't come down the stairs."   40
He sat and fixed his chin between his fists.
"There's something I should like to ask you, dear."

"You don't know how to ask it."

                    "Help me, then."

Her fingers moved the latch for all reply.

"My words are nearly always an offense.
I don't know how to speak of anything
So as to please you. But I might be taught
I should suppose. I can't say I see how.
A man must partly give up being a man
With women-folk. We could have some arrangement   50
By which I'd bind myself to keep hands off
Anything special you're a-mind to name.
Though I don't like such things 'twixt those that love.
Two that don't love can't live together without them.
But two that do can't live together with them."
She moved the latch a little. "Don't—don't go.
Don't carry it to someone else this time.
Tell me about it if it's something human.
Let me into your grief. I'm not so much
Unlike other folks as your standing there   60
Apart would make me out. Give me my chance.
I do think, though, you overdo it a little.
What was it brought you up to think it the thing
To take your mother-loss of a first child
So inconsolably—in the face of love.
You'd think his memory might be satisfied—"

"There you go sneering now!"

                    "I'm not, I'm not!
You make me angry. I'll come down to you.
God, what a woman! And it's come to this,
A man can't speak of his own child that's dead."   70

"You can't because you don't know how to speak.
If you had any feelings, you that dug
With your own hand—how could you?—his little grave;
I saw you from that very window there,
Making the gravel leap and leap in air,
Leap up, like that, like that, and land so lightly
And roll back down the mound beside the hole.
I thought, Who is that man? I didn't know you.
And I crept down the stairs and up the stairs

To look again, and still your spade kept lifting.   80
Then you came in. I heard your rumbling voice
Out in the kitchen, and I don't know why,
But I went near to see with my own eyes.
You could sit there with the stains on your shoes
Of the fresh earth from your own baby's grave
And talk about your everyday concerns.
You had stood the spade up against the wall
Outside there in the entry, for I saw it."

"I shall laugh the worst laugh I ever laughed.
I'm cursed. God, if I don't believe I'm cursed."   90

"I can repeat the very words you were saying.
'Three foggy mornings and one rainy day
Will rot the best birch fence a man can build.'
Think of it, talk like that at such a time!
What had how long it takes a birch to rot
To do with what was in the darkened parlor.
You *couldn't* care! The nearest friends can go
With anyone to death, comes so far short
They might as well not try to go at all.
No, from the time when one is sick to death,   100
One is alone, and he dies more alone.
Friends make pretense of following to the grave,
But before one is in it, their minds are turned
And making the best of their way back to life
And living people, and things they understand.
But the world's evil. I won't have grief so
If I can change it. Oh, I won't, I won't!"

"There, you have said it all and you feel better.
You won't go now. You're crying. Close the door.
The heart's gone out of it: why keep it up.   110
Amy! There's someone coming down the road!"

"*You*—oh, you think the talk is all. I must go—
Somewhere out of this house. How can I make you—"

"If—you—do!" She was opening the door wider.
"Where do you mean to go? First tell me that.
I'll follow and bring you back by force. I *will!*—"

AFTER APPLE–PICKING
(1914)

My long two-pointed ladder's sticking through a tree
Toward heaven still,
And there's a barrel that I didn't fill
Beside it, and there may be two or three
Apples I didn't pick upon some bough.
But I am done with apple-picking now.
Essence of winter sleep is on the night,
The scent of apples: I am drowsing off.
I cannot rub the strangeness from my sight
I got from looking through a pane of glass   10
I skimmed this morning from the drinking trough
And held against the world of hoary grass.
It melted, and I let it fall and break.
But I was well
Upon my way to sleep before it fell,
And I could tell
What form my dreaming was about to take.
Magnified apples appear and disappear,
Stem end and blossom end,
And every fleck of russet showing clear.   20
My instep arch not only keeps the ache,
It keeps the pressure of a ladder-round.
I feel the ladder sway as the boughs bend.
And I keep hearing from the cellar bin
The rumbling sound
Of load on load of apples coming in.
For I have had too much
Of apple-picking: I am overtired
Of the great harvest I myself desired.
There were ten thousand thousand fruit to touch,   30
Cherish in hand, lift down, and not let fall.
For all
That struck the earth,
No matter if not bruised or spiked with stubble,
Went surely to the cider-apple heap
As of no worth.
One can see what will trouble

This sleep of mine, whatever sleep it is.
Were he not gone,
The woodchuck could say whether it's like his   40
death Long sleep, as I describe its coming on,
Or just some human sleep.

THE WOOD–PILE

(1914)

Out walking in the frozen swamp one gray day,
I paused and said, "I will turn back from here.
No, I will go on farther—and we shall see."
The hard snow held me, save where now and then
One foot went through. The view was all in lines
Straight up and down of tall slim trees
Too much alike to mark or name a place by
So as to say for certain I was here
Or somewhere else: I was just far from home.
A small bird flew before me. He was careful   10
To put a tree between us when he lighted,
And say no word to tell me who he was
Who was so foolish as to think what *he* thought.
He thought that I was after him for a feather—
The white one in his tail; like one who takes
Everything said as personal to himself.
One flight out sideways would have undeceived him.
And then there was a pile of wood for which
I forgot him and let his little fear
Carry him off the way I might have gone,   20
Without so much as wishing him good-night.
He went behind it to make his last stand.
It was a cord of maple, cut and split
And piled—and measured, four by four by eight.
And not another like it could I see.
No runner tracks in this year's snow looped near it.
And it was older sure than this year's cutting,
Or even last year's or the year's before.
The wood was gray and the bark warping off it
And the pile somewhat sunken. Clematis   30
Had wound strings round and round it like a bundle.

What held it though on one side was a tree
Still growing, and on one a stake and prop,
These latter about to fall. I thought that only
Someone who lived in turning to fresh tasks
Could so forget his handiwork on which
He spent himself, the labor of his ax,
And leave it there far from a useful fireplace
To warm the frozen swamp as best it could   ) cycles
With the slow smokeless burning of decay.   / dust to   40

THE ROAD NOT TAKEN
(1916)

Two roads diverged in a yellow wood,
And sorry I could not travel both
And be one traveler, long I stood
And looked down one as far as I could
To where it bent in the undergrowth;

Then took the other, as just as fair,
And having perhaps the better claim,
Because it was grassy and wanted wear;
Though as for that the passing there
Had worn them really about the same,   10

And both that morning equally lay
In leaves no step had trodden black.
Oh, I kept the first for another day!
Yet knowing how way leads on to way,
I doubted if I should ever come back.

I shall be telling this with a sigh
Somewhere ages and ages hence:
Two roads diverged in a wood, and I—
I took the one less traveled by,
And that has made all the difference.   20

THE OVEN BIRD
(1916)

There is a singer everyone has heard,
Loud, a mid-summer and a mid-wood bird,
Who makes the solid tree trunks sound again.
He says that leaves are old and that for flowers
Mid-summer is to spring as one to ten.
He says the early petal-fall is past
When pear and cherry bloom went down in showers
On sunny days a moment overcast;
And comes that other fall we name the fall.
He says the highway dust is over all.   10
The bird would cease and be as other birds
But that he knows in singing not to sing.
The question that he frames in all but words
Is what to make of a diminished thing.

THE WITCH OF COÖS
(From "Two Witches")

(1923)

I stayed the night for shelter at a farm
Behind the mountain, with a mother and son,
Two old-believers. They did all the talking.

MOTHER. Folks think a witch who has familiar spirits
She could call up to pass a winter evening,
But won't, should be burned at the stake or something.
Summoning spirits isn't "Button, button,
Who's got the button," I would have them know.

SON. Mother can make a common table rear
And kick with two legs like an army mule.   10

MOTHER. And when I've done it, what good have I done?
Rather than tip a table for you, let me
Tell you what Ralle the Sioux Control once told me.

He said the dead had souls, but when I asked him
How could that be—I thought the dead were souls,
He broke my trance. Don't that make you suspicious
That there's something the dead are keeping back?
Yes, there's something the dead are keeping back.

SON. You wouldn't want to tell him what we have
Up attic, mother?   20

MOTHER. Bones—a skeleton.

SON. But the headboard of mother's bed is pushed
Against the attic door: the door is nailed.
It's harmless. Mother hears it in the night
Halting perplexed behind the barrier
Of door and headboard. Where it wants to get
Is back into the cellar where it came from.

MOTHER. We'll never let them, will we, son! We'll never!

SON. It left the cellar forty years ago
And carried itself like a pile of dishes   30
Up one flight from the cellar to the kitchen,
Another from the kitchen to the bedroom,
Another from the bedroom to the attic,
Right past both father and mother, and neither stopped it.
Father had gone upstairs; mother was downstairs.
I was a baby: I don't know where I was.

MOTHER. The only fault my husband found with me—
I went to sleep before I went to bed,
Especially in winter when the bed
Might just as well be ice and the clothes snow.   40
The night the bones came up the cellar-stairs
Toffile had gone to bed alone and left me,
But left an open door to cool the room off
So as to sort of turn me out of it.
I was just coming to myself enough
To wonder where the cold was coming from,
When I heard Toffile upstairs in the bedroom
And thought I heard him downstairs in the cellar.

The board we had laid down to walk dry-shod on
When there was water in the cellar in spring   50
Struck the hard cellar bottom. And then someone
Began the stairs, two footsteps for each step,
The way a man with one leg and a crutch,
Or a little child, comes up. It wasn't Toffile:
It wasn't anyone who could be there.
The bulkhead double-doors were double-locked
And swollen tight and buried under snow.
The cellar windows were banked up with sawdust
And swollen tight and buried under snow.
It was the bones. I knew them—and good reason.   60
My first impulse was to get to the knob
And hold the door. But the bones didn't try
The door; they halted helpless on the landing,
Waiting for things to happen in their favor.
The faintest restless rustling ran all through them.
I never could have done the thing I did
If the wish hadn't been too strong in me
To see how they were mounted for this walk.
I had a vision of them put together
Not like a man, but like a chandelier.   70
So suddenly I flung the door wide on him.
A moment he stood balancing with emotion,
And all but lost himself. (A tongue of fire
Flashed out and licked along his upper teeth.
Smoke rolled inside the sockets of his eyes.)
Then he came at me with one hand outstretched,
The way he did in life once; but this time
I struck the hand off brittle on the floor,
And fell back from him on the floor myself.
The finger-pieces slid in all directions.   80
(Where did I see one of those pieces lately?
Hand me my button-box—it must be there.)
I sat up on the floor and shouted, "Toffile,
It's coming up to you." It had its choice
Of the door to the cellar or the hall.
It took the hall door for the novelty,
And set off briskly for so slow a thing,
Still going every which way in the joints, though,
So that it looked like lightning or a scribble,

From the slap I had just now given its hand.   90
I listened till it almost climbed the stairs
From the hall to the only finished bedroom,
Before I got up to do anything;
Then ran and shouted, "Shut the bedroom door,
Toffile, for my sake!" "Company?" he said,
"Don't make me get up; I'm too warm in bed."
So lying forward weakly on the handrail
I pushed myself upstairs, and in the light
(The kitchen had been dark) I had to own
I could see nothing. "Toffile, I don't see it.   100
It's with us in the room though. It's the bones."
"What bones?" "The cellar bones—out of the grave."
That made him throw his bare legs out of bed
And sit up by me and take hold of me.
I wanted to put out the light and see
If I could see it, or else mow the room,
With our arms at the level of our knees,
And bring the chalk-pile down. "I'll tell you what—
It's looking for another door to try.
The uncommonly deep snow has made him think   110
Of his old song, *The Wild Colonial Boy*,
He always used to sing along the tote road.
He's after an open door to get outdoors.
Let's trap him with an open door up attic."
Toffile agreed to that, and sure enough,
Almost the moment he was given an opening,
The steps began to climb the attic stairs.
I heard them. Toffile didn't seem to hear them.
"Quick!" I slammed to the door and held the knob.
"Toffile, get nails." I made him nail the door shut   120
And push the headboard of the bed against it.
Then we asked was there anything
Up attic that we'd ever want again.
The attic was less to us than the cellar.
If the bones liked the attic, let them have it.
Let them stay in the attic. When they sometimes
Come down the stairs at night and stand perplexed
Behind the door and headboard of the bed,
Brushing their chalky skull with chalky fingers,
With sounds like the dry rattling of a shutter,   130

That's what I sit up in the dark to say—
To no one any more since Toffile died.
Let them stay in the attic since they went there.
I promised Toffile to be cruel to them
For helping them be cruel once to him.

SON. We think they had a grave down in the cellar.

MOTHER. We know they had a grave down in the cellar.

SON. We never could find out whose bones they were.

MOTHER. Yes, we could too, son. Tell the truth for once.
They were a man's his father killed for me.   140
I mean a man he killed instead of me.
The least I could do was to help dig their grave.
We were about it one night in the cellar.
Son knows the story: but 'twas not for him
To tell the truth, suppose the time had come.
Son looks surprised to see me end a lie
We'd kept all these years between ourselves
So as to have it ready for outsiders.
But tonight I don't care enough to lie—
I don't remember why I ever cared.   150
Toffile, if he were here, I don't believe
Could tell you why he ever cared himself. . . .

She hadn't found the finger-bone she wanted
Among the buttons poured out in her lap.
I verified the name next morning: Toffile.
The rural letter box said Toffile Lajway.

FIRE AND ICE
(1923)

Some say the world will end in fire,
Some say in ice.
From what I've tasted of desire
I hold with those who favor fire.
But if it had to perish twice,

I think I know enough of hate
To say that for destruction ice
Is also great
And would suffice.

STOPPING BY WOODS ON A SNOWY EVENING
(1923)

Whose woods these are I think I know.
His house is in the village though;
He will not see me stopping here
To watch his woods fill up with snow.

My little horse must think it queer
To stop without a farmhouse near
Between the woods and frozen lake
The darkest evening of the year.

He gives his harness bells a shake
To ask if there is some mistake.   10
The only other sound's the sweep
Of easy wind and downy flake.

The woods are lovely, dark and deep,
But I have promises to keep,
And miles to go before I sleep,
And miles to go before I sleep.

THE ONSET
(1923)

Always the same, when on a fated night
At last the gathered snow lets down as white
As may be in dark woods, and with a song
It shall not make again all winter long
Of hissing on the yet uncovered ground,
I almost stumble looking up and round,
As one who overtaken by the end
Gives up his errand, and lets death descend

Upon him where he is, with nothing done
To evil, no important triumph won,   10
More than if life had never been begun.

Yet all the precedent is on my side:
I know that winter death has never tried
The earth but it has failed: the snow may heap
In long storms an undrifted four feet deep
As measured against maple, birch, and oak,
It cannot check the peeper's silver croak;
And I shall see the snow all go down hill
In water of a slender April rill
That flashes tail through last year's withered brake   20
And dead weeds, like a disappearing snake.
Nothing will be left white but here a birch,
And there a clump of houses with a church.

TO EARTHWARD
(1923)

Love at the lips was touch
As sweet as I could bear;
And once that seemed too much;
I lived on air

That crossed me from sweet things
The flow of—was it musk
From hidden grapevine springs
Down hill at dusk?

I had the swirl and ache
From sprays of honeysuckle   10
That when they're gathered shake
Dew on the knuckle.

I craved strong sweets, but those
Seemed strong when I was young;
The petal of the rose
It was that stung.

Now no joy but lacks salt
That is not dashed with pain
And weariness and fault;
I crave the stain   20

Of tears, the aftermark
Of almost too much love,
The sweet of bitter bark
And burning clove.

When stiff and sore and scarred
I take away my hand
From leaning on it hard
In grass and sand,

The hurt is not enough:
I long for weight and strength   30
To feel the earth as rough
To all my length.

TWO LOOK AT TWO
(1923)

Love and forgetting might have carried them
A little further up the mountain side
With night so near, but not much further up.
They must have halted soon in any case
With thoughts of the path back, how rough it was
With rock and washout, and unsafe in darkness;
When they were halted by a tumbled wall
With barbed-wire binding. They stood facing this,
Spending what onward impulse they still had
In one last look the way they must not go,   10
On up the failing path, where, if a stone
Or earthslide moved at night, it moved itself;
No footstep moved it. "This is all," they sighed,
"Good-night to woods." But not so; there was more.
A doe from round a spruce stood looking at them
Across the wall, as near the wall as they.
She saw them in their field, they her in hers.

The difficulty of seeing what stood still,
Like some up-ended boulder split in two,
Was in her clouded eyes: they saw no fear there.   20
She seemed to think that two thus they were safe.
Then, as if they were something that, though strange,
She could not trouble her mind with too long,
She sighed and passed unscared along the wall.
"*This,* then, is all. What more is there to ask?"
But no, not yet. A snort to bid them wait.
A buck from round the spruce stood looking at them
Across the wall, as near the wall as they.
This was an antlered buck of lusty nostril,
Not the same doe come back into her place.   30
He viewed them quizzically with jerks of head,
As if to ask, "Why don't you make some motion?
Or give some sign of life? Because you can't.
I doubt if you're as living as you look."
Thus till he had them almost feeling dared
To stretch a proffering hand—and a spell-breaking.
Then he too passed unscared along the wall.
Two had seen two, whichever side you spoke from.
"This *must* be all." It was all. Still they stood,
A great wave from it going over them,   40
As if the earth in one unlooked-for favor
Had made them certain earth returned their love.

ONCE BY THE PACIFIC
(1928)

The shattered water made a misty din.
Great waves looked over others coming in,
And thought of doing something to the shore
That water never did to land before.
The clouds were low and hairy in the skies,
Like locks blown forward in the gleam of eyes.
You could not tell, and yet it looked as if
The shore was lucky in being backed by cliff,
The cliff in being backed by continent;
It looked as if a night of dark intent   10
Was coming, and not only a night, an age.

Someone had better be prepared for rage.
There would be more than ocean-water broken
Before God's last *Put out the Light* was spoken.

ACQUAINTED WITH THE NIGHT
(1928)

I have been one acquainted with the night.
I have walked out in rain—and back in rain.
I have outwalked the furthest city light.

I have looked down the saddest city lane.
I have passed by the watchman on his beat
And dropped my eyes, unwilling to explain.

I have stood still and stopped the sound of feet
When far away an interrupted cry
Came over houses from another street,

But not to call me back or say good-by;   10
And further still at an unearthly height,
One luminary clock against the sky

Proclaimed the time was neither wrong nor right.
I have been one acquainted with the night.

THE LOVELY SHALL BE CHOOSERS
(1929)

The Voice said, "Hurl her down!"

The Voices, "How far down?"

"Seven levels of the world."

"How much time have we?"

"Take twenty years.
She *would* refuse love safe with wealth and honor!
The lovely shall be choosers, shall they?
Then let them choose!"

"Then we shall let her choose?"

"Yes, let her choose.   10
Take up the task beyond her choosing."

Invisible hands crowded on her shoulder
In readiness to weigh upon her.
But she stood straight still,
In broad round ear-rings, gold and jet with pearls,
And broad round suchlike brooch,
Her cheeks high colored,
Proud and the pride of friends.

The Voice asked, "You can let her choose?"

"Yes, we can let her and still triumph."   20

"Do it by joys, and leave her always blameless.
Be her first joy her wedding,
That though a wedding,
Is yet—well something they know, he and she.
And after that her next joy
That though she grieves, her grief is secret:
Those friends know nothing of her grief to make it shameful.
Her third joy that though now they cannot help but know,
They move in pleasure too far off
To think much or much care.   30
Give her a child at either knee for fourth joy
To tell once and once only, for them never to forget,
How once she walked in brightness,
And make them see it in the winter firelight.
But give her friends for then she dare not tell
For their foregone incredulousness.
And be her next joy this:
Her never having deigned to tell them.
Make her among the humblest even
Seem to them less than they are.   40
Hopeless of being known for what she has been,
Failing of being loved for what she is,
Give her the comfort for her sixth of knowing
She fails from strangeness to a way of life

She came to from too high too late to learn.
Then send some *one* with eyes to see
And wonder at her where she is,
And words to wonder in her hearing how she came there,
But without time to linger for her story.
Be her last joy her heart's going out to this one   50
So that she almost speaks.
You know them—seven in all."

"Trust us," the Voices said.

TWO TRAMPS IN MUD TIME
(1936)

Out of the mud two strangers came
And caught me splitting wood in the yard.
And one of them put me off my aim
By hailing cheerily "Hit them hard!"
I knew pretty well why he dropped behind
And let the other go on a way.
I knew pretty well what he had in mind:
He wanted to take my job for pay.

Good blocks of oak it was I split,
As large around as the chopping block;   10
And every piece I squarely hit
Fell splinterless as a cloven rock.
The blows that a life of self-control
Spares to strike for the common good
That day, giving a loose to my soul,
I spent on the unimportant wood.

The sun was warm but the wind was chill.
You know how it is with an April day
When the sun is out and the wind is still,
You're one month on in the middle of May.   20
But if you so much as dare to speak,
A cloud comes over the sunlit arch,
A wind comes off a frozen peak,
And you're two months back in the middle of March.

A bluebird comes tenderly up to alight
And turns to the wind to unruffle a plume
His song so pitched as not to excite
A single flower as yet to bloom.
It is snowing a flake: and he half knew
Winter was only playing possum.   30
Except in color he isn't blue,
But he wouldn't advise a thing to blossom.

The water for which we may have to look
In summertime with a witching-wand,
In every wheelrut's now a brook,
In every print of a hoof a pond.
Be glad of water, but don't forget
The lurking frost in the earth beneath
That will steal forth after the sun is set
And show on the water its crystal teeth.   40

The time when most I loved my task
These two must make me love it more
By coming with what they came to ask.
You'd think I never had felt before
The weight of an ax-head poised aloft,
The grip on earth of outspread feet.
The life of muscles rocking soft
And smooth and moist in vernal heat.

Out of the woods two hulking tramps
(From sleeping God knows where last night,   50
But not long since in the lumber camps).
They thought all chopping was theirs of right.
Men of the woods and lumberjacks,
They judged me by their appropriate tool.
Except as a fellow handled an ax,
They had no way of knowing a fool.

Nothing on either side was said.
They knew they had but to stay their stay
And all their logic would fill my head:
As that I had no right to play   60
With what was another man's work for gain.

My right might be love but theirs was need.
And where the two exist in twain
Theirs was the better right—agreed.

But yield who will to their separation,
My object in life is to unite
My avocation and my vocation
As my two eyes make one in sight.
Only where love and need are one,
And the work is play for mortal stakes,   70
Is the deed ever really done
For Heaven and the future's sakes.

DESERT PLACES

(1936)

Snow falling and night falling fast, oh, fast
In a field I looked into going past,
And the ground almost covered smooth in snow,
But a few weeds and stubble showing last.

The woods around it have it—it is theirs.
All animals are smothered in their lairs.
I am too absent-spirited to count;
The loneliness includes me unawares.

And lonely as it is that loneliness
Will be more lonely ere it will be less—   10
A blanker whiteness of benighted snow
With no expression, nothing to express.

They cannot scare me with their empty spaces
Between stars—on stars where no human race is.
I have it in me so much nearer home
To scare myself with my own desert places.

NEITHER OUT FAR NOR IN DEEP
(1936)

The people along the sand
All turn and look one way.
They turn their back on the land.
They look at the sea all day.

As long as it takes to pass
A ship keeps raising its hull;
The wetter ground like glass
Reflects a standing gull.

The land may vary more;
But wherever the truth may be—   10
The water comes ashore,
And the people look at the sea.

They cannot look out far.
They cannot look in deep.
But when was that ever a bar
To any watch they keep?

DESIGN
(1936)

worldly death

I found a dimpled spider, fat and white,
nearly blue On a white heal-all, holding up a moth
Like a white piece of rigid satin cloth—
Assorted characters of death and blight
Mixed ready to begin the morning right,
Like the ingredients of a witches' broth—
A snow-drop spider, a flower like a froth,
And dead wings carried like a paper kite.

What had that flower to do with being white,
The wayside blue and innocent heal-all?   10
What brought the kindred spider to that height,

Then steered the white moth thither in the night? *Hardy, chance*
What but design of darkness to appall?—
If design govern in a thing so small.

THE GIFT OUTRIGHT
(1942)

The land was ours before we were the land's.
She was our land more than a hundred years
Before we were her people. She was ours
In Massachusetts, in Virginia,
But we were England's, still colonials,
Possessing what we still were unpossessed by,
Possessed by what we now no more possessed.
Something we were withholding made us weak
Until we found out that it was ourselves
We were withholding from our land of living,   10
And forthwith found salvation in surrender.
Such as we were we gave ourselves outright
(The deed of gift was many deeds of war)
To the land vaguely realizing westward,
But still unstoried, artless, unenhanced,
Such as she was, such as she would become.

DIRECTIVE
(1947)

Back out of all this now too much for us,
Back in a time made simple by the loss
Of detail, burned, dissolved, and broken off
Like graveyard marble sculpture in the weather,
There is a house that is no more a house
Upon a farm that is no more a farm
And in a town that is no more a town.
The road there, if you'll let a guide direct you
Who only has at heart your getting lost,
May seem as if it should have been a quarry—   10
Great monolithic knees the former town
Long since gave up pretense of keeping covered.

And there's a story in a book about it:
Besides the wear of iron wagon wheels
The ledges show lines ruled southeast northwest,
The chisel work of an enormous Glacier
That braced his feet against the Arctic Pole.
You must not mind a certain coolness from him
Still said to haunt this side of Panther Mountain.
Nor need you mind the serial ordeal   20
Of being watched from forty cellar holes
As if by eye pairs out of forty firkins.
As for the woods' excitement over you
That sends light rustle rushes to their leaves,
Charge that to upstart inexperience.
Where were they all not twenty years ago?
They think too much of having shaded out
A few old pecker-fretted apple trees.
Make yourself up a cheering song of how
Someone's road home from work this once was,   30
Who may be just ahead of you on foot
Or creaking with a buggy load of grain.
The height of the adventure is the height
Of country where two village cultures faded
Into each other. Both of them are lost.
And if you're lost enough to find yourself
By now, pull in your ladder road behind you
And put a sign up CLOSED to all but me.
Then make yourself at home. The only field
Now left's no bigger than a harness gall.   40
First there's the children's house of make believe,
Some shattered dishes underneath a pine,
The playthings in the playhouse of the children.
Weep for what little things could make them glad.
Then for the house that is no more a house,
But only a belilaced cellar hole,
Now slowly closing like a dent in dough.
This was no playhouse but a house in earnest.
Your destination and your destiny's
A brook that was the water of the house,   50
Cold as a spring as yet so near its source,
Too lofty and original to rage.
(We know the valley streams that when aroused

Will leave their tatters hung on barb and thorn.)
I have kept hidden in the instep arch
Of an old cedar at the waterside
A broken drinking goblet like the Grail
Under a spell so the wrong ones can't find it,
So can't get saved, as Saint Mark says they mustn't.
(I stole the goblet from the children's playhouse.)   60
Here are your waters and your watering place.
Drink and be whole again beyond confusion.

Wallace Stevens
1879-1955

DOMINATION OF BLACK
(1923)

At night, by the fire,
The colors of the bushes
And of the fallen leaves,
Repeating themselves,
Turned in the room,
Like the leaves themselves
Turning in the wind.
Yes: but the color of the heavy hemlocks
Came striding.
And I remembered the cry of the peacocks.   10

The colors of their tails
Were like the leaves themselves
Turning in the wind,
In the twilight wind.
They swept over the room,
Just as they flew from the boughs of the hemlocks
Down to the ground.
I heard them cry—the peacocks.
Was it a cry against the twilight
Or against the leaves themselves   20
Turning in the wind,
Turning as the flames
Turned in the fire,

Turning as the tails of the peacocks
Turned in the loud fire,
Loud as the hemlocks
Full of the cry of the peacocks?
Or was it a cry against the hemlocks?

Out of the window,
I saw how the planets gathered   30
Like the leaves themselves
Turning in the wind.
I saw how the night came,
Came striding like the color of the heavy hemlocks
I felt afraid.
And I remembered the cry of the peacocks.

THE SNOW MAN
(1923)

One must have a mind of winter
To regard the frost and the boughs
Of the pine-trees crusted with snow;

And have been cold a long time
To behold the junipers shagged with ice,
The spruces rough in the distant glitter

Of the January sun; and not to think
Of any misery in the sound of the wind,
In the sound of a few leaves,

Which is the sound of the land   10
Full of the same wind
That is blowing in the same bare place

For the listener, who listens in the snow,
And, nothing himself, beholds
Nothing that is not there and the nothing that is.

LE MONOCLE DE MON ONCLE
(1923)

"Mother of heaven, regina of the clouds,
O sceptre of the sun, crown of the moon,
There is not nothing, no, no, never nothing,
Like the clashed edges of two words that kill."
And so I mocked her in magnificent measure.
Or was it that I mocked myself alone?
I wish that I might be a thinking stone.
The sea of spuming thought foists up again
The radiant bubble that she was. And then
A deep up-pouring from some saltier well   10
Within me, bursts its watery syllable.

II

A red bird flies across the golden floor.
It is a red bird that seeks out his choir
Among the choirs of wind and wet and wing.
A torrent will fall from him when he finds.
Shall I uncrumple this much-crumpled thing?
I am a man of fortune greeting heirs;
For it has come that thus I greet the spring.
These choirs of welcome choir for me farewell.
No spring can follow past meridian.   20
Yet you persist with anecdotal bliss
To make believe a starry *connaissance*.

III

Is it for nothing, then, that old Chinese
Sat tittivating by their mountain pools
Or in the Yangtse studied out their beards?
I shall not play the flat historic scale.
You know how Utamaro's beauties sought
The end of love in their all-speaking braids.
You know the mountainous coiffures of Bath.
Alas! Have all the barbers lived in vain   30
That not one curl in nature has survived?
Why, without pity on these studious ghosts,
Do you come dripping in your hair from sleep?

IV

This luscious and impeccable fruit of life
Falls, it appears, of its own weight to earth.
When you were Eve, its acrid juice was sweet,
Untasted, in its heavenly, orchard air.
An apple serves as well as any skull
To be the book in which to read a round,
And is as excellent, in that it is composed   40
Of what, like skulls, comes rotting back to ground.
But it excels in this that as the fruit
Of love, it is a book too mad to read
Before one merely reads to pass the time.

V

In the high west there burns a furious star.
It is for fiery boys that star was set
And for sweet-smelling virgins close to them.
The measure of the intensity of love
Is measure, also, of the verve of earth.
For me, the firefly's quick, electric stroke   50
Ticks tediously the time of one more year.
And you? Remember how the crickets came
Out of their mother grass, like little kin,
In the pale nights, when your first imagery
Found inklings of your bond to all that dust.

VI

If men at forty will be painting lakes
The ephemeral blues must merge for them in one,
The basic slate, the universal hue.
There is a substance in us that prevails.
But in our amours amorists discern   60
Such fluctuations that their scrivening
Is breathless to attend each quirky turn.
When amorists grow bald, then amours shrink
Into the compass and curriculum
Of introspective exiles, lecturing.
It is a theme for Hyacinth alone.

VII

The mules that angels ride come slowly down
The blazing passes, from beyond the sun.

Descensions of their tinkling bells arrive.
These muleteers are dainty of their way.   70
Meantime, centurions guffaw and beat
Their shrilling tankards on the table-boards.
This parable, in sense, amounts to this:
The honey of heaven may or may not come,
But that of earth both comes and goes at once.
Suppose these couriers brought amid their train
A damsel heightened by eternal bloom.

VIII

Like a dull scholar, I behold, in love,
An ancient aspect touching a new mind.
It comes, it blooms, it bears its fruit and dies.   80
This trivial trope reveals a way of truth.
Our bloom is gone. We are the fruit thereof.
Two golden gourds distended on our vines,
Into the autumn weather, splashed with frost,
Distorted by hale fatness, turned grotesque.
We hang like warty squashes, streaked and rayed,
The laughing sky will see the two of us
Washed into rinds by rotting winter rains.

IX

In verses wild with motion, full of din,
Loudened by cries, by clashes, quick and sure   90
As the deadly thought of men accomplishing
Their curious fates in war, come, celebrate
The faith of forty, ward of Cupido.
Most venerable heart, the lustiest conceit
Is not too lusty for your broadening.
I quiz all sounds, all thoughts, all everything
For the music and manner of the paladins
To make oblation fit. Where shall I find
Bravura adequate to this great hymn?

X

The fops of fancy in their poems leave   100
Memorabilia of the mystic spouts,
Spontaneously watering their gritty soils.
I am a yeoman, as such fellows go.
I know no magic trees, no balmy boughs,
No silver-ruddy, gold-vermilion fruits.

But, after all, I know a tree that bears
A semblance to the thing I have in mind.
It stands gigantic, with a certain tip
To which all birds come sometime in their time.
But when they go that tip still tips the tree.   110

XI

If sex were all, then every trembling hand
Could make us squeak, like dolls, the wished-for words.
But note the unconscionable treachery of fate,
That makes us weep, laugh, grunt and groan, and shout
Doleful heroics, pinching gestures forth
From madness or delight, without regard
To that first, foremost law. Anguishing hour!
Last night, we sat beside a pool of pink,
Clippered with lilies scudding the bright chromes,
Keen to the point of starlight, while a frog   120
Boomed from his very belly odious chords.

XII

A blue pigeon it is, that circles the blue sky,
On sidelong wing, around and round and round.
A white pigeon it is, that flutters to the ground,
Grown tired of flight. Like a dark rabbi, I
Observed, when young, the nature of mankind,
In lordly study. Every day, I found
Man proved a gobbet in my mincing world.
Like a rose rabbi, later, I pursued,
And still pursue, the origin and course   130
Of love, but until now I never knew
That fluttering things have so distinct a shade.

A HIGH–TONED OLD CHRISTIAN WOMAN
(1923)

Poetry is the supreme fiction, madame.
Take the moral law and make a nave of it
And from the nave build haunted heaven. Thus,
The conscience is converted into palms,
Like windy citherns hankering for hymns.
We agree in principle. That's clear. But take

The opposing law and make a peristyle,
And from the peristyle project a masque
Beyond the planets. Thus, our bawdiness,
Unpurged by epitaph, indulged at last,   10
Is equally converted into palms,
Squiggling like saxophones. And palm for palm,
Madame, we are where we began. Allow,
Therefore, that in the planetary scene
Your disaffected flagellants, well-stuffed,
Smacking their muzzy bellies in parade,
Proud of such novelties of the sublime,
Such tink and tank and tunk-a-tunk-tunk,
May, merely may, madame, whip from themselves
A jovial hullabaloo among the spheres.   20
This will make widows wince. But fictive things
Wink as they will. Wink most when widows wince.

THE EMPEROR OF ICE–CREAM

(1923)

Call the roller of big cigars,
The muscular one, and bid him whip
In kitchen cups concupiscent curds.
Let the wenches dawdle in such dress
As they are used to wear, and let the boys
Bring flowers in last month's newspapers.
Let be be finale of seem.
The only emperor is the emperor of ice-cream.

Take from the dresser of deal,
Lacking the three glass knobs, that sheet   10
On which she embroidered fantails once
And spread it so as to cover her face.
If her horny feet protrude, they come
To show how cold she is, and dumb.
Let the lamp affix its beam.
The only emperor is the emperor of ice-cream.

SUNDAY MORNING
(1923)

I

Complacencies of the peignoir, and late
Coffee and oranges in a sunny chair,
And the green freedom of a cockatoo
Upon a rug mingle to dissipate
The holy hush of ancient sacrifice.
She dreams a little, and she feels the dark
Encroachment of that old catastrophe,
As a calm darkens among water-lights.
The pungent oranges and bright, green wings
Seem things in some procession of the dead,   10
Winding across wide water, without sound. *unimpressed*
The day is like wide water, without sound, —
Stilled for the passing of her dreaming feet
Over the seas, to silent Palestine,
Dominion of the blood and sepulchre.

II

Why should she give her bounty to the dead?
What is divinity if it can come
Only in silent shadows and in dreams?
Shall she not find in comforts of the sun,
In pungent fruit and bright, green wings, or else   20
In any balm or beauty of the earth,
Things to be cherished like the thought of heaven?
Divinity must live within herself:
Passions of rain, or moods in falling snow;
Grievings in loneliness, or unsubdued
Elations when the forest blooms; gusty
Emotions on wet roads on autumn nights;
All pleasures and all pains, remembering
The bough of summer and the winter branch.
These are the measures destined for her soul.   30

III

Jove in the clouds had his inhuman birth.   *History of
No mother suckled him, no sweet land gave   metaphisics*
Large-mannered motions to his mythy mind.
He moved among us, as a muttering king,

Magnificent, would move among his hinds,
Until our blood, commingling, virginal,
With heaven, brought such requital to desire
The very hinds discerned it, in a star.
Shall our blood fail? Or shall it come to be
The blood of paradise? And shall the earth   40
Seem all of paradise that we shall know?
The sky will be much friendlier then than now,
A part of labor and a part of pain,
And next in glory to enduring love,
Not this dividing and indifferent blue.

IV

She says, "I am content when wakened birds,
Before they fly, test the reality
Of misty fields, by their sweet questionings;
But when the birds are gone, and their warm fields
Return no more, where, then, is paradise?"   50
There is not any haunt of prophecy,
Nor any old chimera of the grave,
Neither the golden underground, nor isle
Melodious, where spirits gat them home,
Nor visionary south, nor cloudy palm
Remote on heaven's hill, that has endured
As April's green endures; or will endure
Like her remembrance of awakened birds,
Or her desire for June and evening, tipped
By the consummation of the swallow's wings.   60

V

She says, "But in contentment I still feel
The need of some imperishable bliss."
Death is the mother of beauty; hence from her,
Alone, shall come fulfilment to our dreams
And our desires. Although she strews the leaves
Of sure obliteration on our paths,
The path sick sorrow took, the many paths
Where triumph rang its brassy phrase, or love
Whispered a little out of tenderness,
She makes the willow shiver in the sun   70
For maidens who were wont to sit and gaze
Upon the grass, relinquished to their feet.

She causes boys to pile new plums and pears
On disregarded plate. The maidens taste
And stray impassioned in the littering leaves.

VI

Is there no change of death in paradise?
Does ripe fruit never fall? Or do the boughs
Hang always heavy in that perfect sky,
Unchanging, yet so like our perishing earth,
With rivers like our own that seek for seas   80
They never find, the same receding shores
That never touch with inarticulate pang?
Why set the pear upon those river-banks
Or spice the shores with odors of the plum?
Alas, that they should wear our colors there,
The silken weavings of our afternoons,
And pick the strings of our insipid lutes!
Death is the mother of beauty, mystical,
Within whose burning bosom we devise
Our earthly mothers waiting, sleeplessly.   90

VII

Supple and turbulent, a ring of men
Shall chant in orgy on a summer morn
Their boisterous devotion to the sun,
Not as a god, but as a god might be,
Naked among them, like a savage source.
Their chant shall be a chant of paradise,
Out of their blood, returning to the sky;
And in their chant shall enter, voice by voice,
The windy lake wherein their lord delights,
The trees, like serafin, and echoing hills,   100
That choir among themselves long afterward.
They shall know well the heavenly fellowship
Of men that perish and of summer morn.
And whence they came and whither they shall go
The dew upon their feet shall manifest.

VIII

She hears, upon that water without sound,
A voice that cries, "The tomb in Palestine
Is not the porch of spirits lingering.
It is the grave of Jesus, where he lay."

We live in an old chaos of the sun,   110
Or old dependency of day and night,
Or island solitude, unsponsored, free,
Of that wide water, inescapable.
Deer walk upon our mountains, and the quail
Whistle about us their spontaneous cries;
Sweet berries ripen in the wilderness;
And, in the isolation of the sky,
At evening, casual flocks of pigeons make
Ambiguous undulations as they sink,
Downward to darkness, on extended wings.   120

ANECDOTE OF THE JAR
(1923)

I placed a jar in Tennessee,
And round it was, upon a hill.
It made the slovenly wilderness
Surround that hill.

The wilderness rose up to it,
And sprawled around, no longer wild.
The jar was round upon the ground
And tall and of a port in air.

It took dominion everywhere.
The jar was gray and bare.   10
It did not give of bird or bush,
Like nothing else in Tennessee.

TO THE ONE OF FICTIVE MUSIC
(1923)

Sister and mother and diviner love,
And of the sisterhood of the living dead
Most near, most clear, and of the clearest bloom,
And of the fragrant mothers the most dear
And queen, and of diviner love the day
And flame and summer and sweet fire, no thread

Of cloudy silver sprinkles in your gown
Its venom of renown, and on your head
No crown is simpler than the simple hair.

Now, of the music summoned by the birth   10
That separates us from the wind and sea,
Yet leaves us in them, until earth becomes,
By being so much of the things we are,
Gross effigy and simulacrum, none
Gives motion to perfection more serene
Than yours, out of our imperfections wrought,
Most rare, or ever of more kindred air
In the laborious weaving that you wear.

For so retentive of themselves are men
That music is intensest which proclaims   20
The near, the clear, and vaunts the clearest bloom,
And of all vigils musing the obscure,
That apprehends the most which sees and names,
As in your name, an image that is sure,
Among the arrant spices of the sun,
O bough and bush and scented vine, in whom
We give ourselves our likest issuance.

Yet not too like, yet not so like to be
Too near, too clear, saving a little to endow
Our feigning with the strange unlike, whence springs   30
The difference that heavenly pity brings.
For this, musician, in your girdle fixed
Bear other perfumes. On your pale head wear
A band entwining, set with fatal stones.
Unreal, give back to us what once you gave:
The imagination that we spurned and crave.

PETER QUINCE AT THE CLAVIER
(1923)

I

Just as my fingers on these keys
Make music, so the selfsame sounds
On my spirit make a music, too.

music + sound differ only in organization and person to appreciate.

Music is feeling, then, not sound; *poetry*
And thus it is that what I feel,
Here in this room, desiring you,

Thinking of your blue-shadowed silk,
Is music. It is like the strain
Waked in the elders by Susanna.

Of a green evening, clear and warm,   10
She bathed in her still garden, while
The red-eyed elders watching, felt

The basses of their beings throb
In witching chords, and their thin blood
Pulse pizzicati of Hosanna.

                        II
In the green water, clear and warm,
Susanna lay.
sensual gratification She searched
The touch of springs,
And found   20
Concealed imaginings.
She sighed,
For so much melody.

sexual memories Upon the bank, she stood
In the cool
Of spent emotions.
She felt, among the leaves,
The dew
Of old devotions.

She walked upon the grass,   30
Still quavering.
The winds were like her maids,
On timid feet,
Fetching her woven scarves,
Yet wavering.

A breath upon her hand
Muted the night.

She turned—
A cymbal crashed,
And roaring horns.   40

III

Soon, with a noise like tambourines,   *— false nose*
Came her attendant Byzantines.

They wondered why Susanna cried
Against the elders by her side;

And as they whispered, the refrain
Was like a willow swept by rain.

Anon, their lamps' uplifted flame
Revealed Susanna and her shame.

And then, the simpering Byzantines
Fled, with a noise like tambourines.   50

IV

Beauty is momentary in the mind—
The fitful tracing of a portal;
But in the flesh it is immortal.   *— memories*
The body dies; the body's beauty lives.   *— other beauty like the body lives on*
So evenings die, in their green going,
A wave, interminably flowing.
So gardens die, their meek breath scenting
The cowl of winter, done repenting.
So maidens die, to the auroral
Celebration of a maiden's choral.   60
Susanna's music touched the bawdy strings   *beauty*
Of those white elders; but, escaping,
old age — Left only Death's ironic scraping.
they scorn — Now, in its immortality, it plays
On the clear viol of her memory,
And makes a constant sacrament of praise.
permanent.

THIRTEEN WAYS OF LOOKING AT A BLACKBIRD

(1923)

I

cosmic background

Among twenty snowy mountains,
The only moving thing
Was the eye of the blackbird.

II

psych.
remind ourselves of past birds

I was of three minds,
Like a tree
In which there are three blackbirds.

III

The blackbird whirled in the autumn winds.
It was a small part of the pantomime.   *soundless world*

IV

social humans

A man and a woman
Are one.   10

creation

A man and a woman and a blackbird
Are one.

V

I do not know which to prefer,
The beauty of inflections
Or the beauty of innuendoes,

contrasted w/ silence

The blackbird whistling   *Knowledge of opposites*
Or just after.

VI

Icicles filled the long window
With barbaric glass.

ignorance instills fear

The shadow of the blackbird   20
Crossed it, to and fro.
The mood
Traced in the shadow
An indecipherable cause.

VII

imagination disturbs what we see / vs. reality

O thin men of Haddam,
Why do you imagine golden birds?
Do you not see how the blackbird
Walks around the feet
Of the women about you?

VIII

I know noble accents   30
And lucid, inescapable rhythms;
But I know, too,
That the blackbird is involved
In what I know.

[handwritten annotations in left margin: "poetry", "harmony + in poetry"; right: "the subject matter for the poem"]

IX

When the blackbird flew out of sight,
It marked the edge
Of one of many circles.

X

At the sight of blackbirds   *[handwritten: "eerie"]*
Flying in a green light,
Even the bawds of euphony   *[handwritten: "– slave to rythms in poetry"]*   40
Would cry out sharply.

XI

He rode over Connecticut   *[handwritten: "– vague life."]*
In a glass coach.
Once, a fear pierced him,
In that he mistook
The shadow of his equipage
For blackbirds.

XII

[handwritten: "nature"]
The river is moving.
The blackbird must be flying.

XIII

It was evening all afternoon.   50
It was snowing
And it was going to snow.   *[handwritten: "allways / never"]*
The blackbird sat
In the cedar-limbs.

SEA SURFACE FULL OF CLOUDS

(1931)

I

In that November off Tehuantepec,
The slopping of the sea grew still one night
And in the morning summer hued the deck

And made one think of rosy chocolate
And gilt umbrellas. Paradisal green
Gave suavity to the perplexed machine

Of ocean, which like limpid water lay.
Who, then, in that ambrosial latitude
Out of the light evolved the moving blooms,

Who, then, evolved the sea-blooms from the clouds   10
Diffusing balm in that Pacific calm?
C'était mon enfant, mon bijou, mon âme.

The sea-clouds whitened far below the calm
And moved, as blooms move, in the swimming green
And in its watery radiance, while the hue

Of heaven in an antique reflection rolled
Round those flotillas. And sometimes the sea
Poured brilliant iris on the glistening blue.

                    II
In that November off Tehuantepec
The slopping of the sea grew still one night.   20
At breakfast jelly yellow streaked the deck

And made one think of chop-house chocolate
And sham umbrellas. And a sham-like green
Capped summer-seeming on the tense machine

Of ocean, which in sinister flatness lay.
Who, then, beheld the rising of the clouds
That strode submerged in that malevolent sheen,

Who saw the mortal massives of the blooms
Of water moving on the water-floor?
C'était mon frère du ciel, ma vie, mon or.   30

The gongs rang loudly as the windy booms
Hoo-hooed it in the darkened ocean-blooms.
The gongs grew still. And then blue heaven spread

Its crystalline pendentives on the sea
And the macabre of the water-glooms
In an enormous undulation fled.

III

In that November off Tehuantepec,
The slopping of the sea grew still one night
And a pale silver patterned on the deck

And made one think of porcelain chocolate   40
And pied umbrellas. An uncertain green,
Piano-polished, held the tranced machine

Of ocean, as a prelude holds and holds.
Who, seeing silver petals of white blooms
Unfolding in the water, feeling sure

Of the milk within the saltiest spurge, heard, then,
The sea unfolding in the sunken clouds?
Oh! C'était mon extase et mon amour.

So deeply sunken were they that the shrouds,
The shrouding shadows, made the petals black   50
Until the rolling heaven made them blue,

A blue beyond the rainy hyacinth,
And smiting the crevasses of the leaves
Deluged the ocean with a sapphire blue.

IV

In that November off Tehuantepec
The night-long slopping of the sea grew still.
A mallow morning dozed upon the deck

And made one think of musky chocolate
And frail umbrellas. A too-fluent green
Suggested malice in the dry machine   60

Of ocean, pondering dank stratagem.
Who then beheld the figures of the clouds,
Like blooms secluded in the thick marine?

Like blooms? Like damasks that were shaken off
From the loosed girdles in the spangling must.
C'était ma foi, la nonchalance divine.

The nakedness would rise and suddenly turn
Salt masks of beard and mouths of bellowing,
Would—But more suddenly the heaven rolled

Its bluest sea-clouds in the thinking green,   70
And the nakedness became the broadest blooms,
Mile-mallows that a mallow sun cajoled.

v

In that November off Tehuantepec
Night stilled the slopping of the sea. The day
Came, bowing and voluble, upon the deck,

Good clown. . . . One thought of Chinese chocolate
And large umbrellas. And a motley green
Followed the drift of the obese machine

Of ocean, perfected in indolence.
What pistache one, ingenious and droll,   80
Beheld the sovereign clouds as jugglery

And the sea as turquoise-turbaned Sambo, neat
At tossing saucers—cloudy-conjuring sea?
C'était mon esprit bâtard, l'ignominie.

The sovereign clouds came clustering. The conch
Of loyal conjuration trumped. The wind
Of green blooms turning crisped the motley hue

To clearing opalescence. Then the sea
And heaven rolled as one and from the two
Came fresh transfigurings of freshest blue.   90

THE IDEA OF ORDER AT KEY WEST
(1935)

She sang beyond the genius of the sea.
The water never formed to mind or voice,
Like a body wholly body, fluttering
Its empty sleeves; and yet its mimic motion
Made constant cry, caused constantly a cry,
That was not ours although we understood,
Inhuman, of the veritable ocean.

The sea was not a mask. No more was she.
The song and water were not medleyed sound
Even if what she sang was what she heard,   10
Since what she sang was uttered word by word.
It may be that in all her phrases stirred
The grinding water and the gasping wind;
But it was she and not the sea we heard.

For she was the maker of the song she sang.
The ever-hooded, tragic-gestured sea
Was merely a place by which she walked to sing.
Whose spirit is this? we said, because we knew
It was the spirit that we sought and knew
That we should ask this often as she sang.   20

If it was only the dark voice of the sea
That rose, or even colored by many waves;
If it was only the outer voice of sky
And cloud, of the sunken coral water-walled,
However clear, it would have been deep air,
The heaving speech of air, a summer sound
Repeated in a summer without end
And sound alone. But it was more than that,
More even than her voice, and ours, among
The meaningless plungings of water and the wind,   30
Theatrical distances, bronze shadows heaped
On high horizons, mountainous atmospheres
Of sky and sea.
                    It was her voice that made
The sky acutest at its vanishing.
She measured to the hour its solitude.
She was the single artificer of the world
In which she sang. And when she sang, the sea, *poet as maker*
Whatever self it had, became the self
That was her song, for she was the maker. Then we,   40
As we beheld her striding there alone,
Knew that there never was a world for her
Except the one she sang and, singing, made.

Ramon Fernandez, tell me, if you know,
Why, when the singing ended and we turned

Toward the town, tell why the glassy lights,
The lights in the fishing boats at anchor there,
As the night descended, tilting in the air,
Mastered the night and portioned out the sea,
Fixing emblazoned zones and fiery poles,   50
Arranging, deepening, enchanting night.

Oh! Blessed rage for order, pale Ramon,
The maker's rage to order words of the sea,
Words of the fragrant portals, dimly-starred,
And of ourselves and of our origins,
In ghostlier demarcations, keener sounds.

THE GLASS OF WATER
(1942)

That the glass would melt in heat,
That the water would freeze in cold,
Shows that this object is merely a state,
One of many, between two poles. So,
In the metaphysical, there are these poles.

Here in the centre stands the glass. Light
Is the lion that comes down to drink. There
And in that state, the glass is a pool.
Ruddy are his eyes and ruddy are his claws
When light comes down to wet his frothy jaws   10

And in the water winding weeds move round.
And there and in another state—the refractions,
The *metaphysica*, the plastic parts of poems
Crash in the mind—But, fat Jocundus, worrying
About what stands here in the centre, not the glass,

But in the centre of our lives, this time, this day,
It is a state, this spring among the politicians
Playing cards. In a village of the indigenes,
One would have still to discover. Among the dogs and dung,
One would continue to contend with one's ideas.   20

THE SENSE OF THE SLEIGHT-OF-HAND MAN
(1942)

One's grand flights, one's Sunday baths,
One's tootings at the weddings of the soul
Occur as they occur. So bluish clouds
Occurred above the empty house and the leaves
Of the rhododendrons rattled their gold,
As if someone lived there. Such floods of white
Came bursting from the clouds. So the wind
Threw its contorted strength around the sky.

Could you have said the bluejay suddenly
Would swoop to earth? It is a wheel, the rays   10
Around the sun. The wheel survives the myths.
The fire eye in the clouds survives the gods.
To think of a dove with an eye of grenadine
And pines that are cornets, so it occurs,
And a little island full of geese and stars:
It may be that the ignorant man, alone,
Has any chance to mate his life with life
That is the sensual, pearly spouse, the life
That is fluent in even the wintriest bronze.

CREDENCES OF SUMMER
(1947)

I

Now in midsummer come and all fools slaughtered
And spring's infuriations over and a long way
To the first autumnal inhalations, young broods
Are in the grass, the roses are heavy with a weight
Of fragrance and the mind lays by its trouble.

Now the mind lays by its trouble and considers.
The fidgets of remembrance come to this.
This is the last day of a certain year
Beyond which there is nothing left of time.
It comes to this and the imagination's life.   10

There is nothing more inscribed nor thought nor felt
And this must comfort the heart's core against
Its false disasters—these fathers standing round,
These mothers touching, speaking, being near,
These lovers waiting in the soft dry grass.

II

Postpone the anatomy of summer, as
The physical pine, the metaphysical pine.
Let's see the very thing and nothing else.
Let's see it with the hottest fire of sight.
Burn everything not part of it to ash.   20

Trace the gold sun about the whitened sky
Without evasion by a single metaphor.
Look at it in its essential barrenness
And say this, this is the centre that I seek.
Fix it in an eternal foliage

And fill the foliage with arrested peace,
Joy of such permanence, right ignorance
Of change still possible. Exile desire
For what is not. This is the barrenness
Of the fertile thing that can attain no more.   30

III

It is the natural tower of all the world,
The point of survey, green's green apogee,
But a tower more precious than the view beyond,
A point of survey squatting like a throne,
Axis of everything, green's apogee

And happiest folk-land, mostly marriage-hymns.
It is the mountain on which the tower stands,
It is the final mountain. Here the sun,
Sleepless, inhales his proper air, and rests.
This is the refuge that the end creates.   40

It is the old man standing on the tower,
Who reads no book. His ruddy ancientness
Absorbs the ruddy summer and is appeased,
By an understanding that fulfils his age,
By a feeling capable of nothing more.

IV

One of the limits of reality
Presents itself in Oley when the hay,
Baked through long days, is piled in mows. It is
A land too ripe for enigmas, too serene.
There the distant fails the clairvoyant eye 50

And the secondary senses of the ear
Swarm, not with secondary sounds, but choirs,
Not evocations but last choirs, last sounds
With nothing else compounded, carried full,
Pure rhetoric of a language without words.

Things stop in that direction and since they stop
The direction stops and we accept what is
As good. The utmost must be good and is
And is our fortune and honey hived in the trees
And mingling of colors at a festival. 60

V

One day enriches a year. One woman makes
The rest look down. One man becomes a race,
Lofty like him, like him perpetual.
Or do the other days enrich the one?
And is the queen humble as she seems to be,

The charitable majesty of her whole kin?
The bristling soldier, weather-foxed, who looms
In the sunshine is a filial form and one
Of the land's children, easily born, its flesh,
Not fustian. The more than casual blue 70

Contains the year and other years and hymns
And people, without souvenir. The day
Enriches the year, not as embellishment.
Stripped of remembrance, it displays its strength—
The youth, the vital son, the heroic power.

VI

The rock cannot be broken. It is the truth.
It rises from land and sea and covers them.

It is a mountain half way green and then,
The other immeasurable half, such rock
As placid air becomes. But it is not   80

A hermit's truth nor symbol in hermitage.
It is the visible rock, the audible,
The brilliant mercy of a sure repose,
On this present ground, the vividest repose,
Things certain sustaining us in certainty.

It is the rock of summer, the extreme,
A mountain luminous half way in bloom
And then half way in the extremest light
Of sapphires flashing from the central sky,
As if twelve princes sat before a king.   90

VII

Far in the woods they sang their unreal songs,
Secure. It was difficult to sing in face
Of the object. The singers had to avert themselves
Or else avert the object. Deep in the woods
They sang of summer in the common fields.

They sang desiring an object that was near,
In face of which desire no longer moved,
Nor made of itself that which it could not find . . .
Three times the concentred self takes hold, three times
The thrice concentred self, having possessed   100

The object, grips it in savage scrutiny,
Once to make captive, once to subjugate
Or yield to subjugation, once to proclaim
The meaning of the capture, this hard prize,
Fully made, fully apparent, fully found.

VIII

The trumpet of morning blows in the clouds and through
The sky. It is the visible announced,
It is the more than visible, the more
Than sharp, illustrious scene. The trumpet cries
This is the successor of the invisible.   110

This is its substitute in stratagems
Of the spirit. This, in sight and memory,
Must take its place, as what is possible
Replaces what is not. The resounding cry
Is like ten thousand tumblers tumbling down

To share the day. The trumpet supposes that
A mind exists, aware of division, aware
Of its cry as clarion, its diction's way
As that of a personage in a multitude:
Man's mind grown venerable in the unreal.   120

IX

Fly low, cock bright, and stop on a bean pole. Let
Your brown breast redden, while you wait for warmth.
With one eye watch the willow, motionless.
The gardener's cat is dead, the gardener gone
And last year's garden grows salacious weeds.

A complex of emotions falls apart,
In an abandoned spot. Soft, civil bird,
The decay that you regard: of the arranged
And of the spirit of the arranged, *douceurs,*
Tristesses, the fund of life and death, suave bush   130

And polished beast, this complex falls apart.
And on your bean pole, it may be, you detect
Another complex of other emotions, not
So soft, so civil, and you make a sound,
Which is not part of the listener's own sense.

X

The personae of summer play the characters
Of an inhuman author, who meditates
With the gold bugs, in blue meadows, late at night.
He does not hear his characters talk. He sees
Them mottled, in the moodiest costumes,   140

Of blue and yellow, sky and sun, belted·
And knotted, sashed and seamed, half pales of red,
Half pales of green, appropriate habit for
The huge decorum, the manner of the time,
Part of the mottled mood of summer's whole,

In which the characters speak because they want
To speak, the fat, the roseate characters,
Free, for a moment, from malice and sudden cry,
Complete in a completed scene, speaking
Their parts as in a youthful happiness.   150

William Carlos Williams
1883-1964

TRACT
(1917)

I will teach you my townspeople
how to perform a funeral
for you have it over a troop
of artists—
unless one should scour the world—
you have the ground sense necessary.

See! the hearse leads.
I begin with a design for a hearse.
For Christ's sake not black—
nor white either—and not polished!   10
Let it be weathered—like a farm wagon—
with gilt wheels (this could be
applied fresh at small expense)
or no wheels at all:
a rough dray to drag over the ground.

Knock the glass out!
My God!—glass, my townspeople!
For what purpose? Is it for the dead
to look out or for us to see
how well he is housed or to see   20
the flowers or the lack of them—
or what?
To keep the rain and snow from him?

He will have a heavier rain soon:
pebbles and dirt and what not.
Let there be no glass—
and no upholstery, phew!
and no little brass rollers
and small easy wheels on the bottom—
my townspeople what are you thinking of?   30

A rough plain hearse then
with gilt wheels and no top at all.
On this the coffin lies
by its own weight.

               No wreaths please—
especially no hot house flowers.
Some common memento is better,
something he prized and is known by:
his old clothes—a few books perhaps—
God knows what! You realize   40
how we are about these things
my townspeople—
something will be found—anything
even flowers if he had come to that.
So much for the hearse.

For heaven's sake though see to the driver!
Take off the silk hat! In fact
that's no place at all for him—
up there unceremoniously
dragging our friend out to his own dignity!   50
Bring him down—bring him down!
Low and inconspicuous! I'd not have him ride
on the wagon at all—damn him—
the undertaker's understrapper!
Let him hold the reins
and walk at the side
and inconspicuously too!

Then briefly as to yourselves:
Walk behind—as they do in France,
seventh class, or if you ride   60
Hell take curtains! Go with some show

of inconvenience; sit openly—
to the weather as to grief.
Or do you think you can shut grief in?
What—from us? We who have perhaps
nothing to lose? Share with us
share with us—it will be money
in your pockets.
          Go now
I think you are ready. 70

THE WIDOW'S LAMENT IN SPRINGTIME
(1921)

Sorrow is my own yard
where the new grass
flames as it has flamed
often before but not
with the cold fire
that closes round me this year.
Thirtyfive years
I lived with my husband.
The plumtree is white today
with masses of flowers. 10
Masses of flowers
load the cherry branches
and color some bushes
yellow and some red
but the grief in my heart
is stronger than they
for though they were my joy
formerly, today I notice them
and turned away forgetting.
Today my son told me 20
that in the meadows,
at the edge of the heavy woods
in the distance, he saw
trees of white flowers.
I feel that I would like
to go there
and fall into those flowers
and sink into the marsh near them.

SPRING AND ALL

(1923)

By the road to the contagious hospital
under the surge of the blue
mottled clouds driven from the
northeast—a cold wind. Beyond, the
waste of broad, muddy fields
brown with dried weeds, standing and fallen

patches of standing water
the scattering of tall trees

All along the road the reddish
purplish, forked, upstanding, twiggy   10
stuff of bushes and small trees
with dead, brown leaves under them
leafless vines—

Lifeless in appearance, sluggish
dazed spring approaches—

They enter the new world naked,
cold, uncertain of all
save that they enter. All about them
the cold, familiar wind—

Now the grass, tomorrow   20
the stiff curl of wildcarrot leaf
One by one objects are defined—
It quickens: clarity, outline of leaf

But now the stark dignity of
entrance—Still, the profound change
has come upon them: rooted, they
grip down and begin to awaken

TO ELSIE

(1923)

The pure products of America
go crazy—
mountain folk from Kentucky

or the ribbed north end of
Jersey
with its isolate lakes and

valleys, its deaf-mutes, thieves
old names
and promiscuity between

devil-may-care men who have taken   10
to railroading
out of sheer lust of adventure—

and young slatterns, bathed
in filth
from Monday to Saturday

to be tricked out that night
with gauds
from imaginations which have no

peasant traditions to give them
character   20
but flutter and flaunt

sheer rags—succumbing without
emotion
save numbed terror

under some hedge of choke-cherry
or viburnum—
which they cannot express—

Unless it be that marriage
perhaps
with a dash of Indian blood   30

will throw up a girl so desolate
so hemmed round
with disease or murder

that she'll be rescued by an
agent—
reared by the state and

sent out at fifteen to work in
some hard-pressed
house in the suburbs—

some doctor's family, some Elsie—   40
voluptuous water
expressing with broken

brain the truth about us—
her great
ungainly hips and flopping breasts

addressed to cheap
jewelry
and rich young men with fine eyes

as if the earth under our feet
were   50
an excrement of some sky

and we degraded prisoners
destined
to hunger until we eat filth

while the imagination strains
after deer
going by fields of goldenrod in

the stifling heat of September
Somehow
it seems to destroy us   60

It is only in isolate flecks that
something
is given off

No one
to witness
and adjust, no one to drive the car

RAIN
(1934)

As the rain falls
so does
            your love

bathe every
                  open
object of the world—

In houses
the priceless dry
                  rooms
of illicit love   10
where we live
hear the wash of the
                        rain—

There
      paintings
and fine
      metalware
woven stuffs—
all the whorishness
of our   20
            delight
sees
from its window

the spring wash
of your love
           the falling
rain—

The trees
are become
beasts fresh-risen   30
from the sea—
water

trickles
from the crevices of
their hides—

So my life is spent
              to keep out love
with which
she rains upon

            the world   40

of spring

      drips

so spreads

      the words

far apart to let in

        her love

And running in between

the drops

      the rain

is a kind physician   50

        the rain
of her thoughts over
the ocean
       every

where

    walking with
invisible swift feet
over

    the helpless
        waves—   60

Unworldly love
that has no hope
      of the world

      and that
cannot change the world
to its delight—

    The rain
falls upon the earth
and grass and flowers

come   70
    perfectly

into form from its
      liquid

clearness

    But love is
unworldly

    and nothing
comes of it but love

following
and falling endlessly   80
from
            her thoughts

THE YACHTS

(1935)

contend in a sea which the land partly encloses
shielding them from the too-heavy blows
of an ungoverned ocean which when it chooses

tortures the biggest hulls, the best man knows
to pit against its beatings, and sinks them pitilessly.
Mothlike in mists, scintillant in the minute

brilliance of cloudless days, with broad bellying sails
they glide to the wind tossing green water
from their sharp prows while over them the crew crawls

ant-like, solicitously grooming them, releasing,   10
making fast as they turn, lean far over and having
caught the wind again, side by side, head for the mark.

In a well guarded arena of open water surrounded by
lesser and greater craft which, sycophant, lumbering
and flittering follow them, they appear youthful, rare

as the light of a happy eye, live with the grace
of all that in the mind is feckless, free and
naturally to be desired. Now the sea which holds them

is moody, lapping their glossy sides, as if feeling
for some slightest flaw but fails completely.   20
Today no race. Then the wind comes again. The yachts

move, jockeying for a start, the signal is set and they
are off. Now the waves strike at them but they are too
well made, they slip through, though they take in canvas.

Arms with hands grasping seek to clutch at the prows.
Bodies thrown recklessly in the way are cut aside.
It is a sea of faces about them in agony, in despair

until the horror of the race dawns staggering the mind,
the whole sea become an entanglement of watery bodies
lost to the world bearing what they cannot hold. Broken,   30

beaten, desolate, reaching from the dead to be taken up
they cry out, failing, failing! their cries rising
in waves still as the skillful yachts pass over.

THESE

(1938)

    are the desolate, dark weeks
when nature in its barrenness
equals the stupidity of man.

The year plunges into night
and the heart plunges
lower than night

to an empty, windswept place
without sun, stars or moon
but a peculiar light as of thought

that spins a dark fire—   10
whirling upon itself until,
in the cold, it kindles

to make a man aware of nothing
that he knows, not loneliness
itself—Not a ghost but

would be embraced—emptiness,
despair—(They
whine and whistle) among

the flashes and booms of war;
houses of whose rooms   20
the cold is greater than can be thought,

the people gone that we loved,
the beds lying empty, the couches
damp, the chairs unused—

Hide it away somewhere
out of the mind, let it get roots
and grow, unrelated to jealous

ears and eyes—for itself.
In this mine they come to dig—all.
Is this the counterfoil to sweetest   30

music? The source of poetry that
seeing the clock stopped, says,
The clock has stopped

that ticked yesterday so well?
and hears the sound of lakewater
splashing—that is now stone.

BURNING THE CHRISTMAS GREENS
(1944)

Their time past, pulled down
cracked and flung to the fire
—go up in a roar

All recognition lost, burnt clean
clean in the flame, the green
dispersed, a living red,
flame red, red as blood wakes
on the ash—

and ebbs to a steady burning
the rekindled bed become   10
a landscape of flame

At the winter's midnight
we went to the trees, the coarse
holly, the balsam and
the hemlock for their green

At the thick of the dark
the moment of the cold's
deepest plunge we brought branches
cut from the green trees

to fill our need, and over   20
doorways, about paper Christmas
bells covered with tinfoil
and fastened by red ribbons

we stuck the green prongs
in the windows hung
woven wreaths and above pictures
the living green. On the

mantle we built a green forest
and among those hemlock
sprays put a herd of small   30
white deer as if they

were walking there. All this!
and it seemed gentle and good
to us. Their time past,
relief! The room bare. We

stuffed the dead grate
with them upon the half burnt out
log's smoldering eye, opening
red and closing under them

and we stood there looking down.   40
Green is a solace
a promise of peace, a fort
against the cold (though we

did not say so) a challenge
above the snow's
hard shell. Green (we might
have said) that, where

small birds hide and dodge
and lift their plaintive
rallying cries, blocks for them   50
and knocks down

the unseeing bullets of
the storm. Green spruce boughs
pulled down by a weight of
snow—Transformed!

Violence leaped and appeared.
Recreant! roared to life
as the flame rose through and
our eyes recoiled from it.

In the jagged flames green   60
to red, instant and alive. Green!
those sure abutments . . . Gone!
lost to mind

and quick in the contracting
tunnel of the grate
appeared a world! Black
mountains, black and red—as

yet uncolored—and ash white,
an infant landscape of shimmering
ash and flame and we, in   70
that instant, lost,

breathless to be witnesses,
as if we stood
ourselves refreshed among
the shining fauna of that fire.

PREFACE TO *PATERSON*: BOOK ONE
(1946)

Rigor of beauty is the quest. But how will you find beauty
when it is locked in the mind past all remonstrance?

To make a start,
out of particulars
and make them general, rolling
up the sum, by defective means—

Sniffing the trees,
just another dog
among a lot of dogs. What
else is there? And to do?
The rest have run out—
after the rabbits.   10
Only the lame stands—on
three legs. Scratch front and back.
Deceive and eat. Dig
a musty bone

For the beginning is assuredly
the end—since we know nothing, pure
and simple, beyond
our own complexities.

                    Yet there is
no return: rolling up out of chaos,   20
a nine months' wonder, the city
the man, an identity—it can't be
otherwise—an
interpenetration, both ways. Rolling
up! obverse, reverse;
the drunk the sober; the illustrious
the gross; one. In ignorance
a certain knowledge and knowledge,
undispersed, its own undoing.

                    (The multiple seed,   30
packed tight with detail, soured,
is lost in the flux and the mind,
distracted, floats off in the same
scum)

Rolling up, rolling up heavy with
numbers.

          It is the ignorant sun
rising in the slot of
hollow suns risen, so that never in this
world will a man live well in his body   40

save dying—and not know himself
dying; yet that is
the design. Renews himself
thereby, in addition and subtraction,
walking up and down.

     and the craft,
subverted by thought, rolling up, let
him beware lest he turn to no more than
the writing of stale poems . . .
Minds like beds always made up,   50
         (more stony than a shore)
unwilling or unable.

         Rolling in, top up,
under, thrust and recoil, a great clatter:
lifted as air, boated, multicolored, a
wash of seas—
from mathematics to particulars—

        divided as the dew,
floating mists, to be rained down and
regathered into a river that flows   60
and encircles:

        shells and animalcules
generally and so to man,

     to Paterson.

Ezra Pound

1885-

SESTINA: ALTAFORTE

(1909)

LOQUITUR: *En* Bertrans de Born.
Dante Alighieri put this man in hell for that he was a stirrer
up of strife.
Eccovi!
Judge ye!
Have I dug him up again?
The scene is at his castle, Altaforte. "Papiols" is his jongleur.
"The Leopard," the *device* of Richard Cœur de Lion.

I

Damn it all! all this our South stinks peace.
You whoreson dog, Papiols, come! Let's to music!
I have no life save when the swords clash.
But ah! when I see the standards gold, vair, purple, opposing
And the broad fields beneath them turn crimson,
Then howl I my heart nigh mad with rejoicing.

II

In hot summer have I great rejoicing
When the tempests kill the earth's foul peace,
And the lightnings from black heav'n flash crimson,
And the fierce thunders roar me their music   10
And the winds shriek through the clouds mad, opposing,
And through all the riven skies God's swords clash.

III

Hell grant soon we hear again the swords clash!
And the shrill neighs of destriers in battle rejoicing,

Spiked breast to spiked breast opposing!
Better one hour's stour than a year's peace
With fat boards, bawds, wine and frail music!
Bah! there's no wine like the blood's crimson!

IV

And I love to see the sun rise blood-crimson.
And I watch his spears through the dark clash   20
And it fills all my heart with rejoicing
And pries wide my mouth with fast music
When I see him so scorn and defy peace,
His lone might 'gainst all darkness opposing.

V

The man who fears war and squats opposing
My words for stour, hath no blood of crimson
But is fit only to rot in womanish peace
Far from where worth's won and the swords clash
For the death of such sluts I go rejoicing;
Yea, I fill all the air with my music.   30

VI

Papiols, Papiols, to the music!
There's no sound like to swords swords opposing,
No cry like the battle's rejoicing
When our elbows and swords drip the crimson
And our charges 'gainst "The Leopard's" rush clash.
May God damn for ever all who cry "Peace!"

VII

And let the music of the swords make them crimson!
Hell grant soon we hear again the swords clash!
Hell blot black for alway the thought "Peace"!

A VIRGINAL

(1912)

No, no! Go from me. I have left her lately.
I will not spoil my sheath with lesser brightness,
For my surrounding air hath a new lightness;
Slight are her arms, yet they have bound me straitly
And left me cloaked as with a gauze of æther;

As with sweet leaves; as with a subtle clearness.
Oh, I have picked up magic in her nearness
To sheathe me half in half the things that sheathe her.
No, no! Go from me. I have still the flavour,
Soft as spring wind that's come from birchen bowers.   10
Green come the shoots, aye April in the branches,
As winter's wound with her sleight hand she staunches,
Hath of the trees a likeness of the savour:
As white their bark, so white this lady's hours.

THE RETURN

(1912)

[handwritten: of nero god of past]

> See, they return; ah, see the tentative
> > Movements, and the slow feet,
> > > The trouble in the pace and the uncertain
> > Wavering!

> See, they return, one, and by one,
> With fear, as half-awakened;
> As if the snow should hesitate
> And murmur in the wind,
> > and half turn back;
> These were the "Wing'd-with-Awe,"   10
> > Inviolable.

[handwritten: vanish neros (past tense)]

> Gods of the wingèd shoe!
> With them the silver hounds,
> > sniffing the trace of air!

> Haie! Haie!
> > These were the swift to harry;
> These were the keen-scented;
> These were the souls of blood.

> Slow on the leash,
> > pallid the leash-men!   20

LAMENT OF THE FRONTIER GUARD
(1915)

By the North Gate, the wind blows full of sand,
Lonely from the beginning of time until now!
Trees fall, the grass goes yellow with autumn.
I climb the towers and towers
                to watch out the barbarous land:
Desolate castle, the sky, the wide desert.
There is no wall left to this village.
Bones white with a thousand frosts,
High heaps, covered with trees and grass;
Who brought this to pass?   10
Who has brought the flaming imperial anger?
Who has brought the army with drums and with kettle-drums?
Barbarous kings.
A gracious spring, turned to blood-ravenous autumn,
A turmoil of wars-men, spread over the middle kingdom,
Three hundred and sixty thousand,
And sorrow, sorrow like rain.
Sorrow to go, and sorrow, sorrow returning.
Desolate, desolate fields,
And no children of warfare upon them,   20
                No longer the men for offence and defence.
Ah, how shall you know the dreary sorrow at the North Gate,
With Rihoku's name forgotten,
And we guardsmen fed to the tigers.

                                        By Rihaku

HUGH SELWYN MAUBERLEY
Life and Contacts

(1920)

Vocat æstus in umbram
            —Nemesianus, Ec. IV

I

E. P. ODE POUR L'ELECTION DE SON SEPULCHRE

For three years, out of key with his time,
He strove to resuscitate the dead art
Of poetry; to maintain "the sublime"
In the old sense. Wrong from the start—

No, hardly, but seeing he had been born
In a half savage country, out of date;
Bent resolutely on wringing lilies from the acorn;
Capaneus; trout for factitious bait;

"Ἴδμεν γάρ τοι πάνθ', ὅσ' ἐνὶ Τροίῃ
Caught in the unstopped ear;
Giving the rocks small lee-way   10
The chopped seas held him, therefore, that year.

His true Penelope was Flaubert,
He fished by obstinate isles;
Observed the elegance of Circe's hair
Rather than the mottoes on sun-dials.

Unaffected by "the march of events,"
He passed from men's memory in *l'an trentiesme*
De son eage; the case presents
No adjunct to the Muses' diadem.   20

II

The age demanded an image
Of its accelerated grimace,
Something for the modern stage,
Not, at any rate, an Attic grace;

Not, not certainly, the obscure reveries
Of the inward gaze;
Better mendacities
Than the classics in paraphrase!

The "age demanded" chiefly a mould in plaster,
Made with no loss of time,   30
A prose kinema, not, not assuredly, alabaster
Or the "sculpture" of rhyme.

III

The tea-rose tea-gown, etc.
Supplants the mousseline of Cos,
The pianola "replaces"
Sappho's barbitos.

Christ follows Dionysus,
Phallic and ambrosial
Made way for macerations;
Caliban casts out Ariel.   40

All things are a flowing,
Sage Heracleitus says;
But a tawdry cheapness
Shall outlast our days.

Even the Christian beauty
Defects—after Samothrace;
We see τὸ καλὸν
Decreed in the market place.

Faun's flesh is not to us,
Nor the saint's vision.   50

We have the press for wafer;
Franchise for circumcision.

All men, in law, are equals.
Free of Pisistratus,
We choose a knave or an eunuch
To rule over us.

O bright Apollo,
τίν' ἄνδρα, τίν' ἥρωα, τίνα θεὸν,
What god, man, or hero
Shall I place a tin wreath upon!   60

IV

These fought in any case,
and some believing,
                    pro domo, in any case . . .

Some quick to arm,
some for adventure,
some from fear of weakness,
some from fear of censure,
some for love of slaughter, in imagination,
learning later . . .
some in fear, learning love of slaughter;   70

Died some, pro patria,
                    non "dulce" non "et decor" . . .
walked eye-deep in hell
believing in old men's lies, then unbelieving
came home, home to a lie,
home to many deceits,
home to old lies and new infamy;
usury age-old and age-thick
and liars in public places.

Daring as never before, wastage as never before. 80
Young blood and high blood,
fair cheeks, and fine bodies;

fortitude as never before

frankness as never before,
disillusions as never told in the old days,
hysterias, trench confessions,
laughter out of dead bellies.

V

There died a myriad,
And of the best, among them,
For an old bitch gone in the teeth,   90
For a botched civilization,

Charm, smiling at the good mouth,
Quick eyes gone under earth's lid,

For two gross of broken statues,
For a few thousand battered books.

YEUX GLAUQUES

Gladstone was still respected,
When John Ruskin produced
"King's Treasuries"; Swinburne
And Rossetti still abused.

Fœtid Buchanan lifted up his voice   100
When that faun's head of hers
Became a pastime for
Painters and adulterers.

The Burne-Jones cartons
Have preserved her eyes;
Still, at the Tate, they teach
Cophetua to rhapsodize;

Thin like brook-water,
With a vacant gaze.
The English Rubaiyat was still-born   110
In those days.

The thin, clear gaze, the same
Still darts out faun-like from the half-ruin'd face,
Questing and passive. . . .
"Ah, poor Jenny's case" . . .

Bewildered that a world
Shows no surprise
At her last maquero's
Adulteries.

"SIENA MI FE'; DISFECEMI
MAREMMA"

Among the pickled fœtuses and bottled bones,   120
Engaged in perfecting the catalogue,
I found the last scion of the
Senatorial families of Strasbourg, Monsieur Verog.

For two hours he talked of Gallifet;
Of Dowson; of the Rhymers' Club;
Told me how Johnson (Lionel) died
By falling from a high stool in a pub . . .

But showed no trace of alcohol
At the autopsy, privately performed—
Tissue preserved—the pure mind   130
Arose toward Newman as the whiskey warmed.

Dowson found harlots cheaper than hotels;
Headlam for uplift; Image impartially imbued
With raptures for Bacchus, Terpsichore and the Church.
So spoke the author of "The Dorian Mood,"

M. Verog, out of step with the decade,
Detached from his contemporaries,
Neglected by the young,
Because of these reveries.

BRENNBAUM

The sky-like limpid eyes,   140
The circular infant's face,
The stiffness from spats to collar
Never relaxing into grace;

The heavy memories of Horeb, Sinai and the forty years,
Showed only when the daylight fell
Level across the face
Of Brennbaum "The Impeccable."

MR. NIXON

In the cream gilded cabin of his steam yacht
Mr. Nixon advised me kindly, to advance with fewer
Dangers of delay. "Consider   150
    "Carefully the reviewer.

"I was as poor as you are;
"When I began I got, of course,
"Advance on royalties, fifty at first," said Mr. Nixon,
"Follow me, and take a column,
"Even if you have to work free.

"Butter reviewers. From fifty to three hundred
"I rose in eighteen months;
"The hardest nut I had to crack
"Was Dr. Dundas.   160

"I never mentioned a man but with the view
"Of selling my own works.
"The tip's a good one, as for literature
"It gives no man a sinecure.

"And no one knows, at sight, a masterpiece.
"And give up verse, my boy,
"There's nothing in it."

    .   .   .   .

Likewise a friend of Bloughram's once advised me:
Don't kick against the pricks,
Accept opinion. The "Nineties" tried your game   170
And died, there's nothing in it.

X

Beneath the sagging roof
The stylist has taken shelter,
Unpaid, uncelebrated,
At last from the world's welter

Nature receives him;
With a placid and uneducated mistress
He exercises his talents
And the soil meets his distress.

The haven from sophistications and contentions   180
Leaks through its thatch;
He offers succulent cooking;
The door has a creaking latch.

XI

"Conservatrix of Milésien"
Habits of mind and feeling,
Possibly. But in Ealing
With the most bank-clerkly of Englishmen?

No, "Milésian" is an exaggeration.
No instinct has survived in her
Older than those her grandmother   190
Told her would fit her station.

XII

"Daphne with her thighs in bark
Stretches toward me her leafy hands,"—
Subjectively. In the stuffed-satin drawing-room
I await The Lady Valentine's commands,

Knowing my coat has never been
Of precisely the fashion
To stimulate, in her,
A durable passion;

Doubtful, somewhat, of the value   200
Of well-gowned approbation
Of literary effort,
But never of The Lady Valentine's vocation:

Poetry, her border of ideas,
The edge, uncertain, but a means of blending
With other strata
Where the lower and higher have ending;

A hook to catch the Lady Jane's attention,
A modulation toward the theatre,
Also, in the case of revolution,   210
A possible friend and comforter.

.   .   .   .

Conduct, on the other hand, the soul
"Which the highest cultures have nourished"
To Fleet St. where
Dr. Johnson flourished;

Beside this thoroughfare
The sale of half-hose has
Long since superseded the cultivation
Of Pierian roses.

ENVOI (1919)

Go, dumb-born book,   220
Tell her that sang me once that song of Lawes:
Hadst thou but song
As thou hast subjects known,
Then were there cause in thee that should condone
Even my faults that heavy upon me lie,
And build her glories their longevity.

Tell her that sheds
Such treasure in the air,
Recking naught else but that her graces give
Life to the moment,   230
I would bid them live
As roses might, in magic amber laid,
Red overwrought with orange and all made
One substance and one colour
Braving time.

Tell her that goes
With song upon her lips
But sings not out the song, nor knows
The maker of it, some other mouth,
May be as fair as hers,   240

Might, in new ages, gain her worshippers,
When our two dusts with Waller's shall be laid,
Siftings on siftings in oblivion,
Till change hath broken down
All things save Beauty alone.

MAUBERLEY

1920

Vacuos exercet aera morsus

I

Turned from the "eau-forte
Par Jaquemart"
To the strait head
Of Messalina:

"His true Penelope   250
Was Flaubert,"
And his tool
The engraver's.

Firmness,
Not the full smile,
His art, but an art
In profile;

Colourless
Pier Francesca,
Pisanello lacking the skill   260
To forge Achaia.

II

Qu'est ce qu'ils savent de l'amour, et qu'est ce qu'ils peuvent com-
prendre?
S'ils ne comprennent pas la poésie, s'ils ne sentent pas la
musique, qu'est ce qu'ils peuvent comprendre de cette passion en
comparaison avec laquelle la rose est grossière et le parfum des
violettes un tonnerre?   CAID ALI

For three years, diabolus in the scale,
He drank ambrosia,
All passes, ANANGKE prevails,
Came end, at last, to that Arcadia.

He had moved amid her phantasmagoria,
Amid her galaxies,
NUKTIS 'AGALMA

. . . .

Drifted . . . drifted precipitate,
Asking time to be rid of . . .   270
Of his bewilderment; to designate
His new found orchid. . . .

To be certain . . . certain . . .
(Amid ærial flowers) . . . time for arrangements—
Drifted on
To the final estrangement;

Unable in the supervening blankness
To sift TO AGATHON from the chaff
Until he found his sieve . . .
Ultimately, his seismograph: 280

—Given that is his "fundamental passion,"
This urge to convey the relation
Of eye-lid and cheek-bone
By verbal manifestations;

To present the series
Of curious heads in medallion—

He had passed, inconscient, full gaze,
The wide-banded irides
And botticellian sprays implied
In their diastasis;   290

Which anæthesis, noted a year late,
And weighed, revealed his great affect,
(Orchid), mandate
Of Eros, a retrospect.

.   .   .

Mouths biting empty air,
The still stone dogs,
Caught in metamorphis, were
Left him as epilogues.

"THE AGE DEMANDED"

Vide Poem II. Page 296

For this agility chance found
Him of all men, unfit   300
As the red-beaked steeds of
The Cytheræan for a chain bit.

The glow of porcelain
Brought no reforming sense
To his perception
Of the social inconsequence.

Thus, if her colour
Came against his gaze,
Tempered as if
It were through a perfect glaze   310

He made no immediate application
Of this to relation of the state
To the individual, the month was more temperate
Because this beauty had been.

The coral isle, the lion-coloured sand
Burst in upon the porcelain revery:
Impetuous troubling
Of his imagery.

Mildness, amid the neo-Nietzschean clatter,
His sense of graduations,   320
Quite out of place amid
Resistance to current exacerbations,

Invitation, mere invitation to perceptivity
Gradually led him to the isolation
Which these presents place
Under a more tolerant, perhaps, examination.

By constant elimination
The manifest universe
Yielded an armour
Against utter consternation,   330

A Minoan undulation,
Seen, we admit, amid ambrosial circumstances
Strengthened him against
The discouraging doctrine of chances,

And his desire for survival,
Faint in the most strenuous moods,
Became an Olympian *apathein*
In the presence of selected perceptions.

A pale gold, in the aforesaid pattern,
The unexpected palms   340
Destroying, certainly, the artist's urge,
Left him delighted with the imaginary
Audition of the phantasmal sea-surge,

Incapable of the least utterance or composition,
Emendation, conservation of the "better tradition,"
Refinement of medium, elimination of superfluities,
August attraction or concentration.

Nothing, in brief, but maudlin confession,
Irresponse to human aggression,
Amid the precipitation, down-float   350

Of insubstantial manna,
Lifting the faint susurrus
Of his subjective hosannah.

Ultimate affronts to
Human redundancies;

Non-esteem of self-styled "his betters"
Leading, as he well knew,
To his final
Exclusion from the world of letters.

IV

Scattered Moluccas   360
Not knowing, day to day,
The first day's end, in the next noon;
The placid water
Unbroken by the Simoon;

Thick foliage
Placid beneath warm suns,
Tawn fore-shores
Washed in the cobalt of oblivions;

Or through dawn-mist
The grey and rose   370
Of the juridical
Flamingoes;

A consciousness disjunct,
Being but this overblotted
Series
Of intermittences;

Coracle of Pacific voyages,
The unforecasted beach;
Then on an oar
Read this: 380

"I was
And I no more exist;
Here drifted
An hedonist."

MEDALLION

Luini in porcelain!
The grand piano
Utters a profane
Protest with her clear soprano.

The sleek head emerges
From the gold-yellow frock   390
As Anadyomene in the opening
Pages of Reinach.

Honey-red, closing the face-oval,
A basket-work of braids which seem as if they were
Spun in King Minos' hall
From metal, or intractable amber;

The face-oval beneath the glaze,
Bright in its suave bounding-line, as,
Beneath half-watt rays,
The eyes turn topaz.   400

CANTO I
(1925)

And then went down to the ship,
Set keel to breakers, forth on the godly sea, and
We set up mast and sail on that swart ship,
Bore sheep aboard her, and our bodies also
Heavy with weeping, and winds from sternward
Bore us out onward with bellying canvas,
Circe's this craft, the trim-coifed goddess.
Then sat we amidships, wind jamming the tiller,
Thus with stretched sail, we went over sea till day's end.
Sun to his slumber, shadows o'er all the ocean,   10

Came we then to the bounds of deepest water,
To the Kimmerian lands, and peopled cities
Covered with close-webbed mist, unpierced ever
With glitter of sun-rays
Nor with stars stretched, nor looking back from heaven
Swartest night stretched over wretched men there.
The ocean flowing backward, came we then to the place
Aforesaid by Circe.
Here did they rites, Perimedes and Eurylochus,
And drawing sword from my hip   20
I dug the ell-square pitkin;
Poured we libations unto each the dead,
First mead and then sweet wine, water mixed with white flour.
Then prayed I many a prayer to the sickly death's-heads;
As set in Ithaca, sterile bulls of the best
For sacrifice, heaping the pyre with goods,
A sheep to Tiresias only, black and a bell-sheep.
Dark blood flowed in the fosse,
Souls out of Erebus, cadaverous dead, of brides
Of youths and of the old who had borne much;   30
Souls stained with recent tears, girls tender,
Men many, mauled with bronze lance heads,
Battle spoil, bearing yet dreory arms,
These many crowded about me; with shouting,
Pallor upon me, cried to my men for more beasts;
Slaughtered the herds, sheep slain of bronze;
Poured ointment, cried to the gods,
To Pluto the strong, and praised Proserpine;
Unsheathed the narrow sword,
I sat to keep off the impetuous impotent dead,   40
Till I should hear Tiresias.
But first Elpenor came, our friend Elpenor,
Unburied, cast on the wide earth,
Limbs that we left in the house of Circe,
Unwept, unwrapped in sepulchre, since toils urged other.
Pitiful spirit. And I cried in hurried speech:
"Elpenor, how art thou come to this dark coast?
"Cam'st thou afoot, outstripping seamen?"
                And he in heavy speech:
"Ill fate and abundant wine. I slept in Circe's ingle.   50
"Going down the long ladder unguarded,

"I fell against the buttress,
"Shattered the nape-nerve, the soul sought Avernus.
"But thou, O King, I bid remember me, unwept, unburied,
"Heap up mine arms, be tomb by sea-bord, and inscribed:
"A man of no fortune, and with a name to come.
"And set my oar up, that I swung mid fellows."

And Anticlea came, whom I beat off, and then Tiresias Theban,
Holding his golden wand, knew me, and spoke first:
"A second time? why? man of ill star,   60
"Facing the sunless dead and this joyless region?
"Stand from the fosse, leave me my bloody bever
"For soothsay."
            And I stepped back,
And he strong with the blood, said then: "Odysseus
"Shalt return through spiteful Neptune, over dark seas,
"Lose all companions." And then Anticlea came.
Lie quiet Divus. I mean, that is Andreas Divus,
In officina Wecheli, 1538, out of Homer.
And he sailed, by Sirens and thence outward and away   70
And unto Circe.
            Venerandam,
In the Cretan's phrase, with the golden crown, Aphrodite,
Cypri munimenta sortita est, mirthful, oricalchi, with golden
Girdles and breast bands, thou with dark eyelids
Bearing the golden bough of Argicida. So that:

CANTO II

(1925)

Hang it all, Robert Browning,
there can be but the one "Sordello."
But Sordello, and my Sordello?
Lo Sordels si fo di Mantovana.
So-shu churned in the sea.
Seal sports in the spray-whited circles of cliff-wash,
Sleek head, daughter of Lir,
            eyes of Picasso
Under black fur-hood, lithe daughter of Ocean;

And the wave runs in the beach-groove: 10
"Eleanor, ἐλέναυς and ἑλέπτολις!"
    And poor old Homer blind, blind, as a bat,
Ear, ear for the sea-surge, murmur of old men's voices:
"Let her go back to the ships,
Back among Grecian faces, lest evil come on our own,
Evil and further evil, and a curse cursed on our children,
Moves, yes she moves like a goddess
And has the face of a god
    and the voice of Schoeney's daughters,
And doom goes with her in walking,   20
Let her go back to the ships,
    back among Grecian voices."
And by the beach-run, Tyro,
    Twisted arms of the sea-god,
Lithe sinews of water, gripping her, cross-hold,
And the blue-gray glass of the wave tents them,
Glare azure of water, cold-welter, close cover.
Quiet sun-tawny sand-stretch,
The gulls broad out their wings,
    nipping between the splay feathers;   30
Snipe come for their bath,
    bend out their wing-joints,
Spread wet wings to the sun-film,
And by Scios,
    to left of the Naxos passage,
Naviform rock overgrown,
    algæ cling to its edge,
There is a wine-red glow in the shallows,
    a tin flash in the sun-dazzle.

The ship landed in Scios,   40
    men wanting spring-water,
And by the rock-pool a young boy loggy with vine-must,
    "To Naxos? Yes, we'll take you to Naxos,
Cum' along lad." "Not that way!"
"Aye, that way is Naxos."
    And I said: "It's a straight ship."
And an ex-convict out of Italy
    knocked me into the fore-stays,

(He was wanted for manslaughter in Tuscany)
        And the whole twenty against me,   50
Mad for a little slave money.
        And they took her out of Scios
And off her course . . .
        And the boy came to, again, with the racket,
And looked out over the bows,
        and to eastward, and to the Naxos passage.
God-sleight then, god-sleight:
        Ship stock fast in sea-swirl,
Ivy upon the oars, King Pentheus,
        grapes with no seed but sea-foam,   60
Ivy in scupper-hole.
Aye, I, Acœtes, stood there,
        and the god stood by me,
Water cutting under the keel,
Sea-break from stern forrards,
        wake running off from the bow,
And where was gunwhale, there now was vine-trunk,
And tenthril where cordage had been,
        grape-leaves on the rowlocks,
Heavy vine on the oarshafts,   70
And, out of nothing, a breathing,
        hot breath on my ankles,
Beasts like shadows in glass,
        a furred tail upon nothingness.
Lynx-purr, and heathery smell of beasts,
        where tar smell had been,
Sniff and pad-foot of beasts,
        eye-glitter out of black air.
The sky overshot, dry, with no tempest,
Sniff and pad-foot of beasts,   80
        fur brushing my knee-skin,
Rustle of airy sheaths,
        dry forms in the *æther*.
And the ship like a keel in ship-yard,
        slung like an ox in smith's sling,
Ribs stuck fast in the ways,
        grape-cluster over pin-rack,
        void air taking pelt.

Lifeless air become sinewed,
        feline leisure of panthers,   90
Leopards sniffing the grape shoots by scupper-hole,
Crouched panthers by fore-hatch,
And the sea blue-deep about us,
        green-ruddy in shadows,
And Lyæus: "From now, Accœtes, my altars,
Fearing no bondage,
        fearing no cat of the wood,
Safe with my lynxes,
        feeding grapes to my leopards,
Olibanum is my incense,   100
        the vines grow in my homage."

The back-swell now smooth in the rudder-chains,
Black snout of a porpoise
        where Lycabs had been,
Fish-scales on the oarsmen.
        And I worship.
I have seen what I have seen.
        When they brought the boy I said:
"He has a god in him,
        though I do not know which god."   110
And they kicked me into the fore-stays.
I have seen what I have seen:
        Medon's face like the face of a dory,
Arms shrunk into fins. And you, Pentheus,
Had as well listen to Tiresias, and to Cadmus,
        or your luck will go out of you.
Fish-scales over groin muscles,
        lynx-purr amid sea . . .
And of a later year,
        pale in the wine-red algæ,   120
If you will lean over the rock,
        the coral face under wave-tinge,
Rose-paleness under water-shift,
        Ileuthyeria, fair Dafne of sea-bords,
The swimmer's arms turned to branches,
Who will say in what year,
        fleeing what band of tritons,

The smooth brows, seen, and half seen,
        now ivory stillness.

And So-shu churned in the sea, So-shu also,   130
        using the long moon for a churn-stick . . .
Lithe turning of water,
        sinews of Poseidon,
Black azure and hyaline,
        glass wave over Tyro,
Close cover, unstillness,
        bright welter of wave-cords,
Then quiet water,
        quiet in the buff sands,
Sea-fowl stretching wing-joints,   140
        splashing in rock-hollows and sand-hollows
In the wave-runs by the half-dune;
Glass-glint of wave in the tide-rips against sunlight,
        pallor of Hesperus,
Grey peak of the wave,
        wave, colour of grape's pulp,

Olive grey in the near,
        far, smoke grey of the rock-slide,
Salmon-pink wings of the fish-hawk
        cast grey shadows in water,   150
The tower like a one-eyed great goose
        cranes up out of the olive-grove,

And we have heard the fauns chiding Proteus
        in the smell of hay under the olive-trees,
And the frogs singing against the fauns
        in the half-light.
And . . .

Robinson Jeffers
1887-1962

NIGHT

(1925)

The ebb slips from the rock, the sunken
Tide-rocks lift streaming shoulders
Out of the slack, the slow west
Sombering its torch; a ship's light   *ccean*
Shows faintly, far out,
Over the weight of the prone ocean
On the low cloud.

Over the dark mountain, over the dark pinewood,
Down the long dark valley along the shrunken river,
Returns the splendor without rays, the shining of shadow,   10
Peace-bringer, the matrix of all shining and quieter of shining.
Where the shore widens on the bay she opens dark wings
And the ocean accepts her glory. O soul worshipful of her
You like the ocean have grave depths where she dwells always,
And the film of waves above that takes the sun takes also
Her, with more love. The sun-lovers have a blond favorite,
A father of lights and noises, wars, weeping and laughter,
Hot labor, lust and delight and the other blemishes. Quietness
Flows from her deeper fountain; and he will die; and she is immortal.

Far off from here the slender   20
Flocks of the mountain forest
Move among stems like towers
Of the old redwoods to the stream,

No twig crackling; dip shy
Wild muzzles into the mountain water
Among the dark ferns.

O passionately at peace you being secure will pardon
The blasphemies of glowworms, the lamp in my tower, the fretfulness
Of cities, the cressets of the planets, the pride of the stars.
This August night in a rift of cloud Antares reddens,   30
The great one, the ancient torch, a lord among lost children,
The earth's orbit doubled would not girdle his greatness, one fire
Globed, out of grasp of the mind enormous; but to you O Night
What? Not a spark? What flicker of a spark in the faint far glimmer
Of a lost fire dying in the desert, dim coals of a sand-pit the Bedouins
Wandered from at dawn . . . Ah singing prayer to what gulfs tempted
Suddenly are you more lost? To us the near-hand mountain
Be a measure of height, the tide-worn cliff at the sea-gate a measure of
        continuance.

The tide, moving the night's
Vastness with lonely voices,   40
Turns, the deep dark-shining
Pacific leans on the land,
Feeling his cold strength
To the outmost margins: you Night will resume
The stars in your time.

O passionately at peace when will that tide draw shoreward?
Truly the spouting fountains of light, Antares, Arcturus,
Tire of their flow, they sing one song but they think silence.
The striding winter giant Orion shines, and dreams darkness.
And life, the flicker of men and moths and the wolf on the hill,   50
Though furious for continuance, passionately feeding, passionately
Remaking itself upon its mates, remembers deep inward
The calm mother, the quietness of the womb and the egg,
The primal and the latter silences: dear Night it is memory
Prophesies, prophecy that remembers, the charm of the dark.
And I and my people, we are willing to love the four-score years
Heartily; but as a sailor loves the sea, when the helm is for harbor.

Have men's minds changed,
Or the rock hidden in the deep of the waters of the soul

Broken the surface? A few centuries   60
Gone by, was none dared not to people
The darkness beyond the stars with harps and habitations.
But now, dear is the truth. Life is grown sweeter and lonelier,
And death is no evil.

BIRDS
(1925)

The fierce musical cries of a couple of sparrowhawks hunting on the
    headland,
Hovering and darting, their heads northwestward,
Prick like silver arrows shot through a curtain the noise of the ocean
Trampling its granite; their red backs gleam
Under my window around the stone corners; nothing gracefuller, nothing
Nimbler in the wind. Westward the wave-gleaners,
The old gray sea-going gulls are gathered together, the northwest wind
    wakening
Their wings to the wild spirals of the wind-dance.
Fresh as the air, salt as the foam, play birds in the bright wind, fly
    falcons
Forgetting the oak and the pinewood, come gulls   10
From the Carmel sands and the sands at the river-mouth, from Lobos and
    out of the limitless
Power of the mass of the sea, for a poem
Needs multitude, multitudes of thoughts, all fierce, all flesh-eaters, musically
    clamorous
Bright hawks that hover and dart headlong, and ungainly
Gray hungers fledged with desire of transgression, salt slimed beaks, from the
    sharp
Rock-shores of the world and the secret waters.

HURT HAWKS
(1928)

I

The broken pillar of the wing jags from the clotted shoulder,
The wing trails like a banner in defeat,
No more to use the sky forever but live with famine

And pain a few days: cat nor coyote
Will shorten the week of waiting for death, there is game without talons.
He stands under the oak-bush and waits
The lame feet of salvation; at night he remembers freedom
And flies in a dream, the dawns ruin it.
He is strong and pain is worse to the strong, incapacity is worse.
The curs of the day come and torment him   10
At distance, no one but death the redeemer will humble that head,
The intrepid readiness, the terrible eyes.
The wild God of the world is sometimes merciful to those
That ask mercy, not often to the arrogant.
You do not know him, you communal people, or you have forgotten him;
Intemperate and savage, the hawk remembers him;
Beautiful and wild, the hawks, and men that are dying, remember him.

II

I'd sooner, except the penalties, kill a man than a hawk; but the great
    redtail
Had nothing left but unable misery
From the bone too shattered for mending, the wing that trailed under his
    talons when he moved.   20
We had fed him six weeks, I gave him freedom,
He wandered over the foreland hill and returned in the evening, asking
    for death,
Not like a beggar, still eyed with the old
Implacable arrogance. I gave him the lead gift in the twilight.
    What fell was relaxed,
Owl-downy, soft feminine feathers; but what
Soared: the fierce rush: the night-herons by the flooded river cried fear at
    its rising
Before it was quite unsheathed from reality.

APOLOGY FOR BAD DREAMS

(1935)

I

In the purple light, heavy with redwood, the slopes drop seaward,
Headlong convexities of forest, drawn in together to the steep ravine. Below,
    on the sea-cliff,
A lonely clearing; a little field of corn by the streamside; a roof under
    spared trees. Then the ocean

Like a great stone someone has cut to a sharp edge and polished to shining. Beyond it, the fountain
And furnace of incredible light flowing up from the sunk sun. In the little clearing a woman
Is punishing a horse; she had tied the halter to a sapling at the edge of the wood, but when the great whip
Clung to the flanks the creature kicked so hard she feared he would snap the halter; she called from the house
The young man her son; who fetched a chain tie-rope, they working together
Noosed the small rusty links round the horse's tongue
And tied him by the swollen tongue to the tree.   10
Seen from this height they are shrunk to insect size,
Out of all human relation. You cannot distinguish
The blood dripping from where the chain is fastened,
The beast shuddering; but the thrust neck and the legs
Far apart. You can see the whip fall on the flanks . . .
The gesture of the arm. You cannot see the face of the woman.
The enormous light beats up out of the west across the cloud-bars of the trade-wind. The ocean
Darkens, the high clouds brighten, the hills darken together. Unbridled and unbelievable beauty
Covers the evening world . . . not covers, grows apparent out of it, as Venus down there grows out
From the lit sky. What said the prophet? "I create good: and I create evil: I am the Lord."   20

II
This coast crying out for tragedy like all beautiful places,
(The quiet ones ask for quieter suffering: but here the granite cliff the gaunt cypresses crown
Demands what victim? The dykes of red lava and black what Titan? The hills like pointed flames
Beyond Soberanes, the terrible peaks of the bare hills under the sun, what immolation?)
This coast crying out for tragedy like all beautiful places: and like the passionate spirit of humanity
Pain for its bread: God's, many victims', the painful deaths, the horrible transfigurements: I said in my heart,
"Better invent than suffer: imagine victims
Lest your own flesh be chosen the agonist, or you
Martyr some creature to the beauty of the place." And I said,

"Burn sacrifices once a year to magic   30
Horror away from the house, this little house here
You have built over the ocean with your own hands
Beside the standing boulders: for what are we,
The beast that walks upright, with speaking lips
And little hair, to think we should always be fed,
Sheltered, intact, and self-controlled? We sooner more liable
Than the other animals. Pain and terror, the insanities of desire; not accidents
        but essential,
And crowd up from the core:" I imagined victims for those wolves, I
        made the phantoms to follow,
They have hunted the phantoms and missed the house. It is not good to
        forget over what gulfs the spirit
Of the beauty of humanity, the petal of a lost flower blown seaward by the
        night-wind, floats to its quietness.   40

III

Boulders blunted like an old bear's teeth break up from the headland; below
        them
All the soil is thick with shells, the tide-rock feasts of a dead people.
Here the granite flanks are scarred with ancient fire, the ghosts of the tribe
Crouch in the nights beside the ghost of a fire, they try to remember the
        sunlight,
Light has died out of their skies. These have paid something for the future
Luck of the country, while we living keep old griefs in memory: though
        God's
Envy is not a likely fountain of ruin, to forget evil calls down
Sudden reminders from the cloud: remembered deaths be our redeemers;
Imagined victims our salvation: white as the half moon at midnight
Someone flamelike passed me, saying, "I am Tamar Cauldwell, I have my
        desire,"
                                                                             50
Then the voice of the sea returned, when she had gone by, the stars to their
        towers.
. . . Beautiful country burn again, Point Pinos down to the Sur Rivers
Burn as before with bitter wonders, land and ocean and the Carmel water.

IV

He brays humanity in a mortar to bring the savor
From the bruised root: a man having bad dreams, who invents victims, is only
        the ape of that God.
He washes it out with tears and many waters, calcines it with fire in the red
        crucible,

Deforms it, makes it horrible to itself: the spirit flies out and stands naked, he
    sees the spirit,
He takes it in the naked ecstasy; it breaks in his hand, the atom is broken, the
    power that massed it
Cries to the power that moves the stars, "I have come home to myself, behold
    me.
I bruised myself in the flint mortar and burnt me   60
In the red shell, I tortured myself, I flew forth,
Stood naked of myself and broke me in fragments,
And here am I moving the stars that are me."
I have seen these ways of God: I know of no reason
For fire and change and torture and the old returnings.
He being sufficient might be still. I think they admit no reason; they are the
    ways of my love.
Unmeasured power, incredible passion, enormous craft: no thought apparent
    but burns darkly
Smothered with its own smoke in the human brain-vault: no thought outside:
    a certain measure in phenomena:
The fountains of the boiling stars, the flowers on the foreland, the ever-
    returning roses of dawn.

PROMISE OF PEACE
(1935)

The heads of strong old age are beautiful
Beyond all grace of youth. They have strange quiet,
Integrity, health, soundness, to the full
They've dealt with life and been atempered by it.
A young man must not sleep, his years are war
Civil and foreign but the former's worse;
But the old can breathe in safety now they are
Forgetting what youth meant, the being perverse,
Running the fool's gauntlet and getting cut
By the whips of the five senses. As for me,   10
If I should wish to live long it were but
To trade those fevers for tranquillity,
Thinking though that's entire and sweet in the grave
How shall the dead taste the deep treasure they have?

THE EYE
(1948)

The Atlantic is a stormy moat; and the Mediterranean,
The blue pool in the old garden,
More than five thousand years has drunk sacrifice
Of ships and blood, and shines in the sun; but here the Pacific—
Our ships, planes, wars are perfectly irrelevant.
Neither our present blood-feud with the brave dwarfs
Nor any future world-quarrel of westering
And eastering man, the bloody migrations, greed of power, clash of faiths—
Is a speck of dust on the great scale-pan.
Here from this mountain shore, headland beyond stormy headland plunging
    like dolphins through the blue sea-smoke   10
Into pale sea—look west at the hill of water: it is half the planet: this dome,
    this half-globe, this bulging
Eyeball of water, arched over to Asia,
Australia and white Antarctica: those are the eyelids that never close; this is
    the staring unsleeping
Eye of the earth; and what it watches is not our wars.

OCEAN
(1954)

The gray whales are going south: I see their fountains
Rise from black sea: great dark bulks of hot blood
Plowing the deep cold sea to their trysting-place
Off Mexican California, where water is warm, and love
Finds massive joy: from the flukes to the blowhole the whole giant
Flames like a star. In February storm the ocean
Is black and rainbowed; the high spouts of white spray
Rise and fall over in the wind. There is no April in the ocean;
How do these creatures know that spring is at hand? They remember their
    ancestors
That crawled on earth: the little fellows like otters, who took to sea   10
And have grown great. Go out to the ocean, little ones,
You will grow great or die.

                And here the small trout
Flicker in the streams that tumble from the coast mountain,

Little quick flames of life: but from time to time
One of them goes mad, wanting room and freedom; he slips between the rock
　　jaws
And takes to sea, where from time immemorial
The long sharks wait. If he lives he becomes a steelhead,
A rainbow trout grown beyond nature in the ocean. Go out to the great ocean,
Grow great or die.　　　　　　　　　　　　　　　　　　　20

　　　　　　O ambitious children,
It would be wiser no doubt to rest in the brook
And remain little. But if the devil drives
I hope you will scull far out to the wide ocean and find your fortune, and
　　beware of teeth.

It is not important. There are deeps you will never reach and peaks you will
　　never explore,
Where the great squids and kraken lie in the gates, in the awful twilight
The whip-armed hungers; and mile under mile below,
Deep under deep, on the deep floor, in the darkness
Under the weight of the world: like lighted galleons the ghost-fish,
With phosphorescent portholes along their flanks,　　　　　　　　30
Sail over and eat each other: the condition of life,
To eat each other: but in the slime below
Prodigious worms as great and as slow as glaciers burrow in the sediment,
Mindless and blind, huge tubes of muddy flesh
Sucking not meat but carrion, drippings and offal
From the upper sea. They move a yard in a year,
Where there are no years, no sun, no seasons, darkness and slime;
They spend nothing on action, all on gross flesh.

　　　　　　　　　　　O ambitious ones,
Will you grow great, or die? It hardly matters; the words are comparative;　40
Greatness is but less little; and death's changed life.

Marianne Moore

1887-

POETRY

(1921)

formal

I, too, dislike it: there are things that are important beyond
          all this fiddle. *Slang*
  Reading it, however, with a perfect contempt for it, one
formal   discovers in
    it after all, a place for the genuine. *interpretation y*
      Hands that can grasp, eyes   *explanation*
      that can dilate, hair that can rise
        if it must, these things are important not because a

high-sounding interpretation can be put upon them but be-
          cause they are   *Cliches*   10
concrete
material useful. When they become so derivative as to become
        unintelligible, *unexciting*
    the same thing may be said for all of us, that we
      do not admire what
      we cannot understand: the bat
        holding on upside down or in quest of something to

eat, elephants pushing, a wild horse taking a roll, a tireless
          wolf under
  a tree, the immovable critic twitching his skin like a horse
        that feels a flea, the base-   20
  ball fan, the statistician—
      nor is it valid
        to discriminate against "business documents and

school-books"; all these phenomena are important. One
               must make a distinction
however: when dragged into prominence by half poets, *only literalists*
               the result is not poetry,
nor till the poets among us can be
     "literalists of
     the imagination"—above   30
          insolence and triviality and can present

for inspection, "imaginary gardens with real toads in them,"
               shall we have
it. In the meantime, if you demand on the one hand,
the raw material of poetry in
     all its rawness and
     that which is on the other hand
          genuine, you are interested in poetry.

THE STEEPLE–JACK

(1935)

painter
apocalyptic vision

Dürer would have seen a reason for living
     in a town like this, with eight stranded whales
to look at; with the sweet sea air coming into your house
on a fine day, from water etched
     with waves as formal as the scales — *venture*
on a fish.

One by one, in two's, in three's, the seagulls keep
     flying back and forth over the town clock,
or sailing around the lighthouse without moving their
          wings—   10
rising steadily with a slight
     quiver of the body—or flock
mewing where

a sea the purple of the peacock's neck is
     paled to greenish azure as Dürer changed
the pine green of the Tyrol to peacock blue and guinea
grey. You can see a twenty-five-
     pound lobster and fish-nets arranged
to dry. The

whirlwind fife-and-drum of the storm bends the salt   20
    marsh grass, disturbs stars in the sky and the
star on the steeple; it is a privilege to see so
much confusion.

       A steeple-jack in red, has let
    a rope down as a spider spins a thread;
he might be part of a novel, but on the sidewalk a
sign says C. J. Poole, Steeple-Jack,
    in black and white; and one in red
and white says

Danger. The church portico has four fluted   30
    columns, each a single piece of stone, made
modester by white-wash. This would be a fit haven for
waifs, children, animals, prisoners,
    and presidents who have repaid
sin-driven

senators by not thinking about them. One
    sees a school-house, a post-office in a
store, fish-houses, hen-houses, a three-masted schooner on
the stocks. The hero, the student,
    the steeple-jack, each in his way,   40
is at home.

It scarcely could be dangerous to be living
    in a town like this, of simple people
who have a steeple-jack placing danger-signs by the church
when he is gilding the solid-
    pointed star, which on a steeple
stands for hope.

[handwritten margin note: sarcastic view of society]

NO SWAN SO FINE
(1935)

    "No water so still as the
        dead fountains of Versailles." No swan,
    with swart blind look askance

and gondoliering legs, so fine
    as the chintz china one with fawn-
brown eyes and toothed gold
collar on to show whose bird it was.

Lodged in the Louis Fiftccnth
    candelabrum-tree of cockscomb-
tinted buttons, dahlias,   10
sea-urchins, and everlastings,
    it perches on the branching foam
of polished sculptured
flowers—at ease and tall. The king is dead.

THE PANGOLIN
(1936)

Another armoured animal—scale
    lapping scale with spruce-cone regularity until they
form the uninterrupted central
    tail-row! This near artichoke with heads and legs and
        grit-equipped gizzard,
  the night miniature artist engineer is
    Leonardo's—da Vinci's replica—
      impressive animal and toiler of whom we seldom
        hear.
    Armour seems extra. But for him,   10
    the closing ear-ridge—
      or bare ear lacking even this small
      eminence and similarly safe

contracting nose and eye apertures
    impenetrably closable, are not;—a true ant-eater,
not cockroach-eater, who endures
    exhausting solitary trips through unfamiliar ground at
        night,
    returning before sunrise; stepping in the moonlight,
      on the moonlight peculiarly, that the outside   20
        edges of his hands may bear the weight and save
        the claws

for digging. Serpentined about
    the tree, he draws
        away from danger unpugnaciously,
         with no sound but a harmless hiss; keeping

the fragile grace of the Thomas-
    of-Leighton Buzzard Westminster Abbey wrought-
        iron vine, or
rolls himself into a ball that has   30
    power to defy all effort to unroll it; strongly intailed,
        neat
    head for core, on neck not breaking off, with curled-in
        feet.
        Nevertheless he has sting-proof scales; and nest
        of rocks closed with earth from inside, which he
         can thus darken
        Sun and moon and day and night and man and beast
        each with a splendour
         which man in all his vileness cannot   40
         set aside; each with an excellence!

"Fearful yet to be feared," the armoured
    ant-eater met by the driver-ant does not turn back, but
engulfs what he can, the flattened sword-
    edged leafpoints on the tail and artichoke set leg- and
        body-plates
    quivering violently when it retaliates
        and swarms on him. Compact like the furled
        fringed frill
        on the hat-brim of Gargallo's hollow iron head   50
        of a
    matador, he will drop and will
        then walk away
         unhurt, although if unintruded on,
         he cautiously works down the tree, helped

by his tail. The giant-pangolin-
    tail, graceful tool, as prop or hand or broom or axe,
        tipped like
the elephant's trunk with special skin,

is not lost on this ant- and stone-swallowing uninjurable   60
artichoke which simpletons thought a living fable
    whom the stones had nourished, whereas ants had
        done
    so. Pangolins are not aggressive animals; between
    dusk and day they have the not unchain-like machine-
        like
        form and frictionless creep of a thing
        made graceful by adversities, con-

versities. To explain grace requires
    a curious hand. If that which is at all were not forever,   70
why would those who graced the spires
    with animals and gathered there to rest, on cold luxurious
    low stone seats—a monk and monk and monk—between
        the thus
      ingenious roof-supports, have slaved to confuse
        grace with a kindly manner, time in which to pay
        a debt,
      the cure for sins, a graceful use
      of what are yet
        approved stone mullions branching out across   80
        the perpendiculars? A sailboat

was the first machine. Pangolins, made
    for moving quietly also, are models of exactness,
on four legs; or hind feet plantigrade,
    with certain postures of a man. Beneath sun and moon,
        man slaving
    to make his life more sweet, leaves half the flowers
        worth having,
      needing to chose wisely how to use the strength;
        a paper-maker like the wasp; a tractor of food-   90
        stuffs,
    like the ant; spidering a length
    of web from bluffs
        above a stream; in fighting, mechanicked
        like the pangolin; capsizing in

disheartenment. Bedizened or stark
    naked, man, the self, the being we call human, writing-

master to this world, griffons a dark
  "Like does not like like that is obnoxious"; and writes
    error with four   100
r's. Among animals, one has a sense of humour.
  Humour saves a few steps, it saves years. Un-
    ignorant
  modest and unemotional, and all emotion,
he has everlasting vigour,
  power to grow,
    though there are few creatures who can make one
    breathe faster and make one erecter.

Not afraid of anything is he,
  and then goes cowering forth, tread paced to meet an 110
    obstacle
at every step. Consistent with the
  formula—warm blood, no gills, two pairs of hands and
    a few hairs—that
is a mammal; there he sits in his own habitat,
  serge-clad, strong-shod. The prey of fear, he, always
    curtailed, extinguished, thwarted by the dusk,
    work partly done,
  says to the alternating blaze,
    "Again the sun!   120
    anew each day; and new and new and new,
    that comes into and steadies my soul."

WHAT ARE YEARS?

(1941)

What is our innocence,
  what is our guilt? All.are
    naked, none is safe. And whence
is courage: the unanswered question,
  the resolute doubt,—
    dumbly calling, deafly listening—that
in misfortune, even death,
  encourages others
  and in its defeat, stirs

the soul to be strong? He   10
sees deep and is glad, who
    accedes to mortality
and in his imprisonment rises
upon himself as
the sea in a chasm, struggling to be
free and unable to be,
        in its surrendering
        finds its continuing.

So he who strongly feels,
Behaves. The very bird,   20
    grown taller as he sings, steels
his form straight up. Though he is captive,
his mighty singing
says, satisfaction is a lowly
thing, how pure a thing is joy.
        This is mortality.
        this is eternity.

THE MIND IS AN ENCHANTING THING

(1944)

is an enchanted thing
    like the glaze on a
katydid-wing
        subdivided by sun
        till the nettings are legion.
Like Gieseking playing Scarlatti;

like the apteryx-awl
    as a beak, or the
kiwi's rain-shawl
        of haired feathers, the mind   10
        feeling its way as though blind,
walks along with its eyes on the ground.

It has memory's ear
    that can hear without
having to hear.
        Like the gyroscope's fall,
        truly unequivocal
because trued by regnant certainty,

it is a power of
    strong enchantment. It
is like the dove-
      neck animated by
      sun; it is memory's eye;
it's conscientious inconsistency.

It tears off the veil; tears
    the temptation, the
mist the heart wears,
      from its eyes,—if the heart
      has a face; it takes apart
dejection. It's fire in the dove-neck's

iridescence; in the
    inconsistencies
of Scarlatti.
      Unconfusion submits
      Its confusion to proof; it's
not a Herod's oath that cannot change.

IN DISTRUST OF MERITS
(1944)

Strengthened to live, strengthened to die for
    medals and positioned victories?
They're fighting, fighting, fighting the blind
    man who thinks he sees,—
who cannot see that the enslaver is
enslaved; the hater, harmed. O shining O
    firm star, O tumultuous
      ocean lashed till small things go
    as they will, the mountainous
      wave makes us who look, know

depth. Lost at sea before they fought! O
    star of David, star of Bethlehem,
O black imperial lion
    of the Lord—emblem
of a risen world—be joined at last, be

joined. There is hate's crown beneath which all is
        death; there's love's without which none
            is king; the blessed deeds bless
        the halo. As contagion
            of sickness makes sickness,   20

contagion of trust can make trust. They're
        fighting in deserts and caves, one by
one, in battalions and squadrons;
        they're fighting that I
may yet recover from the disease, My
Self; some have it lightly; some will die. "Man
            wolf to man" and we devour
                ourselves. The enemy could not
            have made a greater breach in our
                defences. One pilot-   30

ing a blind man can escape him, but
        Job disheartened by false comfort knew,
that nothing can be so defeating
        as a blind man who
can see. O alive who are dead, who are
proud not to see, O small dust of the earth
            that walks so arrogantly,
                trust begets power and faith is
            an affectionate thing. We
                vow, we make this promise   40

to the fighting—it's a promise—"We'll
        never hate black, white, red, yellow, Jew,
Gentile, Untouchable." We are
        not competent to
make our vows. With set jaw they are fighting,
fighting, fighting,—some we love whom we know,
            some we love but know not—that
                hearts may feel and not be numb.
        It cures me; or am I what
            I can't believe in? Some   50

in snow, some on crags, some in quicksands,
        little by little, much by much, they

are fighting fighting fighting that where
　　there was death there may
be life. "When a man is prey to anger,
he is moved by outside things; when he holds
　　　　his ground in patience patience
　　　　　　patience, that is action or
　　beauty," the soldier's defence
　　　　and hardest armour for   60

the fight. The world's an orphans' home. Shall
　　we never have peace without sorrow?
without pleas of the dying for
　　help that won't come? O
quiet form upon the dust, I cannot
look and yet I must. If these great patient
　　　　dyings—all these agonies
　　　　　　and woundbearings and bloodshed—
　　can teach us how to live, these
　　　　dyings were not wasted.   70

Hate-hardened heart, O heart of iron,
　　iron is iron till it is rust.
There never was a war that was
　　not inward; I must
fight till I have conquered in myself what
causes war, but I would not believe it.
　　　　I inwardly did nothing.
　　　　　　O Iscariotlike crime!
　　Beauty is everlasting
　　　　and dust is for a time.   80

ARMOUR'S UNDERMINING MODESTY

(1951)

At first I thought a pest
Must have alighted on my wrist.
It was a moth almost an owl,
Its wings were furred so well,
with backgammon-board wedges interlacing
on the wing—

like cloth of gold in a pattern
of scales with a hair-seal Persian
sheen. Once, self-determination
made an axe of a stone   10
and hacked things out with hairy paws. The consequence—
        our mis-set
alphabet.

    Arise, for it is day.
    Even gifted scholars lose their way
    through faulty etymology.
    No wonder we hate poetry,
and stars and harps and the new moon. If tributes cannot
be implicit,

    give me diatribes and the fragrance of iodine,   20
    the cork oak acorn grown in Spain;
    the pale-ale-eyed impersonal look
    which the sales-placard gives the bock beer buck.
What is more precise than precision? Illusion.
Knights we've known,

    like those familiar
    now unfamiliar knights who sought the Grail, were
    ducs in old Roman fashion
    without the addition
of wreaths and silver rods, and armour gilded   30
or inlaid.

    They did not let self bar
    their usefulness to others who were
    different. Though Mars is excessive
    is being preventive,
heroes need not write an ordinall of attributes to enumer-
        ate
what they hate.

    I should, I confess,
    like to have a talk with one of them about excess,   40
    and armour's undermining modesty
    instead of innocent depravity.

A mirror-of-steel uninsistence should countenance
continence,

    objectified and not by chance,
    there in its frame of circumstance
    of innocence and altitude
    in an unhackneyed solitude.
There is the tarnish; and there, the imperishable wish

John Crowe Ransom
1888-

BELLS FOR JOHN WHITESIDE'S DAUGHTER
(1924)

There was such speed in her little body,
And such lightness in her footfall,
It is no wonder that her brown study
Astonishes us all.

Her wars were bruited in our high window.
We looked among orchard trees and beyond,
Where she took arms against her shadow,
Or harried unto the pond

The lazy geese, like a snow cloud
Dripping their snow on the green grass,　　　　　10
Tricking and stopping, sleepy and proud,
Who cried in goose, Alas,

For the tireless heart within the little
Lady with rod that made them rise
From their noon apple-dreams, and scuttle
Goose-fashion under the skies!

But now go the bells, and we are ready,
In one house we are sternly stopped
To say we are vexed at her brown study,
Lying so primly propped.　　　　　20

HERE LIES A LADY

(1924)

Here lies a lady of beauty and high degree.   *change, happy rhythm*
Of chills and fever she died, of fever and chills,
The delight of her husband, her aunts, an infant of three,
And of medicos marveling sweetly on her ills.

For either she burned, and her confident eyes would blaze,
And her fingers fly in a manner to puzzle their heads—
serious tone   What was she making? Why, nothing; she sat in a maze
Of old scraps of laces, snipped into curious shreds—
old aristocratic tattered

Or this would pass, and the light of her fire decline
Till she lay discouraged and cold, like a stalk white and blown,   10
And would not open her eyes, to kisses, to wine;
The sixth of these states was her last; the cold settled down.

old style   poet enters poem   *suffer*

Sweet ladies, long may ye bloom, and toughly I hope ye may thole,
But was she not lucky? In flowers and lace and mourning,
In love and great honor we bade God rest her soul
After six little spaces of chill, and six of burning. *— light tone*

CAPTAIN CARPENTER

(1924)

Captain Carpenter rose up in his prime
Put on his pistols and went riding out
But had got wellnigh nowhere at that time
Till he fell in with ladies in a rout.

It was a pretty lady and all her train
That played with him so sweetly but before
An hour she'd taken a sword with all her main
And twined him of his nose for evermore.

Captain Carpenter mounted up one day
And rode straightway into a stranger rogue   10
That looked unchristian but be that as may
The Captain did not wait upon prologue.

But drew upon him out of his great heart
The other swung against him with a club
And cracked his two legs at the shinny part
And let him roll and stick like any tub.

Captain Carpenter rode many a time
From male and female took he sundry harms
He met the wife of Satan crying "I'm
The she-wolf bids you shall bear no more arms."   20

Their strokes and counters whistled in the wind
I wish he had delivered half his blows
But where she should have made off like a hind
The bitch bit off his arms at the elbows.

And Captain Carpenter parted with his ears
To a black devil that used him in this wise
O Jesus ere his threescore and ten years
Another had plucked out his sweet blue eyes.

Captain Carpenter got up on his roan
And sallied from the gate in hell's despite   30
I heard him asking in the grimmest tone
If any enemy yet there was to fight?

"To any adversary it is fame
If he risk to be wounded by my tongue
Or burnt in two beneath my red heart's flame
Such are the perils he is cast among.

"But if he can he has a pretty choice
From an anatomy with little to lose
Whether he cut my tongue and take my voice
Or whether it be my round red heart he choose."   40

It was the neatest knave that ever was seen
Stepping in perfume from his lady's bower
Who at this word put in his merry mien
And fell on Captain Carpenter like a tower.

I would not knock old fellows in the dust
But there lay Captain Carpenter on his back
His weapons were the old heart in his bust
And a blade shook between rotten teeth alack.

The rogue in scarlet and grey soon knew his mind
He wished to get his trophy and depart   50
With gentle apology and touch refined
He pierced him and produced the Captain's heart.

God's mercy rest on Captain Carpenter now
I thought him Sirs an honest gentleman
Citizen husband soldier and scholar enow
Let jangling kites eat of him if they can.

But God's deep curses follow after those
That shore him of his goodly nose and ears
His legs and strong arms at the two elbows
And eyes that had not watered seventy years.   60

The curse of hell upon the sleek upstart
Who got the Captain finally on his back
And took the red red vitals of his heart
And made the kites to whet their beaks clack clack.

VISION BY SWEETWATER
(1927)

Go and ask Robin to bring the girls over
To Sweetwater, said my Aunt; and that was why
It was like a dream of ladies sweeping by
The willows, clouds, deep meadowgrass, and the river.

Robin's sisters and my Aunt's lily daughter
Laughed and talked, and tinkled light as wrens
If there were a little colony all hens
To go walking by the steep turn of Sweetwater.

Let them alone, dear Aunt, just for one minute
Till I go fishing in the dark of my mind: 10
Where have I seen before, against the wind,
These bright virgins, robed and bare of bonnet,

Flowing with music of their strange quick tongue
And adventuring with delicate paces by the stream,—
Myself a child, old suddenly at the scream
From one of the white throats which it hid among?

PIAZZA PIECE
(1927)

—I am a gentleman in a dustcoat trying
To make you hear. Your ears are soft and small
And listen to an old man not at all,
They want the young men's whispering and sighing.
But see the roses on your trellis dying
And hear the spectral singing of the moon;
For I must have my lovely lady soon,
I am a gentleman in a dustcoat trying. *- make us near death*

—I am a lady young in beauty waiting
Until my truelove comes, and then we kiss.   10
But what grey man among the vines is this
Whose words are dry and faint as in a dream?
Back from my trellis, Sir, before I scream!
I am a lady young in beauty waiting.

ANTIQUE HARVESTERS
(1927)

Scene: Of the Mississippi the bank sinister, and of the
Ohio the bank sinister

Tawny are the leaves turned but they still hold,
And it is harvest; what shall this land produce? *- a grecian*
A meager hill of kernels, a runnel of juice;
Declension looks from our land, it is old.
Therefore let us assemble, dry, grey, spare,
And mild as yellow air.
(old earth)

"I hear the croak of a raven's funeral wing."
The young men would be joying in the song
Of passionate birds; their memories are not long.

What is it thus rehearsed in sable? "Nothing."   10
Trust not but the old endure, and shall be older
Than the scornful beholder.

ritual →
tradition
survive

We pluck the spindling ears and gather the corn.
One spot has special yield? "On this spot stood   – *civil war*
Heroes and drenched it with their only blood."
And talk meets talk, as echoes from the horn
Of the hunter—echoes are the old men's arts, – *old south too*
Ample are the chambers of their hearts.

Here come the hunters, keepers of a rite;
The horn, the hounds, the lank mares coursing by   20
Straddled with archetypes of chivalry;
And the fox, lovely ritualist, in flight
Offering his unearthly ghost to quarry;
And the fields, themselves to harry.   *history*
                              grain –
Resume, harvesters. The treasure is full bronze
Which you will garner for the Lady, and the moon   *south*
Could tinge it no yellower than does this noon;
But the grey will quench it shortly—the fields, men, stones.
Pluck fast, dreamers; prove as you amble slowly
Not less than men, not wholly.   30

Bare the arm, dainty youths, bend the knees
Under bronze burdens. And by an autumn tone
As by a grey, as by a green, you will have known
Your famous Lady's image; for so have these;
And if one say that easily will your hands
More prosper in other lands,

Angry as wasp-music be your cry then:
"Forsake the Proud Lady, of the heart of fire,
The look of snow, to the praise of a dwindled choir,
Song of degenerate specters that were men?   40
The sons of the fathers shall keep her, worthy of
What these have done in love."

True, it is said of our Lady, she ageth.
But see, if you peep shrewdly, she hath not stooped;
Take no thought of her servitors that have drooped,

For we are nothing; and if one talk of death—
Why, the ribs of the earth subsist frail as a breath
If but God wearieth.

THE EQUILIBRISTS

(1927)

Full of her long white arms and milky skin
He had a thousand times remembered sin.
Alone in the press of people traveled he,
Minding her jacinth, and myrrh, and ivory.

Mouth he remembered: the quaint orifice
From which came heat that flamed upon the kiss,
Till cold words came down spiral from the head,
Grey doves from the officious tower illsped.

Body: it was a white field ready for love,
On her body's field, with the gaunt tower above,   10
The lilies grew, beseeching him to take,
If he would pluck and wear them, bruise and break.

Eyes talking: Never mind the cruel words,
Embrace my flowers, but not embrace the swords.
But what they said, the doves came straightway flying
And unsaid: Honor, Honor, they came crying.

Importunate her doves. Too pure, too wise,
Clambering on his shoulder, saying, Arise,
Leave me now, and never let us meet,
Eternal distance now command thy feet.   20

Predicament indeed, which thus discovers
Honor among thieves, Honor between lovers.
O such a little word is Honor, they feel!
But the grey word is between them cold as steel.

At length I saw these lovers fully were come
Into their torture of equilibrium;
Dreadfully had forsworn each other, and yet
They were bound each to each, and they did not forget.

And rigid as two painful stars, and twirled   *gravity & anti-gravity*
About the clustered night their prison world,   30
They burned with fierce love always to come near,
But Honor beat them back and kept them clear.

Ah, the strict lovers, they are ruined now!
I cried in anger. But with puddled brow
Devising for those gibbeted and brave
Came I descanting: Man, what would you have?

For spin your period out, and draw your breath,
A kinder saeculum begins with Death.
Would you ascend to Heaven and bodiless dwell?
Or take your bodies honorless to Hell?   40

In Heaven you have heard no marriage is,
No white flesh tinder to your lecheries,
Your male and female tissue sweetly shaped
Sublimed away, and furious blood escaped.

Great lovers lie in Hell, the stubborn ones
Infatuate of the flesh upon the bones;
Stuprate, they rend each other when they kiss,
The pieces kiss again, no end to this.

But still I watched them spinning, orbited nice.
Their flames were not more radiant than their ice.   50
I dug in the quiet earth and wrought the tomb
And made these lines to memorize their doom:—

Epitaph

Equilibrists lie here; stranger, tread light;
Close, but untouching in each other's sight;
Mouldered the lips and ashy the tall skull,
Let them lie perilous and beautiful.

PRELUDE TO AN EVENING

(1945)

Do not enforce the tired wolf
Dragging his infected wound homeward
To sit tonight with the warm children
Naming the pretty kings of France.

The images of the invaded mind
Being as monsters in the dreams
Of your most brief enchanted headful,
Suppose a miracle of confusion:

That dreamed and undreamt become each other
And mix the night and day of your mind;   10
And it does not matter your twice crying
From mouth unbeautied against the pillow

To avert the gun of the swarthy soldier,
For cry, cock-crow, or the iron bell
Can crack the sleep-sense of outrage,
Annihilate phantoms who were nothing.

But now, by our perverse supposal,
There is a drift of fog on your mornings;
You in your peignoir, dainty at your orange-cup,
Feel poising round the sunny room   20

Invisible evil, deprived and bold.
All day the clock will metronome
Your gallant fear; the needles clicking,
The heels detonating the stair's cavern.

Freshening the water in the blue bowls
For the buckberries with not all your love,
You shall be listening for the low wind,
The warning sibilance of pines.

You like a waning moon, and I accusing
Our too banded Eumenides,   30
You shall make Noes but wanderingly,
Smoothing the heads of the hungry children.

PAINTED HEAD

(1945)

By dark severance the apparition head
Smiles from the air a capital on no
Column or a Platonic perhaps head
On a canvas sky depending from nothing;

Stirs up an old illusion of grandeur
By tickling the instinct of heads to be
Absolute and to try decapitation
And to play truant from the body bush;

But too happy and beautiful for those sorts
Of head (homekeeping heads are happiest)   10
Discovers maybe thirty unwidowed years
Of not dishonoring the faithful stem;

Is nameless and has authored for the evil
Historian headhunters neither book
Nor state and is therefore distinct from tart
Heads with crowns and guilty gallery heads;

So that the extravagant device of art
Unhousing by abstraction this once head
Was capital irony by a loving hand
That knew the no treason of a head like this;   20

Makes repentance in an unlovely head
For having vinegarly traduced the flesh
Till, the hurt flesh recusing, the hard egg
Is shrunken to its own deathlike surface;

And an image thus. The body bears the head
(So hardly one they terribly are two)
Feeds and obeys and unto please what end?
Not to the glory of tyrant head but to

The increase of body. Beauty is of body.
The flesh contouring shallowly on a head   30

Is a rock-garden needing body's love
And best bodiness to colorify

The big blue birds sitting and sea-shell flats
And caves and on the iron acropolis
To spread the hyacinthine hair and rear
The olive garden for the nightingales.

T. S. Eliot
1888-1964

THE LOVE SONG OF J. ALFRED PRUFROCK
(1917)

S'io credesse che mia risposta fosse
A persona che mai tornasse al mondo,
Questa fiamma staria senza piu scosse.
Ma perciocche giammai di questo fondo
Non torno vivo alcun, s'i'odo il vero,
Senza tema d'infamia ti rispondo.

[margin handwritten: "you" = somone as lonely as P. yet unchosen partner in fantasy]

Let us go then, you and I,
When the evening is spread out against the sky
Like a patient etherised upon a table;
Let us go, through certain half-deserted streets,
The muttering retreats
Of restless nights in one-night cheap hotels
And sawdust restaurants with oyster-shells:
Streets that follow like a tedious argument
Of insidious intent

[margin handwritten: wants to rebel against puritanical society - proposes slumming - illiciate places]

To lead you to an overwhelming question . . .   10
Oh, do not ask, "What is it?"
Let us go and make our visit.

In the room the women come and go
Talking of Michelangelo. —

[margin handwritten: ironic - m. full of life subjet of idle chit - chat]

The yellow fog that rubs its back upon the window-panes,
The yellow smoke that rubs its muzzle on the window-panes
Licked its tongue into the corners of the evening,
Lingered upon the pools that stand in drains,

348

Let fall upon its back the soot that falls from chimneys,   *urban London*
Slipped by the terrace, made a sudden leap,   20
And seeing that it was a soft October night,
Curled once about the house, and fell asleep.

And indeed there will be time
For the yellow smoke that slides along the street,
Rubbing its back upon the window-panes;   *hopelessly unable*
There will be time, there will be time   *to act – convinces*
To prepare a face to meet the faces that you meet;   *himself there will*
There will be time to murder and create,   *be time.*
And time for all the works and days of hands
That lift and drop a question on your plate;   30
Time for you and time for me,
And time yet for a hundred indecisions,
And for a hundred visions and revisions,   *decide what to say, do, act*
Before the taking of a toast and tea.

In the room the women come and go *refrain*
Talking of Michelangelo.
                        description of tea party
And indeed there will be time
To wonder, "Do I dare?" and, "Do I dare?"   *the tea party*
Time to turn back and descend the stair,
With a bald spot in the middle of my hair—   40
[They will say: "How his hair is growing thin!"]
My morning coat, my collar mounting firmly to the chin,
My necktie rich and modest, but asserted by a simple pin—
[They will say: "But how his arms and legs are thin!"]
Do I dare   *- upset*
Disturb the universe? – *my world*
In a minute there is time – *I have come close but couldn't?*
For decisions and revisions which a minute will reverse.

For I have known them all already, known them all:— *the social gatherings*
Have known the evenings, mornings, afternoons,   50
I have measured out my life with coffee spoons; - *life has been endless*
I know the voices dying with a dying fall   *tea parties*
Beneath the music from a farther room.
    So how should I presume? – *Its really my life - can I reject it?*

And I have known the eyes already, known them all—
The eyes that fix you in a formulated phrase,
And when I am formulated, sprawling on a pin,
When I am pinned and wriggling on the wall,
Then how should I begin
To spit out all the butt-ends of my days and ways? —tell them of   60
    And how should I presume?   my dreams

    And I have known the arms already, known them all—
Arms that are braceleted and white and bare
[But in the lamplight, downed with light brown hair!]   reminds him
Is it perfume from a dress   of women –
That makes me so digress?   sexual fantasy
Arms that lie along a table, or wrap about a shawl.
    And should I then presume?
    And how should I begin?

change of stream of consciousness
    .   .   .   .

Shall I say, I have gone at dusk through narrow streets   70
And watched the smoke that rises from the pipes   his view of
Of lonely men in shirt-sleeves, leaning out of windows? . . .   life

    I should have been a pair of ragged claws   crab symbolic of the
Scuttling across the floors of silent seas.   self-sefficient · can be
    anti-social

    .   .   .   .   .

And the afternoon, the evening, sleeps so peacefully!
Smoothed by long fingers,
Asleep . . . tired . . . or it malingers,
Stretched on the floor, here beside you and me.   admitting his own
Should I, after tea and cakes and ices,   inadequacy
Have the strength to force the moment to its crisis?   80
But though I have wept and fasted, wept and prayed,
Though I have seen my head [grown slightly bald] brought in upon a platter,
I am no prophet—and here's no great matter;
I have seen the moment of my greatness flicker,
And I have seen the eternal Footman hold my coat, and snicker,
And in short, I was afraid.   ∟ death

And would it have been worth it, after all,
After the cups, the marmalade, the tea,
Among the porcelain, among some talk of you and me,
Would it have been worth while,   90
To have bitten off the matter with a smile,   *— stopped the chit-chat*
To have squeezed the universe into a ball   *\ said something profound*
To roll it toward some overwhelming question, */*
To say: "I am Lazarus, come from the dead,   *\ even if she could say*
Come back to tell you all, I shall tell you all"— *he knew of death*
If one, settling a pillow by her head,
  Should say: "That is not what I meant at all.
  That is not it, at all."

  And would it have been worth it, after all,
  Would it have been worth while,   100
After the sunsets and the dooryards and the sprinkled streets,
After the novels, after the teacups, after the skirts that trail along the floor—
And this, and so much more?—
It is impossible to say just what I mean!
But as if a magic lantern threw the nerves in patterns on a screen: *— ?*
Would it have been worth while
If one, settling a pillow or throwing off a shawl,
And turning toward the window, should say:
  "That is not it at all,
  That is not what I meant, at all."   110

                .   .   .   .   .   .

No! I am not Prince Hamlet, nor was meant to be; *Knows he is no*
Am an attendant lord, one that will do   *hero —*
To swell a progress, start a scene or two,   *intellectualizes*
Advise the prince; no doubt, an easy tool,
Deferential, glad to be of use,
Politic, cautious, and meticulous;
Full of high sentence, but a bit obtuse;
At times, indeed, almost ridiculous—
Almost, at times, the Fool.   *— I know the truth but am not the hero?*

  I grow old . . . I grow old . . .   120
I shall wear the bottoms of my trousers rolled.

Shall I part my hair behind? Do I dare to eat a peach?
I shall wear white flannel trousers, and walk upon the beach.
I have heard the mermaids singing, each to each.

   I do not think that they will sing to me.

   I have seen them riding seaward on the waves
Combing the white hair of the waves blown back
When the wind blows the water white and black.

We have lingered in the chambers of the sea
By sea-girls wreathed with seaweed red and brown   130
Till human voices wake us, and we drown.

SWEENEY AMONG THE NIGHTINGALES
(1919)

ὤμοι, πέπληγμαι καιρίαν πληγὴν ἔσω

Apeneck Sweeney spreads his knees
Letting his arms hang down to laugh,
The zebra stripes along his jaw
Swelling to maculate giraffe.

   The circles of the stormy moon
Slide westward toward the River Plate,
Death and the Raven drift above
And Sweeney guards the hornèd gate.

   Gloomy Orion and the Dog
Are veiled; and hushed the shrunken seas;   10
The person in the Spanish cape
Tries to sit on Sweeney's knees

   Slips and pulls the table cloth
Overturns a coffee-cup,
Reorganized upon the floor
She yawns and draws a stocking up;

   The silent man in mocha brown
Sprawls at the window-sill and gapes;
The waiter brings in oranges
Bananas figs and hothouse grapes;   20

The silent vertebrate in brown
Contracts and concentrates, withdraws;
Rachel *née* Rabinovitch
Tears at the grapes with murderous paws;

She and the lady in the cape
Are suspect, thought to be in league;
Therefore the man with heavy eyes
Declines the gambit, shows fatigue,

Leaves the room and reappears
Outside the window, leaning in,   30
Branches of wistaria
Circumscribe a golden grin;

The host with someone indistinct
Converses at the door apart,
The nightingales are singing near
The Convent of the Sacred Heart,

And sang within the bloody wood
When Agamemnon cried aloud,
And let their liquid siftings fall
To stain the stiff dishonoured shroud.   40

GERONTION
(1920)

Thou hast nor youth nor age
But as it were an after dinner sleep
Dreaming of both.

Here I am, an old man in a dry month,
Being read to by a boy, waiting for rain.
I was neither at the hot gates
Nor fought in the warm rain
Nor knee deep in the salt marsh, heaving a cutlass,
Bitten by flies, fought.
My house is a decayed house,
And the jew squats on the window sill, the owner,

Spawned in some estaminet of Antwerp,
Blistered in Brussels, patched and peeled in London.   10
The goat coughs at night in the field overhead;
Rocks, moss, stonecrop, iron, merds.
The woman keeps the kitchen, makes tea,
Sneezes at evening, poking the peevish gutter.
                              I an old man,
A dull head among windy spaces.

    Signs are taken for wonders. "We would see a sign!"
The word within a word, unable to speak a word,
Swaddled with darkness. In the juvescence of the year
Came Christ the tiger   20

    In depraved May, dogwood and chestnut, flowering judas,
To be eaten, to be divided, to be drunk
Among whispers; by Mr. Silvero
With caressing hands, at Limoges
Who walked all night in the next room;

    By Hakagawa, bowing among the Titians;
By Madame de Tornquist, in the dark room
Shifting the candles; Fräulein von Kulp
Who turned in the hall, one hand on the door.
        Vacant shuttles   30
Weave the wind. I have no ghosts,
An old man in a draughty house
Under a windy knob.

    After such knowledge, what forgiveness? Think now
History has many cunning passages, contrived corridors
And issues, deceives with whispering ambitions,
Guides us by vanities. Think now
She gives when our attention is distracted
And what she gives, gives with such supple confusions
That the giving famishes the craving. Gives too late   40
What's not believed in, or if still believed,
In memory only, reconsidered passion. Gives too soon
Into weak hands, what's thought can be dispensed with
Till the refusal propagates a fear. Think
Neither fear nor courage saves us. Unnatural vices

Are fathered by our heroism. Virtues
Are forced upon us by our impudent crimes.
These tears are shaken from the wrath-bearing tree.

    The tiger springs in the new year. Us he devours. Think at last
We have not reached conclusion, when I   50
Stiffen in a rented house. Think at last
I have not made this show purposelessly
And it is not by any concitation
Of the backward devils.
I would meet you upon this honestly.
I that was near your heart was removed therefrom
To lose beauty in terror, terror in inquisition.
I have lost my passion: why should I need to keep it
Since what is kept must be adulterated?
I have lost my sight, smell, hearing, taste and touch: 60
How should I use them for your closer contact?

    These with a thousand small deliberations
Protract the profit of their chilled delirium,
Excite the membrane, when the sense has cooled,
With pungent sauces, multiply variety
In a wilderness of mirrors. What will the spider do,
Suspend its operations, will the weevil
Delay? De Bailhache, Fresca, Mrs. Cammel, whirled
Beyond the circuit of the shuddering Bear
In fractured atoms. Gull against the wind, in the windy straits
Of Belle Isle, or running on the Horn,   71
White feathers in the snow, the Gulf claims,
And an old man driven by the Trades
To a sleepy corner.

                    Tenants of the house,
Thoughts of a dry brain in a dry season.

THE WASTE LAND

(1922)

Nam Sibyllam quidem Cumis ego ipse oculis meis vidi
in ampulla pendere, et cum illi pueri dicerent: Σίβυλλα
τί θέλεις; respondebat illa: ἀποθανεῖν θέλω.

For Ezra Pound
il miglior fabbro

I. THE BURIAL OF THE DEAD

April is the cruellest month, breeding
Lilacs out of the dead land, mixing
Memory and desire, stirring
Dull roots with spring rain.
Winter kept us warm, covering
Earth in forgetful snow, feeding
A little life with dried tubers.
Summer surprised us, coming over the Starnbergersee
With a shower of rain; we stopped in the colonnade,
And went on in sunlight, into the Hofgarten,   10
And drank coffee, and talked for an hour.
Bin gar keine Russin, stamm' aus Litauen, echt deutsch.
And when we were children, staying at the archduke's,
My cousin's, he took me out on a sled,
And I was frightened. He said, Marie,
Marie, hold on tight. And down we went.
In the mountains, there you feel free.
I read, much of the night, and go south in the winter.

What are the roots that clutch, what branches grow
Out of this stony rubbish? Son of man,   20
You cannot say, or guess, for you know only
A heap of broken images, where the sun beats,
And the dead tree gives no shelter, the cricket no relief,
And the dry stone no sound of water. Only
There is shadow under this red rock,
(Come in under the shadow of this red rock),
And I will show you something different from either

Your shadow at morning striding behind you
Or your shadow at evening rising to meet you;
I will show you fear in a handful of dust.   30
> Frisch weht der Wind
> Der Heimat zu
> Mein Irisch Kind,
> Wo weilest du?
"You gave me hyacinths first a year ago;
"They called me the hyacinth girl."
—Yet when we came back, late, from the Hyacinth garden,
Your arms full, and your hair wet, I could not
Speak, and my eyes failed, I was neither
Living nor dead, and I knew nothing,   40
Looking into the heart of light, the silence.
Oed' und leer das Meer.

Madame Sosostris, famous clairvoyante,
Had a bad cold, nevertheless
Is known to be the wisest woman in Europe,
With a wicked pack of cards. Here, said she,
Is your card, the drowned Phoenician Sailor,
(Those are pearls that were his eyes. Look!)
Here is Belladonna, the Lady of the Rocks,
The lady of situations.   50
Here is the man with three staves, and here the Wheel,
And here is the one-eyed merchant, and this card,
Which is blank, is something he carries on his back,
Which I am forbidden to see. I do not find
The Hanged Man. Fear death by water.
I see crowds of people, walking round in a ring.
Thank you. If you see dear Mrs. Equitone,
Tell her I bring the horoscope myself:
One must be so careful these days.

Unreal City,   60
Under the brown fog of a winter dawn,
A crowd flowed over London Bridge, so many,
I had not thought death had undone so many.
Sighs, short and infrequent, were exhaled,
And each man fixed his eyes before his feet.
Flowed up the hill and down King William Street,

To where Saint Mary Woolnoth kept the hours
With a dead sound on the final stroke of nine.
There I saw one I knew, and stopped him, crying: "Stetson!
"You who were with me in the ships at Mylae!   70
"That corpse you planted last year in your garden,
"Has it begun to sprout? Will it bloom this year?
"Or has the sudden frost disturbed its bed?
"Oh keep the Dog far hence, that's friend to men,
"Or with his nails he'll dig it up again!
"You! hypocrite lecteur!—mon semblable,—mon frère!"

II. A GAME OF CHESS

The Chair she sat in, like a burnished throne,
Glowed on the marble, where the glass
Held up by standards wrought with fruited vines
From which a golden Cupidon peeped out   80
(Another hid his eyes behind his wing)
Doubled the flames of sevenbranched candelabra
Reflecting light upon the table as
The glitter of her jewels rose to meet it,
From satin cases poured in rich profusion;
In vials of ivory and coloured glass
Unstoppered, lurked her strange synthetic perfumes,
Unguent, powdered, or liquid—troubled, confused
And drowned the sense in odours; stirred by the air
That freshened from the window, these ascended   90
In fattening the prolonged candle-flames,
Flung their smoke into the laquearia,
Stirring the pattern on the coffered ceiling.
Huge sea-wood fed with copper
Burned green and orange, framed by the coloured stone,
In which sad light a carvèd dolphin swam.
Above the antique mantel was displayed
As though a window gave upon the sylvan scene
The change of Philomel, by the barbarous king
So rudely forced; yet there the nightingale   100
Filled all the desert with inviolable voice
And still she cried, and still the world pursues,
"Jug Jug" to dirty ears.
And other withered stumps of time

Were told upon the walls; staring forms
Leaned out, leaning, hushing the room enclosed.
Footsteps shuffled on the stair.
Under the firelight, under the brush, her hair
Spread out in fiery points
Glowed into words, then would be savagely still.   110

   "My nerves are bad to-night. Yes, bad. Stay with me.
"Speak to me. Why do you never speak. Speak.
   "What are you thinking of? What thinking? What?
"I never know what you are thinking. Think."

   I think we are in rats' alley
Where the dead men lost their bones.

   "What is that noise?"
                  The wind under the door.
"What is that noise now? What is the wind doing?"
                  Nothing again nothing.   120
                        "Do
"You know nothing? Do you see nothing? Do you remember
"Nothing?"

   I remember
Those are pearls that were his eyes.
"Are you alive, or not? Is there nothing in your head?"
                        But

O O O O that Shakespeherian Rag—
It's so elegant
So intelligent   130
"What shall I do now? What shall I do?"
"I shall rush out as I am, and walk the street
"With my hair down, so. What shall we do to-morrow?
"What shall we ever do?"
                  The hot water at ten.
And if it rains, a closed car at four.
And we shall play a game of chess,
Pressing lidless eyes and waiting for a knock upon the door.

   When Lil's husband got demobbed, I said—
I didn't mince my words, I said to her myself,   140
HURRY UP PLEASE ITS TIME

Now Albert's coming back, make yourself a bit smart.
He'll want to know what you done with that money he gave you
To get yourself some teeth. He did, I was there.
You have them all out, Lil, and get a nice set,
He said, I swear, I can't bear to look at you.
And no more can't I, I said, and think of poor Albert,
He's been in the army four years, he wants a good time,
And if you don't give it him, there's others will, I said.
Oh is there, she said. Something o' that, I said.   150
Then I'll know who to thank, she said, and give me a straight look.
HURRY UP PLEASE ITS TIME
If you don't like it you can get on with it, I said.
Others can pick and choose if you can't.
But if Albert makes off, it won't be for lack of telling.
You ought to be ashamed, I said, to look so antique.
(And her only thirty-one.)
I can't help it, she said, pulling a long face,
It's them pills I took, to bring it off, she said.
(She's had five already, and nearly died of young George.)   160
The chemist said it would be all right, but I've never been the same.
You are a proper fool, I said.
Well, if Albert won't leave you alone, there it is, I said,
What you get married for if you don't want children?
HURRY UP PLEASE ITS TIME
Well, that Sunday Albert was home, they had a hot gammon,
And they asked me in to dinner, to get the beauty of it hot—
HURRY UP PLEASE ITS TIME
HURRY UP PLEASE ITS TIME
Goonight Bill. Goonight Lou. Goonight May. Goonight.   170
Ta ta. Goonight. Goonight.
Good night, ladies, good night, sweet ladies, good night, good night.

III. THE FIRE SERMON

The river's tent is broken: the last fingers of leaf
Clutch and sink into the wet bank. The wind
Crosses the brown land, unheard. The nymphs are departed.
Sweet Thames, run softly, till I end my song.
The river bears no empty bottles, sandwich papers,
Silk handkerchiefs, cardboard boxes, cigarette ends
Or other testimony of summer nights. The nymphs are departed.

And their friends, the loitering heirs of city directors; 180
Departed, have left no addresses.
By the waters of Leman I sat down and wept . . .
Sweet Thames, run softly till I end my song,
Sweet Thames, run softly, for I speak not loud or long.
But at my back in a cold blast I hear
The rattle of the bones, and chuckle spread from ear to ear.
A rat crept softly through the vegetation
Dragging its slimy belly on the bank
While I was fishing in the dull canal
On a winter evening round behind the gashouse 190
Musing upon the king my brother's wreck
And on the king my father's death before him.
White bodies naked on the low damp ground
And bones cast in a little low dry garret,
Rattled by the rat's foot only, year to year.
But at my back from time to time I hear
The sound of horns and motors, which shall bring
Sweeney to Mrs. Porter in the spring.
O the moon shone bright on Mrs. Porter
And on her daughter 200
They wash their feet in soda water
Et O ces voix d'enfants, chantant dans la coupole!

   Twit twit twit
Jug jug jug jug jug jug
So rudely forc'd.
Tereu

   Unreal City
Under the brown fog of a winter noon
Mr. Eugenides, the Smyrna merchant
Unshaven, with a pocket full of currants 210
C.i.f. London: documents at sight,
Asked me in demotic French
To luncheon at the Cannon Street Hotel
Followed by a weekend at the Metropole.

   At the violet hour, when the eyes and back
Turned upward from the desk, when the human engine waits
Like a taxi throbbing waiting,

I Tiresias, though blind, throbbing between two lives,
Old man with wrinkled female breasts, can see
At the violet hour, the evening hour that strives   220
Homeward, and brings the sailor home from sea,
The typist home at teatime, clears her breakfast, lights
Her stove, and lays out food in tins.
Out of the window perilously spread
Her drying combinations touched by the sun's last rays,
On the divan are piled (at night her bed)
Stockings, slippers, camisoles, and stays.
I Tiresias, old man with wrinkled dugs
Perceived the scene, and foretold the rest—
I too awaited the expected guest.   230
He, the young man carbuncular, arrives,
A small house agent's clerk, with one bold stare,
One of the low on whom assurance sits
As a silk hat on a Bradford millionaire.
The time is now propitious, as he guesses,
The meal is ended, she is bored and tired,
Endeavours to engage her in caresses
Which still are unreproved, if undesired.
Flushed and decided, he assaults at once;
Exploring hands encounter no defence;   240
His vanity requires no response,
And makes a welcome of indifference.
(And I Tiresias have foresuffered all
Enacted on this same divan or bed;
I who have sat by Thebes below the wall
And walked among the lowest of the dead.)
Bestows one final patronising kiss,
And gropes his way, finding the stairs unlit . . .

   She turns and looks a moment in the glass,
Hardly aware of her departed lover;   250
Her brain allows one half-formed thought to pass:
"Well now that's done: and I'm glad it's over."
When lovely woman stoops to folly and
Paces about her room again, alone,
She smoothes her hair with automatic hand,
And puts a record on the gramophone.

"This music crept by me upon the waters"
And along the Strand, up Queen Victoria Street.
O City city, I can sometimes hear
Beside a public bar in Lower Thames Street,   260
The pleasant whining of a mandoline
And a clatter and a chatter from within
Where fishmen lounge at noon: where the walls
Of Magnus Martyr hold
Inexplicable splendour of Ionian white and gold.

   The river sweats
  Oil and tar
  The barges drift
  With the turning tide
  Red sails   270
  Wide
  To leeward, swing on the heavy spar.
  The barges wash
  Drifting logs
  Down Greenwich reach
  Past the Isle of Dogs.
    Weialala leia
    Wallala leialala

  Elizabeth and Leicester
  Beating oars   280
  The stern was formed
  A gilded shell
  Red and gold
  The brisk swell
  Rippled both shores
  Southwest wind
  Carried down stream
  The peal of bells
  White towers
    Weialala leia   290
    Wallala leialala

  "Trams and dusty trees.
  Highbury bore me. Richmond and Kew
  Undid me. By Richmond I raised my knees
  Supine on the floor of a narrow canoe."

"My feet are at Moorgate, and my heart
Under my feet. After the event *sex*
He wept. He promised 'a new start.'
I made no comment. What should I resent?" *indifference*

"On Margate Sands.   300
I can connect
Nothing with nothing.
The broken fingernails of dirty hands.
My people humble people who expect
Nothing."
                   la la
        To Carthage then I came

        Burning burning burning burning
O Lord Thou pluckest me out   *ressurection,*
O Lord Thou pluckest ——   310

burning

IV. DEATH BY WATER

conversation
Phlebas the Phoenician, a fortnight dead,
drowned fisher King
Forgot the cry of gulls, and the deep sea swell
And the profit and loss.
                   A current under sea
Picked his bones in whispers. As he rose and fell
He passed the stages of his age and youth
Entering the whirlpool. — *faith*
                   Gentile or Jew
O you who turn the wheel and look to windward,   320
Consider Phlebas, who was once handsome and tall as you.

V. WHAT THE THUNDER SAID

ressurection
After the torchlight red on sweaty faces
After the frosty silence in the gardens   *Gethsemane*
death of Christ
After the agony in stony places
The shouting and the crying
Prison and palace and reverberation
Of thunder of spring over distant mountains

He who was living is now dead
We who were living are now dying
With a little patience   330

   Here is no water but only rock
Rock and no water and the sandy road
The road winding above among the mountains
Which are mountains of rock without water
If there were water we should stop and drink
Amongst the rock one cannot stop or think
Sweat is dry and feet are in the sand
If there were only water amongst the rock
Dead mountain mouth of carious teeth that cannot spit
Here one can neither stand nor lie nor sit   340
There is not even silence in the mountains
But dry sterile thunder without rain
There is not even solitude in the mountains
But red sullen faces sneer and snarl
From doors of mudcracked houses
               If there were water
   And no rock
   If there were rock
   And also water
   And water   350
   A spring
   A pool among the rock
   If there were the sound of water only
   Not the cicada
   And dry grass singing
   But sound of water over a rock
   Where the hermit-thrush sings in the pine trees
   Drip drop drip drop drop drop drop
   But there is no water

   Who is the third who walks always beside you?   360
When I count, there are only you and I together
But when I look ahead up the white road
There is always another one walking beside you
Gliding wrapt in a brown mantle, hooded
I do not know whether a man or a woman
—But who is that on the other side of you?

What is that sound high in the air
Murmur of maternal lamentation
Who are those hooded hordes swarming
Over endless plains, stumbling in cracked earth
Ringed by the flat horizon only   370
What is the city over the mountains
Cracks and reforms and bursts in the violet air
Falling towers
Jerusalem Athens Alexandria
Vienna London
Unreal

the hallucination of destruction then the judgement comes.

A woman drew her long black hair out tight
And fiddled whisper music on those strings
And bats with baby faces in the violet light   380
Whistled, and beat their wings
And crawled head downward down a blackened wall
And upside down in air were towers
Tolling reminiscent bells, that kept the hours
And voices singing out of empty cisterns and exhausted wells.

In this decayed hole among the mountains
In the faint moonlight, the grass is singing
Over the tumbled graves, about the chapel
There is the empty chapel, only the wind's home.
It has no windows, and the door swings,   390
Dry bones can harm no one.
Only a cock stood on the rooftree   — *stops the dream*
Co co rico co co rico
In a flash of lightning. Then a damp gust
Bringing rain   — *hope, fertility*

Ganga was sunken, and the limp leaves
Waited for rain, while the black clouds
Gathered far distant, over Himavant.
The jungle crouched, humped in silence.
Then spoke the thunder   400
DA   — *God speaks*
means "give" Datta: what have we given?   —
My friend, blood shaking my heart
The awful daring of a moment's surrender   *of ourselves to christ to god*

Which an age of prudence can never retract
By this, and this only, we have existed
Which is not to be found in our obituaries
Or in memories draped by the beneficent spider
Or under seals broken by the lean solicitor
In our empty rooms   410
DA
Dayadhvam: I have heard the key
Turn in the door once and turn once only
We think of the key, each in his prison
Thinking of the key, each confirms a prison
Only at nightfall, aethereal rumours
Revive for a moment a broken Coriolanus
DA
Damyata: The boat responded
Gaily, to the hand expert with sail and oar   420
The sea was calm, your heart would have responded
Gaily, when invited, beating obedient
To controlling hands

                        I sat upon the shore
Fishing, with the arid plain behind me
Shall I at least set my lands in order?
London Bridge is falling down falling down falling down
Poi s'ascose nel foco che gli affina
Quando fiam uti chelidon—O swallow swallow
Le Prince d'Aquitaine à la tour abolie
These fragments I have shored against my ruins
Why then Ile fit you. Hieronymo's mad againe.   430
Datta. Dayadhvam. Damyata.
          Shantih   shantih   shantih

THE HOLLOW MEN
(1925)

Mistah Kurtz—he dead.

A penny for the Old Guy

I

We are the hollow men
We are the stuffed men
Leaning together
Headpiece filled with straw. Alas!
Our dried voices, when
We whisper together
Are quiet and meaningless
As wind in dry grass
Or rats' feet over broken glass
In our dry cellar   10

    Shape without form, shade without colour,
Paralyzed force, gesture without motion;

    Those who have crossed
With direct eyes, to death's other Kingdom
Remember us—if at all—not as lost
Violent souls, but only
As the hollow men
The stuffed men.

II

Eyes I dare not meet in dreams
In death's dream kingdom   20
These do not appear:
There, the eyes are
Sunlight on a broken column
There, is a tree swinging
And voices are
In the wind's singing
More distant and more solemn
Than a fading star.

Let me be no nearer
In death's dream kingdom   30
Let me also wear
Such deliberate disguises
Rat's coat, crowskin, crossed staves
In a field
Behaving as the wind behaves
No nearer—

    Not that final meeting
In the twilight kingdom

III

This is the dead land
This is cactus land   40
Here the stone images
Are raised, here they receive
The supplication of a dead man's hand
Under the twinkle of a fading star.

    Is it like this
In death's other kingdom
Waking alone
At the hour when we are
Trembling with tenderness
Lips that would kiss   50
Form prayers to broken stone.

IV

The eyes are not here
There are no eyes here
In this valley of dying stars
In this hollow valley
This broken jaw of our lost kingdoms

    In this last of meeting places
We grope together
And avoid speech
Gathered on this beach of the tumid river   60

    Sightless, unless
The eyes reappear
As the perpetual star

Multifoliate rose
Of death's twilight kingdom
The hope only
Of empty men.

v

Here we go round the prickly pear
Prickly pear prickly pear
Here we go round the prickly pear   70
At five o'clock in the morning.

   Between the idea
And the reality
Between the motion
And the act
Falls the Shadow
        For Thine is the Kingdom

   Between the conception
And the creation
Between the emotion   80
And the response
Falls the Shadow
        Life is very long

   Between the desire
And the spasm
Between the potency
And the existence
Between the essence
And the descent
Falls the Shadow   90
        For Thine is the Kingdom

   For Thine is
Life is
For Thine is the

   This is the way the world ends
This is the way the world ends
This is the way the world ends
Not with a bang but a whimper.

ASH–WEDNESDAY

(1930)

I

Because I do not hope to turn again
Because I do not hope
Because I do not hope to turn
Desiring this man's gift and that man's scope
I no longer strive to strive towards such things
(Why should the agèd eagle stretch its wings?)
Why should I mourn
The vanished power of the usual reign?

　Because I do not hope to know again
The infirm glory of the positive hour   10
Because I do not think
Because I know I shall not know
The one veritable transitory power
Because I cannot drink
There, where trees flower, and springs flow, for there is nothing again

　Because I know that time is always time
And place is always and only place
And what is actual is actual only for one time
And only for one place
I rejoice that things are as they are and   20
I renounce the blessèd face
And renounce the voice
Because I cannot hope to turn again
Consequently I rejoice, having to construct something
Upon which to rejoice

　And pray to God to have mercy upon us
And I pray that I may forget
These matters that with myself I too much discuss
Too much explain
Because I do not hope to turn again   30
Let these words answer
For what is done, not to be done again
May the judgement not be too heavy upon us

Because these wings are no longer wings to fly
But merely vans to beat the air
The air which is now thoroughly small and dry
Smaller and dryer than the will
Teach us to care and not to care
Teach us to sit still.

Pray for us sinners now and at the hour of our death   40
Pray for us now and at the hour of our death.

II

Lady, three white leopards sat under a juniper-tree
In the cool of the day, having fed to satiety
On my legs my heart my liver and that which had been contained
In the hollow round of my skull. And God said
Shall these bones live? shall these
Bones live? And that which had been contained
In the bones (which were already dry) said chirping:
Because of the goodness of this Lady
And because of her loveliness, and because   50
She honours the Virgin in meditation,
We shine with brightness. And I who am here dissembled
Proffer my deeds to oblivion, and my love
To the posterity of the desert and the fruit of the gourd.
It is this which recovers
My guts the strings of my eyes and the indigestible portions
Which the leopards reject. The Lady is withdrawn
In a white gown, to contemplation, in a white gown.
Let the whiteness of bones atone to forgetfulness.
There is no life in them. As I am forgotten   60
And would be forgotten, so I would forget
Thus devoted, concentrated in purpose. And God said
Prophesy to the wind, to the wind only for only
The wind will listen. And the bones sang chirping
With the burden of the grasshopper, saying

Lady of silences
Calm and distressed
Torn and most whole
Rose of memory
Rose of forgetfulness   70
Exhausted and life-giving

Worried reposeful
The single Rose
Is now the Garden
Where all loves end
Terminate torment
Of love unsatisfied
The greater torment
Of love satisfied
End of the endless 80
Journey to no end
Conclusion of all that
Is inconclusible
Speech without word and
Word of no speech
Grace to the Mother
For the Garden
Where all love ends.

Under a juniper-tree the bones sang, scattered and shining
We are glad to be scattered, we did little good to each other, 90
Under a tree in the cool of the day, with the blessing of sand,
Forgetting themselves and each other, united
In the quiet of the desert. This is the land which ye
Shall divide by lot. And neither division nor unity
Matters. This is the land. We have our inheritance.

III

At the first turning of the second stair
I turned and saw below
The same shape twisted on the banister
Under the vapour in the fetid air
Struggling with the devil of the stairs who wears 100
The deceitful face of hope and of despair.

At the second turning of the second stair
I left them twisting, turning below;
There were no more faces and the stair was dark,
Damp, jaggèd, like an old man's mouth drivelling, beyond repair,
Or the toothed gullet of an agèd shark.

At the first turning of the third stair
Was a slotted window bellied like the fig's fruit

And beyond the hawthorn blossom and a pasture scene
The broadbacked figure drest in blue and green   110
Enchanted the maytime with an antique flute.
Blown hair is sweet, brown hair over the mouth blown,
Lilac and brown hair;
Distraction, music of the flute, stops and steps of the mind over the third
    stair,
Fading, fading; strength beyond hope and despair
Climbing the third stair.

    Lord, I am not worthy
Lord, I am not worthy

        but speak the word only.
                            IV
Who walked between the violet and the violet   120
Who walked between
The various ranks of varied green
Going in white and blue, in Mary's colour,
Talking of trivial things
In ignorance and in knowledge of eternal dolour
Who moved among the others as they walked,
Who then made strong the fountains and made fresh the springs

    Made cool the dry rock and made firm the sand
In blue of larkspur, blue of Mary's colour,
Sovegna vos   130

    Here are the years that walk between, bearing
Away the fiddles and the flutes, restoring
One who moves in the time between sleep and waking, wearing

    White light folded, sheathed about her, folded.
The new years walk, restoring
Through a bright cloud of tears, the years, restoring
With a new verse the ancient rhyme. Redeem
The time. Redeem
The unread vision in the higher dream
While jewelled unicorns draw by the gilded hearse.   140

    The silent sister veiled in white and blue
Between the yews, behind the garden god,
Whose flute is breathless, bent her head and signed but spoke no word

But the fountain sprang up and the bird sang down
Redeem the time, redeem the dream
The token of the word unheard, unspoken

Till the wind shake a thousand whispers from the yew

And after this our exile

V

If the lost word is lost, if the spent word is spent
If the unheard, unspoken   150
Word is unspoken, unheard;
Still is the unspoken word, the Word unheard,
The Word without a word, the Word within
The world and for the world;
And the light shone in darkness and
Against the Word the unstilled world still whirled
About the centre of the silent Word.

O my people, what have I done unto thee.

Where shall the word be found, where will the word
Resound? Not here, there is not enough silence   160
Not on the sea or on the islands, not
On the mainland, in the desert or the rain land,
For those who walk in darkness
Both in the day time and in the night time
The right time and the right place are not here
No place of grace for those who avoid the face
No time to rejoice for those who walk among noise and deny the voice

Will the veiled sister pray for
Those who walk in darkness, who chose thee and oppose thee,
Those who are torn on the horn between season and season, time and
        time, between   170
Hour and hour, word and word, power and power, those who wait
In darkness? Will the veiled sister pray
For children at the gate
Who will not go away and cannot pray:
Pray for those who chose and oppose

O my people, what have I done unto thee.

Will the veiled sister between the slender
Yew trees pray for those who offend her
And are terrified and cannot surrender
And affirm before the world and deny between the rocks   180
In the last desert between the last blue rocks
The desert in the garden the garden in the desert
Of drouth, spitting from the mouth the withered apple-seed.

    O my people.

VI

Although I do not hope to turn again
Although I do not hope
Although I do not hope to turn

    Wavering between the profit and the loss
In this brief transit where the dreams cross
The dreamcrossed twilight between birth and dying   190
(Bless me father) though I do not wish to wish these things
From the wide window towards the granite shore
The white sails still fly seaward, seaward flying
Unbroken wings

    And the lost heart stiffens and rejoices
In the lost lilac and the lost sea voices
And the weak spirit quickens to rebel
For the bent golden-rod and the lost sea smell
Quickens to recover
The cry of quail and the whirling plover   200
And the blind eye creates
The empty forms between the ivory gates
And smell renews the salt savour of the sandy earth

    This is the time of tension between dying and birth
The place of solitude where three dreams cross
Between blue rocks
But when the voices shaken from the yew-tree drift away
Let the other yew be shaken and reply.

    Blessèd sister, holy mother, spirit of the fountain, spirit of the garden,
Suffer us not to mock ourselves with falsehood   210
Teach us to care and not to care

Teach us to sit still
Even among these rocks,
Our peace in His will
And even among these rocks
Sister, mother
And spirit of the river, spirit of the sea,
Suffer me not to be separated

And let my cry come unto Thee.

Archibald MacLeish
1892-

THE SILENT SLAIN
(1926)

We too, we too, descending once again
The hills of our own land, we too have heard
Far off—Ah, que ce cor a longue haleine—
The horn of Roland in the passages of Spain,
The first, the second blast, the failing third,
And with the third turned back and climbed once more
The steep road southward, and heard faint the sound
Of swords, of horses, the disastrous war,
And crossed the dark defile at last, and found
At Roncevaux upon the darkening plain   10
The dead against the dead and on the silent ground
The silent slain—

ARS POETICA
(1926)

A poem should be palpable and mute
As a globed fruit,

Dumb
As old medallions to the thumb,

Silent as the sleeve-worn stone
Of casement ledges where the moss has grown—

378

A poem should be wordless
As the flight of birds.

*

A poem should be motionless in time
As the moon climbs,   10

Leaving, as the moon releases
Twig by twig the night-entangled trees,

Leaving, as the moon behind the winter leaves,
Memory by memory the mind—

A poem should be motionless in time
As the moon climbs.

*

A poem should be equal to:
Not true.

For all the history of grief
An empty doorway and a maple leaf.   20

For love
The leaning grasses and two lights above the sea—

A poem should not mean
But be.

THE END OF THE WORLD
(1926)

Quite unexpectedly as Vasserot
The armless ambidextrian was lighting
A match between his great and second toe
And Ralph the lion was engaged in biting
The neck of Madame Sossman while the drum
Pointed, and Teeny was about to cough
In waltz-time swinging Jocko by the thumb—
Quite unexpectedly the top blew off:

And there, there overhead, there, there, hung over
Those thousands of white faces, those dazed eyes,   5
There in the starless dark the poise, the hover,
There with vast wings across the canceled skies,
There in the sudden blackness the black pall
Of nothing, nothing, nothing—nothing at all.

YOU, ANDREW MARVELL

(1930)

And here face down beneath the sun
And here upon earth's noonward height
To feel the always coming on
The always rising of the night:

To feel creep up the curving east
The earthy chill of dusk and slow
Upon those under lands the vast
And ever climbing shadow grow

And strange at Ecbatan the trees
Take leaf by leaf the evening strange   10
The flooding dark about their knees
The mountains over Persia change

And now at Kermanshah the gate
Dark empty and the withered grass
And through the twilight now the late
Few travelers in the westward pass

And Baghdad darken and the bridge
Across the silent river gone
And through Arabia the edge
Of evening widen and steal on   20

And deepen on Palmyra's street
The wheel rut in the ruined stone
And Lebanon fade out and Crete
High through the clouds and overblown

And over Sicily the air
Still flashing with the landward gulls
And loom and slowly disappear
The sails above the shadowy hulls

And Spain go under and the shore
Of Africa the gilded sand   30
And evening vanish and no more
The low pale light across that land

Nor now the long light on the sea:

And here face downward in the sun
To feel how swift how secretly
The shadow of the night comes on . . .

IMMORTAL AUTUMN

(1930)

I speak this poem now with grave and level voice
In praise of autumn, of the far-horn-winding fall.

I praise the flower-barren fields, the clouds, the tall
Unanswering branches where the wind makes sullen noise.

I praise the fall: it is the human season.
                                                Now
No more the foreign sun does meddle at our earth,
Enforce the green and bring the fallow land to birth,
Nor winter yet weigh all with silence the pine bough,

But now in autumn with the black and outcast crows
Share we the spacious world: the whispering year is gone: 10
There is more room to live now: the once secret dawn
Comes late by daylight and the dark unguarded goes.

Between the mutinous brave burning of the leaves
And winter's covering of our hearts with his deep snow
We are alone: there are no evening birds: we know
The naked moon: the tame stars circle at our eaves.

It is the human season. On this sterile air
Do words outcarry breath: the sound goes on and on.
I hear a dead man's cry from autumn long since gone.

I cry to you beyond upon this bitter air.   20

"NOT MARBLE NOR THE GILDED MONUMENTS"
For Adele

(1930)

The praisers of women in their proud and beautiful poems,
Naming the grave mouth and the hair and the eyes,
Boasted those they loved should be forever remembered:
These were lies.

The words sound but the face in the Istrian sun is forgotten.
The poet speaks but to her dead ears no more.
The sleek throat is gone—and the breast that was troubled to listen:
Shadow from door.

Therefore I will not praise your knees nor your fine walking
Telling you men shall remember your name as long   10
As lips move or breath is spent or the iron of English
Rings from a tongue.

I shall say you were young, and your arms straight, and your mouth scarlet:
I shall say you will die and none will remember you:
Your arms change, and none remember the swish of your garments,
Nor the click of your shoe.

Not with my hand's strength, not with difficult labor
Springing the obstinate words to the bones of your breast
And the stubborn line to your young stride and the breath to your breathing
And the beat to your haste   20
Shall I prevail on the hearts of unborn men to remember.

(What is a dead girl but a shadowy ghost
Or a dead man's voice but a distant and vain affirmation
Like dream words most)

Therefore I will not speak of the undying glory of women.
I will say you were young and straight and your skin fair
And you stood in the door and the sun was a shadow of leaves on your
 shoulders
And a leaf on your hair—

I will not speak of the famous beauty of dead women:
I will say the shape of a leaf lay once on your hair.   30
Till the world ends and the eyes are out and the mouths broken
Look! It is there!

POLE STAR
(1936)

Where the wheel of light is turned,
Where the axle of the night is
Turned, is motionless, where holds
And has held ancient sureness always:

Where of faring men the eyes
At oar bench at the rising bow
Have seen—torn shrouds between—the Wain
And that star's changelessness, not changing:

There upon that intent star,
Trust of wandering men, of truth   10
The most reminding witness, we
Fix our eyes also, waylost, the wanderers:

We too turn now to that star:
We too in whose trustless hearts
All truth alters and the lights
Of earth are out now turn to that star:

Liberty of man and mind
That once was mind's necessity
And made the West blaze up has burned
To bloody embers and the lamp's out: 20

Hope that was a noble flame
Has fanned to violence and feeds
On cities and the flesh of men
And chokes where unclean smoke defiles it:

Even the small spark of pride
That taught the tyrant once is dark
Where gunfire rules the starving street
And justice cheats the dead of honor:

Liberty and pride and hope—
And every guide-mark of the mind   30
That led our blindness once has vanished.
This star will not. Love's star will not.

Love that has beheld the face
A man has with a man's eyes in it
Bloody from the slugger's blows
Or heard the cold child cry for hunger—

Love that listens where the good,
The virtuous, the men of faith,
Proclaim the paradise on earth
And murder starve and burn to make it—   40

Love that cannot either sleep
Or keep rich music in the ear
Or lose itself for the wild beat
The anger in the blood makes raging—

Love that hardens into hate,
Love like hatred and as bright,
Love is that one waking light
That leads now when all others darken.

E. E. Cummings

1894-1962

A MAN WHO HAD FALLEN AMONG THIEVES
(1926)

a man who had fallen among thieves
lay by the roadside on his back
dressed in fifteenthrate ideas
wearing a round jeer for a hat

fate per a somewhat more than less
emancipated evening
had in return for consciousness
endowed him with a changeless grin

whereon a dozen staunch and leal
citizens did graze at pause   10
then fired by hypercivic zeal
sought newer pastures or because

swaddled with a frozen brook
of pinkest vomit out of eyes
which noticed nobody he looked
as if he did not care to rise

one hand did nothing on the vest
its wideflung friend clenched weakly dirt
while the mute trouserfly confessed
a button solemnly inert.   20

Brushing from whom the stiffened puke
i put him all into my arms
and staggered banged with terror through
a million billion trillion stars

SOMEWHERE I HAVE NEVER TRAVELLED,GLADLY BEYOND

(1931)

somewhere i have never travelled,gladly beyond
any experience,your eyes have their silence:
in your most frail gesture are things which enclose me,
or which i cannot touch because they are too near

your slightest look easily will unclose me
though i have closed myself as fingers,
you open always petal by petal myself as Spring opens
(touching skilfully,mysteriously)her first rose

or if your wish be to close me,i and
my life will shut very beautifully,suddenly,   10
as when the heart of this flower imagines
the snow carefully everywhere descending;

nothing which we are to perceive in this world equals
the power of your intense fragility:whose texture
compels me with the colour of its countries,
rendering death and forever with each breathing

(i do not know what it is about you that closes
and opens;only something in me understands
the voice of your eyes is deeper than all roses)
nobody,not even the rain,has such small hands   20

ANYONE LIVED IN A PRETTY HOW TOWN

(1940)

anyone lived in a pretty how town
(with up so floating many bells down)
spring summer autumn winter
he sang his didn't he danced his did.

Women and men(both little and small)
cared for anyone not at all
they sowed their isn't they reaped their same
sun moon stars rain

children guessed(but only a few
and down they forgot as up they grew   10
autumn winter spring summer)
that noone loved him more by more

when by now and tree by leaf
she laughed his joy she cried his grief
bird by snow and stir by still
anyone's any was all to her

someones married their everyones
laughed their cryings and did their dance
(sleep wake hope and then)they
said their nevers they slept their dream   20

stars rain sun moon
(and only the snow can begin to explain
how children are apt to forget to remember
with up so floating many bells down)

one day anyone died i guess
(and noone stooped to kiss his face)
busy folk buried them side by side
little by little and was by was

all by all and deep by deep
and more by more they dream their sleep   30
noone and anyone earth by april
wish by spirit and if by yes.

Women and men(both dong and ding)
summer autumn winter spring
reaped their sowing and went their came
sun moon stars rain

MY FATHER MOVED THROUGH DOOMS OF LOVE

(1940)

my father moved through dooms of love
through sames of am through haves of give,
singing each morning out of each night
my father moved through depths of height

this motionless forgetful where
turned at his glance to shining here;
that if(so timid air is firm)
under his eyes would stir and squirm

newly as from unburied which
floats the first who,his april touch   10
drove sleeping selves to swarm their fates
woke dreamers to their ghostly roots

and should some why completely weep
my father's fingers brought her sleep:
vainly no smallest voice might cry
for he could feel the mountains grow.

Lifting the valleys of the sea
my father moved through griefs of joy;
praising a forehead called the moon
singing desire into begin   20

joy was his song and joy so pure
a heart of star by him could steer
and pure so now and now so yes
the wrists of twilight would rejoice

keen as midsummer's keen beyond
conceiving mind of sun will stand,
so strictly(over utmost him
so hugely)stood my father's dream

his flesh was flesh his blood was blood:
no hungry man but wished him food;   30
no cripple wouldn't creep one mile
uphill to only see him smile.

Scorning the pomp of must and shall
my father moved through dooms of feel;
his anger was as right as rain
his pity was as green as grain

septembering arms of year extend
less humbly wealth to foe and friend
than he to foolish and to wise
offered immeasurable is   40

proudly and(by octobering flame
beckoned)as earth will downward climb,
so naked for immortal work
his shoulders marched against the dark

his sorrow was as true as bread:
no liar looked him in the head;
if every friend became his foe
he'd laugh and build a world with snow.

My father moved through theys of we,
singing each new leaf out of each tree   50
(and every child was sure that spring
danced when she heard my father sing)

then let men kill which cannot share,
let blood and flesh be mud and mire,
scheming imagine,passion willed,
freedom a drug that's bought and sold

giving to steal and cruel kind,
a heart to fear,to doubt a mind,
to differ a disease of same,
conform the pinnacle of am   60

though dull were all we taste as bright,
bitter all utterly things sweet,
maggoty minus and dumb death
all we inherit,all bequeath

and nothing quite so least as truth
—i say though hate were why men breathe—

because my father lived his soul
love is the whole and more than all

PITY THIS BUSY MONSTER,MANUNKIND
(1944)

pity this busy monster,manunkind,

not. Progress is a comfortable disease:
your victim(death and life safely beyond)

plays with the bigness of his littleness
—electrons deify one razorblade
into a mountainrange;lenses extend

unwish through curving wherewhen till unwish
returns on its unself.
                    A world of made
is not a world of born—pity poor flesh

and trees,poor stars and stones,but never this   10
fine specimen of hypermagical

ultraomnipotence. We doctors know

a hopeless case if—listen:there's a hell
of a good universe next door;let's go

Hart Crane
1899-1932

BLACK TAMBOURINE
(1926)

The interests of a black man in a cellar
Mark tardy judgment on the world's closed door.
Gnats toss in the shadow of a bottle,
And a roach spans a crevice in the floor.

Æsop, driven to pondering, found
Heaven with the tortoise and the hare;
Fox brush and sow ear top his grave
And mingling incantations on the air.

The black man, forlorn in the cellar,
Wanders in some mid-kingdom, dark, that lies,   10
Between his tambourine, stuck on the wall,
And, in Africa, a carcass quick with flies.

PRAISE FOR AN URN
In Memoriam: Ernest Nelson

(1926)

It was a kind and northern face
That mingled in such exile guise
The everlasting eyes of Pierrot
And, of Gargantua, the laughter.

His thoughts, delivered to me
From the white coverlet and pillow,
I see now, were inheritances—
Delicate riders of the storm.

The slant moon on the slanting hill
Once moved us toward presentiments   10
Of what the dead keep, living still,
And such assessments of the soul

As, perched in the crematory lobby,
The insistent clock commented on,
Touching as well upon our praise
Of glories proper to the time.

Still, having in mind gold hair,
I cannot see that broken brow
And miss the dry sound of bees
Stretching across a lucid space.   20

Scatter these well-meant idioms
Into the smoky spring that fills
The suburbs, where they will be lost.
They are no trophies of the sun.

REPOSE OF RIVERS
(1926)

The willows carried a slow sound,
A sarabande the wind mowed on the mead.
I could never remember
That seething, steady leveling of the marshes
Till age had brought me to the sea.

Flags, weeds. And remembrance of steep alcoves
Where cypresses shared the noon's
Tyranny; they drew me into hades almost.
And mammoth turtles climbing sulphur dreams
Yielded, while sun-silt rippled them   10
Asunder . . .

How much I would have bartered! the black gorge
And all the singular nestings in the hills
Where beavers learn stitch and tooth.
The pond I entered once and quickly fled—
I remember now its singing willow rim.

And finally, in that memory all things nurse;
After the city that I finally passed
With scalding unguents spread and smoking darts
The monsoon cut across the delta   20
At gulf gates . . . There, beyond the dykes

I heard wind flaking sapphire, like this summer,
And willows could not hold more steady sound.

AT MELVILLE'S TOMB
(1926)

Often beneath the wave, wide from this ledge
The dice of drowned men's bones he saw bequeath
An embassy. Their numbers as he watched,
Beat on the dusty shore and were obscured.

And wrecks passed without sound of bells,
The calyx of death's bounty giving back
A scattered chapter, livid hieroglyph,
The portent wound in corridors of shells.

Then in the circuit calm of one vast coil,
Its lashings charmed and malice reconciled,   10
Frosted eyes there were that lifted altars;
And silent answers crept across the stars.

Compass, quadrant and sextant contrive
No farther tides . . . High in the azure steeps
Monody shall not wake the mariner.
This fabulous shadow only the sea keeps.

VOYAGES II

(1926)

And yet this great wink of eternity,
Of rimless floods, unfettered leewardings,
Samite sheeted and processioned where
Her undinal vast belly moonward bends,
Laughing the wrapt inflections of our love;

Take this Sea, whose diapason knells
On scrolls of silver snowy sentences,
The sceptred terror of whose sessions rends
As her demeanors motion well or ill,
All but the pieties of lovers' hands.   10

And onward, as bells off San Salvador
Salute the crocus lustres of the stars,
In these poinsettia meadows of her tides,—
Adagios of islands, O my Prodigal,
Complete the dark confessions her veins spell.

Mark how her turning shoulders wind the hours,
And hasten while her penniless rich palms
Pass superscription of bent foam and wave,—
Hasten, while they are true,—sleep, death, desire,
Close round one instant in one floating flower.   20

Bind us in time, O Seasons clear, and awe.
O minstrel galleons of Carib fire,
Bequeath us to no earthly shore until
Is answered in the vortex of our grave
The seal's wide spindrift gaze toward paradise.

TO BROOKLYN BRIDGE
(Proem to *The Bridge*)

(1930)

[handwritten: principle of liberty]

How many dawns, chill from his rippling rest
The seagull's wings shall dip and pivot him,
Shedding white rings of tumult, building high
Over the chained bay waters Liberty—

Then, with inviolate curve, forsake our eyes *[handwritten: our work with beauty]*
As apparitional as sails that cross
Some page of figures to be filed away;
—Till elevators drop us from our day . . .

I think of cinemas, panoramic sleights *[handwritten: movies move]*
With multitudes bent toward some flashing scene *[handwritten: don't stop + give]*   10
Never disclosed, but hastened to again, *[handwritten: message]*
Foretold to other eyes on the same screen;

And Thee, across the harbor, silver-paced *[handwritten: the bridge saw]*
As though the sun took step of thee, yet left *[handwritten: is re notebook]*
Some motion ever unspent in thy stride,—
Implicitly thy freedom staying thee!

Out of some subway scuttle, cell or loft
A bedlamite speeds to thy parapets,
Tilting there momently, shrill shirt ballooning,
A jest falls from the speechless caravan.   20

Down Wall, from girder into street noon leaks,
A rip-tooth of the sky's acetylene;
All afternoon the cloud-flown derricks turn . . .
Thy cables breathe the North Atlantic still.

And obscure as that heaven of the Jews,
Thy guerdon . . . Accolade thou dost bestow
Of anonymity time cannot raise:
Vibrant reprieve and pardon thou dost show.

O harp and altar, of the fury fused, *[handwritten: creative imagination]*
(How could mere toil align thy choiring strings!)   30

Terrific threshold of the prophet's pledge,
Prayer of pariah, and the lover's cry,—

Again the traffic lights that skim thy swift
Unfractioned idiom, immaculate sigh of stars,
Beading thy path—condense eternity:
And we have seen night lifted in thine arms.

Under thy shadow by the piers I waited;
Only in darkness is thy shadow clear.
The City's fiery parcels all undone,
Already snow submerges an iron year . . .   40

O Sleepless as the river under thee,
Vaulting the sea, the prairies' dreaming sod,
Unto us lowliest sometime sweep, descend
And of the curveship lend a myth to God.

THE RIVER
(From *The Bridge*)

(1930)

Stick your patent name on a signboard
brother—all over—going west—young man   . . . and past
Tintex—Japalac—Certain-teed Overalls ads   the din and
                                            slogans of
and lands sakes! under the new playbill ripped   the year—
in the guaranteed corner—see Bert Williams what?
Minstrels when you steal a chicken just
save me the wing for if it isn't
Erie it ain't for miles around a
Mazda—and the telegraphic night coming on Thomas

a Ediford—and whistling down the tracks   10
a headlight rushing with the sound—can you
imagine—while an EXPRESS makes time like
SCIENCE—COMMERCE and the HOLYGHOST
RADIO ROARS IN EVERY HOME WE HAVE THE NORTHPOLE
WALLSTREET AND VIRGINBIRTH WITHOUT STONES OR
WIRES OR EVEN RUNNing brooks connecting ears
and no more sermons windows flashing roar
Breathtaking—as you like it . . . eh?

                    So the 20th Century—so   20
whizzed the Limited—roared by and left
three men, still hungry on the tracks, ploddingly
watching the tail lights wizen and converge, slip-
ping gimleted and neatly out of sight.

                    *

The last bear, shot drinking in the Dakotas
Loped under wires that span the mountain stream.
Keen instruments, strung to a vast precision
Bind town to town and dream to ticking dream.
But some men take their liquor slow—and count
—Though they'll confess no rosary nor clue—
The river's minute by the far brook's year.   30
Under a world of whistles, wires and steam
Caboose-like they go ruminating through
Ohio, Indiana—blind baggage—
To Cheyenne tagging . . . Maybe Kalamazoo.

Time's rendings, time's blendings they construe
As final reckonings of fire and snow;
Strange bird-wit, like the elemental gist
Of unwalled winds they offer, singing low
My Old Kentucky Home and *Casey Jones,*
Some Sunny Day. I heard a road-gang chanting so.   40
And afterwards, who had a colt's eyes—one said,
"Jesus! Oh I remember watermelon days!" And sped
High in a cloud of merriment, recalled
"—And when my Aunt Sally Simpson smiled," he drawled—
"It was almost Louisiana, long ago."

"There's no place like Booneville though, Buddy,"
One said, excising a last burr from his vest,
"—For early trouting." Then peering in the can,
"—But I kept on the tracks." Possessed, resigned,
He trod the fire down pensively and grinned,   50
Spreading dry shingles of a beard. . . .

                    Behind
My father's cannery works I used to see
Rail-squatters ranged in nomad raillery,

The ancient men—wifeless or runaway
Hobo-trekkers that forever search
An empire wilderness of freight and rails.
—Each seemed a child, like me, on a loose perch,
Holding to childhood like some termless play.
John, Jake or Charley, hopping the slow freight   60
—Memphis to Tallahassee—riding the rods,
Blind fists of nothing, humpty-dumpty clods.

Yet they touch something like a key perhaps.
From pole to pole across the hills, the states
—They know a body under the wide rain;
Youngsters with eyes like fjords, old reprobates
With racetrack jargon,—dotting immensity
They lurk across her, knowing her yonder breast
Snow-silvered, sumac-stained or smoky blue—
Is past the valley-sleepers, south or west.   70
—As I have trod the rumorous midnights, too,

And past the circuit of the lamp's thin flame
(O Nights that brought me to her body bare!)
Have dreamed beyond the print that bound her name.
Trains sounding the long blizzards out—I heard
Wail into distances I knew were hers.
Papooses crying on the wind's long mane
Screamed redskin dynasties that fled the brain,
—Dead echoes! But I knew her body there,
Time like a serpent down her shoulder, dark,   80
And space, an eaglet's wing, laid on her hair.

Under the Ozarks, domed by Iron Mountain,
The old gods of the rain lie wrapped in pools
Where eyeless fish curvet a sunken fountain
And re-descend with corn from querulous crows.
Such pilferings make up their timeless eatage,
Propitiate them for their timber torn
By iron, iron—always the iron dealt cleavage!
They doze now, below axe and powder horn.

And Pullman breakfasters glide glistening steel   90
From tunnel into field—iron strides the dew—
Straddles the hill, a dance of wheel on wheel.

You have a half-hour's wait at Siskiyou,
Or stay the night and take the next train through.
Southward, near Cairo passing, you can see
The Ohio merging,—borne down Tennessee;
And if it's summer and the sun's in dusk
Maybe the breeze will lift the River's musk
—As though the waters breathed that you might know
Memphis Johnny, Steamboat Bill, Missouri Joe.   100
Oh, lean from the window, if the train slows down,
As though you touched hands with some ancient clown,
—A little while gaze absently below
And hum *Deep River* with them while they go.

Yes, turn again and sniff once more—look see,
O Sheriff, Brakeman and Authority—
Hitch up your pants and crunch another quid,
For you, too, feed the River timelessly.
And few evade full measure of their fate;
Always they smile out eerily what they seem.   110
I could believe he joked at heaven's gate—
Dan Midland—jolted from the cold brake-beam.

Down, down—born pioneers in time's despite,
Grimed tributaries to an ancient flow—
They win no frontier by their wayward plight,
But drift in stillness, as from Jordan's brow.

You will not hear it as the sea; even stone
Is not more hushed by gravity . . . But slow,
As loth to take more tribute—sliding prone
Like one whose eyes were buried long ago   120

The River, spreading, flows—and spends your dream.
What are you, lost within this tideless spell?
You are your father's father, and the stream—
A liquid theme that floating niggers swell.

Damp tonnage and alluvial march of days—
Nights turbid, vascular with silted shale
And roots surrendered down of moraine clays:
The Mississippi drinks the farthest dale.

O quarrying passion, undertowed sunlight!
The basalt surface drags a jungle grace   *130*
Ochreous and lynx-barred in lengthening might;
Patience! and you shall reach the biding place!

Over De Soto's bones the freighted floors
Throb past the City storied of three thrones.
Down two more turns the Mississippi pours
(Anon tall ironsides up from salt lagoons)

And flows within itself, heaps itself free.
All fades but one thin skyline 'round . . . Ahead
No embrace opens but the stinging sea;
The River lifts itself from its long bed,   *140*

Poised wholly on its dream, a mustard glow
Tortured with history, its one will—flow!
—The Passion spreads in wide tongues, choked and slow,
Meeting the Gulf, hosannas silently below.

THE HURRICANE

(1933)

Lo, Lord, Thou ridest!
Lord, Lord, Thy swifting heart

Naught stayeth, naught now bideth
But's smithereened apart!

Ay! Scripture flee'th stone!
Milk-bright, Thy chisel wind

Rescindeth flesh from bone
To quivering whittlings thinned—

Swept—whistling straw! Battered,
Lord, e'en boulders now out-leap   *10*

Rock sockets, levin-lathered!
Nor, Lord, may worm out-deep

Thy drum's gambade, its plunge abscond!
Lord God, while summits crashing

Whip sea-kelp screaming on blond
Sky-seethe, high heaven dashing—

Thou ridest to the door, Lord!
Thou bidest wall nor floor, Lord!

THE BROKEN TOWER
(1933)

The bell-rope that gathers God at dawn
Dispatches me as though I dropped down the knell
Of a spent day—to wander the cathedral lawn
From pit to crucifix, feet chill on steps from hell.

Have you not heard, have you not seen that corps
Of shadows in the tower, whose shoulders sway
Antiphonal carillons launched before
The stars are caught and hived in the sun's ray?

The bells, I say, the bells break down their tower;
And swing I know not where. Their tongues engrave   10
Membrane through marrow, my long-scattered score
Of broken intervals. . . . And I, their sexton slave!

Oval encyclicals in canyons heaping
The impasse high with choir. Banked voices slain!
Pagodas, campaniles with reveilles outleaping—
O terraced echoes prostrate on the plain! . . .

And so it was I entered the broken world
To trace the visionary company of love, its voice
An instant in the wind (I know not whither hurled)
But not for long to hold each desperate choice.   20

My word I poured. But was it cognate, scored
Of that tribunal monarch of the air
Whose thigh embronzes earth, strikes crystal Word
In wounds pledged once to hope—cleft to despair?

The steep encroachments of my blood left me
No answer (could blood hold such a lofty tower
As flings the question true?)—or is it she
Whose sweet mortality stirs latent power?—

And through whose pulse I hear, counting the strokes
My veins recall and add, revived and sure   30
The angelus of wars my chest evokes:
What I hold healed, original now, and pure . . .

And builds, within, a tower that is not stone
(Not stone can jacket heaven)—but slip
Of pebbles—visible wings of silence sown
In azure circles, widening as they dip

The matrix of the heart, lift down the eye
That shrines the quiet lake and swells a tower . . .
The commodious, tall decorum of that sky
Unseals her earth, and lifts love in its shower.   40

Theodore Roethke
1908-1964

OPEN HOUSE
(1941)

My secrets cry aloud.
I have no need for tongue.
My heart keeps open house,
My doors are widely swung.
An epic of the eyes
My love, with no disguise.

My truths are all foreknown,
This anguish self-revealed.
I'm naked to the bone,
With nakedness my shield.   10
Myself is what I wear:
I keep the spirit spare.

The anger will endure,
The deed will speak the truth
In language strict and pure.
I stop the lying mouth:
Rage warps my clearest cry
To witless agony.

MOSS–GATHERING
(1948)

To loosen with all ten fingers held wide and limber
And lift up a patch, dark-green, the kind for lining cemetery baskets,
Thick and cushiony, like an old-fashioned door-mat,
The crumbling small hollow sticks on the underside mixed with roots,
And wintergreen berries and leaves still stuck to the top,—
That was moss-gathering.
But something always went out of me when I dug loose those carpets
Of green, or plunged to my elbows in the spongy yellowish moss of the
    marshes:
And afterwards I always felt mean, jogging back over the logging road,
As if I had broken the natural order of things in that swampland;   10
Disturbed some rhythm, old and of vast importance,
By pulling off flesh from the living planet;
As if I had committed, against the whole scheme of life, a desecration.

DOLOR
(1948)

I have known the inexorable sadness of pencils,
Neat in their boxes, dolor of pad and paper-weight,
All the misery of manila folders and mucilage,
Desolation in immaculate public places,
Lonely reception room, lavatory, switchboard,
The unalterable pathos of basin and pitcher,
Ritual of multigraph, paper-clip, comma,
Endless duplication of lives and objects.
And I have seen dust from the walls of institutions,
Finer than flour, alive, more dangerous than silica,   10
Sift, almost invisible, through long afternoons of tedium,
Dropping a fine film on nails and delicate eyebrows,
Glazing the pale hair, the duplicate gray standard faces.

THE LOST SON

(1948)

1 THE FLIGHT

inner psychology
without values

At Woodlawn I heard the dead cry:
cemetary
I was lulled by the slamming of iron,
A slow drip over stones,   *sinister*
symbolistic Toads brooding in wells.
evil
All the leaves stuck out their tongues; — *hostile nature*
I shook the softening chalk of my bones,
Saying,
Snail, snail, glister me forward,
Bird, soft-sigh me home.   (*nature help me!*)
Worm, be with me.   10
This is my hard time.

Fished in an old wound, *a old solutions of problems*
The soft pond of repose;
Nothing nibbled my line,
Not even the minnows came. *not smallest help.*

Sat in an empty house
Watching shadows crawl,
Scratching.
There was one fly. *death*

& prayer

Voice, come out of the silence.   20
Say something.
Appear in the form of a spider *death*
Or a moth beating the curtain.
intelligence

Tell me: *communication   imperative mood*
Which is the way I take;
Out of what door do I go,   *metaphysical questions*
Where and to whom?

Dark hollows said, lee to the wind,
The moon said, back of an eel,
The salt said, look by the sea,   30

Your tears are not enough praise,
You will find no comfort here,
In the kingdom of bang and blab. *nonsense*
                                shows psych.
Running lightly over spongy ground,   *discontent.*
Past the pasture of flat stones,   *not helpful*
The three elms, *no ressurectional help-ironic*
The sheep strewn on a field, *chaos*
Over a rickety bridge *insecurity symbol*
Toward the quick-water, wrinkling and rippling.

Hunting along the river,   40
Down among the rubbish, the bug-riddled foliage,
By the muddy pond-edge, by the bog-holes,
By the shrunken lake, hunting, in the heat of summer.

                            hallucination
The shape of a rat?   *failure to identity*
    It's bigger than that.
    It's less than a leg ✓
    And more than a nose,
    Just under the water
    It usually goes.

Is it soft like a mouse?   50
Can it wrinkle its nose?
Could it come in the house
On the tips of its toes? \   *doesn't know*

    Take the skin of a cat ✓
    And the back of an eel,
    Then roll them in grease,—
    That's the way it would feel.

    It's sleek as an otter
    With wide webby toes
    Just under the water   60
    It usually goes.

        2 THE PIT *womb female symbol)*
                sources   *source of life & death*
Where do the roots go?
    Look down under the leaves.
Who put the moss there? *creationist question*

These stones have been here too long.
Who stunned the dirt into noise? *light*
   Ask the mole, he knows. *father figure*
I feel the slime of a wet nest. *birth, mother*
   Beware Mother Mildew. *unhealthy / nevs back to womb*
Nibble again, fish nerves.   70

3 THE GIBBER — *ish unintelligable world*

At the wood's mouth,
By the cave's door,
I listened to something
I had heard before.

Dogs of the groin *male figure against him*
Barked and howled,
The sun was against me,
The moon would not have me. *mother figure*

The weeds whined,
The snakes cried,   80
The cows and briars
Said to me: Die.

What a small song. What slow clouds. What dark water.
quote Job Hath the rain a father? All the caves are ice. Only the
     snow's here.
theme — I'm cold. I'm cold all over. Rub me in father and mother.
Fear was my father, Father Fear.
His look drained the stones.
orgasm

    What gliding shape
    Beckoning through halls,
    Stood poised on the stair,   90
    Fell dreamily down?

    From the mouths of jugs *vaginal*
    Perched on many shelves,
    I saw substance flowing *sperm*
    That cold morning.

Like a slither of eels   *scene of birth*
That watery cheek
As my own tongue kissed
My lips awake.

chaos of mind

Is this the storm's heart? The ground is unstilling itself.
My veins are running nowhere. Do the bones cast out
        their fire?   101
Is the seed leaving the old bed? These buds are live as
        birds.
Where, where are the tears of the world?
Let the kisses resound, flat like a butcher's palm;
Let the gestures freeze; our doom is already decided.
All the windows are burning! What's left of my life?
I want the old rage, the lash of primordial milk!
Good-by, good-by, old stones, the time-order is going,
I have married my hands to perpetual agitation,
I run, I run to the whistle of money.   110

capitalism — Money money money
Water water water

scenic detail

How cool the grass is.
Has the bird left?
The stalk still sways.
Has the worm a shadow?
What do the clouds say?

first helpful sign

— These sweeps of light undo me.
Look, look, the ditch is running white!
I've more veins than a tree!   120
Kiss me, ashes, I'm falling through a dark swirl.
                            psychic rebirth

4   THE RETURN — *recovery of sanity*

realistic symbol

The way to the boiler was dark,
Dark all the way,
Over slippery cinders
Through the long greenhouse. — *life*
        christ hope

The roses kept breathing in the dark.
They had many mouths to breathe with.

My knees made little winds underneath
Where the weeds slept.

There was always a single light   130
Swinging by the fire-pit,
Where the fireman pulled out roses,
The big roses, the big bloody clinkers.

Once I stayed all night.
The light in the morning came slowly over the white
Snow. ressurection
There were many kinds of cool
Air.
Then came steam.

Pipe-knock.   in grean house   140
fathapipe smokes. return of father
Scurry of warm over small plants.
Ordnung! ordnung!
heavenly — Papa is coming!
+ earthy

A fine haze moved off the leaves;
Frost melted on far panes;
The rose, the chrysanthemum turned toward the
        light.
Even the hushed forms, the bent yellowy weeds
Moved in a slow up-sway.

5

It was beginning winter,
An in-between time,   150
The landscape still partly brown:
The bones of weeds kept swinging in the wind,
Above the blue snow.

It was beginning winter.
The light moved slowly over the frozen field,
Over the dry seed-crowns,
The beautiful surviving bones
Swinging in the wind.

Light traveled over the field;
Stayed.   160
The weeds stopped swinging.
The mind moved, not alone,
Through the clear air, in the silence.

Was it light?
Was it light within?
Was it light within light?   *found light*
Stillness becoming alive,
Yet still?

A lively understandable spirit
Once entertained you.   170
It will come again.
Be still.
Wait.

FOUR FOR SIR JOHN DAVIES

(1953)

I

THE DANCE

Is that dance slowing in the mind of man
That made him think the universe could hum?
The great wheel turns its axle when it can;
I need a place to sing, and dancing-room,
And I have made a promise to my ears
I'll sing and whistle romping with the bears.

For they are all my friends: I saw one slide
Down a steep hillside on a cake of ice,—
Or was that in a book? I think with pride:
A caged bear rarely does the same thing twice   10
In the same way: O watch his body sway!—
This animal remembering to be gay.

I tried to fling my shadow at the moon,
The while my blood leaped with a wordless song.
Though dancing needs a master, I had none

To teach my toes to listen to my tongue.
But what I learned there, dancing all alone,
Was not the joyless motion of a stone.

I take this cadence from a man named Yeats;
I take it, and I give it back again: 20
For other tunes and other wanton beats
Have tossed my heart and fiddled through my brain.
Yes, I was dancing-mad, and how
That came to be the bears and Yeats would know.

II

THE PARTNER

Between such animal and human heat
I find myself perplexed. What is desire?—
The impulse to make someone else complete?
That woman would set sodden straw on fire.
Was I the servant of a sovereign wish,
Or ladle rattling in an empty dish?   30

We played a measure with commingled feet:
The lively dead had taught us to be fond.
Who can embrace the body of his fate?
Light altered light along the living ground.
She kissed me close, and then did something else.
My marrow beat as wildly as my pulse.

I'd say it to my horse: we live beyond
Our outer skin. Who's whistling up my sleeve?
I see a heron prancing in his pond;
I know a dance the elephants believe.   40
The living all assemble! What's the cue?—
Do what the clumsy partner wants to do!

Things loll and loiter. Who condones the lost?
This joy outleaps the dog. Who cares? Who cares?
I gave her kisses back, and woke a ghost.
O what lewd music crept into our ears!
The body and the soul know how to play
In that dark world where gods have lost their way.

III

THE WRAITH

Incomprehensible gaiety and dread
Attended what we did. Behind, before,   50
Lay all the lonely pastures of the dead;
The spirit and the flesh cried out for more.
We two, together, on a darkening day
Took arms against our own obscurity.

Did each become the other in that play?
She laughed me out, and then she laughed me in;
In the deep middle of ourselves we lay;
When glory failed, we danced upon a pin.
The valley rocked beneath the granite hill;
Our souls looked forth, and the great day stood still.   60

There was a body, and it cast a spell,—
God pity those but wanton to the knees,—
The flesh can make the spirit visible;
We woke to find the moonlight on our toes.
In the rich weather of a dappled wood
We played with dark and light as children should.

What shape leaped forward at the sensual cry?—
Sea-beast or bird flung toward the ravaged shore?
Did space shake off an angel with a sigh?
We rose to meet the moon, and saw no more.   70
It was and was not she, a shape alone,
Impaled on light, and whirling slowly down.

IV

THE VIGIL

Dante attained the purgatorial hill,
Trembled at hidden virtue without flaw,
Shook with a mighty power beyond his will,—
Did Beatrice deny what Dante saw?
All lovers live by longing, and endure:
Summon a vision and declare it pure.

Though everything's astonishment at last,
Who leaps to heaven at a single bound?   80
The links were soft between us; still, we kissed;
We undid chaos to a curious sound:
The waves broke easy, cried to me in white;
Her look was morning in the dying light.

The visible obscures. But who knows when?
Things have their thought: they are the shards of me;
I thought that once, and thought comes round again;
Rapt, we leaned forth with what we could not see.
We danced to shining; mocked before the black
And shapeless night that made no answer back.   90

The world is for the living. Who are they?
We dared the dark to reach the white and warm.
She was the wind when wind was in my way;
Alive at noon, I perished in her form.
Who rise from flesh to spirit know the fall:
The word outleaps the world, and light is all.

THE WAKING
(1953)

I wake to sleep, and take my waking slow.
I feel my fate in what I cannot fear.
I learn by going where I have to go.

We think by feeling. What is there to know?
I hear my being dance from ear to ear.
I wake to sleep, and take my waking slow.

Of those so close beside me, which are you?
God bless the Ground! I shall walk softly there,
And learn by going where I have to go.

Light takes the Tree; but who can tell us how?   10
The lowly worm climbs up a winding stair;
I wake to sleep, and take my waking slow.

Great Nature has another thing to do
To you and me; so take the lively air,
And, lovely, learn by going where to go.

This shaking keeps me steady. I should know.
What falls away is always. And is near.
I wake to sleep, and take my waking slow.
I learn by going where I have to go.

Karl Shapiro
1913-

THE DOME OF SUNDAY
(1942)

With focus sharp as Flemish-painted face
In film of varnish brightly fixed
And through a polished hand-lens deeply seen,
Sunday at noon through hyaline thin air
Sees down the street,
And in the camera of my eye depicts
Row-houses and row-lives:
Glass after glass, door after door the same,
Face after face the same, the same,
The brutal visibility the same;   10

As if one life emerging from one house
Would pause, a single image caught between
Two facing mirrors where vision multiplies
Beyond perspective,
A silent clatter in the high-speed eye
Spinning out photo-circulars of sight.

I see slip to the curb the long machines
Out of whose warm and windowed rooms pirouette
Shellacked with silk and light
The hard legs of our women.   20
Our women are one woman, dressed in black.
The carmine printed mouth
And cheeks as soft as muslin-glass belong

Outright to one dark dressy man,
Merely a swagger at her curvy side.
This is their visit to themselves:
All day from porch to porch they weave
A nonsense pattern through the even glare,
Stealing in surfaces
Cold vulgar glances at themselves.   30

And high up in the heated room all day
I wait behind the plate glass pane for one,
Hot as a voyeur for a glimpse of one,
The vision to blot out this woman's sheen;
All day my sight records expensively
Row-houses and row-lives.

But nothing happens; no diagonal
With melting shadow falls across the curb:
Neither the blinded negress lurching through fatigue,
Nor exiles bleeding from their pores,
Nor that bright bomb slipped lightly from its rack   40
To splinter every silvered glass and crystal prism,
Witch-bowl and perfume bottle
And billion candle-power dressing-bulb,
No direct hit to smash the shatter-proof
And lodge at last the quivering needle
Clean in the eye of one who stands transfixed
In fascination of her brightness.

THE POTOMAC

(1942)

The thin Potomac scarcely moves
But to divide Virginia from today;
    Rider, whichever is your way
You go due south and neither South improves;
Not this, of fractured columns and queer rents
    And rags that charm the nationalist,
Not that, the axle of the continents,
Nor the thin sky that flows unprejudiced
This side and that, cleansing the poisoned breath.

For Thomas died a Georgian death   10
And now the legion bones of Arlington
    Laid out in marble alphabets
Stare on the great tombs of the capitol
    Where heroes calcified and cool
    Ponder the soldier named Unknown
Whose lips are guarded with live bayonets.

    Yet he shall speak though sentries walk
And columns with their cold Corinthian stalk
    Shed gold-dust pollen on Brazil
    To turn the world to Roman chalk;   20
Yet he shall speak, yet he shall speak
    Whose sulphur lit the flood-lit Dome,
    Whose hands were never in the kill,
Whose will was furrows of Virginia loam.

But not like London blown apart by boys
Who learned the books of love in English schools,
His name shall strike the fluted columns down;
These shall lie buried deep as fifty Troys,
The money fade like leaves from green to brown,
And embassies dissolve to molecules.   30

NOSTALGIA

(1942)

My soul stands at the window of my room,
    And I ten thousand miles away;
My days are filled with Ocean's sound of doom,
    Salt and cloud and the bitter spray.
Let the wind blow, for many a man shall die.

My selfish youth, my books with gilded edge,
    Knowledge and all gaze down the street;
The potted plants upon the window ledge
    Gaze down with selfish lives and sweet.
Let the wind blow, for many a man shall die.   10

My night is now her day, my day her night,
  So I lie down, and so I rise;
The sun burns close, the star is losing height,
  The clock is hunted down the skies.
Let the wind blow, for many a man shall die.

Truly a pin can make the memory bleed,
  A word explode the inward mind
And turn the skulls and flowers never freed
  Into the air, no longer blind.
Let the wind blow, for many a man shall die.   20

Laughter and grief join hands. Always the heart
  Clumps in the breast with heavy stride;
The face grows lined and wrinkled like a chart,
  The eyes bloodshot with tears and tide.
Let the wind blow, for many a man shall die.

ELEGY FOR A DEAD SOLDIER
(1944)

I

A white sheet on the tail-gate of a truck
Becomes an altar; two small candlesticks
Sputter at each side of the crucifix
Laid round with flowers brighter than the blood,
Red as the red of our apocalypse,
Hibiscus that a marching man will pluck
To stick into his rifle or his hat,
And great blue morning-glories pale as lips
That shall no longer taste or kiss or swear.
The wind begins a low magnificat,   10
The chaplain chats, the palmtrees swirl their hair,
The columns come together through the mud.

II

We too are ashes as we watch and hear
The psalm, the sorrow, and the simple praise
Of one whose promised thoughts of other days
Were such as ours, but now wholly destroyed,
The service record of his youth wiped out,

His dream dispersed by shot, must disappear.
What can we feel but wonder at a loss
That seems to point at nothing but the doubt   20
Which flirts our sense of luck into the ditch?
Reader of Paul who prays beside this fosse,
Shall we believe our eyes or legends rich
With glory and rebirth beyond the void?

III

For this comrade is dead, dead in the war,
A young man out of millions yet to live,
One cut away from all that war can give,
Freedom of self and peace to wander free.
Who mourns in all this sober multitude
Who did not feel the bite of it before   30
The bullet found its aim? This worthy flesh,
This boy laid in a coffin and reviewed—
Who has not wrapped himself in this same flag,
Heard the light fall of dirt, his wound still fresh,
Felt his eyes closed, and heard the distant brag
Of the last volley of humanity?

IV

By chance I saw him die, stretched on the ground,
A tattooed arm lifted to take the blood
Of someone else sealed in a tin. I stood
During the last delirium that stays   40
The intelligence a tiny moment more,
And then the strangulation, the last sound.
The end was sudden, like a foolish play,
A stupid fool slamming a foolish door,
The absurd catastrophe, half-prearranged,
And all the decisive things still left to say.
So we disbanded, angrier and unchanged,
Sick with the utter silence of dispraise.

V

We ask for no statistics of the killed,
For nothing political impinges on   50
This single casualty, or all those gone,
Missing or healing, sinking or dispersed,
Hundreds of thousands counted, millions lost.
More than an accident and less than willed

Is every fall, and this one like the rest.
However others calculate the cost,
To us the final aggregate is *one,*
One with a name, one transferred to the blest;
And though another stoops and takes the gun,
We cannot add the second to the first.   60

VI

I would not speak for him who could not speak
Unless my fear were true: he was not wronged,
He knew to which decision he belonged
But let it choose itself. Ripe in instinct,
Neither the victim nor the volunteer,
He followed, and the leaders could not seek
Beyond the followers. Much of this he knew;
The journey was a detour that would steer
Into the Lincoln Highway of a land
Remorselessly improved, excited, new,   70
And that was what he wanted. He had planned
To earn and drive. He and the world had winked.

VII

No history deceived him, for he knew
Little of times and armies not his own;
He never felt that peace was but a loan,
Had never questioned the idea of gain.
Beyond the headlines once or twice he saw
The gathering of a power by the few
But could not tell their names; he cast his vote,
Distrusting all the elected but not law.   80
He laughed at socialism; *on mourrait*
Pour les industriels? He shed his coat
And not for brotherhood, but for his pay.
To him the red flag marked the sewer main.

VIII

Above all else he loathed the homily,
The slogan and the ad. He paid his bill
But not for Congressmen at Bunker Hill.
Ideals were few and those there were not made
For conversation. He belonged to church
But never spoke of God. The Christmas tree,   90
The Easter egg, baptism, he observed,

Never denied the preacher on his perch,
And would not sign Resolved That or Whereas.
Softness he had and hours and nights reserved
For thinking, dressing, dancing to the jazz.
His laugh was real, his manners were home made.

IX

Of all men poverty pursued him least;
He was ashamed of all the down and out,
Spurned the panhandler like an uneasy doubt,
And saw the unemployed as a vague mass   100
Incapable of hunger or revolt.
He hated other races, south or east,
And shoved them to the margin of his mind.
He could recall the justice of the Colt,
Take interest in a gang-war like a game.
His ancestry was somewhere far behind
And left him only his peculiar name.
Doors opened, and he recognized no class.

X

His children would have known a heritage,
Just or unjust, the richest in the world,   110
The quantum of all art and science curled
In the horn of plenty, bursting from the horn,
A people bathed in honey, Paris come,
Vienna transferred with the highest wage,
A World's Fair spread to Phoenix, Jacksonville,
Earth's capitol, the new Byzantium,
Kingdom of man—who knows? Hollow or firm,
No man can ever prophesy until
Out of our death some undiscovered germ,
Whole toleration or pure peace is born.   120

XI

The time to mourn is short that best becomes
The military dead. We lift and fold the flag,
Lay bare the coffin with its written tag,
And march away. Behind, four others wait
To lift the box, the heaviest of loads.
The anesthetic afternoon benumbs,
Sickens our senses, forces back our talk.
We know that others on tomorrow's roads

Will fall, ourselves perhaps, the man beside,
Over the world the threatened, all who walk: 130
And could we mark the grave of him who died
We would write this beneath his name and date:

EPITAPH

Underneath this wooden cross there lies
A Christian killed in battle. You who read,
Remember that this stranger died in pain;
And passing here, if you can lift your eyes
Upon a peace kept by a human creed,
Know that one soldier has not died in vain.

V–LETTER

(1944)

I love you first because your face is fair,
            Because your eyes Jewish and blue,
Set sweetly with the touch of foreignness
Above the cheekbones, stare rather than dream.
Often your countenance recalls a boy
            Blue-eyed and small, whose silent mischief
Tortured his parents and compelled my hate
                        To wish his ugly death.
Because of this reminder, my soul's trouble,
And for your face, so often beautiful,   10
            I love you, wish you life.

I love you first because you wait, because
            For your own sake, I cannot write
Beyond these words. I love you for these words
That sting and creep like insects and leave filth.
I love you for the poverty you cry
            And I bend down with tears of steel
That melt your hand like wax, not for this war
                        The droplets shattering
Those candle-glowing fingers of my joy,   20
But for your name of agony, my love,
            That cakes my mouth with salt.

And all your imperfections and perfections
        And all your magnitude of grace
And all this love explained and unexplained
Is just a breath. I see you woman-size
And this looms larger and more goddess-like
        Than silver goddesses on screens.
I see you in the ugliness of light,
           Yet you are beautiful,   30
And in the dark of absence your full length
Is such as meets my body to the full
        Though I am starved and huge.

You turn me from these days as from a scene
        Out of an open window far
Where lies the foreign city and the war.
You are my home and in your spacious love
I dream to march as under flaring flags
        Until the door is gently shut.
Give me the tearless lesson of your pride,   40
        Teach me to live and die
As one deserving anonymity,
The mere devotion of a house to keep
        A woman and a man.

Give me the free and poor inheritance
        Of our own kind, not furniture
Of education, nor the prophet's pose,
The general cause of words, the hero's stance,
The ambitions incommensurable with flesh,
        But the drab makings of a room   50
Where sometimes in the afternoon of thought
        The brief and blinding flash
May light the enormous chambers of your will
And show the gracious Parthenon that time
        Is ever measured by.

As groceries in a pantry gleam and smile
        Because they are important weights
Bought with the metal minutes of your pay,
So do these hours stand in solid rows,

The dowry for a use in common life.   60
            I love you first because your years
Lead to my matter-of-fact and simple death
                    Or to our open marriage,
And I pray nothing for my safety back,
Not even luck, because our love is whole
                    Whether I live or fail.

THE SICKNESS OF ADAM

(From "Adam and Eve")

(1953)

In the beginning, at every step, he turned
As if by instinct to the East to praise
The nature of things. Now every path was learned
He lost the lifted, almost flower-like gaze

Of a temple dancer. He began to walk
Slowly, like one accustomed to be alone.
He found himself lost in the field of talk;
Thinking became a garden of its own.

In it were new things: words he had never said,
Beasts he had never seen and knew were not   10
In the true garden, terrors, and tears shed
Under a tree by him, for some new thought.

And the first anger. Once he flung a staff
At softly coupling sheep and struck the ram.
It broke away. And God heard Adam laugh
And for his laughter made the creature lame.

And wanderlust. He stood upon the Wall
To search the unfinished countries lying wide
And waste, where not a living thing could crawl,
And yet he would descend, as if to hide.   20

His thought drew down the guardian at the gate,
To whom man said, "What danger am I in?"
And the angel, hurt in spirit, seemed to hate
The wingless thing that worried after sin,

For it said nothing but marvelously unfurled
Its wings and arched them shimmering overhead,
Which must have been the signal from the world
That the first season of our life was dead.

Adam fell down with labor in his bones,
And God approached him in the cool of day   30
And said, "This sickness in your skeleton
Is longing. I will remove it from your clay."

He said also, "I made you strike the sheep."
It began to rain and God sat down beside
The sinking man. When he was fast asleep
He wet his right hand deep in Adam's side

And drew the graceful rib out of his breast.
Far off, the latent streams began to flow
And birds flew out of Paradise to nest
On earth. Sadly the angel watched them go.   40

Randall Jarrell
1914-1965

90 NORTH
(1942)

At home, in my flannel gown, like a bear to its floe,
I clambered to bed; up the globe's impossible sides
I sailed all night—till at last, with my black beard,
My furs and my dogs, I stood at the northern pole.

There in the childish night my companions lay frozen,
The stiff furs knocked at my starveling throat,
And I gave my great sigh: the flakes came huddling,
Were they really my end? In the darkness I turned to my rest.

—Here, the flag snaps in the glare and silence
Of the unbroken ice. I stand here,   10
The dogs bark, my beard is black, and I stare
At the North Pole . . .
                And now what? Why, go back.

Turn as I please, my step is to the south.
The world—my world spins on this final point
Of cold and wretchedness: all lines, all winds
End in this whirlpool I at last discover.

And it is meaningless. In the child's bed
After the night's voyage, in that warm world
Where people work and suffer for the end
That crowns the pain—in that Cloud-Cuckoo-Land   20

426

I reached my North and it had meaning.
Here at the actual pole of my existence,
Where all that I have done is meaningless,
Where I die or live by accident alone—

Where, living or dying, I am still alone;
Here where North, the night, the berg of death
Crowd me out of the ignorant darkness,
I see at last that all the knowledge

I wrung from the darkness—that the darkness flung me—
Is worthless as ignorance: nothing comes from nothing,   30
The darkness from the darkness. Pain comes from the darkness
And we call it wisdom. It is pain.

SECOND AIR FORCE

(1945)

Far off, above the plain the summer dries,
The great loops of the hangars sway like hills.
Buses and weariness and loss, the nodding soldiers
Are wire, the bare frame building, and a pass
To what was hers; her head hides his square patch
And she thinks heavily: My son is grown.
She sees a world: sand roads, tar-paper barracks,
The bubbling asphalt of the runways, sage,
The dunes rising to the interminable ranges,
The dim flights moving over clouds like clouds.   10
The armorers in their patched faded green,
Sweat-stiffened, banded with brass cartridges,
Walk to the line; their Fortresses, all tail,
Stand wrong and flimsy on their skinny legs,
And the crews climb to them clumsily as bears.
The head withdraws into its hatch (a boy's),
The engines rise to their blind laboring roar,
And the green, made beasts run home to air.
Now in each aspect death is pure.
(At twilight they wink over men like stars   20
And hour by hour, through the night, some see
The great lights floating in—from Mars, from Mars.)
How emptily the watchers see them gone.

They go, there is silence; the woman and her son
Stand in the forest of the shadows, and the light
Washes them like water. In the long-sunken city
Of evening, the sunlight stills like sleep
The faint wonder of the drowned; in the evening,
In the last dreaming light, so fresh, so old,
The soldiers pass like beasts, unquestioning,   30
And the watcher for an instant understands
What there is then no need to understand;
But she wakes from her knowledge, and her stare,
A shadow now, moves emptily among
The shadows learning in their shadowy fields
The empty missions.
                    Remembering,
She hears the bomber calling, *Little Friend!*
To the fighter hanging in the hostile sky,
And sees the ragged flame eat, rib by rib,   40
Along the metal of the wing into her heart:
The lives stream out, blossom, and float steadily
To the flames of the earth, the flames
That burn like stars above the lands of men.

She saves from the twilight that takes everything
A squadron shipping, in its last parade—
Its dogs run by it, barking at the band—
A gunner walking to his barracks, half-asleep,
Starting at something, stumbling (above, invisible,
The crews in the steady winter of the sky   50
Tremble in their wired fur); and feels for them
The love of life for life. The hopeful cells
Heavy with someone else's death, cold carriers
Of someone else's victory, grope past their lives
Into her own bewilderment: The years meant *this?*

But for them the bombers answer everything.

LOSSES

(1945)

It was not dying: everybody died.
It was not dying: we had died before
In the routine crashes—and our fields
Called up the papers, wrote home to our folks,
And the rates rose, all because of us.
We died on the wrong page of the almanac,
Scattered on mountains fifty miles away;
Diving on haystacks, fighting with a friend,
We blazed up on the lines we never saw.
We died like aunts or pets or foreigners.   10
(When we left high school nothing else had died
For us to figure we had died like.)

In our new planes, with our new crews, we bombed
The ranges by the desert or the shore,
Fired at towed targets, waited for our scores—
And turned into replacements and woke up
One morning, over England, operational.
It wasn't different: but if we died
It was not an accident but a mistake
(But an easy one for anyone to make).   20
We read our mail and counted up our missions—
In bombers named for girls, we burned
The cities we had learned about in school—
Till our lives wore out; our bodies lay among
The people we had killed and never seen.
When we lasted long enough they gave us medals;
When we died they said, "Our casualties were low."

They said, "Here are the maps"; we burned the cities.

It was not dying—no, not ever dying;
But the night I died I dreamed that I was dead,   30
And the cities said to me: "Why are you dying?
We are satisfied, if you are; but why did I die?"

THE DEATH OF THE BALL TURRET GUNNER
(1945)

From my mother's sleep I fell into the State,
And I hunched in its belly till my wet fur froze.
Six miles from earth, loosed from its dream of life,
I woke to black flak and the nightmare fighters.
When I died they washed me out of the turret with a hose.

THE ORIENT EXPRESS
(1951)

One looks from the train
Almost as one looked as a child. In the sunlight
What I see still seems to me plain,
I am safe; but at evening
As the lands darken, a questioning
Precariousness comes over everything.

Once after a day of rain
I lay longing to be cold; and after a while
I was cold again, and hunched shivering
Under the quilt's many colors, gray   10
With the dull ending of the winter day.
Outside me there were a few shapes
Of chairs and tables, things from a primer;
Outside the window
There were the chairs and tables of the world. . . .
I saw that the world
That had seemed to me the plain
Gray mask of all that was strange
Behind it—of all that *was*—was all.

But it is beyond belief.   20
One thinks, "Behind everything
An unforced joy, an unwilling
Sadness (a willing sadness, a forced joy)
Moves changelessly"; one looks from the train
And there is something, the same thing
Behind everything: all these little villages,

A passing woman, a field of grain,
The man who says good-bye to his wife—
A path through a wood full of lives, and the train
Passing, after all unchangeable   30
And not now ever to stop, like a heart—

It is like any other work of art.
It is and never can be changed.
Behind everything there is always
The unknown unwanted life.

SEELE IM RAUM
(1951)

[handwritten: Soul in Space]

It sat between my husband and my children.
A place was set for it—a plate of greens.

[handwritten: fantasy world / irony of poem]

It had been there: I had seen it
But not somehow—but this was like a dream—
Not seen it so that I knew I saw it.
It was as if I could not know I saw it
Because I had never once in all my life
Not seen it. It was an eland.
An eland! *That* is why the children
Would ask my husband, for a joke, at Christmas: 10
"Father, is it Donner?" He would say, "No, Blitzen."
It had been there always. Now we put silver
At its place at meals, fed it the same food

[handwritten: psych. disorientation]

We ourselves ate, and said nothing. Many times
When it breathed heavily (when it had tried
A long useless time to speak) and reached to me
So that I touched it—of a different size
And order of being, like the live hard side
Of a horse's neck when you pat the horse—
And looked with its great melting tearless eyes   20
Fringed with a few coarse wire-like lashes
Into my eyes, and whispered to me
So that my eyes turned backward in their sockets
And they said nothing—
                              many times
I have known, when they said nothing,

That it did not exist. If they had heard
They *could* not have been silent. And yet they heard;
Heard many times what I have spoken
When it could no longer speak, but only breathe—   30
When I could no longer speak, but only breathe.

And, after some years, the others came *from the* sanilorium
And took it from me—it was ill, they told me— *she was cured*
And cured it, they wrote me: my whole city
Sent me cards like lilac-branches, mourning
As I had mourned—
                              and I was standing   *buries that part*
By a grave in flowers, by dyed rolls of turf,   *of her life*
And a canvas marquee the last brown of earth.

It is over.   40
It is over so long that I begin to think
That it did not exist, that I have never—
And my son says, one morning, from the paper:
"An eland. Look, an eland!"
                              —It was so.

Today, in a German dictionary, I saw *elend*
And the heart in my breast turned over, it was—

It was a word one translates *wretched.*

It is as if somone remembered saying:
"This is an antimacassar that I grew from seed,"   50
And this were true.
                    And, truly,
One could not wish for anything more strange—
For anything more. And yet it wasn't *interesting* . . .
—It was worse than impossible, it was a joke.   *elend*

And yet when it was, I *was*—   *hallucination*
Even to think that I once thought
That I could see it is to feel the sweat
Like needles at my hair-roots, I am blind

—It was not even a joke, not even a joke.   60

Yet how can I believe it? Or believe that I
Owned it, a husband, children? Is my voice the voice
Of that skin of being—of what owns, is owned
In honor or dishonor, that is borne and bears—
Or of that raw thing, the being inside it
That has neither a wife, a husband, nor a child
But goes at last as naked from this world
As it was born into it—

And the eland comes and grazes on its grave.

                    This is senseless?   7c
Shall I make sense or shall I tell the truth?
Choose either—I cannot do both.

I tell myself that. And yet it is not so,
And what I say afterwards will not be so:
To be at all is to be wrong.
                    Being is being old
And saying, almost comfortably, across a table
From—
        from what I don't know—
                            in a voice   80
Rich with a kind of longing satisfaction:
"To own an eland! That's what I call life!"

Robert Lowell

1917-

COLLOQUY IN BLACK ROCK
(1946)

Here the jack-hammer jabs into the ocean;
My heart, you race and stagger and demand
More blood-gangs for your nigger-brass percussions,
Till I, the stunned machine of your devotion,
Clanging upon this cymbal of a hand,
Am rattled screw and footloose. All discussions

End in the mud-flat detritus of death.
My heart, beat faster, faster. In Black Mud
Hungarian workmen give their blood
For the martyre Stephen, who was stoned to death.   10

Black Mud, a name to conjure with: O mud
For watermelons gutted to the crust,
Mud for the mole-tide harbor, mud for mouse,
Mud for the armored Diesel fishing tubs that thud
A year and a day to wind and tide; the dust
Is on this skipping heart that shakes my house,

House of our Savior who was hanged till death.
My heart, beat faster, faster. In Black Mud
Stephen the martyre was broken down to blood:
Our ransom is the rubble of his death.   20

434

Christ walks on the black water. In Black Mud
Darts the kingfisher. On Corpus Christi, heart,
Over the drum-beat of St. Stephen's choir
I hear him, *Stupor Mundi,* and the mud
Flies from his hunching wings and beak—my heart,
The blue kingfisher dives on you in fire.

THE QUAKER GRAVEYARD IN NANTUCKET

For Warren Winslow, Dead at Sea

(1946)

*Let man have dominion over the fishes of the sea and the
fowls of the air and the beasts and the whole earth, and
every creeping creature that moveth upon the earth.*

I

A brackish reach of shoal off Madaket,—
The sea was still breaking violently and night
Had steamed into our North Atlantic Fleet,
When the drowned sailor clutched the drag-net. Light
Flashed from his matted head and marble feet,
He grappled at the net
With the coiled, hurdling muscles of his thighs:
The corpse was bloodless, a botch of reds and whites,
Its open, staring eyes
Were lustreless dead-lights   10
Or cabin-windows on a stranded hulk
Heavy with sand. We weight the body, close
Its eyes and heave it seaward whence it came,
Where the heel-headed dogfish barks its nose
On Ahab's void and forehead; and the name
Is blocked in yellow chalk.
Sailors, who pitch this portent at the sea
Where dreadnaughts shall confess
Its hell-bent deity,
When you are powerless   20
To sand-bag this Atlantic bulwark, faced
By the earth-shaker, green, unwearied, chaste
In his steel scales: ask for no Orphean lute

To pluck life back. The guns of the steeled fleet
Recoil and then repeat
The hoarse salute.

II

Whenever winds are moving and their breath
Heaves at the roped-in bulwarks of this pier,
The terns and sea-gulls tremble at your death
In these home waters. Sailor, can you hear   30
The Pequod's sea wings, beating landward, fall
Headlong and break on our Atlantic wall
Off 'Sconset, where the yawing S-boats splash
The bellbuoy, with ballooning spinnakers,
As the entangled, screeching mainsheet clears
The blocks: off Madaket, where lubbers lash
The heavy surf and throw their long lead squids
For blue-fish? Sea-gulls blink their heavy lids
Seaward. The winds' wings beat upon the stones,
Cousin, and scream for you and the claws rush   40
At the sea's throat and wring it in the slush
Of this old Quaker graveyard where the bones
Cry out in the long night for the hurt beast
Bobbing by Ahab's whaleboats in the East.

III

All you recovered from Poseidon died
With you, my cousin, and the harrowed brine
Is fruitless on the blue beard of the god,
Stretching beyond us to the castles in Spain,
Nantucket's westward haven. To Cape Cod
Guns, cradled on the tide,   50
Blast the eelgrass about a waterclock
Of bilge and backwash, roil the salt and sand
Lashing earth's scaffold, rock
Our warships in the hand
Of the great God, where time's contrition blues
Whatever it was these Quaker sailors lost
In the mad scramble of their lives. They died
When time was open-eyed,
Wooden and childish; only bones abide
There, in the nowhere, where their boats were tossed 60
Sky-high, where mariners had fabled news

Of IS, the whited monster. What it cost
Them is their secret. In the sperm-whale's slick
I see the Quakers drown and hear their cry:
"If God himself had not been on our side,
If God himself had not been on our side,
When the Atlantic rose against us, why,
Then it had swallowed us up quick."

IV

This is the end of the whaleroad and the whale
Who spewed Nantucket bones on the thrashed swell   70
And stirred the troubled waters to whirlpools
To send the Pequod packing off to hell:
This is the end of them, three-quarters fools,
Snatching at straws to sail
Seaward and seaward on the turntail whale,
Spouting out blood and water as it rolls,
Sick as a dog to these Atlantic shoals:
Clamavimus, O depths. Let the sea-gulls wail

For water, for the deep where the high tide
Mutters to its hurt self, mutters and ebbs.   80
Waves wallow in their wash, go out and out,
Leave only the death-rattle of the crabs,
The beach increasing, its enormous snout
Sucking the ocean's side.
This is the end of running on the waves;
We are poured out like water. Who will dance
The mast-lashed master of Leviathans
Up from this field of Quakers in their unstoned graves?

V

When the whale's viscera go and the roll
Of its corruption overruns this world   90
Beyond tree-swept Nantucket and Wood's Hole
And Martha's Vineyard, Sailor, will your sword
Whistle and fall and sink into the fat?
In the great ash-pit of Jehoshaphat
The bones cry for the blood of the white whale,
The fat flukes arch and whack about its ears,
The death-lance churns into the sanctuary, tears
The gun-blue swingle, heaving like a flail,

And hacks the coiling life out: it works and drags
And rips the sperm-whale's midriff into rags,   100
Gobbets of blubber spill to wind and weather,
Sailor, and gulls go round the stoven timbers
Where the morning stars sing out together
And thunder shakes the white surf and dismembers
The red flag hammered in the mast-head. Hide
Our steel, Jonas Messias, in Thy side.

VI

OUR LADY OF WALSINGHAM

There once the penitents took off their shoes
And then walked barefoot the remaining mile;
And the small trees, a stream and hedgerows file
Slowly along the munching English lane,   110
Like cows to the old shrine, until you lose
Track of your dragging pain.
The stream flows down under the druid tree,
Shiloah's whirlpools gurgle and make glad
The castle of God. Sailor, you were glad
And whistled Sion by that stream. But see:

Our Lady, too small for her canopy,
Sits near the altar. There's no comeliness
At all or charm in that expressionless
Face with its heavy eyelids. As before,   120
This face, for centuries a memory,
Non est species, neque decor,
Expressionless, expresses God: it goes
Past castled Sion. She knows what God knows,
Not Calvary's Cross nor crib at Bethlehem
Now, and the world shall come to Walsingham.

VII

The empty winds are creaking and the oak
Splatters and splatters on the cenotaph,
The boughs are trembling and a gaff
Bobs on the untimely stroke   130
Of the greased wash exploding on a shoal-bell
In the old mouth of the Atlantic. It's well;
Atlantic, you are fouled with the blue sailors,
Sea-monsters, upward angel, downward fish:

Unmarried and corroding, spare of flesh,
Mart once of supercilious, wing'd clippers,
Atlantic, where your bell-trap guts its spoil
You could cut the brackish winds with a knife
Here in Nantucket, and cast up the time
When the Lord God formed man from the sea's slime   140
And breathed into his face the breath of life,
And blue-lung'd combers lumbered to the kill.
The Lord survives the rainbow of His will.

AS A PLANE TREE BY THE WATER
(1946)

Darkness has called to darkness, and disgrace
Elbows about our windows in this planned
Babel of Boston where our money talks
And multiplies the darkness of a land
Of preparation where the Virgin walks
And roses spiral her enamelled face
Or fall to splinters on unwatered streets.
Our Lady of Babylon, go by, go by,
I was once the apple of your eye;
Flies, flies are on the plane tree, on the streets.   10

The flies, the flies, the flies of Babylon
Buzz in my ear-drums while the devil's long
Dirge of the people detonates the hour
For floating cities where his golden tongue
Enchants the masons of the Babel Tower
To raise tomorrow's city to the sun
That never sets upon these hell-fire streets
Of Boston, where the sunlight is a sword
Striking at the withholder of the Lord:
Flies, flies are on the plane tree, on the streets.   20

Flies strike the miraculous waters of the iced
Atlantic and the eyes of Bernadette
Who saw Our Lady standing in the cave
At Massabielle, saw her so squarely that
Her vision put out reason's eyes. The grave

Is open-mouthed and swallowed up in Christ.
O walls of Jericho! And all the streets
To our Atlantic wall are singing: "Sing,
Sing for the resurrection of the King."
Flies, flies are on the plane tree, on the streets.   30

AFTER THE SURPRISING CONVERSIONS
(1946)

September twenty-second, Sir: today
I answer. In the latter part of May,
Hard on our Lord's Ascension, it began
To be more sensible. A gentleman
Of more than common understanding, strict
In morals, pious in behavior, kicked
Against our goad. A man of some renown,
An useful, honored person in the town,
He came of melancholy parents; prone
To secret spells, for years they kept alone—   10
His uncle, I believe, was killed of it:
Good people, but of too much or little wit.
I preached one Sabbath on a text from Kings;
He showed concernment for his soul. Some things
In his experience were hopeful. He
Would sit and watch the wind knocking a tree
And praise this countryside our Lord has made.
Once when a poor man's heifer died, he laid
A shilling on the doorsill; though a thirst
For loving shook him like a snake, he durst   20
Not entertain much hope of his estate
In heaven. Once we saw him sitting late
Behind his attic window by a light
That guttered on his Bible; through that night
He meditated terror, and he seemed
Beyond advice or reason, for he dreamed
That he was called to trumpet Judgment Day
To Concord. In the latter part of May
He cut his throat. And though the coroner
Judged him delirious, soon a noisome stir   30
Palsied our village. At Jehovah's nod

Satan seemed more let loose amongst us: God
Abandoned us to Satan, and he pressed
Us hard, until we thought we could not rest
Till we had done with life. Content was gone.
All the good work was quashed. We were undone.
The breath of God had carried out a planned
And sensible withdrawal from this land;
The multitude, once unconcerned with doubt,
Once neither callous, curious nor devout,   40
. Jumped at broad noon, as though some peddler groaned
At it in its familiar twang: "My friend,
Cut your own throat. Cut your own throat. Now! Now!"
September twenty-second, Sir, the bough
Cracks with the unpicked apples, and at dawn
The small-mouth bass breaks water, gorged with spawn.

WHERE THE RAINBOW ENDS
(1946)

I saw the sky descending, black and white,
Not blue, on Boston where the winters wore
The skulls to jack-o'-lanterns on the slates,
And Hunger's skin-and-bone retrievers tore
The chickadee and shrike. The thorn tree waits
Its victim and tonight
The worms will eat the deadwood to the foot
Of Ararat: the scythers, Time and Death,
Helmed locusts, move upon the tree of breath;
The wild ingrafted olive and the root   10

Are withered, and a winter drifts to where
The Pepperpot, ironic rainbow, spans
Charles River and its scales of scorched-earth miles.
I saw my city in the Scales, the pans
Of judgment rising and descending. Piles
Of dead leaves char the air—
And I am a red arrow on this graph
Of Revelations. Every dove is sold
The Chapel's sharp-shinned eagle shifts its hold
On serpent-Time, the rainbow's epitaph.   20

In Boston serpents whistle at the cold.
The victim climbs the altar steps and sings:
"Hosannah to the lion, lamb, and beast
Who fans the furnace-face of IS with wings:
I breathe the ether of my marriage feast."
At the high altar, gold
And a fair cloth. I kneel and the wings beat
My cheek. What can the dove of Jesus give
You now but wisdom, exile? Stand and live,
The dove has brought an olive branch to eat.   30

FALLING ASLEEP OVER THE AENEID
(1950)

An old man in Concord forgets to go to morning service.
He falls asleep, while reading Vergil, and dreams that he is
Aeneas at the funeral of Pallas, an Italian prince.

The sun is blue and scarlet on my page,
And *yuck-a, yuck-a, yuck-a, yuck-a,* rage
The yellowhammers mating. Yellow fire
Blankets the captives dancing on their pyre,
And the scorched lictor screams and drops his rod.
Trojans are singing to their drunken God,
Ares. Their helmets catch on fire. Their files
Clank by the body of my comrade—miles
Of filings! Now the scythe-wheeled chariot rolls
Before their lances long as vaulting poles,   10
And I stand up and heil the thousand men,
Who carry Pallas to the bird-priest. Then
The bird-priest groans, and as his birds foretold,
I greet the body, lip to lip. I hold
The sword that Dido used. It tries to speak,
A bird with Dido's sworded breast. Its beak
Clangs and ejaculates the Punic word
I hear the bird-priest chirping like a bird.
I groan a little. "Who am I, and why?"
It asks, a boy's face, though its arrow-eye   20
Is working from its socket. "Brother, try,
O Child of Aphrodite, try to die:

To die is life." His harlots hang his bed
With feathers of his long-tailed birds. His head
Is yawning like a person. The plumes blow;
The beard and eyebrows ruffle. Face of snow,
You are the flower that country girls have caught,
A wild bee-pillaged honey-suckle brought
To the returning bridegroom—the design
Has not yet left it, and the petals shine;   30
The earth, its mother, has, at last, no help:
It is itself. The broken-winded yelp
Of my Phoenician hounds, that fills the brush
With snapping twigs and flying, cannot flush
The ghost of Pallas. But I take his pall,
Stiff with its gold and purple, and recall
How Dido hugged it to her, while she toiled,
Laughing—her golden threads, a serpent coiled
In cypress. Now I lay it like a sheet;
It clinks and settles down upon his feet,   40
The careless yellow hair that seemed to burn
Beforehand. Left foot, right foot—as they turn,
More pyres are rising: armored horses, bronze,
And gagged Italians, who must file by ones
Across the bitter river, when my thumb
Tightens into their wind-pipes. The beaks drum;
Their headman's cow-horned death's-head bites its tongue,
And stiffens, as it eyes the hero slung
Inside his feathered hammock on the crossed
Staves of the eagles that we winged. Our cost   50
Is nothing to the lovers, whoring Mars
And Venus, father's lover. Now his car's
Plumage is ready, and my marshals fetch
His squire, Acoetes, white with age, to hitch
Aethon, the hero's charger, and its ears
Prick, and it steps and steps, and stately tears
Lather its teeth; and then the harlots bring
The hero's charms and baton—but the King,
Vain-glorious Turnus, carried off the rest.
"I was myself, but Ares thought it best   60
The way it happened." At the end of time,
He sets his spear, as my descendants climb
The knees of Father Time, his beard of scalps,

His scythe, the arc of steel that crowns the Alps.
The elephants of Carthage hold those snows,
Turms of Numidian horse unsling their bows,
The flaming turkey-feathered arrows swarm
Beyond the Alps. "Pallas," I raise my arm
And shout, "Brother, eternal health. Farewell
Forever." Church is over, and its bell   70
Frightens the yellowhammers, as I wake
And watch the whitecaps wrinkle up the lake.
Mother's great-aunt, who died when I was eight,
Stands by our parlor sabre. "Boy, it's late.
Vergil must keep the Sabbath." Eighty years!
It all comes back. My Uncle Charles appears.
Blue-capped and bird-like. Phillips Brooks and Grant
Are frowning at his coffin, and my aunt,
Hearing his colored veterans parade
Through Concord, laughs, and tells her English maid   80
To clip his yellow nostril hairs, and fold
His colors on him. . . . It is I, I hold
His sword to keep from falling, for the dust
On the stuffed birds is breathless, for the bust
Of young Augustus weighs on Vergil's shelf:
It scowls into my glasses at itself.

COMMENTARY

LIST OF ABBREVIATIONS

Am. Lit.	*American Literature*
Am. Schol.	*American Scholar*
Atlantic	*Atlantic Monthly*
Coll. Eng.	*College English*
Essays in Crit.	*Essays in Criticism*
Eng. Jour.	*English Journal*
Hud. Rev.	*Hudson Review*
Jour. Aesth. & Art Crit.	*Journal of Aesthetics and Art Criticism*
Ken. Rev.	*Kenyon Review*
Mod. Lang. Notes	*Modern Language Notes*
Mod. Phil.	*Modern Philology*
New Statesman	*New Statesman and Nation*
PMLA	*Publications of the Modern Language Association of America*
Part. Rev.	*Partisan Review*
Rev. Eng. Stud.	*Review of English Studies*
So. Atl. Quart.	*South Atlantic Quarterly*
So. Rev.	*Southern Review*
Sewanee Rev.	*Sewanee Review*
Times Lit. Sup.	*The [London] Times Literary Supplement*
U. Kans. City Rev.	*University of Kansas City Review*
Va. Quart. Rev.	*Virginia Quarterly Review*
West. Hum. Rev.	*Western Humanities Review*
West. Rev.	*Western Review*
Yale Rev.	*Yale Review*

Notes

W. H. AUDEN (1907–   )

LIFE

Wystan Hugh Auden was born February 21 at York, England, the son of a doctor. After attending Gresham's School, Holt, he went up to Christ Church College, Oxford, in 1925 and took his degree in 1928. He then visited Berlin, taught school in England and Scotland, visited Iceland with MacNeice, drove an ambulance for the Loyalists in Spain, and visited China in 1938 with Christopher Isherwood. In January, 1939, he came to the United States and took out citizenship papers. Although he has taught briefly at several American colleges and was made Professor of Poetry at Oxford in 1955, he is primarily a poet, critic, and editor.

BIBLIOGRAPHY

Clancy, J. P. "A W. H. Auden Bibliography, 1924–1955," *Thought*, XXX (1955), 260–70.

MAJOR WRITINGS

The Collected Poetry of W. H. Auden (1945)
Collected Shorter Poems, 1930–1944 (1950)

Poems (1930)
The Orators: An English Study (1932)
Poems (2d ed., 1934)
Look, Stranger (1936; published in New York in 1937 as *On This Island*)
Another Time (1940)
The Double Man (1941; published in London as *New Year Letter*)
For the Time Being (1944)
The Age of Anxiety: A Baroque Eclogue (1947)
Nones (1951)
The Shield of Achilles (1955)

449

Some Poems (1940)

The Enchafèd Flood, or The Romantic Iconography of the Sea (1950)

Letters from Iceland (1937; with Louis MacNeice)
Journey to a War (1939; with Christopher Isherwood)

BIOGRAPHY

None.

CRITICISM

Beach, J. W. *The Making of the Auden Canon.* Minneapolis, Minn.: University of Minnesota Press, 1957.

Bradbury, J. M. "Auden and the Tradition," *West. Rev.,* XII (1948), 223–29.

Enright, D. J. "Reluctant Admiration: A Note on Auden and Rilke," *Essays in Crit.,* II (1952), 180–95.

Hoggart, Richard. *Auden: An Introductory Essay.* London: Chatto & Windus, 1951.

Jarrell, Randall. "Changes of Attitude and Rhetoric in Auden's Poetry," *So. Rev.,* VII (1941), 326–49.

———, "Freud to Paul: Stages of Auden's Ideology," *Part. Rev.,* XII (1945), 437–57.

Roth, Robert. "The Sophistication of W. H. Auden: A Sketch in Longinian Method," *Mod. Phil.,* XLVIII (1951), 193–204.

Scarfe, Francis. *W. H. Auden.* Monaco: Lyrebird Press, 1949.

Spears, M. K. "The Dominant Symbols of Auden's Poetry," *Sewanee Rev.,* LIX (1951), 392–425.

———, "Late Auden: The Satirist as Lunatic Clergyman," *Sewanee Rev.,* LIX (1951), 50–74.

Spender, Stephen. "W. H. Auden and His Poetry," *Atlantic,* CXCII (1953), 74–79.

Stauffer, Donald. "Which Side Am I Supposed to Be On?: The Search for Beliefs in Auden's Poetry," *Va. Quart. Rev.,* XXII (1946), 570–80.

Wilson, Edmund. "W. H. Auden in America," *New Statesman,* LI (June 9, 1956), 658–59.

COMMENTS ON POEMS

PETITION

Discussed in Beach, *The Making of the Auden Canon,* pp. 35–36; Brooks, *Modern Poetry and the Tradition* (U. of No. Carolina Press, 1939), pp. 1–2; W. C. Brown, *Explicator,* III (1945), 38; Isherwood, *Lions and Shadows* (Hogarth, 1938), pp. 217, 303; D. A. Robertson, W. K. Wimsatt, Jr., and Hallett Smith, *Explicator,* III (1945), 51.

3. *sovereign touch*: That is, like the king's touch, which was supposed to cure one of the "king's evil," or scrofula.

WHICH SIDE AM I SUPPOSED TO BE ON?

Originally entitled "Ode V: To My Pupils" in *The Orators* (1932).

Discussed in Bayley, *The Romantic Survival* (Constable, 1957), p. 161; Beach, *The Making of the Auden Canon*, pp. 85–92; Brooks, *Modern Poetry and the Tradition* (U. of N. Carolina Press, 1939), pp. 132–33; C. B. LeCompte, Jr., *Explicator*, VIII (1949), 21; R. A. Long, *Explicator*, VI (1948), 39; Spears, *Sewanee Rev.*, LIX (1951), 393–94.

37. *questions won't help*: Cf. Tennyson, "Charge of the Light Brigade": "Theirs not to reason why, / Theirs but to do and die."

45. *wine-dark conquerors*: Conquerors of the wine-dark (sea), that is, the Navy.

57–58. *"Heart and head . . ."*: A close paraphrase of the words spoken by Byrhtwold, at the death of Byrhtnoth, earl of Essex, at the battle of Maldon, 991 A.D., against the Danes. Lines 312–13 of the Anglo-Saxon poem, "The Battle of Maldon," may be translated: "Our hearts must be the stronger, heads the keener, spirit the greater as our forces diminish."

SOMETHING IS BOUND TO HAPPEN

This poem was entitled "Chorus from a Play" when it first appeared in *Poems* (1933). It is called "The Wanderer" in *Collected Shorter Poems, 1930–1944*, perhaps to remind us of the famous Anglo-Saxon poem of the same name.

Discussed in Beach, *The Making of the Auden Canon*, p. 213; M. W. Bloomfield, *Mod. Lang. Notes*, LXIII (1948), 548–52.

1. *Doom is dark*: This beginning echoes the thirteenth-century West Midlands prose homily, *Sawles Warde*, lines 318–20, which may be translated: "Those who dwell in God's sight are so wise that they know all God's counsels, his mysteries and his dooms which are secret and deeper than any sea-dingle."

1. *sea-dingle*: Deep, narrow cleft between hills.

11. *chat*: A species of warbler.

LAW LIKE LOVE

Discussed in Spears, *Sewanee Rev.*, LIX (1951), 408.

LAY YOUR SLEEPING HEAD, MY LOVE

Discussed in Hoggart, *Auden*, pp. 30–31; Roth, *Mod. Phil.*, XLVIII (1951), 197–98.

MUSÉE DES BEAUX ARTS

This poem first appeared with the title, "Palais des Beaux Arts," which is the popular name for the *Palais des Musées Royaux de Peinture et*

de Sculpture in Brussels, where is hung "The Fall of Icarus" by Pieter
Brueghel the Elder (c.1525–69). The present title has no basis in fact.
Discussed in Hoggart, *Auden,* pp. 29–30, 215–16; Roth, *Mod. Phil.,*
XLVIII (1951), 196–97.

IN MEMORY OF W. B. YEATS

Considerable light on this poem is cast by Auden's article, "The Public
and the Late Mr. William Butler Yeats," *Part. Rev.,* VI (1939), 46–51.
Discussed in Dell Hymes, *Folio,* XVIII (1951), 69–78; Roth, *Mod. Phil.,*
XLVIII (1951), 198–202.

42–47. *Earth, receive:* The meter of this section follows that of parts V and
VI of Yeats's "obituary" poem, "Under Ben Bulben."

55. *Pardoned Kipling:* Kipling has largely ceased to be reproached as the
poet of British imperialism.

56. *Paul Claudel:* French diplomat, poet, and dramatist (1868–1955). His
political conservatism was anathema to liberals in the thirties.

SEPTEMBER 1, 1939

On September 1, 1939, Germany invaded Poland to touch off World War
II.

Discussed in Phyllis Bartlett and John Pollard, *Explicator,* XIV (1955),
8; Beach, *The Making of the Auden Canon,* pp. 49–52; D. N. Bennett,
Quarterly Journal of Speech, XLII (1956), 1–13.

12–15. The concept of the state as an end in itself and as superior to the
individuals who compose it began to flourish when Lutheran doctrines
freed the German states from ecclesiastical control.

16. *what occurred at Linz:* As a boy, Hitler was an unhappy student at
the *Realschule* in Linz. The *Anschluss* took place at Linz, Sunday,
March 13, 1938. On that day Seyss-Inquart met Hitler and got President
Miklas' resignation. The Austrian Republic was dissolved and its ter-
ritories annexed to the Third Reich.

23–29. In *The Peloponnesian War,* book iii, chaps. 82–83, Thucydides,
exiled for failing to prevent the capture of a city by the Spartan general,
Brasidas, gives a terrifying analysis of democracy in Athens after the
death of Pericles.

47. *The lights must never go out:* On August 3, 1914, the British Foreign
Secretary, Viscount Grey of Fallodon, was reported to have said, "The
lamps are going out all over Europe; we shall not see them lit again in
our life-time" (Viscount Grey of Fallodon, *Twenty-Five Years, 1892–
1916,* Vol. II [New York: Frederick A. Stokes Co., 1925], p. 20).

59–66. *What mad Nijinsky wrote . . . loved alone:* "Some politicians
are hypocrites like Diaghilev, who does not want universal love, but to
be loved alone. I want universal love" (*The Diary of Vaslav Nijinsky,*
ed. Romola Nijinsky [New York: Simon & Schuster, 1936], p. 27).

IN PRAISE OF LIMESTONE

Discussed in Spears, *Sewanee Rev.*, LIX (1951), 399–401; Stephen Spender, *Poetry*, LXXVIII (1951), 355–56.

ROBERT BRIDGES (1844–1930)

LIFE

Born October 23 at Walmer, Kent, the son of a prosperous landowner. In September, 1854, he went to Eton, and in October, 1863, to Corpus Christi College, Oxford, where he made friends with Gerard Manley Hopkins, distinguished himself as stroke on the college crew, and took a second class in *literae humaniores*. In 1869 he entered St. Bartholomew's Hospital, London, as a medical student and followed a medical career until 1881, when illness forced his retirement to Yattendon, Berkshire. Thereafter he was exclusively a man of letters. In 1913 he succeeded Alfred Austin as Poet Laureate, and in the same year he founded the Society for Pure English. In 1918 he edited *Poems of Gerard Manley Hopkins*. He died at Chilswell, Oxford, on April 21, 1930.

BIBLIOGRAPHY

McKay, G. L. *A Bibliography of Robert Bridges.* New York: Columbia University Press, 1933.

MAJOR WRITINGS

Poetical Works of Robert Bridges (1920; 6 vols.)
The Shorter Poems of Robert Bridges (enlarged ed., 1931)

Poems (1873)
The Growth of Love (1876)
Eros and Psyche (1885)
Shorter Poems (Books I–IV, 1890; Book V, 1894)
October and Other Poems (1920)
New Verse (1925)
The Testament of Beauty (1929)

Robert Bridges: Poetry and Prose (1955; ed. John Sparrow)

Milton's Prosody (1893)
Collected Essays and Papers (1927–29; 4 vols.)

Three Friends: Memoirs of Digby Mackworth Dolben, Richard Watson Dixon, Henry Bradley (1932; contains much autobiographical material)

Correspondence of Robert Bridges and Henry Bradley (1940)
"Coventry Patmore and Bridges: Some Letters," *Fortnightly Review*,
N.S., CLXIII (1948), 196–204 (ed. Derek Patmore)

BIOGRAPHY

None (as requested in Bridges' will).

CRITICISM

Cohen, J. M. "The Road Not Taken: A Study in the Poetry of Robert
Bridges," *Cambridge Journal*, IV (1951), 555–64.
Garrod, H. W. "The Testament of Beauty," pp. 129–47 in *Poetry and the
Criticism of Life*. Cambridge, Mass.: Harvard University Press, 1931.
Gordon, G. S. *Robert Bridges*. Cambridge: At the University Press, 1946.
Guérard, A. J. *Robert Bridges: A Study of Traditionalism*. Cambridge, Mass.:
Harvard University Press, 1942.
Smith, N. C. *Notes on The Testament of Beauty*. London: Oxford University Press, 1931; rev. ed., 1940.
Symons, Arthur. "Robert Bridges," pp. 105–11 in *Studies in Prose and Verse*.
London: J. M. Dent & Sons, Ltd., 1904.
Thompson, E. J. *Robert Bridges, 1844–1930*. London: Oxford University
Press, 1945.
Winters, Yvor. "Traditional Mastery: The Lyrics of Robert Bridges," *Hound
and Horn*, V (1932), 324–25.
Wright, E. C. *Metaphor, Sound and Meaning in Bridges' The Testament
of Beauty*. Philadelphia, Pa.: University of Pennsylvania Press, 1951.

COMMENTS ON POEMS

ELEGY

Discussed in Guérard, *Robert Bridges*, pp. 13, 44, 110–11.

A PASSER-BY

Discussed in Guérard, *Robert Bridges*, pp. 107–8.

LONDON SNOW

This poem was intended by Bridges as an imitation of Hopkins' "sprung
rhythm." For Hopkins' criticism see pp. 122–23 in C. C. Abbott (ed.),
Letters of Gerard Manley Hopkins to Robert Bridges (London: Oxford
University Press, 1935).
29. *Paul's high dome*: Dome of St. Paul's Cathedral.

NIGHTINGALES

Discussed in Guérard, *Robert Bridges*, p. 49.

LOW BAROMETER

Discussed in Yvor Winters, *The Function of Criticism* (Alan Swallow,
1957), pp. 105–7.

HART CRANE (1899–1932)

LIFE

Harold Hart Crane was born July 21 in Garrettsville, Ohio, the son of a prosperous manufacturer. He grew up in Cleveland, but in 1916 went to New York and began a series of jobs both there and in several Midwestern cities to support himself while writing poetry. With financial help from Otto Kahn from 1925 on, he worked for several years at *The Bridge,* his most important achievement. After a year in Mexico on a Guggenheim Fellowship, he committed suicide on April 26, 1932, by jumping into the Gulf of Mexico from the ship that was returning him to the United States.

BIBLIOGRAPHY

Rowe, H. D. *Hart Crane: A Bibliography.* Denver: Alan Swallow, 1955.

MAJOR WRITINGS

The Collected Poems of Hart Crane (1933; ed. Waldo Frank)

White Buildings: Poems (1926)
The Bridge: A Poem (1930)

The Letters of Hart Crane, 1916–1932 (1952; ed. Brom Weber)

BIOGRAPHY

Horton, Philip. *Hart Crane: The Life of an American Poet.* New York: W. W. Norton & Co., Inc., 1937. Republished in Compass Books, The Viking Press, Inc., 1957.

CRITICISM

Blackmur, R. P. *The Double Agent,* pp. 121–40. New York: Arrow Editions, 1935. Reprinted in Blackmur, *Form and Value in Modern Poetry,* pp. 269–85. New York: Anchor Books, Doubleday & Co., Inc., 1957.
Herman, Barbara. "The Language of Hart Crane," *Sewanee Rev.,* LVIII (1950), 52–67.
Munson, G. B. *Destinations,* pp. 160–77. New York: J. H. Sears & Co., Inc., 1928.
Tate, Allen. *On the Limits of Poetry,* pp. 225–37. New York: The Swallow Press, 1948. Reprinted in Tate, *The Man of Letters in the Modern World,* pp. 283–94. New York: Meridian Books, The Noonday Press, 1955.
Weber, Brom. *Hart Crane: A Biographical and Critical Study.* New York: The Bodley Press, 1948.
Winters, Yvor. "The Progress of Hart Crane," *Poetry,* XXXVI (1930), 153–65.

Zabel, M. D. "The Book of Hart Crane," *Poetry,* XLII (1933), 33–39.

COMMENTS ON POEMS

PRAISE FOR AN URN

Ernest Nelson, who died and was cremated in December, 1921, was a friend of Crane's.
Discussed in Alan Swallow, *U. Kans. City Rev.,* XVI (1949), 115.

AT MELVILLE'S TOMB

Herman Melville (1819–91) was the American novelist and poet.
Discussed in Harriet Monroe and Hart Crane, *Poetry,* XXIX (1926), 34–41 (reprinted in Appendix B of Weber, *Hart Crane,* pp. 416–22).

VOYAGES II

Discussed in H. C. Morris, *Accent,* XIV (1954), 291–99; O'Connor, *Sense and Sensibility in Modern Poetry* (U. of Chicago Press, 1948), pp. 73–75; M. F. Schulz, *Explicator,* XIV (1956), 46; James Zigerell, *Explicator,* XIII (1954), 7.

TO BROOKLYN BRIDGE

For discussions of *The Bridge,* of which "To Brooklyn Bridge" and "The River" are parts, see S. K. Coffman, Jr., *PMLA,* LXVI (1951), 65–77; Lawrence Dembo, *Am. Lit.,* XXVII (1955), 203–24; Brewster Ghiselin, *Part. Rev.,* XVI (1949), 679–86; F. J. Hoffman, *The Twenties* (New York: The Viking Press, Inc., 1955), pp. 223–39; Howard Moss, *Poetry,* LXII (1943), 32–45; O'Connor, *Sense and Sensibility in Modern Poetry* (U. of Chicago Press, 1948), pp. 19–25; Quinn, *The Metamorphic Tradition in Modern Poetry* (Rutgers U. Press, 1955), pp. 147–67; Waggoner, *The Heel of Elohim* (U. of Oklahoma Press, 1950, pp. 155–92; Winters, *In Defense of Reason* (Swallow & Morrow, 1947), pp. 577–603.
21. *Wall:* Wall Street in New York City.

THE RIVER

For discussions see "To Brooklyn Bridge."
5. *Bert Williams:* Negro vaudeville comedian who died in 1922.
9–10. *Thomas a Ediford:* A combined name for Thomas A. Edison and Henry Ford, selected as representative of a machine civilization.
112. *Dan Midland:* A famous hobo, who was killed in the manner described while "riding the rods."
133. *De Soto's bones:* When Hernando de Soto, discoverer of the Mississippi River, died in 1542, his men buried him in the Mississippi near the future site of New Orleans.

134. *the City*: New Orleans, which in its history has been under French, Spanish, and finally American government. "Throne" applies to the last only by extension from the other two, of course.

THE BROKEN TOWER

Discussed in Herbert Martey, *U. Kans. City Rev.*, XVIII (1952), 199–205; Muriel Rukeyser, *The Life of Poetry* (New York: A. A. Wyn, Inc., 1949), pp. 32–33.

E. E. CUMMINGS (1894–1962)

LIFE

Edward Estlin Cummings was born October 14 in Cambridge, Massachusetts. His father was then teaching at Harvard and later became minister of the Old South Church in Boston. Cummings took his A.B. from Harvard in 1915 and his M.A. in 1916. During World War I he was in the Norton Harjes Ambulance Corps until, through a military censor's error, he was placed for three months in a French detention camp. After the war he studied painting in Paris. Later he moved back to New York, where he continues to paint and to write poetry that is more traditional in form than his typographical experiments at first appear to indicate.

BIBLIOGRAPHY

Lauter, Paul. *E. E. Cummings: Index to First Lines and Bibliography of Works by and about the Poet*. Denver: Alan Swallow, 1955.

MAJOR WRITINGS

Poems, 1923–1954 (1954)

Tulips and Chimneys (1923)
& (1925)
is 5 (1926)
W (Viva) (1931)
no thanks (1935)
50 POEMS (1940)
1 x 1 (1944)
XAIPE (1950)

Him (1927; a play)
Eimi (1933; a report on a trip to the U.S.S.R.)

The Enormous Room (1922; autobiographical)
i: six nonlectures (1953)

BIOGRAPHY

None.

CRITICISM

Arthos, John. "The Poetry of E. E. Cummings," *Am. Lit.,* XIV (1943), 372–90.

Axelrod, Joseph. "Cummings and Phonetics," *Poetry,* LXV (1944), 88–94.

Baum, S. V. "E. E. Cummings: The Technique of Immediacy," *So. Atl. Quart.,* LIII (1954), 70–88.

Blackmur, R. P. *Form and Value in Modern Poetry,* pp. 287–312. New York: Anchor Books, Doubleday & Co., Inc., 1957.

Frankenberg, Lloyd. *Pleasure Dome,* pp. 159–94. Boston: Houghton Mifflin Co., 1949.

Harvard Wake, No. 5 (1946). Cummings number.

Sickels, E. M. "The Unworld of E. E. Cummings," *Am. Lit.,* XXVI (1954), 223–38.

Spencer, Theodore. "Technique as Joy," *Perspectives USA,* No. 2 (1953), pp. 23–29.

Von Abele, Rudolph. " 'Only to Grow': Change in the Poetry of E. E. Cummings," *PMLA,* LXX (1955), 913–33.

Watson, Barbara. "The Dangers of Security: E. E. Cummings' Revolt against the Future," *Ken. Rev.,* XVIII (1956), 519–37.

COMMENTS ON POEMS

ANYONE LIVED IN A PRETTY HOW TOWN

Discussed in H. C. Barrows, Jr., and W. R. Steinhoff, *Explicator,* IX (1950), 1; Arthur Carr, *Explicator,* XI (1952), 6; George Haines, *Sewanee Rev.,* LIX (1951), 216–17.

MY FATHER MOVED THROUGH DOOMS OF LOVE

Discussed in Haines, *Sewanee Rev.,* LIX (1951), 215–16.

WALTER DE LA MARE (1873–1956)

LIFE

Born April 25 at Charlton, Kent, the son of a churchwarden. He was educated at St. Paul's Cathedral Choir School, London, and in 1890 became a bookkeeper for the Anglo-American (Standard) Oil Company in London.

While there he began writing poems and stories in his free time. In 1908 he received a government Civil List pension which enabled him to devote full time to writing. He died June 22, 1956.

BIBLIOGRAPHY

Clark, L. A. "A Handlist of the Writings in Book Form (1902–1953) of Walter de la Mare," *Studies in Bibliography*, VI (1954), 197–217.
———. "Addendum: A Check-List of Walter de la Mare," *Studies in Bibliography*, VII (1955), 269–70.

MAJOR WRITINGS

Collected Poems (1941)
Collected Rhymes and Verses (1944; primarily for children)

Songs of Childhood (1902)
The Listeners and Other Poems (1912)
Motley and Other Poems (1918)
The Veil and Other Poems (1921)
The Burning Glass and Other Poems (1945)
Inward Companion (1950)

Walter de la Mare: A Selection from His Writings (1956; ed. Kenneth Hopkins)

Pleasures and Speculations (1940)
Private View (1953)

BIOGRAPHY

Brain, Russell. *Tea with Walter de la Mare*. London: Faber & Faber, Ltd., 1957.
Mégroz, R. L. *Walter de la Mare: A Biographical and Critical Study*. New York: George H. Doran Co., 1924.

CRITICISM

Atkins, John. *Walter de la Mare*. London: C. & J. Temple, 1947.
Brown, E. K. "The Epilogue to Mr. de la Mare's Poetry," *Poetry*, LXVIII (1946), 90–96.
Duffin, H. C. *Walter de la Mare: A Study of His Poetry*. London: Sidgwick & Jackson, 1949.
Endicott, N. J. "Walter de la Mare, 1873–1956," *University of Toronto Quarterly*, XXVI (1957), 109–21.
Gregory, Horace. "Contemporary Portrait No. 1: Walter de la Mare," *Poetry London–New York*, I (1956), 30–33.
———. "The Nocturnal Traveller: Walter de la Mare," *Poetry*, LXXX (1952), 213–32.

Hopkins, Kenneth. *Walter de la Mare*. London: Longmans, Green & Co., Ltd., 1953.

Johnson, M. C. "Fantasy and a Real World, in the Poetry of Walter de la Mare," pp. 75–85 in *Art and Scientific Thought*. New York: Columbia University Press, 1949.

Pritchett, V. S. "Walter de la Mare," *New Statesman*, LI (1956), 567–68.

Reid, Forrest. *Walter de la Mare: A Critical Study*. New York: Henry Holt & Co., Inc., 1929.

COMMENTS ON POEMS

THE LISTENERS

This is "the first of the three poems Thomas Hardy asked his wife to read to him as he lay on his deathbed" (Duffin, *Walter de la Mare*, p. 72 n.).

Discussed in Duffin, *Walter de la Mare*, pp. 19–21, 37–38; De Lancey Ferguson, *Explicator*, IV (1945), 15; F. L. Gwynn and R. W. Condee, *Explicator*, XII (1954), 26; Alfred Noyes, *Contemporary Review*, CXC (1956), 70–73; J. M. Purcell, *Explicator*, III (1945), 42, and IV (1946), 31; Reid, *Walter de la Mare*, pp. 155–58.

FARE WELL

Discussed in Deutsch, *Poetry in Our Time* (Holt, 1952), p. 234.

MAERCHEN

The title is a German word meaning "fairy tale." The poem's central idea resembles that expressed in Hardy's "Nature's Questioning," lines 19–20.

Discussed in Elisabeth Schneider, *Explicator*, IV (1946), 29.

SUNK LYONESSE

In Arthurian legend Lyonesse is the land, now submerged, between Land's End, Cornwall, and the Scilly Isles.

NOSTALGIA

Discussed in Brown, *Poetry*, LXVIII (1946), 90–92.

THE CHART

Discussed in Jarrell, *Poetry and the Age* (Vintage Books, 1955), p. 138.

T. S. ELIOT (1888–1964)

LIFE

Thomas Stearns Eliot was born September 26 in St. Louis, Missouri, of a family originally long in New England. At first more interested in philosophy and theology than in literature, he graduated from Harvard in 1910, spent a year in Paris at the Sorbonne, and returned for three years of graduate study at Harvard in philosophy and Indic philology. He left the United States in 1914, and did not return until 1932, when he made the first of several visits to this country. From 1914 to 1915 he studied at Oxford and subsequently worked as a bank clerk in London for a number of years. He was assistant editor of the *Egoist* from 1917 to 1919 and editor of the influential *Criterion* from 1923 until it ceased publication in 1939. For a number of years he has been a director of Faber and Faber, the London publishing house. In 1927 he became a British subject and soon attracted attention as a spokesman for the Anglo-Catholic branch of the Church of England. He is almost as well known for his essays as he is for his poetry, and since the middle 1930's he has shown an increasing interest in writing verse dramas. In 1948 he became one of the few American writers to receive the Nobel Prize for Literature.

BIBLIOGRAPHY

Gallup, D. C. *T. S. Eliot: A Bibliography Including Contributions to Periodicals and Foreign Translations.* New York: Harcourt, Brace & Co., Inc., 1953.

MAJOR WRITINGS

The Complete Poems and Plays, 1909–1950 (1952)

Prufrock and Other Observations (1917)
Poems (1919)
Ara Vos Prec (1920)
The Waste Land (1922)
Poems, 1909–25 (1925)
Ash-Wednesday (1930)
Four Quartets (1943)

Murder in the Cathedral (1935; verse drama)
The Family Reunion: A Play (1939; verse drama)
The Cocktail Party: A Comedy (1950; verse drama)
The Confidential Clerk: A Play (1954; verse drama)

Selected Essays (1932; enlarged ed., 1950)
On Poetry and Poets (1957)

BIOGRAPHY

None

CRITICISM

Bradbrook, M. C. *T. S. Eliot.* London: Longmans, Green & Co., Ltd., 1950.
Drew, Elizabeth. *T. S. Eliot: The Design of His Poetry.* New York: Charles Scribner's Sons, 1950.

Gardner, Helen. *The Art of T. S. Eliot.* London: Cresset Press, 1949.

Harvard Advocate, CXXV (1938). "For T. S. Eliot."

March, Richard, and Tambimuttu, M. J. *T. S. Eliot: A Symposium.* Chicago: Henry Regnery Co., 1949.

Martin, P. M. *Mastery and Mercy: A Study of Two Religious Poems.* London: Oxford University Press, 1957.

Matthiessen, F. O. *The Achievement of T. S. Eliot: An Essay on the Nature of Poetry,* rev. ed. New York: Oxford University Press, 1947.

Maxwell, D. E. S. *The Poetry of T. S. Eliot.* London: Routledge & Kegan Paul, Ltd., 1952.

Preston, Raymond. *'Four Quartets' Rehearsed: A Commentary on T. S. Eliot's Cycle of Poems.* London: Sheed & Ward, Ltd., 1946.

Rajan, B. (ed.). *T. S. Eliot: A Study of His Writings by Several Hands.* London: Dennis Dobson, Ltd., 1947.

Smidt, Kristian. *Poetry and Belief in the Work of T. S. Eliot.* Oslo: Jacob Dybwad, 1949.

Smith, Grover. *T. S. Eliot's Poetry and Plays: A Study in Sources and Meaning.* Chicago: The University of Chicago Press, 1956.

Unger, Leonard (ed.). *T. S. Eliot: A Selected Critique.* New York: Rinehart & Co., Inc., 1948.

Williamson, George. *A Reader's Guide to T. S. Eliot: A Poem-by-Poem Analysis.* New York: The Noonday Press, 1953. Reprinted as a paperback, The Noonday Press, 1957.

COMMENTS ON POEMS

Because the critical literature on Eliot is so vast, no listing of discussions will be made for the individual poems. Probably the two most valuable books for detailed discussions are those by Matthiessen and by Williamson, already listed under the criticism.

THE LOVE SONG OF J. ALFRED PRUFROCK

The epigraph is from Dante's *Inferno,* XXXVII, 61–66: "If I thought my answer were to one who ever could return to the world, this flame should shake no more; but since none ever did return alive from this depth, if what I hear be true, without fear of infamy I answer thee."

82–83. *Though I . . . no prophet:* Cf. Matthew 14:3–11. The "prophet" is John the Baptist.

94. *Lazarus:* See John 11:1–44 for the resurrection of Lazarus by Christ.

113. *swell a progress:* Increase the number in the prince's retinue on a journey.

121. *I shall . . . rolled:* With the bottoms turned up into cuffs in the manner of the young dandies of the 1900's. At that time trousers were customarily worn without cuffs.

SWEENEY AMONG THE NIGHTINGALES

The epigraph is from Aeschylus' *Agamemnon,* line 1343: "Ay me! I am smitten deep with a mortal blow."

6. *River Plate:* British for Rio de la Plata, the estuary on which is situated the city of Buenos Aires, Argentina.

7. *Raven:* The constellation of Corvus.

8. *hornèd gate:* Cf. Vergil's *Aeneid,* book vi, lines 893–96, where Aeneas, in Hades, is told that there are two gates of Sleep—the gate of horn, through which true dreams pass, and the gate of ivory, through which the false pass. This part of the *Aeneid* is taken from the *Odyssey,* xix, lines 562–67, where Penelope describes the two gates of Dreams. In Eliot's poem "the hornèd gate" is also perhaps the gate of death.

9. *Orion and the Dog:* Constellations.

38. *Agamemnon:* Leader of the Greeks at the siege of Troy, who on his return home is killed by Aegisthus, his wife's lover. Dying, Agamemnon speaks the words here used as epigraph.

GERONTION

The title, coined from the Greek *geron,* means "little old man."

The epigraph is from the Duke's speech to Claudio in Shakespeare's *Measure for Measure,* Act III, scene 1, lines 32–34.

12. *merds:* Dung.

17. *"We . . . sign":* Cf. Matthew 12:38–39.

18–19. *The word . . . darkness:* Cf. John 1:1 and Luke 2:12.

23. *Mr. Silvero:* Like those which follow, the name of an acquaintance recalled by the old man "speaking" the poem.

48. *wrath-bearing tree:* Cf. Genesis 2:16–17; 3.

53. *concitation:* Excitation or stirring up.

55. *you:* Christ.

68. *De Bailhache . . . Cammel:* Other remembered acquaintances.

69. *Bear:* Either of the constellations also known as the Dippers.

THE WASTE LAND

The epigraph, in Latin and Greek, is from chapter 48 of the *Satyricon* by Petronius: "For I myself saw with my own eyes the Sibyl of Cumae hanging in a cage; and when the boys cried to her: 'Sibyl, what do you want?'; she would reply: 'I want to die.'"

The Italian dedication, "the better craftsman," is from Dante's *Purgatorio,* XXVI, 117, where the reference is to Arnaut Daniel, the twelfth-century Provençal poet. Pound had helped Eliot compress the original version of *The Waste Land* from some eight-hundred lines into the present length.

The notes that Eliot appended to his poem follow, interspersed with additional editorial comment. After the introductory statement by Eliot himself, each of his notes has been designated by inserting his name in brackets immediately after the line number and by placing the note itself in quotation marks.

NOTES ON "THE WASTE LAND"

Not only the title, but the plan and a good deal of the incidental symbolism of the poem were suggested by Miss Jessie L. Weston's book on the Grail legend: *From Ritual to Romance* (Cambridge). Indeed, so deeply am I indebted, Miss Weston's book will elucidate the difficulties of the poem much better than my notes can do; and I recommend it (apart from the great interest of the book itself) to any who think such elucidation of the poem worth the trouble. To another work of anthropology I am indebted in general, one which has influenced our generation profoundly; I mean *The Golden Bough;* I have used especially the two volumes *Adonis, Attis, Osiris.* Anyone who is acquainted with these works will immediately recognize in the poem certain references to vegetation ceremonies.

I. THE BURIAL OF THE DEAD

8. *Starnbergersee:* A resort lake near Munich in Germany.

10. *Hofgarten:* A public park in Munich with a zoo and outdoor cafés.

12. *Bin . . . deutsch:* (German) "I am not Russian, I come from Lithuania, pure German."

20: [Eliot] "Cf. Ezekiel II, i."

23: [Eliot] "Cf. Ecclesiastes XII, v."

25. *There is . . . rock:* Cf. Isaiah 32:1–2.

31–34: [Eliot] "V. Tristan und Isolde, I, verses 5–8." The translation from the German is: "Fresh blows the wind / to the homeland; / my Irish child, / where are you waiting?"

42: [Eliot] "Id. III, verse 24." The translation of this verse from the German is: "Desolate and empty is the sea."

46: [Eliot] "I am not familiar with the exact constitution of the Tarot pack of cards, from which I have obviously departed to suit my own convenience. The Hanged Man, a member of the traditional pack, fits my purpose in two ways: because he is associated in my mind with the Hanged God of Frazer, and because I associate him with the hooded figure in the passage of the disciples to Emmaus in Part V. The Phoenician Sailor and the Merchant appear later; also the 'crowds of people,' and Death by Water is executed in Part IV. The Man with Three Staves (an authentic member of the Tarot pack) I associate, quite arbitrarily, with the Fisher King himself." Originally the Tarot pack of cards was used by Eastern magicians, but it is now employed by fortune-tellers like the fictitious Madame Sosostris (accent on the second syllable). The pack is still used in central Europe in playing the popular game of tarok (in French, *tarot*).

48. *Those . . . eyes:* From Shakespeare's *The Tempest*, Act I, scene 2, line 398, Ariel's song.

60: [Eliot] "Cf. Baudelaire:
> 'Fourmillante cité, cité pleine de rêves,
> 'Où le spectre en plein jour raccroche le passant.' "

These are the opening lines of "Les Sept Vieillards" ("The Seven Old Men"), Poem 90 in Charles Baudelaire's *Les Fleurs du Mal* (*Flowers of Evil*). The translation from the French is: "Swarming city, city full of dreams, / where the ghost in broad daylight hails the passerby."

63: [Eliot] "Cf. Inferno III, 55–57:
> 'si lunga tratta
> di gente, ch'io non avrei mai creduto
> che morte tanta n' avesse disfatta.' "

(Italian) "so long a train of people, I should never have believed Death had undone so many."

64: [Eliot] "Cf. Inferno IV, 25–27:
> 'Quivi, secondo che per ascoltare,
> 'non avea pianto, ma' che di sospiri,
> 'che l'aura eterna facevan tremare.' "

(Italian) "Here was no plaint, that could be heard, except of sighs, which caused the eternal air to tremble."

67. *St. Mary Woolnoth:* An Anglican church built in the eighteenth century at the corner of King William and Lombard streets.

68: [Eliot] "A phenomenon which I have often noticed."

70. *Mylae:* A naval battle (260 B.C.) in the Punic Wars in which the Romans defeated the Carthaginians.

74: [Eliot] "Cf. the Dirge in Webster's *White Devil*." See John Webster's *The White Devil*, Act V, scene 4, lines 97–98.

76: [Eliot] "V. Baudelaire, Preface to *Fleurs du Mal*." The translation of this line from the French is: " 'hypocritical reader!—my likeness,— my brother!' "

II. A GAME OF CHESS

77: [Eliot] "Cf. *Antony and Cleopatra*, II, ii, l. 190."

92: [Eliot] "Laquearia. V. *Aeneid*, I, 726:
> dependent lychni laquearibus aureis incensi, et noctem
> flammis funalia vincunt."

(Latin) "lighted lamps hang from the golden laquearia (fretted ceiling), and flaming torches drive out the night."

98: [Eliot] "Sylvan scene. V. Milton, *Paradise Lost*, IV, 140."

99: [Eliot] "V. Ovid, *Metamorphoses*, VI, Philomela." King Tereus of Thrace, according to this passage in Ovid's poem, rapes Philomela, sister of his wife, Procne, and then cuts off her tongue. In revenge the sisters kill Tereus' son and feed him to Tereus. When Tereus pursues them, the gods change him into a hoopoe, Philomela into a nightingale, and Procne into a swallow.

100: [Eliot] "Cf. Part III, l. 204."

115: [Eliot] "Cf. Part III, l. 195."

118: [Eliot] "Cf. Webster: 'Is the wind in that door still?'" See John Webster, *The Devil's Law Case,* Act III, scene 2, line 162.

126: [Eliot] "Cf. Part I, l. 37, 48."

128. *that Shakespeherian Rag:* B. R. McElderry, Jr., has pointed out that "That Shakespearian Rag" was a popular ragtime piece in 1912. The first two lines of the chorus are: "That Shakespearian rag— / Most intelligent, very elegant. . . ."

138: [Eliot] "Cf. the game of chess in Middleton's *Women beware Women.*" See Act II, scene 2 of this play by Thomas Middleton.

139. *demobbed:* (British slang) Demobilized from the army.

161. *chemist:* (British) Druggist.

172. *Good . . . night:* Cf. Shakespeare's *Hamlet,* Act IV, scene 5, lines 72–74.

III. THE FIRE SERMON

176: [Eliot] "V. Spenser, *Prothalamion.*"

182. *By . . . wept:* Cf. Psalm 137:1.

182. *Leman:* Archaic English word meaning "lover."

185. *But . . . hear:* See note to line 196.

192: [Eliot] "Cf. *The Tempest,* I, ii." The reference is to lines 389–90 in this scene of *The Tempest.*

196: [Eliot] "Cf. Marvell, *To His Coy Mistress.*" The reference is to lines 21–22 of the poem by Andrew Marvell. Cf. MacLeish's use of this passage in "You, Andrew Marvell" (p. 380).

197: [Eliot] "Cf. Day, *Parliament of Bees:*
'When of the sudden, listening, you shall hear,
'A noise of horns and hunting, which shall bring
'Actaeon to Diana in the spring,
'Where all shall see her naked skin . . .'"

199: [Eliot] "I do not know the origin of the ballad from which these lines are taken: it was reported to me from Sydney, Australia."

202: [Eliot] "V. Verlaine, *Parsifal.*" The translation of this verse from the French is: "And O those children's voices, singing in the cupola!"

204 and 206. *Jug . . . Tereu:* The words used by the Elizabethans to represent the song of the nightingale. Cf. Trico's song in Act V, scene 1 of *Campaspe* by John Lyly (1554?–1606), English novelist and dramatist.

210: [Eliot] "The currants were quoted at a price 'carriage and insurance free to London'; and the Bill of Lading etc. were to be handed to the buyer upon payment of the sight draft."

218: [Eliot] "Tiresias, although a mere spectator and not indeed a 'character,' is yet the most important personage in the poem, uniting all the rest. Just as the one-eyed merchant, seller of currants, melts into the Phoenician Sailor, and the latter is not wholly distinct from Ferdinand Prince of Naples, so all the women are one woman, and the two sexes meet in Tiresias. What Tiresias *sees*, in fact, is the substance of the poem. The whole passage from Ovid is of great anthropological interest. . . ." Eliot then quotes nineteen lines in Latin from Ovid's *Metamorphoses* iii. 320–38, which may be translated as follows: "He [Jupiter] jested with Juno and said: 'Certainly your [women's] pleasure is greater than men's [in love].' She denies it. They decided to ask the opinion of the learned Tiresias: both kinds of love had been known to him [as a man and as a woman]. For he had struck with his staff the bodies of two great serpents mating in a green wood; from a man he was changed, marvelous to say, and spent seven autumns as a woman. In the eighth year he saw the same serpents again and said: If there is such potency in striking you that it changes the lot of the striker to the opposite [sex], now I will strike you again!' When he had struck the same snakes, his original form and the shape with which he was born returned. He, then, chosen as arbiter for the playful dispute, confirms the words of Jupiter; it is said that Saturn's daughter [Juno] was more annoyed than she should have been in accordance with the situation and condemned the eyes of her own judge to eternal night. But the almighty father (for it is not permitted to any god to render vain the action of another god), in restitution for his loss of sight, gave [Tiresias] knowledge of the future and so relieved his punishment with dignity."

221: [Eliot] "This may not appear as exact as Sappho's lines, but I had in mind the 'longshore' or 'dory' fisherman, who returns at nightfall." Sappho's "lines" are probably those of a fragment addressed to Hesperus, the Evening Star.

234. *Bradford*: An industrial city in north central England.

245–46. I . . . *dead*: Tiresias lived and prophesied for several generations in Thebes before he was killed in the destruction of the city. After death he continued to prophesy in Hades, where Ulysses consulted him.

253: [Eliot] "V. Goldsmith, the song in *The Vicar of Wakefield*."

257: [Eliot] "V. *The Tempest*, as above." See Act I, scene 2, line 391.

258. *Strand*: A street in London.

264: [Eliot] "The interior of St. Magnus Martyr is to my mind one of the finest among Wren's interiors. See *The Proposed Demolition of Nineteen City Churches*: (P. S. King & Son, Ltd.)."

266: [Eliot] "The Song of the (three) Thames-daughters begins here. From line 292 to 306 inclusive they speak in turn. V. *Götterdämmerung*,

III, i: the Rhine-daughters." The reference is to the opera, *Twilight of the Gods,* by the German composer, Richard Wagner (1813–83).

275. *Greenwich reach:* A section of the Thames bordered by Greenwich, a borough of southeastern London on the south side of the river.

276. *Isle of Dogs:* A peninsula in the Thames opposite Greenwich.

277–78. *Weialala . . . leialala:* The refrain in the song of the Rhine-daughters in Wagner's opera.

279: [Eliot] "V. Froude, *Elizabeth,* Vol. I, ch. iv, letter of De Quadra to Philip of Spain: 'In the afternoon we were in a barge, watching the games on the river. (The queen) was alone with Lord Robert and myself on the poop, when they began to talk nonsense, and went so far that Lord Robert at last said, as I was on the spot there was no reason why they should not be married if the queen pleased.' "

293: [Eliot] "Cf. *Purgatorio,* V, 133:

> 'Ricorditi di me, che son la Pia;
> 'Siena mi fe', disfecemi Maremma.' "

(Italian) "Remember me, who am La Pia; Siena made me, Maremma unmade me." La Pia, a woman of Siena, was killed by her husband in the Sienese Maremma. Her soul here addresses Dante in purgatory. Cf. Pound's *Hugh Selwyn Mauberley,* the poem entitled, "Siena Mi Fe'; Disfecemi Maremma" (pp. 299 and 513).

293. *Highbury . . . Kew:* Districts in London.

296: *Moorgate:* A slum area in London.

300. *Margate Sands:* A seaside resort on the Thames estuary.

307: [Eliot] "V. St. Augustine's *Confessions:* 'to Carthage then I came, where a cauldron of unholy loves sang all about mine ears.' "

308: [Eliot] "The complete text of the Buddha's Fire Sermon (which corresponds in importance to the Sermon on the Mount) from which these words are taken, will be found translated in the late Henry Clarke Warren's *Buddhism in Translation* (Harvard Oriental Series). Mr. Warren was one of the great pioneers of Buddhist studies in the Occident."

309: [Eliot] "From St. Augustine's *Confessions* again. The collocation of these two representatives of eastern and western asceticism, as the culmination of this part of the poem, is not an accident."

V. WHAT THE THUNDER SAID

[Eliot] "In the first part of Part V three themes are employed: the journey to Emmaus, the approach to the Chapel Perilous (see Miss Weston's book) and the present decay of eastern Europe."

357: [Eliot] "This is *Turdus aonalaschkae pallasii,* the hermit-thrush which I have heard in Quebec Province. Chapman says (*Handbook of Birds of Eastern North America*) 'it is most at home in secluded woodland and thickety retreats. . . . Its notes are not remarkable for variety or volume, but in purity and sweetness of tone and exquisite modulation they are unequalled.' Its 'water-dripping song' is justly celebrated."

360: [Eliot] "The following lines were stimulated by the account of one of the Antarctic expeditions (I forget which, but I think one of Shackleton's): it was related that the party of explorers, at the extremity of their strength, had the constant delusion that there was *one more member* than could actually be counted." Cf. also Luke 24:13–34.

367–77: [Eliot] "Cf. Hermann Hesse, *Blick ins Chaos. . . .*" Eliot quotes a passage from Hesse's *A Glimpse into Chaos,* the translation of which from the German reads as follows: "Already half of Europe, at least half of Eastern Europe, is on the way to chaos, travels drunken in sacred madness along the edge of the abyss and the while sings, sings drunken and ecstatic as Dmitri Karamazov sang [cf. Dostoevski's *The Brothers Karamazov*]. Shocked by these songs the bourgeois laughs; the saint and the prophet listen to them with tears."

388. *chapel:* The Chapel Perilous of the Grail legends, where the knight must meet terrifying and supernatural adventures in order to be granted the sight of the Grail.

396. *Ganga:* Sanscrit name for the Ganges River.

398. *Himavant:* The Himalaya Mountains.

402: [Eliot] " 'Datta, dayadhvam, damyata' (Give, sympathize, control). The fable of the meaning of the Thunder is found in the *Brihada-ranyaka–Upanishad,* 5, 1. A translation is found in Deussen's *Sechzig Upanishads des Veda,* p. 489."

408: [Eliot] "Cf. Webster, *The White Devil,* V, vi:
'. . . they'll remarry
Ere the worm pierce your winding-sheet, ere the spider
Make a thin curtain for your epitaphs.' "

412: [Eliot] "Cf. *Inferno,* XXXIII, 46:
'ed io sentii chiavar l'uscio di sotto
all'orribile torre.' "
[(Italian) "And below I heard being locked the door of the horrible tower."]

"Also F. H. Bradley, *Appearance and Reality,* p. 346. 'My external sensations are no less private to myself than are my thoughts or my feelings. In either case my experience falls within my own circle, a circle closed on the outside; and, with all its elements alike, every sphere is opaque to the others which surround it. . . . In brief, regarded as an existence which appears in a soul, the whole world for each is peculiar and private to that soul.' "

417. *Coriolanus:* Gaius Marcius Coriolanus, Roman general of the fifth century B.C. Cf. Shakespeare's *Coriolanus.*

425: [Eliot] "V. Weston: *From Ritual to Romance;* chapter on the Fisher King."

426. *Shall . . . order?:* Cf. Isaiah 38:1.

428: [Eliot] "V. *Purgatorio*, XXVI, 148.

'"Ara vos prec per aquella valor

"que vos guida al som de l'escalina,

"sovegna vos a temps de ma dolor."

Poi s'ascose nel foco che gli affina.'"

Dante's Italian may be translated as follows: "'Now I pray you, by the Goodness that guides you to the summit of this stairway, be mindful in due season of my pain.' Then he hid him in the fire that refines them." The lines are spoken to Dante by Arnaut Daniel (cf. note to the dedication of *The Waste Land*). For another use of the "stairway" figure, cf. Part III of *Ash-Wednesday*.

429: [Eliot] "V. *Pervigilium Veneris*. Cf. Philomela in Parts II and III." The Latin poem "Pervigilium Veneris" ("The Eve of St. Venus") has been dated variously as belonging to the second through fourth centuries A.D. This phrase from near the end of the poem means: "When shall I be as the swallow?"

430: [Eliot] "V. Gerard de Nerval, Sonnet *El Desdichado*." This line from the sonnet "The Unfortunate One," by the French man of letters, Gérard de Nerval (1808–55) means "The Prince of Aquitaine at the ruined tower."

432: [Eliot] "V. Kyd's *Spanish Tragedy*." The subtitle of this play by Thomas Kyd (1557?–95?) is "Hieronymo's Mad Againe."

434: [Eliot] "Shantih. Repeated as here, a formal ending to an Upanishad. 'The Peace which passeth understanding' is our equivalent to this word."

THE HOLLOW MEN

George Williamson suggests that the title may come from Shakespeare's *Julius Caesar*, Act IV, scene 2, lines 20–27.

Mistah Kurtz—he dead: In this way is announced the death of the "lost" and "violent" Kurtz, central figure in Joseph Conrad's long short story, *Heart of Darkness*.

A penny . . . Guy: On Guy Fawkes Day (November 5) English children exhibit stuffed effigies of Fawkes and use this phrase to beg pennies for fireworks (cf. the ending of the poem). Fawkes (1570–1606) was one of the main figures in the Gunpowder Plot, a conspiracy to blow up King James I of England and Parliament on November 5, 1605. The plot was discovered and the leaders executed.

52–67. The eyes . . . empty men: For some details cf. Dante's *Inferno*, III, and *Paradiso*, XXXI–XXXII.

88–89. Between . . . descent: Cf. Dante's *Purgatorio*, XXXI, 107.

ASH-WEDNESDAY

4. Desiring . . . scope: Except for the change of "art" to "gift" this is line 7 in Shakespeare's Sonnet XXIX.

6. *agèd eagle:* Cf. Psalm 103:5 and Isaiah 40:31.

40. *Pray . . . death:* From the Ave Maria.

42. *Lady:* An idealized woman who may lead the penitent to God, as Beatrice did Dante.

42. *three white leopards:* Cf. the leopard, the lion, and the she-wolf in Dante's *Inferno,* I, symbolizing worldly pleasure, ambition, and avarice.

42. *juniper-tree:* Cf. I Kings 19:4.

43. *cool of the day:* Cf. Genesis 3:8.

46. *Shall . . . live?:* Cf. Ezekiel 37:1–14.

65. *burden of the grasshopper:* Cf. Ecclesiastes 12:5. "Burden" is also to be taken in its musical sense as an accompaniment or a refrain.

69. *Rose:* Often a symbol for the Virgin Mary. Cf. also the Mystic Rose of Dante's *Paradiso,* XXXI–XXXII.

93–94. *This . . . lot:* Cf. Ezekiel 45:1.

96. *stair:* Part III was published separately in 1929 under the title "Som de l'Escalina" ("The Summit of the Stairway"). Cf. the note to line 428 of *The Waste Land* (p. 470).

117–19. *Lord . . . only:* Cf. Matthew 8:8.

123. *Mary:* The Virgin Mary.

130. *Sovegna vos:* (Italian) "Be mindful." Cf. the note to line 428 of *The Waste Land.*

137–38. *Redeem the time:* Cf. Ephesians 5:14–16.

142. *yews:* The yew tree is a symbol of immortality.

148. *And . . . exile:* From the prayer Salve Regina, which reads in part: "And after this our exile, show unto us the blessed fruit of thy womb Jesus."

151. *Word:* Cf. John 1:1–5.

158. *O my people . . . thee:* Cf. Micah 6:3.

191. *Bless me father:* The beginning of the Catholic confession.

202. *ivory gates:* Cf. the note on line 8 of "Sweeney Among the Nightingales" (p. 463).

214. *Our peace in His will:* Dante's lesson. Cf. *Paradiso,* III, 85.

WILLIAM EMPSON (1906–   )

LIFE

Born September 27 at Howden, Yorkshire. He was educated at Winchester and Magdalene College, Cambridge, from which he graduated in mathematics. In 1929 he completed a fourth year in which he took a First in English literature. From 1931 to 1934 he taught English at the University of Tokyo. From 1937 to 1939 he taught at the National University, Peking, which had become a refugee university at Changsha. During World

War II he worked for the British Broadcasting Corporation in London. From 1947 to 1952 he was again at the Peking National University, and since 1953 he has been professor of English literature at Sheffield University. Best known as a literary critic, Empson has written poetry ever since college.

BIBLIOGRAPHY

None.

MAJOR WRITINGS

Collected Poems (1949; republished in London in 1955)

Poems (1935)
The Gathering Storm (1940)

Seven Types of Ambiguity (1930; rev. ed. 1947)
Some Versions of Pastoral (1935)
The Structure of Complex Words (1951)

BIOGRAPHY

None.

CRITICISM

Alvarez, A. "A Style from a Despair," *Twentieth Century*, CLXI (1957), 344–53.

Eberhart, Richard. "Empson's Poetry," pp. 571–88 in *Accent Anthology*, ed. Kerker Quinn and Charles Shattuck. New York: Harcourt, Brace & Co., Inc., 1946.

Madge, Charles. "Empson Agonistes," *Listen*, II (1956), 19–22.

Richards, I. A. "William Empson," *Furioso*, Vol. I, No. 3 (Spring, 1940), Suppl.

Singer, Burns. "In Stars or in Ourselves," *Encounter*, No. 28 (January, 1956), pp. 82–86.

Wain, John. "Ambiguous Gifts: Notes on the Poetry of William Empson," pp. 169–80 in *Preliminary Essays*. London: Macmillan & Co., Ltd., 1957.

Wanning, Andrews. "Neither Cassandra nor Comrade," *Furioso*, Vol. I, No. 4 (Summer, 1941), pp. 53–54.

COMMENTS ON POEMS

THE WORLD'S END

Discussed in Wain, *Preliminary Essays*, p. 173.

8. *Blind Satan's voice:* Satan is represented as blind, like his author, Milton, who wrote of Satan in *Paradise Lost*, I, 314–15: "He called so loud that all the hollow deep / Of Hell resounded."

14. *differential:* "They follow his movements exactly, as if calculated like the differential coefficients used in forming this view of the world" (Empson, *Collected Poems,* Notes, p. 90).

TO AN OLD LADY

This poem is addressed to the poet's mother.

1. *Ripeness is all:* Edgar's words to his father, the blinded old Gloucester (*King Lear,* Act V, scene 2, line 11).

5. *Our earth alone given no name of god:* Other planets bear names of such deities as Saturn, Neptune, Venus, and Mars.

17. *her precession:* "Her *precession* is some customary movement of the planet, meant to suggest the dignity of 'procession'" (Empson, *Collected Poems,* Notes, p. 94).

THIS LAST PAIN

Discussed in Eberhart, *Accent Anthology,* pp. 582–85; Wain, *Preliminary Essays,* pp. 178–79.

9–10. *"What is conceivable . . . ,"* Said Wittgenstein: *"Ein Sachverhalt ist denkbar" heist: Wir können uns ein Bild von ihm machen.* The German is translated "'An atomic fact is thinkable' means: we can imagine it" (Ludwig Wittgenstein, *Tractatus Logico-Philosophicus* [London: Kegan Paul, 1933], p. 42).

MISSING DATES

This poem is a *villanelle,* an old French form introduced into English poetry by Austin Dobson in the 1870's.

Discussed in Wanning, *Furioso,* Vol. I, No. 4 (1941), pp. 53–54.

3. *The waste remains:* I. A. Richards says that this phrase is an unconscious echo of the line in Tennyson's "Tithonus": "The woods decay, the woods decay and fall."

MANCHOULI

The title is the Chinese name of a town in Manchuria on the Siberian border. The English name is "Lupin."

ROBERT FROST (1874–1963)

LIFE

Born March 26 in San Francisco, of New England parentage. After his father's death, when Frost was eleven, his mother took him back to her parents' home in Lawrence, Massachusetts, where she taught school. Frost studied at Harvard for two years, then tried teaching, newspaper work, shoemaking, and farming. From 1912 to 1915 he lived in England, where he first achieved reputation as a poet. Returning to the United States, he taught at several different colleges and universities, including about twenty years at Amherst. He has received the Pulitzer Prize for Poetry four times, as well as numerous other awards. In his eighties he still travels much about the country, lecturing and reading his poetry.

BIBLIOGRAPHY

Clymer, W. B. S., and Green, C. R. *Robert Frost: A Bibliography*. Amherst, Mass.: Jones Library, Inc., 1937.
Mertins, Louis, and Mertins, Esther. *The Intervals of Robert Frost: A Critical Bibliography*. Berkeley, Cal.: University of California Press, 1947.

MAJOR WRITINGS

Complete Poems of Robert Frost, 1949 (1949)

A Boy's Will (1913)
North of Boston (1914)
Mountain Interval (1916)
New Hampshire: A Poem (1923)
West-Running Brook (1928)
A Further Range (1936)
A Witness Tree (1942)
A Masque of Reason (1945)
Steeple Bush (1947)
A Masque of Mercy (1947)

Selected Poems (1923; 3d ed. 1934)
The Road Not Taken: An Introduction to Robert Frost (1951; ed. Louis Untermeyer)

BIOGRAPHY

Cox, Sidney. *A Swinger of Birches: A Portrait of Robert Frost*. New York: New York University Press, 1957.
Munson, G. B. *Robert Frost: A Study in Sensibility and Good Sense*. New York: George H. Doran Co., 1927.

CRITICISM

Coffin, R. P. T. *New Poetry of New England: Frost and Robinson*. Baltimore, Md.: The Johns Hopkins Press, 1938.
Elliott, G. R. *The Cycle of Modern Poetry*, pp. 112–34. Princeton, N.J.: Princeton University Press, 1929.
Jarrell, Randall. *Poetry and the Age*, pp. 26–62. New York: Vintage Books, 1955.

Lowell, Amy. *Tendencies in Modern American Poetry*, pp. 79–136. New York: The Macmillan Co., 1917.

Newdick, R. S. "Robert Frost and the Classics," *Classical Journal*, XXXV (1940), 403–16.

O'Donnell, W. G. "Robert Frost and New England: A Revaluation," *Yale Rev.*, XXXVII (1948), 698–712.

Thompson, Lawrance. *Fire and Ice: The Art and Thought of Robert Frost*. New York: Henry Holt & Co., Inc., 1942.

Thornton, Richard (ed.). *Recognition of Robert Frost, Twenty-Fifth Anniversary*. New York: Henry Holt & Co., Inc., 1937.

Untermeyer, Louis. *From Another World*, pp. 206–28. New York: Harcourt, Brace & Co., Inc., 1939.

Van Doren, Mark. "The Permanence of Robert Frost," *Am. Schol.*, V (1936), 190–98.

Warren, R. P. "The Themes of Robert Frost," pp. 218–33 in *The Writer and His Craft: Being the Hopwood Lectures, 1932–1952*. Ann Arbor, Mich.: University of Michigan Press, 1954.

COMMENTS ON POEMS

THE TUFT OF FLOWERS

In *A Boy's Will* and the collected editions before that of 1949, the following couplet appears between lines 24 and 25:

> "I left my place to know them by their name,
> Finding them butterfly weed when I came."

MENDING WALL

Discussed in J. C. Broderick, *Explicator*, XIV (1956), 24; Deutsch, *This Modern Poetry* (Norton, 1935), p. 42.

AFTER APPLE-PICKING

Discussed in Brooks, *Modern Poetry and the Tradition* (U. of N. Carolina Press, 1939), pp. 114–16; R. L. Cook, *Accent*, X (1949), 36; Warren, *The Writer and His Craft*, pp. 226–31.

THE WOOD-PILE

Discussed in Brooks, *Modern Poetry and the Tradition* (U. of N. Carolina Press, 1939), pp. 113–14.

THE ROAD NOT TAKEN

Discussed in B. W. Griffith, *Explicator*, XII (1954), 55; Yvor Winters, *Sewanee Rev.*, LVI (1948), 568–70 (reprinted in Winters, *The Function of Criticism* [Alan Swallow, 1957], pp. 163–65).

THE WITCH OF COÖS

Coös is the northernmost county of New Hampshire, usually spelled "Coos," but pronounced as two syllables.

Discussed in C. M. Bowra, *Adelphi*, XXVII (1950), 56.

13. *Ralle the Sioux Control:* In spiritualism, a control is the particular spirit or intelligence which supposedly takes charge of and uses a medium during trance. Indians are popular as controls.

STOPPING BY WOODS ON A SNOWY EVENING

Discussed in C. A. McLaughlin, *U. Kans. City Rev.*, XXII (1956), 312–15; C. C. Walcutt, *Coll. Eng.*, XIV (1953), 450; Warren, *The Writer and His Craft*, pp. 220–23.

ACQUAINTED WITH THE NIGHT

Discussed in Yvor Winters, *Sewanee Rev.*, LVI (1948), pp. 590–91 (reprinted in Winters, *The Function of Criticism* [Alan Swallow, 1957], p. 182).

THE LOVELY SHALL BE CHOOSERS

Discussed in Elizabeth Nitchie and W. L. Werner, *Explicator*, XIII (1955), 39; Edward Schwartz, *Explicator*, XIII (1954), 3.

TWO TRAMPS IN MUD TIME

Discussed in Brooks, *Modern Poetry and the Tradition* (U. of N. Carolina Press, 1939), pp. 112–13; Charles Kaplan, *Explicator*, XII (1954), 51; G. F. Whicher, *Am. Schol.*, XIV (1945), 412–14.

34. *witching-wand:* A forked stick by which, it is believed, underground water may be detected.

DESERT PLACES

Discussed in R. P. Blackmur, *Nation*, CXLII (1936), 818–19; W. C. Brown, *U. Kans. City Rev.*, XV (1948), 62–63.

NEITHER OUT FAR NOR IN DEEP

Discussed in H. H. Corbin, Jr., and C. H. Hendricks, *Explicator*, I (1943), 58; Jarrell, *Poetry and the Age* (Vintage Books, 1955), pp. 38–40; Laurence Perrine, *Explicator*, VII (1949), 46.

DESIGN

Discussed in Jarrell, *Poetry and the Age* (Vintage Books, 1955), pp. 42–45.

DIRECTIVE

Discussed in Jarrell, *Poetry and the Age* (Vintage Books, 1955), pp. 46–49.

59. *Saint Mark says:* See Mark 4:11–12.

ROBERT GRAVES (1895–   )

LIFE

Born July 24 in London, the son of A. P. Graves, poet and inspector of schools. He was educated at a number of private schools and Charterhouse, and won an exhibition to St. John's College, Oxford, which he was prevented from taking up by the outbreak of World War I. He enlisted in the Royal Welch Fusiliers (in which Siegfried Sassoon was also an officer), began to write poetry, and was wounded in France. After the war he studied at Oxford, then taught English for a year at the University of Cairo. Since 1930, with a long interruption due to the Spanish Civil War and World War II, he has lived on the island of Majorca. Though poetry is most important to him, he has written brilliant historical novels, such as *I, Claudius,* and many scholarly and critical works.

BIBLIOGRAPHY

Seymour-Smith, Martin. "Robert Graves: A Select Bibliography," pp. 30–32 in *Robert Graves.* London: Longmans, Green & Co., Ltd., 1956.

MAJOR WRITINGS

Collected Poems (1955; contains all the poems that Graves wishes to preserve)

The White Goddess: An Historical Grammar of Poetic Myth (1948)
The Common Asphodel: Collected Essays on Poetry, 1922–1949 (1949)
The Crowning Privilege (1955)
Goodbye to All That (1929; revised and extended, 1957)

BIOGRAPHY

None.

CRITICISM

Gregory, Horace. "Robert Graves: A Parable for Writers," *Part. Rev.,* XX (1953), 44–54.
Hayman, Ronald. "Robert Graves," *Essays in Crit.,* V (1955), 32–43.
Muir, Edwin. "Robert Graves," pp. 163–76 in *Transition: Essays on Contemporary Literature.* New York: The Viking Press, Inc., 1926.
Schwartz, Delmore. "Graves in Dock: The Case for Modern Poetry," *New Republic,* CXXXIV (March 19, 1956), 20–21.
Seymour-Smith, Martin. *Robert Graves.* London: Longmans, Green & Co., Ltd., 1956.
Trilling, Lionel. "A Ramble on Graves," pp. 20–30 in *A Gathering of Fugitives.* Boston: Beacon Press, 1956.

COMMENTS ON POEMS

TO JUAN AT THE WINTER SOLSTICE

Background for reading this poem is amply provided by Graves's *The White Goddess,* especially chap. 24, "The Single Poetic Theme."
Discussed in Jarrell, *Poetry and the Age* (Vintage Books, 1955), pp. 202–3.

THOMAS HARDY (1840–1928)

LIFE

Born June 2 at Higher Bockhampton, Dorset, the son of a builder. After attending schools in Bockhampton and Dorchester, he was apprenticed in 1856 to John Hicks, a Dorchester architect. In 1862 he went to London to study architecture and work under Sir Arthur Blomfield, but in 1867 ill health drove him back to Dorset. There he remained until his death on January 11, 1928. Although he devoted himself primarily to writing fiction from 1868 to 1896, poetry was always his favorite means of expression.

BIBLIOGRAPHY

Purdy, Richard Little. *Thomas Hardy: A Bibliographical Study.* London: Oxford University Press, 1954.
Weber, C[arl] J. *The First Hundred Years of Thomas Hardy, 1840–1940: A Centenary Bibliography of Hardiana.* Waterville, Me.: Colby College Library, 1942.

MAJOR WRITINGS

Collected Poems of Thomas Hardy (1953)

Wessex Poems and Other Verses (1898)
Poems of the Past and the Present (1902)
The Dynasts: A Drama of the Napoleonic Wars (Part One, 1903; Part Two, 1905; Part Three, 1908)
Time's Laughingstocks and Other Verse (1909)
Satires of Circumstance: Lyrics and Reveries with Miscellaneous Pieces (1914)
Moments of Vision and Miscellaneous Verses (1917)
Late Lyrics and Earlier with Many Other Verses (1922)
Human Shows, Far Phantasies, Songs, and Trifles (1925)
Winter Words in Various Moods and Metres (1928)

Selected Poems of Thomas Hardy (1916)
Selected Poems (1940; ed. G. M. Young)

Thomas Hardy's Notebooks (1955; ed. Evelyn Hardy)
Letters (1954; ed. C. J. Weber)

BIOGRAPHY

Blunden, Edmund. *Thomas Hardy*. New York: The Macmillan Co., 1952.
Hardy, Evelyn. *Thomas Hardy: A Critical Biography*. London: Hogarth Press, Ltd., 1954.
Hardy, Florence E. *The Early Life of Thomas Hardy, 1840–1891*. London: Macmillan & Co., Ltd., 1928.
————. *The Later Years of Thomas Hardy, 1892–1928*. London: Macmillan & Co., Ltd., 1930.
Weber, C. J. *Hardy of Wessex*. New York: Columbia University Press, 1940.

CRITICISM

Bailey, J. O. *Thomas Hardy and the Cosmic Mind: A New Reading of The Dynasts*. Chapel Hill, N.C.: University of North Carolina Press, 1956.
Barzun, Jacques. "Hardy's One World," pp. 177–94 in *The Energies of Art*. New York: Harper & Bros., 1956.
Blackmur, R. P. "The Shorter Poems of Thomas Hardy," pp. 1–31 in *Form and Value in Modern Poetry*. New York: Anchor Books, Doubleday & Co., Inc., 1957.
Bowra, C. M. "The Lyrical Poetry of Thomas Hardy," pp. 220–41 in *Inspiration and Poetry*. London: Macmillan & Co., Ltd., 1955.
Brown, Douglas. *Thomas Hardy*. London: Longmans, Green & Co., Ltd., 1954.
Chew, S. C. *Thomas Hardy, Poet and Novelist*, rev. ed. New York: Alfred A. Knopf, Inc., 1928.
De la Mare, Walter. "Thomas Hardy's Lyrics," pp. 95–103 in *Private View*. London: Faber & Faber, Ltd., 1953.
Holloway, John. "Hardy," pp. 244–89 in *The Victorian Sage*. London: Macmillan & Co., Ltd., 1953.
Ransom, J. C. "Old Age of an Eagle," pp. 79–87 in *Poems and Essays*. New York: Vintage Books, 1955.
Rutland, W. R. *Thomas Hardy: A Study of His Writings and Their Background*. Oxford: Basil Blackwell, 1938.
Southern Review, VI (Summer, 1940). Hardy centennial number. Contains essays by such critics as Auden, Howard Baker, Leavis, Ransom, Schwartz, Tate, and Zabel.
Southworth, J. G. *The Poetry of Thomas Hardy*. New York: Columbia University Press, 1947.
Webster, H. C. *On a Darkling Plain: The Art and Thought of Thomas Hardy*. Chicago: The University of Chicago Press, 1947.

COMMENTS ON POEMS

HAP

Written in 1866. The manuscript is entitled "Chance."
Discussed in Howard Baker, *So. Rev.*, VI (1940), 52–53; C. I. Glicksberg,

West. Hum. Rev., VI (1952), 273–83; Webster, *On a Darkling Plain*, pp. 47–48.

12. *Doomsters:* Masters of fate.

NEUTRAL TONES

Written in 1867.

Discussed in Pinto, *Crisis in English Poetry* (Hutchinson's, 1951), pp. 41–42; Ransom, *Poems and Essays*, pp. 81–82.

FRIENDS BEYOND

Discussed in Ransom, *Poems and Essays*, pp. 82–83.

1. *William Dewy:* This name was used in *Tess of the D'Urbervilles* (1891), chap. 17.

1. *Tranter:* A carrier, one who carries goods or persons for hire. Dewy was also a tranter.

3. *Mellstock:* Hardy's name for the village of Stinsford, near Dorchester.

9. *stillicide:* Continuous dripping.

13. *terrestial:* Terrestrial.

16. *mid:* The permissive may.

23. *grinterns:* Granary bins.

24. *ho:* Fuss, bother.

32. *Trine:* The Trinity, or, possibly, the Three Fates.

NATURE'S QUESTIONING

Discussed in Pinto, *Crisis in English Poetry* (Hutchinson's, 1951), pp. 42–43; Tate, *On the Limits of Poetry* (Swallow, 1948), pp. 191–94.

DRUMMER HODGE

This poem on the Boer War was entitled "The Dead Drummer" when it first appeared in *Literature,* Nov. 25, 1899, p. 513.

Discussed in Pinto, *Crisis in English Poetry* (Hutchinson's, 1951), pp. 45–46.

3. *kopje-crest:* (South African) Top of a small hill.

8. *Wessex:* Covering almost exactly the area ruled by West Saxon kings of the eighth century, Hardy's Wessex was a fictitious county encompassing his native Dorset and including all or part of Devon, Somerset, Wiltshire, Hampshire, and Berkshire.

9. *Karoo:* A high plateau of 100,000 square miles in what is now Cape of Good Hope province, Union of South Africa.

SHELLEY'S SKYLARK

Shelley wrote his ode "To a Skylark" in Leghorn, Italy, in 1820.

TO AN UNBORN PAUPER CHILD

Discussed in Bowra, *Inspiration and Poetry*, pp. 239–40; Lewis, *The Poetic Image* (Oxford, 1947), pp. 150–53; Pinto, *Crisis in English Poetry* (Hutchinson's, 1951), p. 44.

THE DARKLING THRUSH

First printed under the title, "By the Century's Deathbed."
10. *Century's corpse:* A reference to the ending of the nineteenth century, which some took to be in 1899 but which Hardy believed was in 1900.

THE CURATE'S KINDNESS

4. *Pummery:* Poundbury pond, near Dorchester.
4. *Ten-Hatches Weir:* A dam to a pond near Dorchester.
5. *Union:* Poorhouse supported by a number of parishes.

THE MAN HE KILLED

Written in 1902.

CHANNEL FIRING

3. *chancel:* That part of a church in which the altar stands.
9. *glebe cow:* Cow grazing on land owned by a parish church.

THE CONVERGENCE OF THE TWAIN

On the night of April 14–15, 1912, the "unsinkable" White Star liner "Titanic," bound for America on her maiden voyage, sank after colliding with an iceberg.
Discussed in Brooks, *Modern Poetry and the Tradition* (U. of N. Carolina Press, 1939), pp. 242–43; Bowra, *Inspiration and Poetry,* pp. 226–27; W. S. Johnson, *Jour. Aesth. & Art Crit.,* XIII (1955), 496–506; Donat O'Donnell, *Spectator,* CXCV (July 8, 1955), 52; Pinto, *Crisis in English Poetry* (Hutchinson's, 1951), pp. 46–47; P. N. Siegel, *Explicator,* XI (1952), 13.
5. *salamandrine:* Unscathed or untouchable, as the mythical salamander which was supposed to be able to live in fire.

RAIN ON A GRAVE

Written January 31, 1913; inspired by the death of Hardy's first wife, Emma Lavinia Gifford, November 27, 1912. The manuscript is entitled "Rain on Her Grave."

THE SATIN SHOES

First printed with subtitle "A Quiet Tragedy."

THE OXEN

First printed in *The Times,* December 24, 1915.
Discussed in Delmore Schwartz, *So. Rev.,* VI (1940), 70–71; Stephen Spender, *Penguin New Writing,* No. 19 (1944), p. 129.
2. *they are all on their knees:* The elder is referring to a folk belief that as the ox fell on its knees in Bethlehem when Christ was born, so oxen

ever since fall on their knees at midnight Christmas Eve. Hardy had ridiculed the belief in *Tess of the D'Urbervilles* (1891), chap. 17, with his story of William Dewy making the bull kneel by fiddling the Nativity hymn, yet he had Angel Clare remark, "It's a curious story; it carries us back to medieval times, when faith was a living thing."

13. *barton:* Farmyard.

13. *coomb:* Deep valley.

IN TIME OF "THE BREAKING OF NATIONS"

The title refers to Jeremiah 51:20: "Thou art my battle axe and weapons of war; for with thee I break in pieces the nations, and with thee will I destroy kingdoms." This poem, written in 1915, was not inspired by World War I, but was a reminiscence of August, 1870, when the Franco-Prussian War was in progress.

Discussed in De Lancey Ferguson, *Explicator*, IV (1946), 25.

THE PEDIGREE

Written in 1916.

MIDNIGHT ON THE GREAT WESTERN

1. *journeying boy:* This boy appeared in *Jude the Obscure* (1896) as Little Father Time.

AN ANCIENT TO ANCIENTS

25. *"Sir Roger":* An old-fashioned country dance, named after Sir Roger de Coverley of the *Spectator*. Bright Young Things of the 1920's were doing the Charleston.

26. *The "Girl"* . . . *"Bohemian":* Opera by Balfe.

27. *"Trovatore":* Opera by Verdi.

29. *This season's paintings:* Probably late cubism and free form.

31. *Etty, Mulready, Maclise:* Early nineteenth-century painters.

38. *roof-wrecked:* A reference to the depreciation of Tennyson's reputation in the early twentieth century. Lytton Strachey had done some notable "roof-wrecking" in *Queen Victoria* (1921). Yet Hardy had not seen the worst that might befall Tennyson—that came in 1923, with Harold Nicolson's *Tennyson* and Hugh I'Anson Fausset's *Tennyson: A Modern Portrait.*

47. *Aïdes:* Hades or Pluto, mythical Greek god of the underworld.

64. *ye:* Youth, the "ancients' " young successors.

GERARD MANLEY HOPKINS (1844–1889)

LIFE

Born June 11 in Stratford, Essex, the son of a London adjuster. After studying at home and at Highgate Grammar School, he went up to Balliol College, Oxford, from which he took his degree in 1867. Born an Anglican, he was received into the Roman Catholic Church on October 21, 1866; in 1868 he became a Jesuit; and in 1877 he was ordained priest. After serving in several parishes, he taught classics at Stonyhurst College, Lancashire, from 1882 to 1884 and held the chair of Greek at the Royal University, Dublin, from 1884 until his death of typhoid fever on June 8, 1889.

BIBLIOGRAPHY

Bischoff, D. A. "The Manuscripts of Gerard Manley Hopkins," *Thought,* XXVI (1951), 551–80.
Charney, Maurice. "A Bibliographical Study of Hopkins Criticism," *Thought,* XXV (1950), 297–326.
Weyand, Norman. "A Chronological Hopkins Bibliography," pp. 393–436 in *Immortal Diamond: Studies in Gerard Manley Hopkins,* ed. Norman Weyand. London: Sheed & Ward, Ltd., 1949.

MAJOR WRITINGS

Poems (1918; ed. Robert Bridges)
Poems (1930; ed. Charles Williams)
Poems (1948; ed. W. H. Gardner)

A Hopkins Reader (1953; ed. John Pick)

"Unpublished Journal of Fr. G. M. Hopkins," *Month,* N.S., IV (1950), 375–84.
The Notebooks and Papers of Gerard Manley Hopkins (1937; ed. Humphry House)
Letters of Gerard Manley Hopkins to Robert Bridges (1935; ed. C. C. Abbott)
The Correspondence of Gerard Manley Hopkins and Richard Watson Dixon (1935; ed. C. C. Abbott)
Further Letters of Gerard Manley Hopkins (1938; rev. and enl. ed. 1956; ed. C. C. Abbott)

BIOGRAPHY

Lahey, G. F. *Gerard Manley Hopkins.* London: Oxford University Press, 1930.

CRITICISM

Gardner, W. H. *Gerard Manley Hopkins* (1844–1889): *A Study of Poetic Idiosyncrasy in Relation to Poetic Tradition.* 2 vols. London: Secker & Warburg, 1948–49.
Gerard Manley Hopkins, by the Kenyon Critics. New York: New Directions, 1945. Essays by F. R. Leavis, Robert Lowell, H. M. McLuhan,

Josephine Miles, Arthur Mizener, Austin Warren, and Harold White-hall.

Hartmann, G. H. "Hopkins," pp. 47–67 in *The Unmediated Vision.* New Haven, Conn.: Yale University Press, 1954.

Leavis, F. R. "Gerard Manley Hopkins," pp. 44–58 in *The Common Pursuit.* London: Chatto & Windus, 1953.

Peters, W. A. M. *Gerard Manley Hopkins.* New York: Oxford University Press, 1948.

Pick, John. *Gerard Manley Hopkins, Priest and Poet.* London: Oxford University Press, 1942.

Read, Herbert. "Gerard Manley Hopkins," pp. 331–53 in *The Nature of Literature.* New York: Horizon Press, Inc., 1956.

Richards, I. A. "Gerard Hopkins," *Dial,* LXXXI (1926), 195–203.

Weyand, Norman° (ed.). *Immortal Diamond: Studies in Gerard Manley Hopkins.* London: Sheed & Ward, Ltd., 1949.

Winters, Yvor. "The Poetry of Gerard Manley Hopkins," pp. 101–56 in *The Function of Criticism.* Denver, Col.: Alan Swallow, 1957.

COMMENTS ON POEMS

THE HABIT OF PERFECTION

Originally called "The Kind Betrothal," the first draft of this poem is dated January 18–19, 1866, nine months before Hopkins was received into the Roman Catholic Church.

Discussed in Leavis, *The Common Pursuit,* pp. 44–46, 53; Boyd Litzinger, *Explicator,* XVI (1957), 1; Pick, *Gerard Manley Hopkins,* p. 16; Winters, *The Function of Criticism,* p. 146.

THE WRECK OF THE DEUTSCHLAND

The "Deutschland," which was wrecked on a sandbank off the mouth of the Thames, had sailed from Bremen, Germany, bearing, among others, five Franciscan nuns. They had been exiled by the Falk Laws, under which all members of Catholic orders except doctors and nurses were expelled. Hopkins began this poem in December, 1875. It marks the resumption of his career as poet.

Discussed by R. R. Boyle, pp. 333–50 in Weyand (ed.), *Immortal Diamond;* W. H. Gardner, *Essays and Studies,* XXI (1935), 124–52; F. R. Leavis, *New Bearings* (Chatto & Windus, 1954), pp. 175–80; F. R. Leavis, *Scrutiny,* XII (1944), 82–93; P. M. Martin, *Mastery and Mercy: A Study of Two Religious Poems* (London: Oxford University Press, 1957); Pick, *Gerard Manley Hopkins,* pp. 40–51; F. B. Thornton, *Catholic World,* CLX (1944), 41–46.

31. *voel:* A hill near St. Beuno's College, North Wales, where Hopkins wrote his poem.

77. *at a crash Paul:* Acts 9:1–9 tells how Saul of Tarsus (St. Paul) suddenly was converted to Christianity by a light from heaven on the road to Damascus.

78. *Austin:* St. Augustine (354–430), perhaps the greatest of the Fathers of the Church, describes in his *Confessions* how he was slowly converted.

96. *reeve:* A nautical image, meaning to tie fast by passing a rope through holes.

108. *Kentish Knock:* A sandbank in the English Channel near the mouth of the Thames.

111. *whorl:* Screw, propeller of a ship.

157. *Gertrude . . . and Luther:* Gertrude (1256?–1302), saint and mystic, lived near Eisleben, birthplace of Martin Luther.

165. *Orion:* In Greek myth a famous hunter who after death became a constellation.

177. *father Francis:* St. Francis of Assisi (1181?–1226), founder of the Franciscan order.

180. *Lovescape:* Stigmata received by St. Francis. Their pattern is that of Christ's five wounds.

186. *pastoral forehead of Wales:* St. Beuno's College, on a hill in North Wales.

198. *weather of Gennesareth:* Matthew 14:22–34 describes the storm on the Sea of Galilee, which Jesus calmed and on which Simon Peter walked.

232. *Tarpeian-fast:* As secure as is the Tarpeian Rock on the Capitoline Hill, Rome.

237. *Feast of the one woman:* Feast of the Immaculate Conception of the Blessed Virgin Mary, December 8.

THE WINDHOVER

Dated May 30, 1877, at Pantasaph, North Wales. Hopkins called this poem "the best thing I ever wrote" and consequently dedicated it "To Christ our Lord."

This poem has probably attracted more critical discussion in the last thirty years than any other. The word "buckle" has been interpreted in a remarkable number of ways. Important analyses are to be found in Empson, *Seven Types of Ambiguity* (New Directions, 1947), pp. 284–86; F. L. Gwynn, *Mod. Lang. Notes,* LXVI (1951), 366–70; Hartmann, *Unmediated Vision,* pp. 49–67; F. N. Lees, *Scrutiny,* XVII (1950), 32–38; H. M. McLuhan, *Ken. Rev.,* VI (1944), 326–29; Pick, *Gerard Manley Hopkins,* pp. 70–71; Richards, *Dial,* LXXXI (1926), 197–99; R. V. Schoder, pp. 276–306 in Weyand (ed.), *Immortal Diamond;* Dennis Ward, pp. 138–52 in John Wain (ed.), *Interpretations* (London: Routledge & Kegan Paul, Ltd., 1955); Winters,

The Function of Criticism, pp. 127–39; C. R. Woodring, *West. Rev.,* XV (1950), 61–64.

1. *minion:* Favorite.
12. *sillion:* Furrow.

PIED BEAUTY

Written in the summer of 1877.
Discussed in Samuel Kliger, *Mod. Lang. Notes,* LIX (1944), 408–10; Pick, *Gerard Manley Hopkins,* pp. 53–56.

BINSEY POPLARS

Written at Oxford in March, 1879, when Hopkins was a parish priest.
Discussed in Leavis, *The Common Pursuit,* pp. 48–49.

THE LEADEN ECHO AND THE GOLDEN ECHO

This poem, dated October 13, 1882, at Stonyhurst College, Blackburn, Lancashire, is the song of the maidens which Hopkins wrote as part of an unfinished play, *St. Winefred's Well.*
Discussed in Leavis, *New Bearings* (Chatto & Windus, 1954), pp. 172–75; Pick, *Gerard Manley Hopkins,* pp. 93–95.

SPELT FROM SIBYL'S LEAVES

Written in Dublin about 1884. The title refers to the reckoning spelled out by the Cumaean Sibyl to Aeneas (*Aeneid* vi. 95–97).
Discussed in Leavis, *New Bearings* (Chatto & Windus, 1954), pp. 182–86; Pick, *Gerard Manley Hopkins,* pp. 141–43; Richards, *Dial,* LXXXI (1926), 199–201; W. J. Rooney, *Jour. Aesth. & Art Crit.,* XIII (1955), 507–19; R. V. Schoder, *Thought,* XIX (1944), 634–48; H. C. Sherwood, *Explicator,* XV (1956), 5.
6. *throughther:* Dialectal telescoping of "through other."

TO SEEM THE STRANGER LIES MY LOT

This is one of a group of seven sonnets written in 1884–85 in Dublin, the most introspective of all Hopkins' verse. They are generally known as "the terrible sonnets." On the general background to these sonnets, see Peters, *Gerard Manley Hopkins,* pp. 45–49.
Discussed in Pick, *Gerard Manley Hopkins,* pp. 143–45; Winters, *The Function of Criticism,* p. 149.

I WAKE AND FEEL THE FELL OF DARK

Another of "the terrible sonnets."
Discussed in Leavis, *New Bearings* (Chatto & Windus, 1954), p. 188; S. C. Pepper, *The Basis of Criticism in the Arts* (Cambridge, Mass.: Harvard University Press, 1945), pp. 127–40; Pick, *Gerard Manley Hopkins,* pp. 145–46; Winters, *The Function of Criticism,* pp. 149–50.

PATIENCE, HARD THING!

A third "terrible sonnet."
Discussed in Pick, *Gerard Manley Hopkins,* pp. 149–50; Winters, *The Function of Criticism,* p. 150.

MY OWN HEART LET ME MORE HAVE PITY ON

A fourth "terrible sonnet."
Discussed in Pick, *Gerard Manley Hopkins,* p. 148; Riding and Graves, *A Survey of Modernist Poetry* (Doubleday, 1928), pp. 90–92; Elisabeth Schneider, *Explicator,* V (1947), 51; Winters, *The Function of Criticism,* p. 150.

THAT NATURE IS A HERACLITEAN FIRE

Written in Dublin in 1888. Heraclitus, Greek philosopher of the sixth to the fifth century B.C., conceived everything as the result of the flux, eternal change, from an essence he called "fire."
Discussed in Pick, *Gerard Manley Hopkins,* pp. 154–55.

THOU ART INDEED JUST, LORD

Written early in 1889. The Vulgate version of Jeremiah 12:1 is translated in the first three lines of the poem.
Discussed in R. A. Brower, *The Fields of Light* (New York: Oxford University Press, 1951), pp. 26–27; Leavis, *The Common Pursuit,* p. 56; Winters, *The Function of Criticism,* p. 151.

TO R. B.

Dated April 22, 1889. "R. B." is Robert Bridges, the friend who brought out the first edition of Hopkins' poems in 1918.
Discussed in W. M. Gibson, *Explicator,* VI (1947), 12; Stauffer, *The Nature of Poetry* (Norton, 1946), pp. 40–41; Winters, *The Function of Criticism,* p. 151.

A. E. HOUSMAN (1859–1936)

LIFE

Alfred Edward Housman was born March 26 near Bromsgrove, Worcestershire, the son of a solicitor. After private schooling he entered St. John's College, Oxford, but although he excelled in classical studies, he failed to graduate with distinction. From 1882 until 1892 he was in London, clerking at the Patent Office and working in his free time on classical studies. In 1892 he became professor in Latin at University College, London, and in

1911 he took up the Kennedy professorship in Latin at Trinity College, Cambridge, a position he held until his death on April 30, 1936. His poetical career was sporadic. His scholarly career, devoted chiefly to the study of Manilius, was unceasing.

BIBLIOGRAPHY

Carter, John, and Sparrow, John. *A. E. Housman: An Annotated Hand-List*. London: Rupert Hart-Davis, 1952.
Stallman, R. W. "Annotated Bibliography of A. E. Housman: A Critical Study," *PMLA*, LV (1945), 463–502.

CONCORDANCE

Hyder, C. K. (ed.). *A Concordance to the Poems of A. E. Housman*. Lawrence, Kans.: University of Kansas Press, 1940.

MAJOR WRITINGS

The Collected Poems of A. E. Housman (1939)

A Shropshire Lad (1896)
Last Poems (1922)
More Poems (1936)

A Shropshire Lad (1946; ed. C. J. Weber; with Notes and Bibliography)

The Name and Nature of Poetry (1933)

BIOGRAPHY

Gow, A. S. F. *A. E. Housman: A Sketch*. Cambridge: At the University Press, 1936.
Housman, Laurence. *A.E.H.: Some Poems, Some Letters, and a Personal Memoir by His Brother, Laurence Housman*. London: Jonathan Cape, Ltd., 1937.
Richards, Grant. *Housman, 1897–1936*. New York: Oxford University Press, 1942.
Watson, George. *A. E. Housman: A Divided Life*. London: Rupert Hart-Davis, 1957.
Withers, Percy. *A Buried Life: Personal Recollections of A. E. Housman*. London: Jonathan Cape, Ltd., 1940.

CRITICISM

Connolly, Cyril. "A. E. Housman: A Controversy," pp. 47–62 in *The Condemned Playground*. London: George Routledge & Sons, Ltd., 1945.
Jarrell, Randall. "Texts from Housman," *Ken. Rev.*, I (1939), 260–71.

Jones, H. M. "A. E. Housman, Last of the Romans," *Double Dealer*, III (1922), 136–41.
Scott-Kilvert, Ian. *A. E. Housman*. London: Longmans, Green & Co., Ltd., 1955.
Tinker, C. B. "Housman's Poetry," *Yale Rev.*, XXV (1936), 84–95.
Wilson, Edmund. "A. E. Housman," pp. 60–71 in *The Triple Thinkers*, rev. ed. New York: Harcourt, Brace & Co., Inc., 1948.

COMMENTS ON POEMS

1887

Discussed in T. S. K. Scott-Craig, C. C. Walcutt, and Cleanth Brooks, *Explicator*, II (1944), 34; W. L. Werner, *Coll. Eng.*, VI (1944), 165–66.
1. *Clee:* Town in southern Shropshire.
1. *beacon:* Bonfire.
7. *'tis fifty years to-night:* In 1887 Victoria completed fifty years of her reign. This achievement was signalized by the Golden Jubilee.
17. *dawns in Asia:* From 1878 to 1880 the British fought in Afghanistan, and from 1885 to 1887 in Upper Burma.
19. *Nile:* In 1882 Wolseley crushed the revolt in Egypt of Arabi Pasha at Tel-el-Kebir, and in 1885 Gordon and his forces were massacred at Khartoum.
20. *Severn:* Shropshire's principal river.
28. *Fifty-third:* The Fifty-third Shropshire Regiment of Foot.

LOVELIEST OF TREES

Discussed in George Arms, *Explicator*, I (1943), 57; Winifred Lynskey, *Explicator*, IV (1946), 59.

IS MY TEAM PLOUGHING?

Discussed in O'Connor, *Sense and Sensibility in Modern Poetry* (U. of Chicago Press, 1948), pp. 133–34.

ON WENLOCK EDGE

Discussed in De Lancey Ferguson, *Explicator*, IV (1945), 15; Spiro Peterson, *Explicator*, XV (1957), 46; R. W. Stallman, *Explicator*, III (1945), 26.
1. *Wenlock Edge:* A ridge in southern Shropshire.
2. *the Wrekin:* An extinct volcano.
6. *Uricon:* Roman city, Uriconium, which served as the capital of Britannia Secunda during the Roman occupation and was burned by the Saxons in 584 A.D.

TERENCE, THIS IS STUPID STUFF

Originally Housman planned to entitle his book *The Poems of Terence Hearsay*. His friend A. W. Pollard suggested that a better title would be *A Shropshire Lad*.

Discussed in B. W. Griffith, Jr., *Explicator*, XIII (1954), 16; W. L. Werner and Fred Dudley, *Explicator*, XIV (1955), 2.

18. *Burton:* Burton-upon-Trent, Derbyshire, is a great brewing center. Several rich brewers have been elevated to the peerage.

21. *Milton can:* Milton said his purpose in writing *Paradise Lost* was to "justify God's ways to man" by asserting Divine Providence (I, 26).

76. *Mithridates:* Mithridates VI, king of Pontus (120–63 B.C.), of whom Pliny wrote in his *Natural History* that he inured himself to poison by the method Housman describes.

EPITAPH ON AN ARMY OF MERCENARIES

This poem was written to honor the heroism of the British Regular Army in the First Battle of Ypres, October, 1914. Housman published his poem in *The Times* on the third anniversary of the turning point of the battle, October 31, 1917.

Discussed in Vincent Freimarck, *Mod. Lang. Notes*, LXVII (1952), 548–50; W. L. Werner, *Explicator*, II (1944), 38.

RANDALL JARRELL (1914–1965)

LIFE

Born May 6 in Nashville, Tennessee. He studied psychology and English at Vanderbilt, where he had two years of graduate work. After teaching at Kenyon College (1937–39) and the University of Texas (1939–42), he enlisted in the Army Air Corps. In 1946–47 he taught at Sarah Lawrence College and was literary editor of *The Nation*. Since 1947 he has been an associate professor of English at the Women's College of the University of North Carolina, and in addition has taught at Princeton, the University of Illinois, and the Salzburg (Austria) Seminar in American Civilization.

BIBLIOGRAPHY

None.

MAJOR WRITINGS

Blood for a Stranger (1942)
Little Friend, Little Friend (1945)
Losses (1948)
The Seven-League Crutches (1951)

Selected Poems (1955)

Poetry and the Age (1953; criticism)
Pictures from an Institution: A Comedy (1954; novel)

BIOGRAPHY

None.

CRITICISM

Maguire, C. E. "Shape of the Lightning: Randall Jarrell," *Renascence*, VII (1955), 115–20 and 181–86, 195.

Quinn, Sister M. B. *The Metamorphic Tradition in Modern Poetry*, pp. 168–206. New Brunswick, N.J.: Rutgers University Press, 1955.

Tyler, Parker. "The Dramatic Lyrism of Randall Jarrell," *Poetry*, LXXIX (1952), 335–46.

COMMENTS ON POEMS

90 NORTH

20. *Cloud-Cuckoo-Land:* In Aristophanes' *The Birds,* an imaginary city built in the clouds by the cuckoos; hence any fantastic, illusionary world.

SECOND AIR FORCE

[Jarrell's note from *Selected Poems*] "In 'Second Air Force' the woman visiting her son remembers what she has read on the front page of her newspaper the week before, a conversation between a bomber, in flames over Germany, and one of the fighters protecting it: 'Then I heard the bomber call me in: "Little Friend, Little Friend, I got two engines on fire. Can you see me, Little Friend?" I said, "I'm crossing right over you. Let's go home." ' "

51. *wired fur:* Electrically heated flying suits.

THE DEATH OF THE BALL TURRET GUNNER

Discussed in I. C. Hungerland, *Jour. Aesth. & Art Crit.*, XIII (1955), 353–54.

[Jarrell's note from *Selected Poems*] "A ball turret was a plexiglass sphere set into the belly of a B-17 or B-24, and inhabited by two .50 caliber machine-guns and one man, a short small man. When this gunner tracked with his machine-guns a fighter attacking his bomber from below, he revolved with the turret; hunched upside-down in his little sphere, he looked like the foetus in the womb. The fighters which attacked him were armed with cannon firing explosive shells. The hose was a steam hose."

SEELE IM RAUM

[Jarrell's note from *Selected Poems*] " 'Seele im Raum' is the title of one of Rilke's poems; 'Soul in Space' sounded so glib that I couldn't use it instead. An eland is the largest sort of African antelope—the males are as big as a horse, and you often see people gazing at them, at the zoo, in uneasy wonder."

ROBINSON JEFFERS (1887–1962)

LIFE

Born January 10 in Pittsburgh, Pennsylvania, where his father was a teacher of theology. After attending schools at home and abroad, he graduated from Occidental College in 1905. He did graduate work at several institutions and then turned entirely to writing poetry, being supported from 1912 on by a legacy. In 1914 he settled at Tor House on Carmel Bay, south of Monterey, California. Overlooking the bay Jeffers himself built a stone tower, where he still does most of his writing. Many of his poems are in some way concerned with the harshly beautiful coastal country around Carmel.

BIBLIOGRAPHY

Alberts, S. S. *A Bibliography of the Works of Robinson Jeffers.* New York: Random House, Inc., 1933.

MAJOR WRITINGS

Tamar and Other Poems (1924)
Roan Stallion, Tamar, and Other Poems (1925)
Cawdor and Other Poems (1928)
Give Your Heart to the Hawks and Other Poems (1933)
Solstice and Other Poems (1935)
Such Counsels You Gave to Me & Other Poems (1937)
Be Angry at the Sun and Other Poems (1941)
The Double Axe & Other Poems (1948)
Hungerfield and Other Poems (1954)

The Selected Poetry of Robinson Jeffers (1938)

Medea: Freely Adapted from the Medea of Euripides (1946; translation)

BIOGRAPHY

Sterling, George. *Robinson Jeffers, the Man and the Artist.* New York: Boni & Liveright, Inc., 1926.

CRITICISM

Carpenter, F. I. "The Values of Robinson Jeffers," *Am. Lit.*, XI (1940), 353–66.

Gierasch, Walter. "Robinson Jeffers," *Eng. Jour.* (College ed.), XXVIII (1939), 284–95.

Gilbert, Rudolph. *Shine, Perishing Republic: Robinson Jeffers and the Tragic Sense in Modern Poetry.* Boston: Bruce Humphries, Inc., 1936.

Gregory, Horace. "Poets without Critics: A Note on Robinson Jeffers," *New World Writing*, 7th Mentor Selection (1955), pp. 40–52.

Powell, L. C. *Robinson Jeffers: The Man & His Work.* Los Angeles: The Primavera Press, 1934; rev. ed., Pasadena, Cal.: San Pasqual Press, 1940.

Schwartz, Delmore, and Taylor, Frajam. "The Enigma of Robinson Jeffers," *Poetry*, LV (1939), 30–46.

Short, R. W. "The Tower beyond Tragedy," *So. Rev.*, VII (1941), 132–44.

Squires, Radcliffe. *The Loyalties of Robinson Jeffers.* Ann Arbor, Mich.: University of Michigan Press, 1956.

Waggoner, H. H. "Science and the Poetry of Robinson Jeffers," *Am. Lit.*, X (1938), 275–88.

COMMENTS ON POEMS

BIRDS

11. *Lobos:* A point of land on Carmel Bay.

APOLOGY FOR BAD DREAMS

The first book of poems solely by Jeffers to include this poem was the Modern Library reprint of *Roan Stallion, Tamar, and Other Poems* (1935), but "Apology for Bad Dreams" was published, with several other poems by Jeffers, in Louis Untermeyer (ed.), *A Miscellany of American Poetry* (New York: Harcourt, Brace & Co., Inc., 1927).

24. *Soberanes:* A point of land just south of Carmel Bay.

31. *this little house:* Tor House, Jeffers' home.

50. *Tamar Cauldwell:* The incestuous heroine of *Tamar*, the title poem of the volume published by Jeffers in 1924.

52. *Point Pinos:* A point of land just north of Monterey.

52. *Sur Rivers:* About twenty miles south of Carmel along the California coast. The coastal strip between Point Pinos and the Sur Rivers is the "Jeffers Country."

PROMISE OF PEACE

The first book of poems solely by Jeffers to include this poem was the Modern Library reprint of *Roan Stallion, Tamar, and Other Poems* (1935), but "Promise of Peace" was published, with several other poems by Jeffers, in Louis Untermeyer (ed.), *A Miscellany of American Poetry* (New York: Harcourt, Brace & Co., Inc., 1927).

THE EYE

6. *brave dwarfs*: The Japanese. This poem was written during World War II.

D. H. LAWRENCE (1885–1930)

LIFE

Born September 11 in Eastwood, Nottinghamshire, the son of a coal miner. After attending school in Nottingham and Eastwood and receiving a teaching certificate from University College, Nottingham, he taught briefly at Croydon, near London. He devoted most of his life to writing fiction, but also painted and wrote poetry, studies in psychology, and literary criticism. His nomadic life carried him to Australia, New Mexico, Mexico, Italy, and Sicily. He died of tuberculosis in southern France on March 2, 1930.

BIBLIOGRAPHY

McDonald, E. D. *A Bibliography of the Writings of D. H. Lawrence.* Philadelphia: The Centaur Book Shop, 1925.
———. *The Writings of D. H. Lawrence, 1925–1930: A Bibliographical Supplement.* Philadelphia: The Centaur Book Shop, 1931.
White, William. *D. H. Lawrence: A Checklist, 1931–1950.* Detroit, Mich.: Wayne University Press, 1950.

MAJOR WRITINGS

The Collected Poems of D. H. Lawrence (1928; 2 vols.)

Love Poems and Others (1913)
Amores: Poems (1916)
Look! We Have Come Through (1917)
New Poems (1918)
Tortoises (1921)
Birds, Beasts and Flowers (1923)
Pansies (1929)
Nettles (1930)
Last Poems (1932)
Fire and Other Poems (1940)

Selected Poems (1947; ed. Kenneth Rexroth)
Selected Poems (1951; ed. James Reeves)

The Portable D. H. Lawrence (1947; ed. Diana Trilling)

Selected Literary Criticism (1955; ed. Anthony Beal)

The Letters of D. H. Lawrence (1932; ed. Aldous Huxley)
The Selected Letters of D. H. Lawrence (1958; ed. Diana Trilling)

BIOGRAPHY

Aldington, Richard. *Portrait of a Genius, But—*. London: Wm. Heinemann, Ltd., 1950.
Moore, H. T. *The Intelligent Heart: The Story of D. H. Lawrence*. New York: Farrar, Straus & Cudahy, 1954.
Nehls, Edward (ed.). *D. H. Lawrence: A Composite Biography*. Vol. I, 1885–1919. Madison, Wis.: University of Wisconsin Press, 1957.

CRITICISM

Blackmur, R. P. "D. H. Lawrence and Expressive Form," pp. 253–67 in *Form and Value in Modern Poetry*. New York: Anchor Books, Doubleday & Co., Inc., 1957.
Fisher, W. J. "Peace and Passivity: The Poetry of D. H. Lawrence," *So. Atl. Quart.*, LV (1956), 337–48.
Hoffman, F. J., and Moore, H. T. (eds.). *The Achievement of D. H. Lawrence*. Norman, Okla.: University of Oklahoma Press, 1953. Includes essays on Lawrence's poetry by Richard Ellmann and Horace Gregory.
Hough, Graham. *The Dark Sun: A Study of D. H. Lawrence*. London: Gerald Duckworth & Co., Ltd., 1957.
Jarrett-Kerr, Martin (Father William Tiverton [*pseud.*]). *D. H. Lawrence and Human Existence*. New York: Philosophical Library, Inc., 1951.
Kenmare, Dallas (*pseud.*). *Fire-Bird: A Study of D. H. Lawrence*. London: J. James Barrie, Ltd., 1951. On the poems.
Moore, H. T. *The Life and Works of D. H. Lawrence*. New York: Twayne Publishers, Inc., 1951.

COMMENTS ON POEMS

THE WILD COMMON

Discussed in Blackmur, *Form and Value in Modern Poetry*, pp. 259–60.

C. DAY LEWIS (1904–   )

LIFE

Born April 27 in Ballintogher, Ireland, the only child of an Anglican clergyman. He attended Sherborne School and Wadham College, Oxford.

After teaching at schools in England and Scotland until 1935, he devoted all his time to editing and writing poetry and literary criticism. Under the pseudonym "Nicholas Blake" he also writes detective fiction. During World War II he was Clark lecturer at Trinity College, Cambridge, and from 1951 to 1955, Professor of Poetry at Oxford. He is a director of the London publishers Chatto and Windus.

BIBLIOGRAPHY

Dyment, Clifford. "C. Day Lewis: A Bibliography," pp. 46–48 in *C. Day Lewis*. London: Longmans, Green & Co., Ltd., 1955.

MAJOR WRITINGS

Collected Poems of C. Day Lewis (1954)

Transitional Poem (1929)
From Feathers to Iron (1931)
The Magnetic Mountain (1933)
A Time to Dance (1935)
Overtures to Death (1938)
Word Over All (1943)
Poems, 1943–1947 (1948)
An Italian Visit (1953)
Pegasus and Other Poems (1957)

A Hope for Poetry (1934)
The Poetic Image (1947)

The Georgics of Virgil (1941; a translation)
The Aeneid of Virgil (1952; a translation)

BIOGRAPHY

None.

CRITICISM

Dupee, F. W. "Cecil Day Lewis and Louis MacNeice," *Nation,* CLXI (Oct. 13, 1945), 380.
Dyment, Clifford. *C. Day Lewis.* London: Longmans, Green & Co., Ltd., 1955.
Gregory, Horace. "The Proletarian Poet," *Part. Rev.,* III (1936), 27–28.
Nairne, Campbell. "The New Professor of Poetry," *John O' London's,* LX (March 16, 1951), 1–2.
Strong, L. A. G. "Cecil Day Lewis," pp. 193–97 in *Personal Remarks.* New York: Liveright Publishing Corp., 1953.

COMMENTS ON POEMS

REST FROM LOVING AND BE LIVING

Discussed in William Elton, *Explicator*, VI (1947), 16, and VII (1948), 25; Walter Gierasch and D. C. Sheldon, *Explicator*, VI (1948), 34.

NEARING AGAIN THE LEGENDARY ISLE

The "legendary isle" is the Sirens' Isle. In the *Odyssey*, book xii, is recounted how Odysseus plugged his men's ears with wax and had himself lashed to the mast lest the Sirens' sweet song entice them ashore (or aground).

COME, LIVE WITH ME AND BE MY LOVE

An ironical political parody of Marlowe's poem bearing the same title. Discussed in R. W. Stallman, *Explicator*, II (1944), 46.

ROBERT LOWELL (1917–   )

LIFE

Born March 1 in Boston, the son of a naval officer and a member of the family which includes James Russell Lowell and Amy Lowell. He attended Harvard for two years and then transferred to Kenyon College, where he majored in classics and graduated in 1940. In the same year he entered the Roman Catholic Church. During World War II he was a conscientious objector and served a jail sentence. In 1947 he was appointed Consultant in Poetry at the Library of Congress for a year, was awarded a Guggenheim Fellowship, and received the Pulitzer Prize for Poetry. He has taught at the State University of Iowa and at Kenyon, and now lives in Boston.

BIBLIOGRAPHY

None.

MAJOR WRITINGS

Land of Unlikeness (1944)
Lord Weary's Castle (1946; with text changes, 1947)
The Mills of the Kavanaughs (1951)

Poems, 1938–1949 (1950)

BIOGRAPHY

None.

CRITICISM

Bewley, Marius. *The Complex Fate,* pp. 158–66. London: Chatto & Windus, 1952.
Jarrell, Randall. *Poetry and the Age,* pp. 188–99, 230–36. New York: Vintage Books, 1955.
Jones, T. H. "The Poetry of Robert Lowell," *Month,* N.S., IX (1953), 133–42.
Jumper, W. C. "Whom Seek Ye? A Note on Robert Lowell's Poetry," *Hud. Rev.,* IX (1956), 117–25.
McCormick, John. "Falling Asleep over Grillparzer: An Interview with Robert Lowell," *Poetry,* LXXXI (1953), 269–79.
Standerwick, DeSales. "Notes on Robert Lowell," *Renascence,* VIII (1955), 75–83.

COMMENTS ON POEMS

COLLOQUY IN BLACK ROCK

Black Rock is a part of Bridgeport, the industrial city in Connecticut on Long Island Sound.

10. *the martyre Stephen:* Christianity's first martyr, who was stoned to death about 36 A.D. in Jerusalem on the charge of blasphemy. He is to be distinguished from the second St. Stephen (977–1038), who was Stephen I, king of Hungary (cf. line 23).

22. *kingfisher:* A symbol for Christ.

24. *Stupor Mundi:* (Latin) "The Astonishment of the World."

THE QUAKER GRAVEYARD IN NANTUCKET

Warren Winslow was a cousin of the poet.

Let man . . . upon the earth: Cf. Genesis 1:26. Lowell, a Roman Catholic convert, quotes from the Douay Version of the Bible.

Discussed in Paul Engle, *Eng. Jour.,* XXXVIII (1949), 64.

1. *Madaket:* Maddaket, a town and a harbor on the west end of the island of Nantucket.

15. *Ahab:* The monomaniacal captain of the whaler "Pequod" (cf. line 31) in Herman Melville's novel *Moby Dick* (1851). References to the novel, which describes Ahab's vengeful pursuit of Moby Dick, the White Whale, recur throughout this poem. Cf. especially lines 43–44, 61–64, 69–77, and 94–106. The "Pequod" sailed from Nantucket, which a century ago was the center of the whaling industry.

33. *'Sconset:* Siasconset, a town on the east end of the island of Nantucket.

78. *Clamavimus:* (Latin) "We have cried out."

91. *Wood's Hole:* Woods Hole, a town on the southwestern end of Cape Cod.

92. *Martha's Vineyard:* An island south of Cape Cod and west of Nantucket.

94. *ash-pit of Jehoshaphat:* Jehoshaphat here is the valley where, according to chapter three of the Book of Joel, at the end of the world the Lord will sit in judgment on the heathen nations for their oppression of Israel.

106. *Jonas Messias:* Cf. Matthew 12:40. Near the beginning of *Moby Dick,* Father Mapple preaches a sermon on Jonah (Jonas).

Our Lady of Walsingham: The Chapel of Our Lady in Walsingham Priory, situated a few miles from the sea in Norfolk, England, was one of the great shrines of medieval England. It was much resorted to until its destruction by Henry VIII in 1538. Since 1921 parts of the Priory have been restored.

In a prefatory note to *Lord Weary's Castle,* Lowell states that the "Our Lady of Walsingham" section of this poem "is an adaptation of several paragraphs from E. I. Watkin's *Catholic Art and Culture.*" Cf. E. I. Watkin, *Catholic Art and Culture* (New York: Sheed & Ward, 1944), pp. 213–14.

114. *Shiloah:* Shiloh, a town in ancient Palestine, the first Israelite sanctuary for the Tabernacle and the Ark of the Covenant.

116. *Sion:* Zion, a hill in Jerusalem on which the Temple was built; later a synonym for the whole city of Jerusalem.

122. *Non est . . . decor:* (Latin) "There is no form nor comeliness." Cf. Isaias (Isaiah) 53:2.

AS A PLANE TREE BY THE WATER

22. *Bernadette:* St. Bernadette (1843–1879), who claimed that the Virgin Mary appeared to her in the grotto of Massabieille near Lourdes, France.

AFTER THE SURPRISING CONVERSIONS

The details of this poem are drawn mainly from two paragraphs near the end of the *Narrative of Surprising Conversions,* an expanded form of a letter originally written on May 30, 1735, to the Reverend Dr. Benjamin Colman of Boston by Jonathan Edwards (1703–58), the great Calvinist preacher and theologian. Edwards was at that time minister at Northampton, Massachusetts, which had been undergoing a religious revival. The expanded form of the letter is dated November 6, 1736. Cf. *The Works of President Edwards,* Vol. III. (New York: Robert Carter & Brothers, 1881), pp. 269–70.

Discussed in G. Giovannini and Others, *Explicator,* IX (1951), 53.

WHERE THE RAINBOW ENDS

Discussed in Jarrell, *Poetry and the Age* (Vintage Books, 1955), pp. 190–91.

12. *Pepperpot:* One of the bridges across the Charles River between Boston and Cambridge, so called because of the "pepperpot" shape of its towers.

FALLING ASLEEP OVER THE AENEID

Vergil's Latin epic, the *Aeneid,* describes the escape of the Trojan Aeneas from the fall of Troy, his subsequent wanderings in the Mediterranean, his love affair with Queen Dido of Carthage, her suicide after his desertion of her, and his final establishment of the Roman state in Italy.

12. *Pallas:* A native Italian prince, who helps Aeneas conquer the Rutulians under the leadership of Turnus (cf. line 59). Turnus kills Pallas and is then himself killed by Aeneas in single combat.

22. *Aphrodite:* Aeneas' mother, the Greek name for the Latin Venus (cf. line 52).

66. *Turms:* Cavalry companies.

85. *Augustus:* Augustus Caesar (63 B.C.–14 A.D.), first Roman emperor, whom Vergil glorifies in the *Aeneid.*

ARCHIBALD MAC LEISH (1892–   )

LIFE

Born May 7 in Glencoe, Illinois. He graduated from Yale in 1915 and received his law degree from the Harvard Law School in 1919, after seeing service as an officer of field artillery in World War I. For three years he practiced law in Boston and then in 1923 went to France for five years. In the 1930's he worked for several years on the staff of *Fortune.* In 1933 his long poem *Conquistador* brought him the Pulitzer Prize. From 1939 to 1944 he was Librarian of Congress and concurrently held other governmental positions. Since 1949 he has been a professor of English at Harvard. In 1953 his *Collected Poems* received the Pulitzer and other prizes.

BIBLIOGRAPHY

Mizener, Arthur. *A Catalogue of the First Editions of Archibald MacLeish.* New Haven, Conn.: Yale University Library, 1938.
Thurber, Gerrish. "MacLeish's Published Books," *Library Journal,* LXIV (1939), 864, 866.

MAJOR WRITINGS

Collected Poems, 1917–1952 (1952)

The Pot of Earth (1925)
Streets in the Moon (1926)
The Hamlet of A. MacLeish (1928)
New Found Land: Fourteen Poems (1930)

Conquistador (1932)
Frescoes for Mr. Rockefeller's City (1933)
Public Speech (1936)
Actfive and Other Poems (1948)
Songs for Eve (1954)

A Time to Speak: The Selected Prose of Archibald MacLeish (1941)
A Time to Act: Selected Addresses (1943)

BIOGRAPHY

None.

CRITICISM

Honig, Edwin. "History, Document, and Archibald MacLeish," *Sewanee Rev.*, XLVIII (1940), 385–96.
Jones, Llewellyn. "Archibald MacLeish: A Modern Metaphysical," *Eng. Jour.* (College ed.), XXIV (1935), 441–51.
Kohler, Dayton. "MacLeish and the Modern Temper," *So. Atl. Quart.*, XXXVIII (1939), 416–26.
Mizener, Arthur. "The Poetry of Archibald MacLeish," *Sewanee Rev.*, XLVI (1938), 501–19.
Rosenberg, Harold. "The God in the Car," *Poetry*, LII (1938), 334–42.
Zabel, M. D. "The Poet on Capitol Hill," *Part. Rev.*, VIII (1941), 2–19, and VIII (1941), 128–45.

COMMENTS ON POEMS

THE SILENT SLAIN

Published in *Streets in the Moon* under the title "The Too-Late Born."
3. *Ah . . . haleine:* (French) "Ah, how long a blast has this horn!" Quoted from the translation into modern French by Joseph Bédier of *La Chanson de Roland* (Paris: H. Piazza, 1921); cf. line 1789.
4. *Roland:* The hero of the medieval French romance, *The Song of Roland.* Left as rear guard of Charlemagne's army as it retreats from Spain, Roland and his men are overwhelmed by the Saracen enemy in the valley of Roncevaux in the Pyrenees. Before he dies, Roland unwillingly blows his horn to summon help. Charlemagne's army returns, but too late to save the hero or his men.

ARS POETICA

Discussed in Stauffer, *The Nature of Poetry* (Norton, 1946), pp. 121–25.

THE END OF THE WORLD

1. *Vasserot:* An imaginary personage, like the others named in the poem,

YOU, ANDREW MARVELL

Andrew Marvell (1621–78) was an English lyric poet. MacLeish was thinking specifically of lines 21–24 in Marvell's "To His Coy Mistress":
"But at my back I always hear
Time's wingèd chariot hurrying near;
And yonder all before us lie
Deserts of vast eternity."
Cf. Eliot's use of this passage in *The Waste Land,* lines 185–86 and 196–98 (p. 361).

Discussed in Brooks, *Modern Poetry and the Tradition* (U. of N. Carolina Press, 1939), p. 122.

1. *here:* According to MacLeish, on the Illinois shore of Lake Michigan.
9. *Ecbatan:* Ecbatana (now Hamadan), ancient capital of the Medes in northwestern Iran. Note that each succeeding place name lies farther to the west, suggesting the turn of the earth and the approach of night.

"NOT MARBLE NOR THE GILDED MONUMENTS"

The title is the first line of Shakespeare's Sonnet LV.

POLE STAR

Published in *Public Speech* under the title "Pole star for this year."

LOUIS MAC NEICE (1907–1963)

LIFE

Born September 12 in Belfast, Ireland, the son of an Anglican clergyman. After Marlborough School, he attended Merton College, Oxford, from which he received a degree in 1930 with highest honors in Greats (classics). From 1930 to 1936 he taught classics at the University of Birmingham and from 1936 to 1940, at Bedford College for Women, London. Since 1940, except for a period in 1950 and 1951 when he was director of the British Institute in Athens, he has been a script-writer and producer for the British Broadcasting Corporation.

BIBLIOGRAPHY

None.

MAJOR WRITINGS

Collected Poems, 1925–1948 (1949)

Blind Fireworks (1929)
Poems (1935)

The Earth Compels (1938)
Autumn Journal (1939)
Springboard (1944)
Holes in the Sky (1948)
Ten Burnt Offerings (1952)
Autumn Sequel (1954)
Visitations (1957)

Modern Poetry: A Personal Essay (1938)
The Poetry of W. B. Yeats (1941)

The Agamemnon of Aeschylus (1936; a translation)
Goethe's Faust (1951; a translation)

BIOGRAPHY

None.

CRITICISM

Brown, S. G. "Some Poems of Louis MacNeice," *Sewanee Rev.*, LI (1943), 62–72.
Matthiessen, F. O. "Louis MacNeice," pp. 106–11 in *The Responsibilities of the Critic*. New York: Oxford University Press, 1952.
Savage, D. S. "Poet's Perspectives," pp. 206–16 in *Modern British Writing*, ed. Denys Val Baker. New York: Vanguard Press, Inc., 1947.
Schwartz, Delmore. "Adroitly Naïve," *Poetry*, XLVIII (1936), 115–17.

COMMENTS ON POEMS

PERSEUS

Perseus was a hero of Greek mythology who slew the Gorgon Medusa. For his exploit he got considerable help from the gods: Pluto lent him a helmet which made him invisible, Athena a very shiny buckler which served as a mirror to save his looking directly at the Medusa, and Hermes wings for his feet.
Discussed in Drew and Sweeney, *Directions in Modern Poetry* (Norton, 1940), pp. 247–49.

THE SUNLIGHT ON THE GARDEN

18. *We are dying, Egypt, dying:* The dying Antony twice says to Cleopatra, "I am dying, Egypt, dying" (*Antony and Cleopatra*, Act IV, scene 15, lines 18 and 40).

LES SYLPHIDES

The title refers to the ballet by Alexandr Glazunov based on the "Nocturne in A-flat Major, Opus 32, No. 2" by Frédéric Chopin.

Discussed in Drew and Sweeney, *Directions in Modern Poetry* (Norton, 1940), pp. 247–49.

NEUTRALITY

1. *The neutral island:* Ireland, which remained neutral in World War II.
5. *County Sligo:* The west of Ireland county idealized in the early poems of W. B. Yeats; e.g., "The Lake Isle of Innisfree."
6. *Knocknarea:* A small mountain near Sligo Town with legendary associations, dealt with by Yeats in early poems.

MARIANNE MOORE (1887–   )

LIFE

Born November 15 in St. Louis, Missouri, though she spent much of her girlhood in Carlisle, Pennsylvania. After graduating from Bryn Mawr in 1909, she taught at the government Indian school at Carlisle from 1911 to 1915, worked as an assistant in a branch of the New York Public Library, and from 1925 to 1929 was acting editor of the *Dial*. In 1924 her book, *Observations,* won the *Dial* Award, and in 1952 her *Collected Poems* received the Pulitzer Prize and other awards.

BIBLIOGRAPHY

None.

MAJOR WRITINGS

Collected Poems (1951)

Poems (1921)
Observations (1924)
The Pangolin and Other Verse (1936)
What Are Years (1941)
Nevertheless (1944)
Like a Bulwark (1956)

Selected Poems (1935)

The Fables of La Fontaine (1954; translations)
Predilections (1955; essays)

BIOGRAPHY

None.

CRITICISM

Blackmur, R. P. *Form and Value in Modern Poetry,* pp. 225–52. New York: Anchor Books, Doubleday & Co., Inc., 1957.

Burke, Kenneth. "Motives and Motifs in the Poetry of Marianne Moore," *Accent*, II (1942), 157–69.

Fowlie, Wallace. "Marianne Moore," *Sewanee Rev.*, LX (1952), 537–47.

Hoffman, F. J. "Marianne Moore: Imaginary Gardens and Real Toads," *Poetry*, LXXXIII (1953), 152–57.

Jarrell, Randall. *Poetry and the Age*, pp. 162–87. New York: Vintage Books, 1955.

Monroe, Harriet. "Symposium on Marianne Moore," *Poetry*, XIX (1922), 208–16.

Quarterly Review of Literature, IV (1948). Marianne Moore issue.

Williams, W. C. "Marianne Moore," *Dial*, LXXVIII (1925), 393–401.

Zabel, M. D. (ed.). *Literary Opinion in America*, rev. ed., pp. 385–92. New York: Harper & Bros., 1951.

COMMENTS ON POEMS

POETRY

Discussed in Frankenberg, *Pleasure Dome* (Houghton Mifflin, 1949), pp. 137–41.

23–24. *"business documents and school-books"*: Quoted, according to Miss Moore, from Leo Tolstoi's *Diary*. Cf. *The Diaries of Leo Tolstoy*, translated from the Russian by C. J. Hogarth and A. Sirnis (New York: E. P. Dutton & Co., Inc., 1917), p. 94. "Where the boundary between prose and poetry lies, I shall never be able to understand. The question is raised in manuals of style, yet the answer to it lies beyond me. Poetry is verse: prose is not verse. Or else poetry is everything with the exception of business documents and school books."

In the notes placed at the end of *Observations* and subsequent volumes, Miss Moore herself identifies the source of most of the quotations in her poems and some of the details.

29–30. *"literalists of the imagination"*: Quoted, according to Miss Moore, from William Butler Yeats, *Ideas of Good and Evil* (London: A. H. Bullen, 1903), from the essay, "William Blake and the Imagination," p. 182. "The limitation of his view was from the very intensity of his vision; he was a too literal realist of imagination, as others are of nature; and because he believed that the figures seen by the mind's eye, when exalted by inspiration, were 'eternal existences,' symbols of divine essences, he hated every grace of style that might obscure their lineaments."

THE STEEPLE-JACK

A 12-stanza version of this poem was published in *Selected Poems* (1935) under the title, "Part of a Novel, Part of a Poem, Part of a Play," with the first subtitle, "The Steeple-Jack." Stanzas 5 through 8 were eliminated to make the present 8-stanza version.

Discussed in Louise Bogan, *Coll. Eng.*, XIV (1953), 257–58; Charles Tomlinson, *Sewanee Rev.*, LXV (1957), 682–84.

1. *Dürer:* Albrecht Dürer (1471–1528), German painter and engraver.

39. *The hero, the student:* For amplification see the version in *Selected Poems.*

NO SWAN SO FINE

1–2. *"No water . . . Versailles":* Quoted, according to Miss Moore, from an article in the *New York Times Magazine,* May 10, 1931.

9. *candelabrum-tree:* Miss Moore notes that she had in mind an actual pair of candelabra with figures of swans in Dresden china.

THE PANGOLIN

27–28. *Thomas . . . vine:* According to Miss Moore's note, "a fragment of ironwork in Westminster Abbey."

50–52. *Gargallo's . . . matador:* Pablo Gargallo (1881–1934), Spanish abstractionist sculptor, who worked in forged iron. Actually the "matador" was probably one of Gargallo's heads of a picador; for the picador, unlike the matador, wears a hat with a brim.

WHAT ARE YEARS?

Discussed in Lloyd Frankenberg, *Saturday Review of Literature*, XXIX (March 23, 1946), 5; O'Connor, *Sense and Sensibility in Modern Poetry* (U. of Chicago Press, 1948), pp. 229–30.

THE MIND IS AN ENCHANTING THING

6. *Gieseking:* Walter Gieseking (1895–1956), German concert pianist.

6. *Scarlatti:* Alessandro Scarlatti (1659–1725), Italian composer.

36. *Herod's oath:* Cf. Matthew 14:3–11.

IN DISTRUST OF MERITS

Discussed in M. E. Allentuck, *Explicator*, X (1952), 42; Wallace Fowlie, *Quarterly Review of Literature*, IV (1948), 176–77.

ARMOUR'S UNDERMINING MODESTY

12–13. *our mis-set / alphabet:* In her note Miss Moore quotes from Oscar Ogg's *The 26 Letters,* which explains the ideographic origin of the letter *E,* originally drawn lying on its side.

14. *Arise, for it is day:* The motto, Miss Moore notes, of The John Day Company, a New York publishing house.

28–31. Quoted, according to Miss Moore, from *The Book of the Ranks and Dignities of British Society,* attributed to Charles Lamb. Before the Norman Conquest, Saxon commanders of armies were called "dukes." After the Conquest the title died out until it was revived by

Edward III, who made his son, the Black Prince, Duke of Cornwall, using in the ceremony a wreath and a silver rod.

WILFRED OWEN (1893–1918)

LIFE

Born March 18 at Oswestry, Shropshire. He was educated at the Birkenhead Institute, Liverpool, and served from 1913 to 1915 as tutor to a family in Bordeaux, France. When England entered the war, he enlisted in the Artists' Rifles, served in France, was invalided home, and then returned to the front, where he won the Military Cross and was killed in action November 4, 1918, just a week before the Armistice. Although he wrote poems before the war, most of his writing grew out of his experiences as a soldier.

BIBLIOGRAPHY

Welland, D. S. R. "Wilfred Owen's Manuscripts," *Times Lit. Sup.*, June 15, 1956, p. 368, and June 22, 1956, p. 384.

MAJOR WRITINGS

Poems by Wilfred Owen (1921; ed. Siegfried Sassoon)
The Poems of Wilfred Owen (1931; ed. Edmund Blunden; republished in New York, 1949)

BIOGRAPHY

Blunden, Edmund. "Memoir," pp. 1–40 in *The Poems of Wilfred Owen*, ed. Edmund Blunden. London: Chatto & Windus, 1931.

CRITICISM

Daiches, David. "The Poetry of Wilfred Owen," pp. 52–68 in *New Literary Values*. Edinburgh: Oliver & Boyd, 1936.
Dickinson, Patrick. "The Poetry of Wilfred Owen," *Fortnightly*, CLXII (1944), 327–31.
Fletcher, I. K. "Wilfred Owen," *Welsh Outlook*, XV (1928), 332–33.
Lehmann, John. "But for Beaumont Hamel," pp. 87–95 in *Open Night*. New York: Harcourt, Brace & Co., Inc., 1952.
Parsons, I. M. "The Poems of Wilfred Owen," *New Criterion*, X (1931), 658–99.
Sitwell, Osbert. "Wilfred Owen," *Penguin New Writing*, No. 27 (1946), pp. 114–32.
Thomas, Dylan. "Wilfred Owen," pp. 117–33 in *Quite Early One Morning*. New York: New Directions, 1954.

Welland, D. S. R. "Half-rhyme in Wilfred Owen: Its Derivation and Use," *Rev. Eng. Stud.,* N.S., I (1950), 226–41.

———. "Wilfred Owen: Poetry, Pity and Prophecy," *Northern Review,* VI (1953), 29–36.

COMMENTS ON POEMS

FROM MY DIARY, JULY 1914

This poem exemplifies what Blunden called the "Endymion" phase of Owen's poetical career.

DULCE ET DECORUM EST

The title is taken from Horace, *Odes* iii. 2. 13. A translation of the full quotation in Owen's last line and a half runs: "It is sweet and honorable to die for one's country." This poem was composed at the Craiglockhart War Hospital for Nervous Cases, near Edinburgh, in August, 1917.

FUTILITY

First published in *Nation,* June 15, 1918, one of the few poems published during Owen's lifetime.

ANTHEM FOR DOOMED YOUTH

Completed in September, 1917.

APOLOGIA PRO POEMATE MEO

The Latin title means "Justification of My Poetry."

STRANGE MEETING

An unfinished poem. Welland, *Times Lit. Sup.,* June 22, 1956, p. 384, says that "title and situation seem . . . to have their origin in Shelley's *The Revolt of Islam,* Canto V, stanzas IX to XIII inclusive."

Discussed in D. S. Savage, *West. Rev.,* XIII (1949), 67–78; Welland, *Northern Review,* VI (1953), 34–36.

14–44: Stephen Spender has written: "If one turns from [Yeats's] *Prayer for My Daughter* to Wilfred Owen's poem, *Strange Meeting,* one sees that Owen was already a poet of far deeper understanding. These lines seem almost like an answer to Yeats's *fortissimo* lyrics" (*The Permanence of Yeats,* ed. James Hall and Martin Steinmann [New York: The Macmillan Co., 1950], p. 191).

EZRA POUND (1885–   )

LIFE

Born October 30 in Hailey, Idaho, but brought up in Pennsylvania. He was educated at the University of Pennsylvania and at Hamilton College, from which he graduated in 1905. After teaching romance languages and literatures at Pennsylvania and, briefly, Wabash College, Indiana, he left for Europe, soon settling in London. A leading figure in the new poetry movements, he helped found and edit *Blast* (1914–15) and from 1917 to 1919 was London editor of *The Little Review*. He left London for Paris in 1920, and from 1924 on lived in Italy. During these years he published, in addition to his poetry, books on art, literature, and economics. In 1941 he began to broadcast fascist propaganda from Rome. Brought back a prisoner to the United States in 1945 on the charge of treason, he was declared insane and placed in St. Elizabeth's Hospital, Washington, D.C., before he could be tried. When his *Pisan Cantos* received the Bollingen Award in 1949, he became the subject of national controversy. He continues to write and publish sections of *The Cantos*, his nearly completed epic poem.

BIBLIOGRAPHY

Edwards, John. *A Preliminary Checklist of the Writings of Ezra Pound, Especially his Contributions to Periodicals*. New Haven, Conn.: Kirgo-Books, 1953.

MAJOR WRITINGS

Personae: The Collected Poems of Ezra Pound (1926)

A Lume Spento (1908)
Personae of Ezra Pound (1909)
Exultations of Ezra Pound (1909)
The Ripostes of Ezra Pound (1912)
Cathay: Translations by Ezra Pound (1915)
Lustra of Ezra Pound (1916)
Quia Pauper Amavi (1919)
Hugh Selwyn Mauberley (1920)
A Draft of XVI Cantos (1925)
A Draft of XXX Cantos (1930)
Eleven New Cantos: XXXI–XLI (1934)
The Fifth Decad of Cantos (1937)
Cantos LII–LXXI (1940)
The Pisan Cantos (1948)
The Cantos of Ezra Pound (1948)
Section: Rock-Drill: 85–95 de los Cantares (1955)

Selected Poems (1928, 1949)

The Letters of Ezra Pound, 1907–1941 (1950; ed. D. D. Paige)
The Literary Essays of Ezra Pound (1954; ed. T. S. Eliot)

BIOGRAPHY

None.

CRITICISM

Amdur, A. S. The Poetry of Ezra Pound. Cambridge, Mass.: Harvard University Press, 1936.
Eliot, T. S. Ezra Pound: His Metric and Poetry. New York: Alfred A. Knopf, Inc., 1917.
Espey, J. J. Ezra Pound's "Mauberley": A Study in Composition. Berkeley, Cal.: University of California Press, 1955.
Kenner, Hugh. The Poetry of Ezra Pound. London: Faber & Faber, Ltd., 1951.
Leary, Lewis (ed.). Motive and Method in The Cantos of Ezra Pound. New York: Columbia University Press, 1954.
MacLeish, Archibald. Poetry and Opinion: The Pisan Cantos of Ezra Pound, a Dialogue on the Role of Poetry. Urbana, Ill.: University of Illinois Press, 1950.
Quarterly Review of Literature, V (1949). Ezra Pound issue.
Russell, Peter (ed.). An Examination of Ezra Pound: A Collection of Essays. Norfolk, Conn.: New Directions, 1950.
Viereck, Peter. Dream and Responsibility: Four Test Cases of the Tension between Poetry and Society, pp. 3–22. Washington, D.C.: University Press of Washington, D.C., 1953.
Watts, H. H. Ezra Pound and the Cantos. London: Routledge & Kegan Paul, Ltd., 1951.

COMMENTS ON POEMS

SESTINA: ALTAFORTE

Pound adapted this sestina from "In Praise of War," a poem in Provençal by Bertrans de Born, a twelfth-century troubadour and warrior.
Loquitur: (Latin) "Speaks."
Dante . . . strife: Cf. Inferno, XXVIII, 134.
Eccovi!: (Italian) "Behold!"
device: (French) The emblem on a shield.
Richard Cœur de Lion: Richard I (the Lionheart), king of England, 1189–99.
4. vair: Heraldic design showing a series of small shields alternately silver and blue.

14. *destriers:* War horses.
16. *stour:* Fight.

THE RETURN

Discussed in Deutsch, *Poetry in Our Time* (Holt, 1952), pp. 124–25; "Experiment in Verse," *Times Lit. Sup.* (Special Number), Aug. 17, 1956, p. iii; Taupin, *L'influence du symbolisme français* (Champion, 1929), pp. 142–44.

LAMENT OF THE FRONTIER GUARD

Like the other poems in *Cathay,* this is a translation from a Chinese original made on the basis of the manuscripts of the American scholar of the Orient, Ernest Fenollosa (1853–1908), for whom Pound had become unofficial literary executor.
Discussed in Deutsch, *Poetry in Our Time* (Holt, 1952), pp. 131–32.
15. *middle kingdom:* That part of China including the central and lower part of the Yangtze valley.
23. *Rihoku:* A variant of "Rihaku" (cf. the "signature" at the end of the poem), the Japanese form of the name of Li Po (701–62), one of China's greatest poets. Li Po lived during the years when the T'ang Dynasty, under which China had become through military conquest the largest empire on earth, reached its climax of power and began a disastrous decline marked by rebellions and invasions.

HUGH SELWYN MAUBERLEY

The editors are glad to acknowledge their indebtedness to John J. Espey's *Ezra Pound's "Mauberley": A Study in Composition* as a source of information for many of the following notes. Espey's book is the most detailed examination of this sequence of poems yet published and is indispensable for anyone who wishes to study it thoroughly. *Hugh Selwyn Mauberley* is also discussed in Blackmur, *Form and Value in Modern Poetry* (Anchor Books, 1957), pp. 81–85; T. E. Connolly, *Accent,* XVI (1956), 59–67; Deutsch, *Poetry in Our Time* (Holt, 1952), 129–31; F. J. Hoffman, *The Twenties* (New York: The Viking Press, Inc., 1955), pp. 36–46.
At the bottom of the title-page of *Personae: The Collected Poems of Ezra Pound* appears the following note by Pound: "The sequence is so distinctly a farewell to London that the reader who chooses to regard this as an exclusively American edition may as well omit it and turn at once to page 205" (that is, to the next group of poems in the book, *Homage to Sextus Propertius*).
Vocat æstus in umbram: (Latin) "The heat calls us into the shade." The quotation is from the *Fourth Eclogue* of Nemesianus, a Roman poet who flourished in the late third century A.D.

E. P. ODE POUR L'ELECTION DE SON SEPULCHRE

The title is French: "E. P. [that is, Ezra Pound] Ode for the Choice of His Tomb." Adapted from the poem "De l'élection de son sepulchre" in the *Odes* of Pierre de Ronsard (1524–85), French poet.

8. *Capaneus:* One of the Seven who marched against the city of Thebes. Because he defied Zeus, the god killed him with a thunderbolt.

9. Ἴδμεν . . . Τροίῃ: (Greek) "For we know all the things that are in Troy." This is substantially what is sung by the Sirens in the *Odyssey* xii. 189. In order to sail past the Sirens without being drawn to disaster by their song, Odysseus plugs his sailors' ears with wax and has himself, with "unstopped ear," bound to the mast. Note that Penelope (line 13) and Circe (line 15) are also characters in the *Odyssey*.

18–19. *l'an . . . eage:* (French) "the thirtieth year of his life." Except for the change of "my" to "his" this is the opening line of the *Grand Testament* of François Villon (1431–63?), French poet.

II

31. *kinema:* (Greek) "Motion." Cf. "cinema."

III

34. *mousseline of Cos:* Muslin from the Greek island of Cos.

35. *pianola:* A "player" (mechanical) piano.

36. *barbitos:* A Greek lyre.

42. *Heracleitus:* Heraclitus, a Greek philosopher (*ca.* 535–*ca.* 475 B.C.).

46. *Samothrace:* A Greek island.

47. τὸ καλὸν: (Greek) "The Beautiful."

54. *Pisistratus:* An Athenian dictator (d. 527 B.C.).

58. τίν' . . . θεὸν: (Greek) "What man, what hero, what god." Adapted from Pindar's *Second Olympian Ode,* line 2, where the word order reads, "what god, what hero, what man." To catch Pound's bilingual pun, note that the Greek τίν' is pronounced like the English word "tin" (see line 60).

IV

63. *pro domo:* (Latin) "For home."

71–72. *pro patria . . . decor:* The whole Latin line adapted here is, "Dulce et decorum est pro patria mori" ("It is sweet and fitting to die for one's country") from Horace, *Odes* iii. 2. 13. Pound adds the Latin "non," meaning "not."

YEUX GLAUQUES

The title is French: "glaucous (yellow-green) eyes."

98. *"King's Treasuries":* "Of Kings' Treasuries" is the title of the first lecture in John Ruskin's *Sesame and Lilies* (1865).

100. *Buchanan:* Robert Buchanan (1841–1901), English man of letters who in 1871 attacked the "Pre-Raphaelites"—Dante Gabriel Rossetti and others—in an article entitled "The Fleshly School of Poetry."

101. *hers:* Elizabeth Siddal, a model for the Pre-Raphaelite painters and later wife of Dante Gabriel Rossetti (1828–82), English painter and poet.

104–7. *Burne-Jones . . . rhapsodize:* Sir Edward Coley Burne-Jones (1833–98), Pre-Raphaelite painter, whose painting, "King Cophetua and the Beggar Maid," hangs in the Tate Gallery in London.

110. *English Rubaiyat:* Edward Fitzgerald published his translation of *The Rubáiyát of Omar Khayyám* in 1859, but it was at first disregarded by the public.

115. *Jenny:* One of the poems attacked by Buchanan was Rossetti's "Jenny," which concerns a London prostitute.

118. *maquero: Maquereau* (French), a pimp.

"SIENA MI FE'; DISFECEMI MAREMMA"

The title is Italian: "Siena made me; Maremma unmade me." Cf. note to Eliot's *The Waste Land,* lines 293–94 (p. 468).

123. *Verog:* Pound's name for Victor Gustave Plarr (1863–1929), author of a book of poems, *In the Dorian Mood* (cf. line 135), and librarian of the Royal College of Surgeons.

124. *Gallifet:* Presumably Gaston Alexandre Auguste, marquis de Galliffet (1830–1909), French general who suppressed the Paris Commune in 1871 and who in 1899–1900, during the Dreyfus Affair, was French minister of war.

125. *Dowson:* Ernest Dowson (1867–1900), British poet.

125. *Rhymers' Club:* A literary group founded in 1891 by a number of English "Decadent" poets, including Dowson and Lionel Johnson (cf. line 126).

131. *Newman:* John Henry Cardinal Newman (1801–90), who like Johnson had been converted to Roman Catholicism.

133. *Headlam:* The Reverend Stewart D. Headlam (1847–1924), a friend of many of the Decadent poets.

133. *Image:* Selwyn Image (1849–1930), an editor of *The Hobby Horse,* a "little magazine" which published the Decadent poets.

BRENNBAUM

The title is probably Pound's name for Max Beerbohm (1872–1956), English essayist and caricaturist, who was known as "The Incomparable Max."

MR. NIXON

The title is probably Pound's name for Arnold Bennett (1867–1931), English editor and novelist.

168. *Bloughram:* A reference to Robert Browning's satirical poem, *Bishop Blougram's Apology.*

173. *stylist:* Probably Ford Madox Ford (1873–1939), English novelist.

XI

184. *Milésien:* The reference is both to the *Milesian Tales,* a collection of erotic romances by Aristides of Miletus, the ancient city of Asia Minor, and to a phrase by the French writer, Remy de Gourmont (1858–1915): "Femmes, conservatrices des traditions milésiennes" ("Women, conservators of Milesian traditions").

186. *Ealing:* A suburb to the west of London.

XII

192. *Daphne:* While Apollo was pursuing the nymph Daphne, she was transformed into a laurel tree. Here Daphne is extending "laurels" to "me."

214. *Fleet St.:* A London street distinguished in the eighteenth century by much literary activity.

215. *Dr. Johnson:* Samuel Johnson (1709–84), English lexicographer and man of letters.

ENVOI

This poem is based on the lyric "Go, Lovely Rose," by the English poet Edmund Waller (1606–87), who is named in line 242.

221. *Lawes:* Henry Lawes (1596–1662), English musician, who set many of Waller's lyrics to music, including "Go, Lovely Rose."

MAUBERLEY

Vacuos exercet aera morsus: (Latin) "He bites emptily at the air."

246–47. *"eau-forte / Par Jaquemart":* (French) "Etching by Jaquemart." Jules Jacquemart (1837–80) was a French artist.

249. *Messalina:* Valeria Messalina, the dissolute third wife of the Roman emperor Claudius.

259. *Pier Francesca:* Piero della Francesca (1420?–92), Italian painter.

260. *Pisanello:* The common name for Vittore Pisano (1397–1455), Italian medalist and painter.

261. *Achaia:* The name of ancient Greece.

II

Qu'est . . . un tonnerre?: (French) "What do they know of love, and what can they understand?

"If they do not understand poetry, if they do not feel music, what can they understand of that passion in comparison with which the rose is gross and the perfume of violets a crash of thunder?"

Caid Ali: A pseudonym for Pound himself.

262. *diabolus in the scale:* The devil in the (musical) scale; a term, according to Espey, for "the augmented fourth, which gave the medieval musicians great difficulty."

264. *ANANGKE:* (Greek) "Fate."

268. *NUKTIS 'AGALMA:* (Greek) "Night's ornament." *NUKTIS* should read *NUKTOS.*

278. *TO AGATHON:* (Greek) "The Good."

288. *irides:* Plural of iris, with reference to its meaning both as part of the eye and as a kind of flower.

289. *botticellian:* Pertaining to Sandro Botticelli (1444?–1510), Italian painter, particularly well known for his painting "The Birth of Venus."

290. *diastasis:* Here meaning both "dilation" and "wide-spaced."

291. *anæthesis:* Anesthesia, "loss of feeling or sensation."

THE AGE DEMANDED

302. *Cytheræan:* Aphrodite, whose chariot was drawn by doves.

337. *apathein:* (Greek) "Apathy."

IV

360. *Moluccas:* The Spice Islands, near New Guinea.

MEDALLION

385. *Luini:* Bernardino Luini (ca. 1475–ca. 1532), Italian painter.

391. *Anadyomene:* Aphrodite, the "foam-born."

392. *Reinach:* Salomon Reinach (1858–1932), French archaeologist, who published his lectures on art as a book entitled *Apollo* (1904).

CANTO I

The present Canto I did not always stand at the beginning of the poem, but was adapted by Pound from what was originally the third of the series. The "Canto III" of *Poetry,* X (1917), 248–54, is a poem of 175 lines, of which the last 95 have become the 76 of the present text. The old "Canto III" was given book publication for the first time in *Quia Pauper Amavi* (1919) but Canto I, like Canto II, first received book publication in *A Draft of XVI Cantos* (1925).

For much of the information in the following notes to Cantos I and II the editors gratefully acknowledge their indebtedness to their former colleague, Edgar M. Glenn of Chico State College, California, and to Robert Mayo, editor of the Northwestern University "Analyst," which has been publishing a series of explications on the Cantos. Numbers I and VII of "The Analyst" are particularly useful.

The first two and other Cantos are also discussed in Blackmur, *Form and Value in Modern Poetry* (Anchor Books, 1957), pp. 92–112; Deutsch, *Poetry in Our Time* (Holt, 1952), pp. 133–45; Leary (ed.), *Motive and Method in The Cantos of Ezra Pound*; Quinn, *The Metamorphic Tradition in Modern Poetry* (Rutgers U. Press, 1955), pp. 14–48; Tate, *On the Limits of Poetry* (Swallow, 1948), pp. 350–57 (reprinted in Tate, *The Man of Letters in the Modern World* [Meridian Books, 1955], pp. 257–63); Watts, *Ezra Pound and the Cantos*. Also useful is J. H. Edwards and William Vasse, Jr., *Annotated Index to "The Cantos of Ezra Pound"* (Berkeley, Cal.: University of California Press, 1957).

1–67. [*Analyst*] "This passage is a free rend[er]ing in English of the opening lines of the eleventh book of the *Odyssey*, called the 'Nekuia,' or 'Book of the Dead,' because it describes Odysseus' visit to the underworld. . . . Actually the poet is not translating directly from the *Odyssey*, but from a Renaissance Latin translation by Andreas Divus, but this fact does not emerge until line 68. . . ." One reason for Pound's introduction of Odysseus at the beginning of the Cantos is that Odysseus appears to represent for him "a union of the inquiring mind and the effective will."

3. *We*: Odysseus, who is speaking, and his companions.

7. *Circe's this craft*: [*Analyst*] "The reference is to Circe's powers of magic which provide the wind so that Odysseus' ship may reach its destination."

12. *Kimmerian*: Pertaining to the Cimmerians, an ancient people originally living in the Crimea.

17. *the place*: Hades, which Circe had told Odysseus he must visit in order to learn from Tiresias, the dead prophet of Thebes, how he might return to Ithaca, his home. Cf. Eliot's use of Tiresias in *The Waste Land*, Part III.

19. *Perimedes and Eurylochus*: Two of Odysseus' men.

21. *pitkin*: A little pit.

33. *dreory*: (Anglo-Saxon) "Bloody."
[*Analyst*] "In rendering Homer into English, as earlier commentators have pointed out, the poet gives his lines a pronounced Old English flavor. This is expressed not only in the diction of lines 1–67 (e.g., *pitkin* and *dreory*), but in the rhythm and metrical structure, the alliteration and assonance, the use of epithets, and so on."

42. *Elpenor*: One of Odysseus' companions, who had died as his spirit describes in lines 50–54.

58. *Anticlea*: [*Analyst*] "The mother of Odysseus, whose death has occurred in his absence. Odysseus weeps to behold her, but, as instructed by Circe, will not let her drink the blood until Tiresias has first done so."

68. *Lie quiet Divus*: [*Analyst*] "The command is cryptic. It may mean: 'That's enough of that. Let's change the subject.' Or perhaps: 'Divus, rest in peace,' or 'Don't turn over in your grave!' "

68. *Andreas Divus:* The author of a Latin version of the *Odyssey*, published in Paris in 1538, which Pound states that he found in a Paris bookstall sometime between 1906 and 1910.

69. *In officina Wecheli:* (Latin) "At the workshop of Wechel." This is part of the imprint of the Divus volume.

72. *Venerandam:* (Latin) "Compelling admiration." The term is applied to Aphrodite, line 73.

73–76. [*Analyst*] "Without making an allegory of *Canto I* we may point out that Aphrodite seems to present a contrast to Odysseus, whose nature differs from hers as the style of lines 1–67 differs from that of lines 73–75. They represent, so to speak, complementary principles. Odysseus is action and intelligence; Aphrodite is feminine beauty, passion, and perhaps creative force."

73. *the Cretan:* Georgius Dartona Cretensis, whose *Hymni Deorum* (*Hymns of the Gods*), Latin translations of the *Homeric Hymns*, were included in the Divus volume. The Latin words used by Pound are from the second Homeric hymn to Aphrodite, as translated by Dartona.

74. *Cypri . . . est:* "The citadels of Cyprus were her appointed realm."

74. *oricalchi:* Pound's spelling of "orichalchi" (Latin), "of copper." The reference is to a votive gift of copper and gold described in the hymn to Aphrodite as being placed on the goddess.

76. *Argicida:* (Latin) Either "slayer of Argus" or "slayer of Greeks." The first would refer to Hermes, herald of the gods, who killed the hundred-eyed Argus at Zeus's command. The second would refer to Aphrodite, who supported the Trojans against the Greeks in the Trojan War.

76. *So that:* [*Analyst*] "Possibly from an *ut* in the Latin of Divus or Georgius Dartona. But it can also be construed as a phrase which can only be completed by the cantos which follow. John Drummond believes that it is an allusion to Browning's *Sordello*. (*v.* line 2 of *Canto II*). The words 'So that Sordello . . .' occur in *Sordello*, I, 567."

CANTO II

1. *Robert Browning:* The English poet (1812–89), whose long poem *Sordello* (1840) is often obscure in meaning.

2–3. *Sordello:* [Note by Edgar M. Glenn] "The word is used to refer to three or four things: (1) Browning's poem; (2) the actual man; (3) Browning's fabrication (the character in Browning's poem); (4) Pound's grasp of Sordello." Historically, Sordello was a thirteenth-century Italian troubadour, who wrote in Provençal.

4. *Lo . . . Mantovana:* (Provençal) "Sordello was from the region around Mantua."

5. *So-shu:* Possibly the Japanese version of the name of Chuang Tzǔ, a Chinese Taoist philosopher. Cf. Pound's poem "Ancient Wisdom, Rather Cosmic," which deals with So-Shu.

5. *churned in the sea:* [Note by Edgar M. Glenn] "Since *churned* seems to be a metaphor, perhaps *sea* is, too. It may stand for the welter (change and multiplicity) of phenomena and of experience.

"In short, I would paraphrase line 5 something like this: Chuang Tzŭ dealt ineffectually with life (phenomena, experience)."

7. *Lir:* A form of the Celtic word for "ocean." In Irish mythology the son of Lir, likewise called Lir, was a god or hero.

8. *Picasso:* The Spanish painter (1881–   ).

11. *"Eleanor . . .* ἐλέπτολις *!":* [*Analyst*] "Eleanor of Aquitaine, deliberately confused with Helen of Troy because of their similarity as sources of discord and war between great powers. The parallel is displayed in the Greek words *elenaus* (ship-destroying) and *eleptolis* (city-destroying), puns used by Aeschylus to describe Helen of Troy in the *Agamemnon.* . . . Pound extends the pun sequence with the proper name *Eleanor,* implying that it means "destroyer of man" (Gr., *ele aner*) and parallels Aeschylus' *elandros* (man-destroying), a third pun used by Aeschylus to describe Helen."

14–22. *"Let her . . . voices":* Cf. *Iliad* iii. 139–60. The old men of Troy speak thus of Helen as they watch the combat between Paris and Menelaus.

19. *Schoeney's daughters:* The beautiful Atalanta, daughter of Schoeneus, caused the death of a number of her suitors.

23. *Tyro:* A mortal woman with whom Poseidon (the "sea-god" of line 24) lay, meanwhile making a wave arch over and hide them.

34. *Scios:* [*Analyst*] "Ancient Chios, modern Scio; an Ionic Greek island off the coast of Asia Minor, about 70 miles north and slightly east of Naxos."

35. *Naxos:* Greek island in the Aegean, known for its wine and for the worship of Dionysus, with whom Bacchus is identified.

36. *Naviform:* Shiplike.

40–118. *The ship . . . amid sea:* [Note by Edgar M. Glenn] "The story of the attempted rape of Bacchus (Dionysus) is told in the second Homeric hymn to Dionysus and, very briefly, in *The Library* of Apollodorus, but Pound seems to be relying here on the version given in Ovid's *Metamorphoses,* III, 582–691. There Acoetes [cf. line 62] tells his story to Pentheus [cf. line 59], using the first person viewpoint. It is a story of conversion to worship of the god and is intended as a warning to Pentheus, the king of Thebes. Pound limits himself to Acoetes' tale and ignores the larger context of the narrative."

42. *young boy:* Bacchus. [Note by Edgar M. Glenn] "The plants commonly associated with the god are the ivy and the grape vine; his attendant animals are the lynx, panther, tiger, leopard, and dolphin."

47. *ex-convict:* Lycabas, the "Lycabs" of line 104.

59. *Pentheus:* King of Thebes and, though he is unaware of it, cousin of Bacchus, whose worship he opposes.

83. *æther:* (Latin) "Air."

95. *Lyæus:* An epithet for Bacchus-Dionysus, meaning "the deliverer from care."

113. *Medon:* Like Lycabas, one of Acœtes' shipmates.

113. *dory:* The sea fish.

115. *Tiresias:* Cf. Canto I, note to line 17.

115. *Cadmus:* Grandfather of Pentheus and founder of Thebes. Both Tiresias and Cadmus had warned Pentheus against suppressing the cult of Dionysus.

124. *Ileuthyeria:* Unidentified. The reference is to some nymph or woman turned into coral.

124. *Dafne:* Daphne, the nymph who, pursued by Apollo, was transˌ formed into a laurel tree.

JOHN CROWE RANSOM (1888–   )

LIFE

Born April 30 in Pulaski, Tennessee, the son of a minister. After graduating from Vanderbilt in 1909, he spent three years at Oxford as a Rhodes Scholar. Most of the time from 1914 until 1937 he taught in the Vanderbilt English Department, although he served in the field artillery during World War I and was a Guggenheim Fellow in England from 1931 to 1932. He was a founder and editor of the *Fugitive* in Nashville from 1922 to 1925, and he founded the *Kenyon Review* in 1938 after he had become professor of English in the previous year at Kenyon College. He continues to teach at Kenyon, to edit the *Review,* and to act as one of the leaders of the "New Criticism."

BIBLIOGRAPHY

Stallman, R. W. (ed.). "John Crowe Ransom: A Checklist," *Sewanee Rev.,* LVI (1948), 442–76.

MAJOR WRITINGS

Poems About God (1919)
Chills and Fever: Poems (1924)
Two Gentlemen in Bonds (1927)

Selected Poems (1945)
Poems and Essays (1955)

The World's Body (1938; criticism)
The New Criticism (1941)

BIOGRAPHY

None.

CRITICISM

Beatty, R. C. "John Crowe Ransom as Poet," *Sewanee Rev.*, LII (1944), 344–66.

Blum, Morgan. "The Fugitive Particular: John Crowe Ransom, Critic," *West. Rev.*, XIV (1950), 85–102.

Brooks, Cleanth. *Modern Poetry and the Tradition*, pp. 88–95. Chapel Hill, N.C.: University of North Carolina Press, 1939.

Gamble, Isabel. "Ceremonies of Bravery: John Crowe Ransom," *Hopkins Review*, Vol. VI, No. 3–4 (1953), pp. 105–15.

Koch, Vivienne. "The Achievement of John Crowe Ransom," *Sewanee Rev.*, LVIII (1950), 227–61.

Sewanee Review, LVI (1948). "Homage to John Crowe Ransom."

Warren, R. P. "John Crowe Ransom: A Study in Irony," *Va. Quart. Rev.*, XI (1935), 93–112.

COMMENTS ON POEMS

BELLS FOR JOHN WHITESIDE'S DAUGHTER

Discussed in R. B. Heilman, *Pacific Spectator*, V (1951), 458–60; Warren, *Va. Quart. Rev.*, XI (1935), 105–6; R. P. Warren, *Ken. Rev.*, V (1943), pp. 237–40 (reprinted in Schorer [ed.], *Criticism* [Harcourt, Brace, 1948], pp. 370–72, and in Stallman [ed.], *Critiques and Essays in Criticism* [Ronald, 1949], pp. 92–94).

HERE LIES A LADY

Discussed in William Bleifuss, *Explicator*, XI (1953), 51; J. M. Bradbury, *Accent*, XI (1951), 52–54; F. H. Stocking and Ellsworth Mason, *Explicator*, VIII (1949), 1.

13. *thole:* Endure.

CAPTAIN CARPENTER

Discussed in Brooks, *Modern Poetry and the Tradition* (U. of N. Carolina Press, 1939), pp. 35–37; Riding and Graves, *A Survey of Modernist Poetry* (Doubleday, 1928), pp. 103–9.

ANTIQUE HARVESTERS

Discussed in F. O. Matthiessen, *Sewanee Rev.*, LVI (1948), 394–95.

26. *Lady:* A symbol for the South. Here the word has overtones of both earthly love and religious veneration as found in the chivalric romance.

THE EQUILIBRISTS

Discussed in Beatty, *Sewanee Rev.*, LII (1944), 359–60; Drew and Sweeney, *Directions in Modern Poetry* (Norton, 1940), pp. 208–11; Howard Nemerov, *Sewanee Rev.*, LVI (1948), 419–20; G. P. Wasserman, *U. Kans. City Rev.*, XXIII (1956), 153, 158–59.

47. *stuprate*: An obsolete word meaning "sexually violated."

PRELUDE TO AN EVENING

Discussed in Cleanth Brooks, *Sewanee Rev.*, LVI (1948), 412–14.

PAINTED HEAD

Discussed in Beatty, *Sewanee Rev.*, LII (1944), 365–66; J. M. Bradbury, *Accent*, XI (1951), 55–56; Brooks, *Modern Poetry and the Tradition* (U. of N. Carolina Press, 1939), pp. 94–95; Charles Moorman, *Explicator*, X (1951), 15; Virginia Wallach, *Explicator*, XIV (1956), 45.

EDWIN ARLINGTON ROBINSON (1869–1935)

LIFE

Born December 22 in Head Tide, Maine, but grew up in Gardiner, Maine, the "Tilbury Town" of his poems. He studied at Harvard from 1891 to 1893 and subsequently worked in New York and Boston. Through the assistance of President Theodore Roosevelt he became a clerk in the New York Custom House from 1905 to 1910, after which year he gave himself entirely to writing. Wide recognition came finally with *The Man Against the Sky* (1916), and in the 1920's he received the Pulitzer Prize three times, as well as other awards; yet he continued, as in his years of obscurity, to be the completely dedicated artist. He died on April 6, 1935, in New York City.

BIBLIOGRAPHY

Hogan, C. B. *A Bibliography of Edwin Arlington Robinson.* New Haven, Conn.: Yale University Press, 1936.
Lippincott, Lillian. *A Bibliography of the Writings and Criticisms of Edwin Arlington Robinson.* Boston: The F. W. Faxon Co., Inc., 1937.

MAJOR WRITINGS

Collected Poems of Edwin Arlington Robinson (1937)

The Torrent and The Night Before (1896)
The Children of the Night: A Book of Poems (1897)

The Town Down the River: A Book of Poems (1910)
The Man Against the Sky: A Book of Poems (1916)
Merlin: A Poem (1917)
The Three Taverns: A Book of Poems (1920)
Lancelot: A Poem (1920)
Avon's Harvest (1921)
Roman Bartholow (1923)
Dionysus in Doubt: A Book of Poems (1925)
Tristram (1927)
Matthias at the Door (1931)
King Jasper: A Poem (1935)

Edwin Arlington Robinson, Poems (1931; ed. Bliss Perry)
Tilbury Town: Selected Poems of Edwin Arlington Robinson (1953; ed. Lawrance Thompson)

Letters of Edwin Arlington Robinson to Howard George Schmitt (1943; ed. C. J. Weber)
Selected Letters of Edwin Arlington Robinson (1940; ed. Ridgely Torrence)
Untriangulated Stars: Letters of Edwin Arlington Robinson to Harry de Forest Smith, 1890–1905 (1947; ed. Denham Sutcliffe)

BIOGRAPHY

Hagedorn, Hermann. *Edwin Arlington Robinson: A Biography.* New York: The Macmillan Co., 1938.
Neff, Emery. *Edwin Arlington Robinson.* New York: William Sloane Associates, Inc., 1948.

CRITICISM

Barnard, Ellsworth. *Edwin Arlington Robinson: A Critical Study.* New York: The Macmillan Co., 1952.
Cestre, Charles. *An Introduction to Edwin Arlington Robinson.* New York: The Macmillan Co., 1930.
Coffin, R. P. T. *New Poetry of New England: Frost and Robinson.* Baltimore, Md.: The Johns Hopkins Press, 1938.
Coxe, L. O. "E. A. Robinson: The Lost Tradition," *Sewanee Rev.,* LXII (1954), 247–66.
Fussell, E. S. *Edwin Arlington Robinson: The Literary Background of a Traditional Poet.* Berkeley, Cal.: University of California Press, 1954.
Kaplan, Estelle. *Philosophy in the Poetry of Edwin Arlington Robinson.* New York: Columbia University Press, 1940.
Lowell, Amy. *Tendencies in Modern American Poetry,* pp. 3–75. New York: The Macmillan Co., 1917.

Morris, Lloyd. *The Poetry of Edwin Arlington Robinson: An Essay in Appreciation.* New York: George H. Doran Co., 1923.
Waggoner, H. H. "E. A. Robinson and the Cosmic Chill," *New England Quarterly,* XIII (1940), 65–84.
Winters, Yvor. *Edwin Arlington Robinson.* Norfolk, Conn.: New Directions, 1946.

COMMENTS ON POEMS

GEORGE CRABBE

George Crabbe (1754–1832) was an English poet, who in *The Village* and other poems described the life of common people with realistic grimness.

LUKE HAVERGAL

Discussed in Richard Crowder, *Explicator,* VII (1948), 15; Walter Gierasch, *Explicator,* III (1944), 8; M. M. Parlett, *Explicator,* III (1945), 57; A. A. Raven, *Explicator,* III (1944), 24.

FOR A DEAD LADY

Discussed in Richard Crowder, *Explicator,* V (1946), 19; E. S. Fussell, *Explicator,* IX (1951), 33; R. H. Super, *Explicator,* V (1947), 60.

THE GIFT OF GOD

Discussed in Coxe, *Sewanee Rev.,* LXII (1954), 250, 261–65.

HILLCREST

Hillcrest was the name of the home of Edward MacDowell, the composer, and his wife at Peterborough, New Hampshire. After her husband's death in 1908, Mrs. MacDowell made Hillcrest the center of the MacDowell Colony, where composers, writers, and artists might live in the summer. From 1911 on Robinson habitually spent his summers there.

EROS TURANNOS

The Latin title means "Love, the tyrant."
Discussed in Coxe, *Sewanee Rev.,* LXII (1954), 252–57; Lawrence Perrine, *Explicator,* VIII (1949), 20.

THE MAN AGAINST THE SKY

Discussed in Waggoner, *The Heel of Elohim* (U. of Oklahoma Press, 1950), pp. 29–36; Yvor Winters, *Arizona Quarterly,* I (1945), 74–75. 42–46. *As on a day . . . a bird:* Cf. Daniel 3 and 4.
136. *Curse God and die:* Cf. Job 2:9.

177–78. *Nahum's . . . soon lost:* Cf. Nahum 3:17
229. *Word:* Cf. John 1:1.

MR. FLOOD'S PARTY

8. *Tilbury Town:* The fictitious name assigned by Robinson in a number of his poems to Gardiner, Maine.

11. *poet:* Omar Khayyám. Cf. Edward Fitzgerald's translation of *The Rubáiyát,* stanza VII.

20. *Roland:* The hero of the medieval French romance, *The Song of Roland.* Cf. note to line 4 of MacLeish's "The Silent Slain" (p. 501).

THE SHEAVES

Discussed in Richard Crowder, *Explicator,* IV (1946), 38.

KARMA

Karma is the Buddhist doctrine that every act inevitably receives its just retribution.

THEODORE ROETHKE (1908–1964)

LIFE

Born May 25 in Saginaw, Michigan, and grew up, as he says, "in and around a beautiful green-house owned by my father and uncle." He graduated from the University of Michigan in 1929 and received his M.A. there in 1936. He has taught English at Lafayette, Pennsylvania State University, and Bennington, and is now a professor of English at the University of Washington. He held a Guggenheim Fellowship in 1945, was a Fulbright lecturer in Italy in 1955, and in 1953 received the Pulitzer and other prizes for *The Waking.*

BIBLIOGRAPHY

None.

MAJOR WRITINGS

Open House (1941)
The Lost Son and Other Poems (1948)
Praise to the End! (1951)

The Waking: Poems 1933–1953 (1953)

BIOGRAPHY

None.

CRITICISM

Burke, Kenneth. "The Vegetal Radicalism of Theodore Roethke," *Sewanee Rev.*, LVIII (1950), 68–108.
Kramer, Hilton. "The Poetry of Theodore Roethke," *West. Rev.*, XVIII (1954), 131–46.
Kunitz, Stanley. "News of the Root," *Poetry*, LXXIII (1949), 222–25.

COMMENTS ON POEMS

THE LOST SON

1. *Woodlawn:* The name of a cemetery.
142. *Ordnung!:* (German) "Order!"

FOUR FOR SIR JOHN DAVIES

Sir John Davies (1569–1626), an English poet, was the author of *Orchestra,* in which natural phenomena are described in terms of "dancing" or ordered motion; and *Nosce Teipsum,* a philosophic poem on the nature of man and the soul.
19. *Yeats:* William Butler Yeats.

KARL SHAPIRO (1913–   )

LIFE

Born November 10 in Baltimore, Maryland. He was an undergraduate at the University of Virginia and Johns Hopkins, and spent a year at the Enoch Pratt Free Library in Baltimore as a library student. From 1941 to 1945 he served in the U.S. Army. While in Australia, New Guinea, and other South Pacific areas, he sent poems back to his fiancée in New York, who arranged for their publication. In 1946–47 he was Consultant in Poetry at the Library of Congress, and from 1947 to 1950 he lectured at Johns Hopkins. He edited *Poetry* from 1950 to 1955, and is now in the English Department at the University of Nebraska, where he also is editor of the *Schooner.*

BIBLIOGRAPHY

Quesnel, Louise, and Webster, W. G. "A Bibliography of the Work of Karl Jay Shapiro, 1935–1949." Mimeographed. Baltimore: Enoch Pratt Free Library, 1950.

MAJOR WRITINGS

Person Place and Thing (1942)
V-Letter and Other Poems (1944)

Essay on Rime (1945)
Trial of a Poet and Other Poems (1947)

Poems, 1940–1953 (1953)

BIOGRAPHY

None.

CRITICISM

Daiches, David. "The Poetry of Karl Shapiro," *Poetry*, LXVI (1945), 266–73.
Fussell, Edwin. "Karl Shapiro: The Paradox of Prose and Poetry," *West. Rev.*, XVIII (1954), 225–44.
Glicksberg, C. I. "Karl Shapiro and the Personal Accent," *Prairie Schooner*, XXII (1948), 44–52.
Kohler, Dayton. "Karl Shapiro: Poet in Uniform," *Coll. Eng.*, VII (1946), 243–49.
O'Connor, W. V. "Shapiro on Rime," *Ken. Rev.*, VIII (1946), 113–22.
Seif, Morton. "Poet's Journey: The Struggle in the Soul of Karl Shapiro," *Menorah Journal*, XXXVII (1949), 51–58.

COMMENTS ON POEMS

THE POTOMAC

This poem, with an extra stanza, was included in *Person Place and Thing* under the title "Alexandria" (that is, the city in Virginia just across the Potomac River from Washington, D.C.).
10. *Thomas:* Thomas Jefferson of Virginia, who died in 1826 at his home, Monticello, which may roughly be called "Georgian" in architecture.
11. *Arlington:* The National Cemetery, on the south bank of the Potomac in the District of Columbia. The Tomb of the Unknown Soldier, located in this cemetery, is kept under constant guard by single sentries.

ELEGY FOR A DEAD SOLDIER

Discussed in Paul Engle, *Eng. Jour.*, XXXVIII (1949), 62–63.
22. *Paul:* The chaplain is reading from one of the epistles of Paul in the New Testament.
81–82. *on mourrait . . . industriels?:* (French) "Would one die for the industrialists?"

EDITH SITWELL (1887–1965)

LIFE

Edith Sitwell was born in Scarborough, Yorkshire, the daughter and oldest child of Sir George Sitwell, fourth baronet. Educated privately at the family estate, Renishaw Park, she had as her most brilliant governess Helen Rootham, the translator of Rimbaud's *Les Illuminations*. Miss Sitwell captured general attention in 1916 when she edited the first of a series of six annual anthologies of poetry entitled *Wheels*. Since then her life has been primarily devoted to poetry. In 1937 she received the medal for poetry from the Royal Society of Literature. She holds honorary degrees of Doctor of Letters from the universities of Leeds, Durham, and Oxford, and she is a Dame of the British Empire.

BIBLIOGRAPHY

Wykes-Joyce, Max. "Checklist of the Chief Works of Edith Sitwell," pp. 236–38 in *Triad of Genius. Part I. Edith and Osbert Sitwell*. London: Peter Owen, Ltd., 1953.

MAJOR WRITINGS

The Collected Poems of Edith Sitwell (1954)

Facade (1922)
Bucolic Comedies (1923)
Rustic Elegies (1927)
Gold Coast Customs (1929)
Street Songs (1942)
Green Song and Other Poems (1944)

The Canticle of the Rose: Selected Poems, 1920–1947 (1949)
Facade and Other Poems, 1920–1935 (1950)

Aspects of Modern Poetry (1934)
A Notebook on William Shakespeare (1948)

A Poet's Notebook (1943)

BIOGRAPHY

Sitwell, Osbert [autobiography in five volumes]. Vol. I, *Left Hand Right Hand!* (1945); Vol. II, *The Scarlet Tree* (1946); Vol. III, *Great Morning* (1948); Vol. IV, *Laughter in the Next Room* (1949); Vol. V, *Noble Essences, or Courteous Revelations* (1950). London: Macmillan & Co., Ltd.

Wykes-Joyce, Max. *Triad of Genius. Part I. Edith and Osbert Sitwell*. London: Peter Owen, Ltd., 1953.

CRITICISM

Bogan, Louise. "Edith Sitwell," pp. 21–27 in *Selected Criticism*. New York: The Noonday Press, 1955.

Bowra, C. M. *Edith Sitwell*. Monaco: Lyrebird Press, 1947.

Clark, Kenneth. "On the Development of Miss Sitwell's Later Style," *Horizon*, XVI (1947), 7–17.

Lehmann, John. *Edith Sitwell*. London: Longmans, Green & Co., Ltd., 1952.

Lindsay, Jack. "The Poetry of Edith Sitwell," *Life and Letters*, LXIV (1950), 39–52.

Muir, Edwin. "Edith Sitwell," pp. 147–59 in *Transition: Essays on Contemporary Literature*. New York: The Viking Press, Inc., 1926.

Reed, Henry. "The Poetry of Edith Sitwell," *Penguin New Writing*, No. 21 (1944), pp. 109–22.

Sister M. Jeremy. "Clown and Canticle: The Achievement of Edith Sitwell," *Renascence*, III (1951), 128–37, 144.

Sitwell, Edith. "Some Notes on My Own Poetry," pp. xv–l in *The Collected Poems of Edith Sitwell*. New York: Vanguard Press, Inc., 1954.

Villa, José Garcia (ed.). *Celebration for Edith Sitwell*. New York: New Directions, 1948. Essays by Gordon Bottomley, C. M. Bowra, Richard Church, Kenneth Clark, Horace Gregory, L. P. Hartley, John Lehmann, Jack Lindsay, Charles Morgan, John Piper, Frederic Prokosch, John Russell, Sir Osbert Sitwell, Stephen Spender, Gertrude Stein, and Arthur Waley.

COMMENTS ON POEMS

(Notes so designated are Edith Sitwell's own, from *The Collected Poems of Edith Sitwell*, 1954.)

AN OLD WOMAN

Discussed in Bowra, *Edith Sitwell*, pp. 41–42; Lehmann, *Edith Sitwell*, pp. 26–27.

119–23: [Sitwell] " 'It is obvious that the heat contained in animals is not fire, neither does it derive its origin from fire': Aristotle, quoted by William Harvey (*The Works of William Harvey, M.D.*, translated from the Latin by R. Willis Sydenham Society, 1847). Harvey continues: 'I maintain the same thing of the innate heat and the blood: I say that they are not fire and neither do they derive their origin from fire. They rather share the nature of some other, and that a more divine body and substance. They act by no faculty or property of the elements . . . as, in producing an animal, it' (the generative factor) 'surpasses the power of the elements—as it is a spirit, namely, and the inherent nature of that spirit corresponds to the essence of the stars, so is there a spirit, or certain force, inherent in the blood, acting superiorly to the power of the elements.' "

127–29: [Sitwell] " 'The inferior world, according to Aristotle, is so continuous and connected with the superior orbits, that all its motions and changes appear to take their rise and to receive directions from thence. . . . Inferior and corruptible things wait upon superior and incorruptible things; but all are subservient to the will of the supreme, omnipotent, and eternal creator.'—*Ibid.*"

139–40: [Sitwell] " 'Best is water of all, and gold, as a flaming sun in the night shineth eminent.'—Pindar." (*Olympian* 1. 1–2.)

162–64: [Sitwell] " 'He gives us men for our refreshment the bread of angels. . . . On the breaking of the Bread thou art not broken, nor art Thou divided, Thou art eaten, but like the Burning Bush, Thou are not consumed.'—St. Thomas Aquinas, *Sermon of the Body of Our Lord.*"

STILL FALLS THE RAIN

Discussed in Bowra, *Edith Sitwell,* pp. 35–37; Pinto, *Crisis in English Poetry* (Hutchinson's, 1951), pp. 205–6.

25–26. O *Ile . . . firmament:* A direct quotation from Christopher Marlowe, *The Tragical History of Doctor Faustus,* Act V, scene 2, lines 1430–31.

STREET SONG

Discussed in Bowra, *Edith Sitwell,* pp. 37–38.

THE SHADOW OF CAIN

Dame Edith has described the origin of the poem in "Some Notes on My Own Poetry" in *The Collected Poems:* "On the tenth of September, 1945, nearly five weeks after the fall of the first atom bomb, my brother Sir Osbert Sitwell and I were in the train going to Brighton, where we were to give a reading. He pointed out to me a paragraph in the *Times,* a description by an eye-witness of the immediate effect of the atomic bomb upon Hiroshima. That witness saw a totem pole of dust arise to the sun as a witness against the murder of mankind. . . . A totem pole, the symbol of creation, the symbol of generation.

"From that moment the poem began, although it was not actually written until April of the next year."

Discussed in Clark, *Horizon,* XVI (1947), 16–17; Lehmann, *Edith Sitwell,* pp. 29–31; Lindsay, *Life and Letters,* LXIV (1950), 51–52; Sister M. Jeremy, *Renascence,* III (1951), 135–36; Sitwell, *Collected Poems,* pp. xlvi–l.

8–11: [Sitwell] "A reference to Oken: *op. cit.*" (That is, Lorenz Oken, *Elements of Physiophilosophy.*)

19–20: [Sitwell] "Arthur Rimbaud's 'Metropolitan.' " Dame Edith follows closely Helen Rootham's translation of lines in the last stanza of Rimbaud's poem.

73: [Sitwell] " '. . . monstrous bull-voices of unseen fearful mimes.'— A fragment of the lost play by Aeschylus, *The Edonians.*" (See Fragment 27, lines 8–9 in *Aeschylus,* Vol. II, tr. H. W. Smyth [Cambridge, Mass.: Harvard University Press, 1952], pp. 399–400.)

77. *For the Son . . . furrow!*: [Sitwell] "Irenaeus expressed it so elegantly as it is almost pity if it be not true. *'Inseminaties est ubique in Scripturis, Filius Dei,'* says he. 'The Son of God is sowed in every furrow.'—John Donne, Sermon XI."

83: [Sitwell] "Transcript of an actual report by an eye-witness of the bomb falling on Hiroshima.—*The Times,* September 10, 1945."

92–93, 95: [Sitwell] "Founded on a passage in Burnet's *Theory of the Earth.*"

116–18: [Sitwell] "These are references to descriptions given by Lombroso and Havelock Ellis of the marks and appearance borne by prenatally disposed criminals."

127–29: [Sitwell] " 'Also we must say that this or that is a disease of Gold, and not that it is leprosy.'—*Paracelsus,* Appendix I, Chapter VI."

135–54: [Sitwell] " 'Gold is the most noble of all, the most precious and primary metal. . . . And we are not prepared to deny that leprosy, in all its forms, can be thereby removed from the human frame.'—*Paracelsus.*"

157–58: [Sitwell] "John Donne, Sermon CXXXVI."

STEPHEN SPENDER (1909–   )

LIFE

Born February 28 in London, the son of a prominent journalist. He was educated at private and public schools and at University College, Oxford, from which he went down in 1931 without a degree. During the thirties he wrote poetry and criticism and traveled in Germany and Spain. In World War II he edited, with Cyril Connolly, the magazine *Horizon,* and served as a fireman in the London Auxiliary Fire Service. Since the war Spender, while continuing to write poetry, has done his most important work as critic and editor. In 1953 he became coeditor, with Irving Kristol, of *Encounter,* an international monthly magazine.

BIBLIOGRAPHY

None.

MAJOR WRITINGS

Collected Poems, 1928–1953 (1955)

Poems (1933)
Vienna (1934)
The Still Centre (1939)
Ruins and Visions (1942)

Poems of Dedication (1946)
The Edge of Being (1949)

The Destructive Element (1934)
The Creative Element (1954)
The Making of a Poem (1955)
World Within World (1948; autobiography)

BIOGRAPHY

None.

CRITICISM

Jacobs, W. D. "The Moderate Poetical Success of Stephen Spender," *Coll. Eng.*, XVII (1956), 374–78.
"A Poetry of Search," *Times Lit. Sup.*, January 28, 1955, p. 56.
Seif, Morton. "The Influence of T. S. Eliot on Auden and Spender," *So. Atl. Quart.*, LIII (1954), 61–69.
Tate, Allen. "Stephen Spender's 'Poems,'" pp. 71–73 in *The Hovering Fly*. Cummington, Mass.: The Cummington Press, 1949.

COMMENTS ON POEMS

WHAT I EXPECTED

Discussed in Jacobs, *Coll. Eng.*, XVII (1956), 375.

THE LANDSCAPE NEAR AN AERODROME

Discussed in Jacobs, *Coll. Eng.*, XVII (1956), 375–76; C. C. Walcutt, *Explicator*, V (1947), 37.

AN ELEMENTARY SCHOOL CLASSROOM IN A SLUM

Discussed in Phyllis Bartlett, *Poems in Process* (New York: Oxford University Press, 1951), pp. 217–19.

TWO ARMIES

On the Spanish Civil War.

SEASCAPE

Discussed in Barbara Gibbs, *Poetry*, LXXXVI (1955), 239; Lewis, *The Poetic Image* (Oxford, 1947), pp. 136–40.

WALLACE STEVENS (1879-1955)

LIFE

Born October 2 in Reading, Pennsylvania. He attended Harvard from 1897 to 1900 and then studied law at the New York Law School. After he was admitted to the bar in 1904, he engaged in general practice in New York. From 1916 on he was employed by the Hartford Accident and Indemnity Company of Hartford, Connecticut. In 1934 he became a vice-president of the company and continued throughout the rest of his life the two occupations of insurance executive and poet. Little known to the general public for most of his career, he received a number of awards in the 1950's, including the Bollingen Prize (1950) and the Pulitzer Prize (1955). He died on August 2, 1955, in Hartford.

BIBLIOGRAPHY

Morse, S. F. *Wallace Stevens: A Preliminary Checklist of His Published Writings, 1898-1954.* New Haven, Conn.: Yale University Library, 1954.

MAJOR WRITINGS

Collected Poems (1954)

Harmonium (1923; enlarged ed., 1931)
Ideas of Order (1935)
Owl's Clover (1936)
The Man with the Blue Guitar and Other Poems (1937)
Parts of a World (1942)
Transport to Summer (1947)
The Auroras of Autumn (1950)
Opus Posthumous (1957)

The Necessary Angel: Essays on Reality and the Imagination (1951)

BIOGRAPHY

None.

CRITICISM

Baker, Howard. "Wallace Stevens and Other Poets," *So. Rev.,* I (1935), 373-89.
Bewley, Marius. "The Poetry of Wallace Stevens," *Part. Rev.,* XVI (1949), 895-915.
Blackmur, R. P. *Form and Value in Modern Poetry,* pp. 183-223. New York: Anchor Books, Doubleday & Co., Inc., 1957.

Frye, Northrop. "The Realistic Oriole: A Study of Wallace Stevens," *Hud. Rev.*, X (1957), 353–70.
Harvard Advocate, CXXVII (1940). Wallace Stevens number.
Martz, L. L. "Wallace Stevens: The Romance of the Precise," *Yale Poetry Review*, Vol. II, No. 5 (1946), pp. 13–20.
Moore, Marianne. *Predilections*, pp. 32–46. New York: The Viking Press, Inc., 1955.
Morse, S. F. "Motive for Metaphor," *Origin*, II (1952), complete issue.
Nemerov, Howard. "The Poetry of Wallace Stevens," *Sewanee Rev.*, LXV (1957), 1–14.
O'Connor, W. V. *The Shaping Spirit: A Study of Wallace Stevens*. Chicago: Henry Regnery Co., 1950.
Pearce, R. H. "Wallace Stevens: The Life of the Imagination," *PMLA*, LXVI (1951), 561–82.
Perspective, VII (1954). Wallace Stevens issue.
Simons, Hi. "The Genre of Wallace Stevens," *Sewanee Rev.*, LIII (1945), 566–79.
Sypher, Wylie. "Connoisseur in Chaos: Wallace Stevens," *Part. Rev.*, XIII (1946), 83–94.

COMMENTS ON POEMS

DOMINATION OF BLACK

Discussed in W. J. Rooney, *Jour. Aesth. & Art Crit.*, XIII (1955), 511–14, 517–18.

THE SNOW MAN

Discussed in Blackmur, *Form and Value in Modern Poetry*, pp. 200–201.

LE MONOCLE DE MON ONCLE

The title is French: "My Uncle's Monocle."
Discussed in Blackmur, *Form and Value in Modern Poetry*, pp. 191–92, 203–4; Donald Davie, *Twentieth Century*, CLIII (1953), 457, 462; Richard Ellmann, *Ken. Rev.*, XIX (1957), 97–99; W. A. Fahey, *Explicator*, XV (1956), 16; Frankenberg, *Pleasure Dome* (Houghton Mifflin, 1949), pp. 205–7; R. M. Gay, *Explicator*, VI (1948), 27; Robert Pack, *West. Rev.*, XX (1955), 57–59.
22. *connaissance*: (French) "Knowledge" or "acquaintanceship."
27. *Utamaro*: Kitagawa Utamaro (1753–1806), Japanese master of woodblock prints, particularly famous for his portraits of courtesans, shown wearing elaborate hairdresses.
29. *mountainous coiffures of Bath*: An exceptionally lofty style of hairdress affected by English beauties of the mid-eighteenth century at Bath, a fashionable watering place. For a discussion of stanza III, see E. R. Miner, *Explicator*, XIII (1955), 28.

A HIGH-TONED OLD CHRISTIAN WOMAN

W. V. O'Connor, *U. Kans. City Rev.*, XV (1948), 110; Winters, *In Defense of Reason* (Swallow & Morrow, 1947), pp. 434–35.

THE EMPEROR OF ICE-CREAM

Discussed in Blackmur, *Form and Value in Modern Poetry*, pp. 189–91; Drew and Sweeney, *Directions in Modern Poetry* (Norton, 1940), pp. 227–31; Richard Ellmann, *Ken. Rev.*, XIX (1957), 92–95; Max Herzberg and Wallace Stevens, *Explicator*, VII (1948), 18; Kenneth Lash and Robert Thackaberry, *Explicator*, VI (1948), 36; Elder Olson, *Coll. Eng.*, XVI (1955), 397–98.

SUNDAY MORNING

Discussed in Blackmur, *Form and Value in Modern Poetry*, pp. 198–200, 202; J. V. Cunningham, *Poetry*, LXXV (1949), 149–65; Frankenberg, *Pleasure Dome* (Houghton Mifflin, 1949), pp. 215–17; Robert Pack, *West Rev.*, XX (1955), 53–55; Winters, *In Defense of Reason* (Swallow & Morrow, 1947), pp. 431–34 and 447–56.

ANECDOTE OF THE JAR

Discussed in G. W. Arms and Others, *Explicator*, III (1944), 16; Howard Baker, *So. Rev.*, I (1935), 376–77; Winters, *In Defense of Reason* (Swallow & Morrow, 1947), 435–37.

TO THE ONE OF FICTIVE MUSIC

Discussed in R. E. Amacher, *Explicator*, XI (1953), 43.

PETER QUINCE AT THE CLAVIER

In Shakespeare's *Midsummer Night's Dream*, Peter Quince is the director of the clownish interlude on the "most cruel death of Pyramus and Thisbe."

Discussed in W. S. Johnson, *Jour. Aesth. & Art Crit.*, XIII (1955), 501–3; O'Connor, *Sense and Sensibility in Modern Poetry* (U. of Chicago Press, 1948), pp. 149–50; F. H. Stocking, *Explicator*, V (1947), 47; M. J. Storm, *Explicator*, XIV (1955), 9.

9. *Susanna:* According to the History of Susanna, a book of the Apocrypha, two Hebrew elders attempted to seduce Susanna, the wife of Joachim, after watching her at her bath. When she brought charges against them, they countercharged that she had attempted to seduce them. About to be executed, she was proved innocent by the prophet Daniel, and the elders were executed instead.

THIRTEEN WAYS OF LOOKING AT A BLACKBIRD

Discussed in W. R. Keast, *Chicago Review*, VIII (1954), 48–63.
25. *Haddam:* A town in Connecticut, southeast of Hartford.

SEA SURFACE FULL OF CLOUDS

Discussed in Blackmur, *Form and Value in Modern Poetry*, pp. 192–94; D. R. Ferry, *Explicator*, VI (1948), 56; John Pauker, *Furioso*, Vol. V, No. 4 (1950), pp. 34–46; Ransom, *The World's Body* (Scribner's, 1938), pp. 58–60.

12. *C'était . . . âme:* (French) "It was my child, my darling, my soul."

30. *C'était . . . or:* (French) "It was my heavenly brother, my life, my gold."

48. *Oh! . . . amour:* (French) "Oh! It was my ecstasy and my love."

66. *C'était . . . divine:* (French) "It was my faith, divine carelessness."

84. *C'était . . . l'ignominie:* (French) "It was my bastard spirit, ignominy."

THE IDEA OF ORDER AT KEY WEST

44. *Ramon Fernandez:* (1894–1944), French exponent of philosophic literary criticism.

THE GLASS OF WATER

Discussed in D. H. Owen, *Perspective*, VII (1954), 181–83.

13. *metaphysica:* (Latin) "After (or beyond) those things which relate to external nature."

14. *Jocundus:* (Latin) "The pleasant (or cheerful) man."

CREDENCES OF SUMMER

Discussed in H. H. Watts, *Ken. Rev.*, XIV (1952), 122–40.

47. *Oley:* Village in Bucks County, Pennsylvania, near Reading.

129. *douceurs:* (French) "Sweetnesses" or "sweet acts."

130. *Tristesses:* (French) "Sadnesses."

DYLAN THOMAS (1914–1953)

LIFE

Born October 22 in Carmarthenshire, Wales, the son of a teacher of English. He was educated at the Swansea Grammar School, and was briefly a reporter before he turned to serious writing of prose and poetry. After World War II, during which he worked for the British Broadcasting Corporation and served as an antiaircraft gunner, he continued to write and began to give readings of his own and others' poetry. He made three successful lecture tours of the United States. The third was abruptly terminated November 9, 1953, by his death in New York City of a cerebral ailment.

BIBLIOGRAPHY

Huff, W. H. "Appendix C: Bibliography," pp. 102–46 in Elder Olson, *The Poetry of Dylan Thomas*. Chicago: The University of Chicago Press, 1954. Works by and about Thomas.
Rolph, J. A. *Dylan Thomas: A Bibliography*. London: J. M. Dent & Sons, Ltd., 1956.

MAJOR WRITINGS

The Collected Poems of Dylan Thomas (1953)

18 Poems (1934)
Twenty-five Poems (1936)
The Map of Love: Verse and Prose (1939)
New Poems (1943)
Deaths and Entrances (1946)
In Country Sleep and Other Poems (1951)

Selected Writings of Dylan Thomas (1946; ed. J. L. Sweeney)

Portrait of the Artist as a Young Dog (1940; stories and autobiographical sketches)
"Reminiscences of Childhood," *Encounter*, No. 10 (July, 1954), pp. 3–7.
Dylan Thomas: Letters to Vernon Watkins (1957; ed. Vernon Watkins)

BIOGRAPHY

None. There is some biographical material in Caitlin Thomas, *Leftover Life to Kill* (London: Putnam & Co., 1957), and J. M. Brinnin has given a view of Thomas' last years in *Dylan Thomas in America* (Boston: Little, Brown & Co., 1955).

CRITICISM

Daiches, David. "The Poetry of Dylan Thomas," pp. 50–61 in *Literary Essays*. Edinburgh: Oliver & Boyd, 1956.
Huddlestone, Linden. "An Approach to Dylan Thomas," *Penguin New Writing*, No. 35 (1948), pp. 123–60.
Maud, R. N. "Dylan Thomas's Poetry," *Essays in Crit.*, IV (1954), 411–20.
Mayhead, Robin. "Dylan Thomas's Poetry," *Scrutiny*, XIX (1953), 142.
Moore, Geoffrey. "Dylan Thomas," *Ken. Rev.*, XVII (1955), 258–77.
Olson, Elder. *The Poetry of Dylan Thomas*. Chicago: The University of Chicago Press, 1954.
Stanford, Derek. *Dylan Thomas: A Literary Study*. London: Neville Spearman, 1954.
Stearns, M. W. "Unsex the Skeleton: Notes on the Poetry of Dylan Thomas," *Sewanee Rev.*, LII (1944), 424–40.

Tindall, W. Y. "The Poetry of Dylan Thomas," *Am. Schol.*, XVII (1948), 431–39.
Treece, Henry. *Dylan Thomas: "Dog among the Fairies."* London: Lindsay Drummond, Ltd., 1949; 2d ed., London: Ernest Benn, 1956.

COMMENTS ON POEMS

THE FORCE THAT THROUGH THE GREEN FUSE DRIVES THE FLOWER

Discussed in David Aivaz, *Hud. Rev.*, III (1950), 389–91; G. Giovannini, *Explicator*, VIII (1950), 59; S. F. Johnson, *Explicator*, VIII (1950), 60, and X (1952), 26.

ALTARWISE BY OWL-LIGHT

Discussed as a whole or in part in R. M. Adams, *Hud. Rev.*, VIII (1955), 71–75; Daiches, *Literary Essays*, p. 57; Bernard Kniger, *Explicator*, XV (1956), 18; R. N. Maud, *Essays in Crit.*, IV (1954), 415, and *Explicator*, XIV (1955), 16; Olson, *The Poetry of Dylan Thomas*, pp. 64–87, 153–61; Francis Scarfe, *Auden and After* (Routledge, 1942), pp. 106–10; Stearns, *Sewanee Rev.*, LII (1944), 9–12.

AFTER THE FUNERAL

Ann Jones was Dylan Thomas' aunt.
Discussed in Deutsch, *Poetry in Our Time* (Holt, 1952), p. 342; Lewis, *The Poetic Image* (Oxford, 1947), pp. 123–25; Marshall Stearns, *Explicator*, III (1945), 52; Tindall, *Am. Schol.*, XVII (1948), 434.

BALLAD OF THE LONG-LEGGED BAIT

Discussed in Bayley, *Romantic Survival* (Constable, 1957), p. 222; Glauco Cambon, *English Miscellany*, VII (1956), 251–59; Olson, *The Poetry of Dylan Thomas*, pp. 50–52; Tindall, *Forces in Modern British Literature* (Knopf, 1947), pp. 354–55.
107. *Sussanah's drowned:* Cf. Wallace Stevens, "Peter Quince at the Clavier" (p. 259).
110. *Sin who had a woman's shape:* Milton gives this description of Sin in *Paradise Lost*, II, 650–51: "The one seem'd Woman to the waist, and fair, / But ended foul in many a scaly fold."

A REFUSAL TO MOURN

Discussed in Daiches, *Literary Essays*, pp. 54–56; Deutsch, *Poetry in Our Time* (Holt, 1952), pp. 335–37; William Empson, *Essays in Crit.*, V (1955), 89; Henry Gibson, *Critic*, I (1947), 19–20; R. N. Maud, *Essays in Crit.*, IV (1954), 413–14, 419–20; Edith Sitwell, *Critic*, I (1947), 18.

POEM IN OCTOBER

Discussed in Daiches, *Literary Essays,* pp. 59–60; Deutsch, *Poetry in Our Time* (Holt, 1952), pp. 332–33.

CEREMONY AFTER A FIRE RAID

Discussed in Tindall, *Am. Schol.,* XVII (1948), 437.

FERN HILL

Discussed in William Blissett, *Queens Quarterly,* LXIII (1956), 52–54; Sister M. Laurentia, *Explicator,* XIV (1955), 1; Stanford, *Dylan Thomas,* pp. 105, 110–13.

DO NOT GO GENTLE INTO THAT GOOD NIGHT

Discussed in Oliver Evans, *English Miscellany,* VII (1955), 163–73.

WILLIAM CARLOS WILLIAMS (1883–1964)

LIFE

Born September 17 in Rutherford, New Jersey. He attended schools in this city and in Geneva, Switzerland, took his M.D. degree in 1906 at the University of Pennsylvania, interned for two years in New York, studied pediatrics at Leipzig for a year, and returned in 1910 to Rutherford, where he has continued to practice pediatrics as well as to publish many volumes of verse. In 1926 he received the *Dial* Award and in 1931 the Guarantors Prize given by *Poetry.* He is particularly interested in creating a specifically American idiom. Besides his poems he has published several novels and volumes of short stories and essays.

BIBLIOGRAPHY

None.

MAJOR WRITINGS

The Collected Earlier Poems of William Carlos Williams (1951)
The Collected Later Poems of William Carlos Williams (1950)

A Book of Poems: Al Que Quiere! (1917)
Sour Grapes: A Book of Poems (1921)
Spring and All (1923)
Collected Poems, 1921–1931 (1934)
An Early Martyr and Other Poems (1935)
The Complete Collected Poems of William Carlos Williams, 1906–1938 (1938)

The Wedge (1944)
Paterson (Book One, 1946; Book Two, 1948; Book Three, 1949; Book Four, 1951)
The Desert Music and Other Poems (1954)

William Carlos Williams: Selected Poems (1949; ed. Randall Jarrell)

In the American Grain (1925; essays)
White Mule (1937; a novel)
Selected Essays (1954)

The Autobiography of William Carlos Williams (1951)
The Selected Letters of William Carlos Williams (1957; ed. J. C. Thirlwall)

BIOGRAPHY

None.

CRITICISM

Bennett, John. "The Lyre and the Sledgehammer," *Hud. Rev.*, V (1952), 295–307.
Briarcliff Quarterly, III (1946). Williams number.
Burke, Kenneth. "The Methods of William Carlos Williams," *Dial*, LXXXII (1927), 94–98.
Jarrell, Randall. *Poetry and the Age*, pp. 215–26, 236–46. New York: Vintage Books, 1955.
Koch, Vivienne. *William Carlos Williams*. Norfolk, Conn.: New Directions, 1950.
———, "William Carlos Williams: The Man and the Poet," *Ken. Rev.*, XIV (1952), 502–10.
Lechlitner, Ruth. "The Poetry of William Carlos Williams," *Poetry*, LIV (1939), 326–35.
Perspective, VI (1953). "William Carlos Williams."

COMMENTS ON POEMS

TRACT

Discussed in Walter Gierasch, *Explicator*, III (1945), 35.

THE WIDOW'S LAMENT IN SPRINGTIME

19. *turned*: Probably a misprint for "turn." The latter is given in *The Complete Collected Poems* (1938).

SPRING AND ALL

Discussed in Winters, *In Defense of Reason* (Swallow & Morrow, 1947), pp. 78–82.

Discussed in Deutsch, *Poetry in Our Time* (Holt, 1952), pp. 102–4.

PREFACE TO PATERSON, BOOK ONE

For discussions of the entire poem, *Paterson*, see: Deutsch, *Poetry in Our Time* (Holt, 1952), pp. 104–9; Sister M. B. Quinn, "William Carlos Williams: A Testament of Perpetual Change," *PMLA*, LXX (1955), 292–322 (reprinted in Quinn, *The Metamorphic Tradition in Modern Poetry* [Rutgers U. Press, 1955], pp. 89–129); Frank Thompson, "The Symbolic Structure of *Paterson*," *West. Rev.*, XIX (1955), 285–93.

Paterson attempts to describe the whole culture of Paterson, New Jersey, from Indian times to the present, in order to show, as Williams writes, "that a man in himself is a city, beginning, seeking, achieving and concluding his life in ways which the various aspects of a city may embody—if imaginatively conceived—any city, all the details of which may be made to voice his most intimate convictions."

WILLIAM BUTLER YEATS (1865–1939)

LIFE

Born June 13 in Dublin, Ireland, the son of a painter. Educated in London and Dublin, he went on to art school rather than to a university. Although he contributed to the cause of Irish nationalism and wrote and produced plays for the Abbey Theater in Dublin, his life was primarily devoted to poetry. He was a senator of the Irish Free State from 1922 to 1928, and received the Nobel Prize for Literature in 1923. He died on the French Riviera, January 28, 1939.

BIBLIOGRAPHY

Wade, Allan. *A Bibliography of the Writings of W. B. Yeats.* Rev. ed. London: Rupert Hart-Davis, 1958.

MAJOR WRITINGS

The Collected Poems of W. B. Yeats (1933; 2d ed., with later poems added, 1950; definitive ed., with author's final revisions, 1956)
The Variorum Edition of the Poems of W. B. Yeats (1957; ed. Peter Allt and R. K. Alspach)

The Wanderings of Oisin and Other Poems (1889)
The Countess Kathleen and Various Legends and Lyrics (1892)
The Wind among the Reeds (1899)

In the Seven Woods (1903)
The Green Helmet and Other Poems (1910)
Responsibilities: Poems and a Play (1914)
The Wild Swans at Coole (1919)
Michael Robartes and the Dancer (1921)
The Tower (1928)
Words for Music Perhaps and Other Poems (1932)
The Winding Stair and Other Poems (1933)
New Poems (1938)
Last Poems and Plays (1940)

The Collected Plays of W. B. Yeats (1934; rev. ed., 1952)

Essays (1924)
Essays (1937)

A Vision (1925; drastically revised, 1937)

The Autobiography of William Butler Yeats (1938; reissued, 1953)
The Letters of W. B. Yeats (1954; ed. Allan Wade)

BIOGRAPHY

Ellmann, Richard. *Yeats: The Man and the Masks.* New York: The Macmillan Co., 1948.
Hone, J. M. *W. B. Yeats, 1865–1939.* New York: The Macmillan Co., 1943.
Jeffares, A. N. *W. B. Yeats, Man and Poet.* New Haven, Conn.: Yale University Press, 1949.

CRITICISM

Brooks, Cleanth. "Yeats: The Poet as Myth-Maker," pp. 173–202 in *Modern Poetry and the Tradition.* Chapel Hill, N.C.: University of North Carolina Press, 1939.
Eliot, T. S. "Yeats," pp. 295–308 in *On Poetry and Poets.* New York: Farrar, Straus & Cudahy, 1957.
Ellmann, Richard. *The Identity of Yeats.* New York: Oxford University Press, 1954.
Hall, James, and Steinmann, Martin (eds.). *The Permanence of Yeats: Selected Criticism.* New York: The Macmillan Co., 1950. Essays by twenty-four modern critics.
Henn, T. R. *The Lonely Tower: Studies in the Poetry of W. B. Yeats.* London: Methuen & Co., Ltd., 1950.
MacNeice, Louis. *The Poetry of W. B. Yeats.* London: Oxford University Press, 1941.
Parkinson, Thomas. *W. B. Yeats, Self-Critic.* Berkeley, Cal.: University of California Press, 1951.

Southern Review, Vol. VII, No. 3 (Winter, 1941). William Butler Yeats memorial issue. Essays by fifteen critics.

Stauffer, D. A. *The Golden Nightingale: Essays on Some Principles of Poetry in the Lyrics of William Butler Yeats.* New York: The Macmillan Co., 1949.

COMMENTS ON POEMS

THE LAKE ISLE OF INNISFREE

Innisfree is an island in Lough Gill, County Sligo. Sligo is the county in the west of Ireland where Yeats spent much of his boyhood.

Discussed in Robert Graves, *The Common Asphodel* (London: Hamish Hamilton, 1949), pp. 186–88 (an attack on its "muzziness"); Hone, *W. B. Yeats,* pp. 81–82; Jeffares, *W. B. Yeats,* p. 64; MacNeice, *The Poetry of W. B. Yeats,* p. 80; J. C. Ransom, *So. Rev.,* VII (1941), 526–30.

ADAM'S CURSE

The situation which inspired this poem, a call by Yeats on Maud Gonne and her sister, Mrs. Pilcher, in the latter's London flat, is described in Hone, *W. B. Yeats,* pp. 164–65.

Discussed in Kermode, *Romantic Image* (Routledge, 1957), pp. 55–56; Stephen Spender, p. 181 in Hall and Steinmann (eds.), *The Permanence of Yeats.*

SEPTEMBER 1913

Inspired by a speech Yeats himself made in July, 1913, in which he exalted the old Ireland and upbraided his contemporaries for failing to house the French paintings acquired by Hugh Lane.

Discussed in Bowra, *The Heritage of Symbolism* (Macmillan, 1947), p. 121; Jeffares, *W. B. Yeats,* p. 171.

8. *O'Leary:* John O'Leary, who died in 1907, was one of the Triumvirate of the Fenian Society. He was imprisoned by the British for five years and was an exile in Paris for fifteen more. His personal influence on Yeats was great.

20. *Edward Fitzgerald:* Lord Edward Fitzgerald (1763–98), member of the United Irishmen, betrayed by an informer.

21. *Robert Emmet:* Irishman hanged as a rebel in 1803.

21. *Wolfe Tone:* Theobald Wolfe Tone (1763–98), a founder of United Irishmen. Adjutant-general of a French expedition invading Ireland, he was captured by the British and committed suicide.

THE MAGI

Discussed in Blackmur, *Form and Value in Modern Poetry* (Anchor Books, 1957), pp. 42–43.

THE FISHERMAN

Discussed in Deutsch, *Poetry in Our Time* (Holt, 1952), p. 259; Jeffares, *W. B. Yeats*, pp. 173–74; Edmund Wilson, pp. 21–23 in Hall and Steinmann (eds.), *The Permanence of Yeats*.

AN IRISH AIRMAN FORESEES HIS DEATH

Written in memory of Major Robert Gregory, son of Yeats's friend, Lady Augusta Gregory. Gregory joined the Royal Flying Corps and was killed on the Italian front, January 23, 1918.
Discussed by Delmore Schwartz, p. 322 in Hall and Steinmann (eds.), *The Permanence of Yeats*.

EASTER 1916

On the Easter Rising of the Irish Republicans, who seized a number of public buildings in Dublin but were soon put down by the British. The leaders were hanged.
Discussed in Bowra, *Heritage of Symbolism* (Macmillan, 1947), pp. 202–3; Hone, *W. B. Yeats*, pp. 318–21; Lewis, *The Poetic Image* (Oxford, 1947), p. 94; Arnold Stein, *Sewanee Rev.*, LVII (1949), 623–26.
15. *all changed*: Yeats takes back his gibe in "September 1913" about those who "fumbled in a greasy till."
17. *That woman*: Constance Markievicz (1876–1927), who for involvement in the Rising received a death sentence which was commuted to life imprisonment. She was released after the amnesty of 1917.
24. *This man*: Patrick Pearse (1879–1916), the schoolmaster who led the fighting in the Post Office.
26. *This other*: James Connolly (1870–1916), commander-in-chief of the Rising.
31. *This other man*: Major John MacBride, who had led the Irish Brigade with the Boers against the English and had married Maud Gonne, Yeats's early love.
75. *MacDonagh*: Thomas MacDonagh (1878–1916), poet and author of a book on Gaelic influences on English prosody.

THE SECOND COMING

The title seems to suggest the second coming of Christ, predicted in Matthew 24.
Discussed in E. A. Bloom, *U. Kans. City Rev.*, XXI (1954), 103–10; Blackmur, *Form and Value in Modern Poetry* (Anchor Books, 1957), pp. 37–43; Ellmann, *Identity of Yeats*, pp. 257–60; Jeffares, *W. B. Yeats*, pp. 197–98; J. C. Ransom, pp. 102–4 in Hall and Steinmann (eds.), *The Permanence of Yeats*; D. S. Savage, *West. Rev.*, XIII (1949), 67–78; Donald Weeks, *PMLA*, LXIII (1948), 281–92.
5. *The blood-dimmed tide*: Violence, war.

12. *Spiritus Mundi:* What the seventeenth-century Cambridge Platonist, Henry More, called *Anima Mundi,* a collective imagination, a communal storehouse of images.

21. *rough beast:* The promise of the title is deceptive. What comes is the rough "beast of the Apocalypse," or Antichrist, predicted by St. John in Revelation.

A PRAYER FOR MY DAUGHTER

This poem was begun a few weeks after the birth of Yeats's first child, Anne Butler Yeats, February 24, 1919.

Discussed in Warren Beck, *Coll. Eng.,* IV (1943), 349–50.

59. *the loveliest woman born:* A reference to the effect of political activity on Maud Gonne.

LEDA AND THE SWAN

This poem was founded upon Michelangelo's painting, which Yeats had seen in Venice.

Discussed in Blackmur, *Form and Value in Modern Poetry* (Anchor Books, 1957), pp. 56–57; Kenneth Burke, pp. 256–58 in Hall and Steinmann (eds.), *The Permanence of Yeats;* Ellmann, *Identity of Yeats,* pp. 176–79; MacNeice, *The Poetry of Yeats,* pp. 144, 162–63; G. Melchiori, *English Miscellany,* VII (1956), pp. 147–239; Leo Spitzer, *Mod. Phil.,* LII (1954), 271–76; Hoyt Trowbridge, *Mod. Phil.,* LI (1953), 118–29.

9. *engenders:* Born to Leda from this union were Helen of Troy and Castor and Pollux, twin gods of war.

10. *The broken wall, the burning roof:* A reference to the sack of Troy by the victorious Greeks.

11. *Agamemnon dead:* On his return from Troy, Agamemnon was treacherously killed by Clytemnestra and her lover, Aegisthus.

SAILING TO BYZANTIUM

Discussed in Blackmur, *Form and Value in Modern Poetry* (Anchor Books, 1957), pp. 52–53; Cleanth Brooks, pp. 82–85 in Hall and Steinmann (eds.), *The Permanence of Yeats;* A. N. Jeffares, *Rev. Eng. Stud.,* XXII (1949), 44–49; Knights, *Explorations* (Stewart, 1947), pp. 202–3; Elder Olson, pp. 290–300 in Hall and Steinmann (eds.), *The Permanence of Yeats;* J. C. Ransom, *Ken. Rev.,* I (1939), 318–20; Stauffer, *The Nature of Poetry* (Norton, 1946), pp. 243–46.

16. *the holy city of Byzantium:* Literally the Holy City of the Eastern Church, Byzantium symbolized for Yeats the realm of art. Yeats wrote in *A Vision* (1937), p. 279: "I think if I could be given a month of Antiquity and leave to spend it where I chose, I would spend it in

Byzantium a little before Justinian opened St. Sophia and closed the Academy of Plato. I think I could find in some little wine-shop some philosophical worker in mosaic who could answer all my questions. . . ."

27–30: In his note to this poem in *Collected Poems* (1933) Yeats wrote: "I have read somewhere that in the Emperor's palace at Byzantium was a tree made of gold and silver, and artificial birds that sang."

THE TOWER

This poem is about Yeats's home, a seventeenth-century Norman tower located next to Lady Gregory's estate in County Galway.
Discussed by J. C. Ransom, pp. 105–7 in Hall and Steinmann (eds.), *The Permanence of Yeats*; D. A. Stauffer, *Ken. Rev.*, XI (1949), 434–35; Rosemond Tuve, *Elizabethan and Metaphysical Imagery* (Chicago: The University of Chicago Press, 1947), pp. 269–71.
9. *Ben Bulben:* A mountain in County Sligo.
12. *Plotinus:* Neo-Platonist of the third century who regarded true reality as abstract.
25. *Mrs. French:* An eighteenth-century lady Yeats had read about in Sir Jonah Barrington's *Sketches of His Own Time* (1827).
34. *a peasant girl:* Mary Hynes, a local beauty celebrated by the blind poet, Raftery.
49. *the man who made the song:* Raftery, blind Irish poet of the mid-nineteenth century.
57. *Hanrahan:* "Possessed" poet and schoolmaster. Yeats had written of the card game described in lines 64–72 in his story, "Red Hanrahan."
65. *bawn:* Barn.
132. *Grattan:* Henry Grattan (1746–1820), Irish champion of independence in British Parliament.
136. *fabulous horn:* Roland, leader of Charlemagne's rear guard, proudly refused to blow his horn when he was cut off at Roncevaux.

TWO SONGS FROM A PLAY

These songs are from Yeats's play, *The Resurrection*.
Discussed by Cleanth Brooks, pp. 75–76 in Hall and Steinmann (eds.). *The Permanence of Yeats*; Ellmann, *Identity of Yeats*, pp. 260–73.
1. *staring virgin:* Athena.
7. *Magnus Annus:* The Great Year, the Platonic Year, a period of approximately two thousand years; a new historical cycle.
9. *Another Troy:* This prophecy recalls Vergil's *Fourth Eclogue* and Shelley's *Chorus from Hellas*.
11. *Argo's painted prow:* The "Argo" was the vessel in which Jason and his Argonauts sailed to obtain the Golden Fleece.
15. *her Star:* Athena's star is Virgo.

AMONG SCHOOL CHILDREN

The background to this poem is described in Hone, *W. B. Yeats*, p. 399.
Discussed in Brooks, *The Well Wrought Urn* (Reynal, 1947), pp. 163–75;
  Richard Chase, "Myth as Literature," pp. 18–21 in Clifford, Kirk,
  Robertson, and Wiggins (eds.), *English Institute Essays, 1947* (New
  York: Columbia University Press, 1948); Hugh Kenner, *Sewanee Rev.*,
  LXIV (1956), 574–90; Arthur Mizener, pp. 158–60 in Hall and Stein-
  mann (eds.), *The Permanence of Yeats*; Delmore Schwartz, pp. 327–29
  in *The Permanence of Yeats*; D. A. Stauffer, *Ken. Rev.*, XI (1949),
  436–37.
15. *Plato's parable:* See Plato's *Symposium.*
26. *Quattrocento:* (Italian) Fifteenth century.
43. *Solider Aristotle:* Aristotle spanked his pupil who was to become
  Alexander the Great.
45. *golden-thighed Pythagoras:* Pre-Socratic philosopher whom Diogenes
  Laertius reported as having a thigh of gold.
47. *What a star sang:* Pythagoras assumed "the music of the spheres."

BYZANTIUM

Discussed in Blackmur, *Form and Value in Modern Poetry* (Anchor
  Books, 1957), pp. 52–53; Cleanth Brooks, pp. 85–92 in Hall and Stein-
  mann (eds.), *The Permanence of Yeats*; Daiches, *Poetry and the Mod-
  ern World* (U. of Chicago Press, 1940), pp. 181–85; Drew and Sweeney,
  Directions in Modern Poetry (Norton, 1940), pp. 166–71; Ellmann,
  Identity of Yeats, pp. 219–22; William Empson, *Ken. Rev.*, XI (1949),
  576–77; A. N. Jeffares, *Rev. Eng. Stud.*, XXII (1946), 49–52; Stauffer,
  Nature of Poetry (Norton, 1946), pp. 172–75.

CRAZY JANE TALKS WITH THE BISHOP

This poem took its origin from the pronouncement of the Bishop of
  Connaught that his people should never read stories about the degrad-
  ing passion of love.
Discussed in Blackmur, *Form and Value in Modern Poetry* (Anchor
  Books, 1957), pp. 76–77; Ellmann, *Identity of Yeats*, pp. 278–79; W. E.
  Houghton, pp. 376–77 in Hall and Steinmann (eds.), *The Permanence
  of Yeats*.
15. *But Love has pitched his mansion in:* Probably an echo of Blake's
  Jerusalem which contains the line: "For I will make their places of love
  and joy excrementitious."

LAPIS LAZULI

Discussed in Ellmann, *Identity of Yeats*, pp. 185–87; A. N. Jeffares, *Mod.
  Lang. Notes*, LXV (1950), 488–91; D. S. Savage, p. 211 in Hall and
  Steinmann (eds.), *The Permanence of Yeats*.

UNDER BEN BULBEN

Discussed in Blackmur, *Form and Value in Modern Poetry* (Anchor Books, 1957), pp. 67–73; C. B. Bradford, *Va. Quart. Rev.*, XXV (1949), 212–14.

25. *Mitchel's prayer:* John Mitchel wrote, "Give us war in our time, O Lord" (*Jail Journal* [Dublin: M. H. Gill, 1913], p. 358).

NEWS FOR THE DELPHIC ORACLE

Yeats here edits the Delphic oracle's report on the destination of Plotinus' soul.

Discussed in Ellmann, *Identity of Yeats*, pp. 284–85; Henn, *The Lonely Tower*, pp. 235–36.

26. *Peleus on Thetis stares:* A description of Poussin's painting, "The Marriage of Peleus and Thetis," which Yeats had seen in the Dublin National Gallery.

Selected Bibliography*

ABBOTT, C. D. (ed.). *Poets at Work*. New York: Harcourt, Brace & Co., Inc., 1948. Essays by Auden, Stauffer, Shapiro, and Arnheim.

BAYLEY, JOHN. *The Romantic Survival*. London: Constable & Co., Ltd., 1957.

BLACKMUR, R. P. *The Double Agent*. New York: Arrow Editions, 1935.

———. *The Expense of Greatness*. New York: Arrow Editions, 1940.

———. *Form and Value in Modern Poetry*. New York: Anchor Books, Doubleday & Co., Inc., 1957.

———. *Language as Gesture*. London: George Allen & Unwin, Ltd., 1954.

BODKIN, MAUD. *Archetypal Patterns in Poetry*. London: Oxford University Press, 1934.

BOGAN, LOUISE. *Achievement in American Poetry*. Chicago: Henry Regnery Co., 1951.

———. *Selected Criticism*. New York: The Noonday Press, 1955.

BOWRA, C. M. *The Background of Modern Poetry*. London: Oxford University Press, 1946.

———. *The Creative Experiment*. London: Macmillan & Co., Ltd., 1949.

———. *The Heritage of Symbolism*. London: Macmillan & Co., Ltd., 1947.

BROOKS, CLEANTH. *Modern Poetry and the Tradition*. Chapel Hill, N.C.: University of North Carolina Press, 1939.

———. *The Well Wrought Urn*. New York: Reynal & Hitchcock, 1947.

BURKE, KENNETH. *Counterstatement*. New York: Harcourt, Brace & Co., Inc., 1931.

COFFMAN, S. K. *Imagism: A Chapter for the History of Modern Poetry*. Norman, Okla.: University of Oklahoma Press, 1951.

DAICHES, DAVID. *Poetry and the Modern World*. Chicago: The University of Chicago Press, 1940.

DEUTSCH, BABETTE. *Poetry in Our Time*. New York: Henry Holt & Co., Inc., 1952.

———. *This Modern Poetry*. New York: W. W. Norton & Co., Inc., 1935.

DREW, ELIZABETH, and SWEENEY, J. L. *Directions in Modern Poetry*. New York: W. W. Norton & Co., Inc., 1940.

ELIOT, T. S. *On Poetry and Poets*. New York: Farrar, Straus & Cudahy, 1957.

* Reference is made in the Notes to the books listed here.

ELIOT, T. S. *The Use of Poetry and the Use of Criticism.* Cambridge, Mass.: Harvard University Press, 1933.

EMPSON, WILLIAM. *Seven Types of Ambiguity,* 2d ed. New York: New Directions, 1947.

FRANKENBURG, LLOYD. *Pleasure Dome.* Boston: Houghton Mifflin Co., 1949.

FRASER, G. S. *The Modern Writer and His World.* London: Derek Verschoyle, 1953.

GREGORY, HORACE, and ZATURENSKA, MARYA. *A History of American Poetry, 1900–1940.* New York: Harcourt, Brace & Co., Inc., 1946.

HULME, T. E. *Further Speculations.* Minneapolis, Minn.: University of Minnesota Press, 1955.

———. *Speculations.* New York: Harcourt, Brace & Co., Inc., 1924.

HYMAN, S. E. *The Armed Vision.* New York: Alfred A. Knopf, Inc., 1948.

ISHERWOOD, CHRISTOPHER. *Lions and Shadows.* London: Hogarth Press, Ltd., 1938.

JARRELL, RANDALL. *Poetry and the Age.* New York: Vintage Books, 1955.

KERMODE, FRANK. *Romantic Image.* London: Routledge & Kegan Paul, Ltd., 1957.

KNIGHTS, L. C. *Explorations: Essays in Criticism.* New York: G. W. Stewart, 1947.

LANGBAUM, ROBERT. *The Poetry of Experience: The Dramatic Monologue in Modern Literary Tradition.* London: Chatto & Windus, 1957.

LEAVIS, F. R. *The Common Pursuit.* London: Chatto & Windus, 1952.

———. *New Bearings in English Poetry.* London: Chatto & Windus, 1932; new ed., 1954.

LEWIS, C. DAY. *A Hope for Poetry.* Oxford: Basil Blackwell, 1934.

———. *The Poetic Image.* London: Oxford University Press, 1947.

LOWELL, AMY. *Tendencies in Modern American Poetry.* New York: The Macmillan Co., 1917.

MONROE, HARRIET. *A Poet's Life.* New York: The Macmillan Co., 1938.

MOORE, MARIANNE. *Predilections.* New York: The Viking Press, Inc., 1955.

O'CONNOR, WILLIAM VAN. *Sense and Sensibility in Modern Poetry.* Chicago: The University of Chicago Press, 1948.

PINTO, VIVIAN DE SOLA. *Crisis in English Poetry, 1880–1940.* London: Hutchinson's University Library, 1951.

QUINN, SISTER M. B. *The Metamorphic Tradition in Modern Poetry.* New Brunswick, N.J.: Rutgers University Press, 1955.

RAIZISS, SONA. *The Metaphysical Passion: Seven Modern American Poets and the Seventeenth-Century Tradition.* Philadelphia, Pa.: University of Pennsylvania Press, 1952.

RANSOM, J. C. "The Poetry of 1900–1950," *Kenyon Review,* XIII (1951), 445–57.

———. *The World's Body.* New York: Charles Scribner's Sons, 1938.

READ, HERBERT. *Form in Modern Poetry.* London: Sheed & Ward, Ltd., 1932.

RICHARDS, I. A. *Practical Criticism*. New York: Harcourt, Brace & Co., Inc., 1929.
———. *Principles of Literary Criticism*. London: Kegan Paul, Trench, Trubner & Co., 1926.
———. *Science and Poetry*. London: Kegan Paul, Trench, Trubner & Co., 1935.
RIDING, LAURA, and GRAVES, ROBERT. *A Survey of Modernist Poetry*. New York: Doubleday, Doran & Co., 1928.
ROBERTS, MICHAEL. *Critique of Poetry*. London: Jonathan Cape, Ltd., 1934.
SAVAGE, D. S. *The Personal Principle: Studies in Modern Poetry*. London: George Routledge & Sons, Ltd., 1944.
SCARFE, FRANCIS. *Auden and After*. London: George Routledge & Sons, Ltd., 1942.
SHAPIRO, KARL. *Beyond Criticism*. Lincoln, Neb.: University of Nebraska Press, 1953.
———. *English Prosody and Modern Poetry*. Baltimore, Md.: The Johns Hopkins Press, 1947.
SITWELL, EDITH. *Aspects of Modern Poetry*. London: Gerald Duckworth & Co., Ltd., 1934.
———. *Poetry and Criticism*. New York: Henry Holt & Co., Inc., 1926.
SPENDER, STEPHEN. *The Creative Element*. London: Hamish Hamilton, 1953.
———. *The Destructive Element*. London: Jonathan Cape, Ltd., 1935.
———. *Poetry since 1939*. London: Longmans, Green & Co., Ltd., 1949.
SPRIGG, C. ST. JOHN (Christopher Caudwell [pseud.]). *Illusion and Reality*. New York: The Macmillan Co., 1937.
STAUFFER, DONALD. *The Nature of Poetry*. New York: W. W. Norton & Co., Inc., 1946.
SYMONS, ARTHUR. *The Symbolist Movement in Literature*. New York: E. P. Dutton & Co., Inc., 1918.
TATE, ALLEN. *The Man of Letters in the Modern World*. New York: Meridian Books, The Noonday Press, 1955.
———. *On the Limits of Poetry*. New York: The Swallow Press, 1948.
———. *Reactionary Essays on Poetry and Ideas*. New York: Charles Scribner's Sons, 1936.
———. *Reason in Madness*. London: Putnam & Co., 1941.
TAUPIN, RENÉ. *L'influence du symbolisme français sur la poésie américaine (de 1910 à 1920)*. Paris: H. Champion, 1929.
TINDALL, W. Y. *Forces in Modern British Literature*. New York: Alfred A. Knopf, Inc., 1947.
TURNELL, MARTIN. *Poetry and Crisis*. London: Sands, The Paladin Press, 1938.
WAGGONER, H. H. *The Heel of Elohim: Science and Values in Modern American Poetry*. Norman, Okla.: University of Oklahoma Press, 1950.

WILDER, A. N. *Modern Poetry and the Christian Tradition*. New York: Charles Scribner's Sons, 1952.

WILSON, EDMUND. *Axel's Castle*. New York: Charles Scribner's Sons, 1931.

WINTERS, YVOR. *In Defense of Reason*. New York: The Swallow Press & William Morrow & Co., Inc., 1947.

———. *The Function of Criticism: Problems and Exercises*. Denver, Col.: Alan Swallow, 1957.

ANTHOLOGIES OF CRITICISM

RANSOM, J. C. (ed.). *The Kenyon Critics*. Cleveland, Ohio: World Publishing Co., 1951.

SCHORER, MARK, *et al.* (eds.). *Criticism*. New York: Harcourt, Brace & Co., Inc., 1948.

STALLMAN, R. W. (ed.). *Critiques and Essays in Criticism*. New York: Ronald Press Co., 1949.

ZABEL, M. D. (ed.). *Literary Opinion in America*, rev. ed. New York: Harper & Bros., 1951.

BIBLIOGRAPHIES

ARMS, GEORGE, and KUNTZ, J. M. *Poetry Explication*. New York: The Swallow Press, 1950.

The Explicator (annual checklists of explication issued each June).

SPILLER, R. E., AND OTHERS (eds.). *Literary History of the United States*, Vol. III. New York: The Macmillan Co., 1948.

MILLETT, F. B. *Contemporary American Authors*. New York: Harcourt, Brace & Co., Inc., 1944.

Modern Humanities Research Association (annual bibliography).

PMLA (annual bibliography issued each April).

TATE, ALLEN (ed.). *Sixty American Poets, 1896–1944*, rev. ed. Washington, D.C.: Library of Congress, 1954.

Twentieth Century Literature (short bibliographies in each number).

Other Important Poets

BRITISH

George Barker (1913–   )
  Collected Poems, 1930–1956
    (1957)
Rupert Brooke (1887–1915)
  Poetical Works (1946; ed. Geof-
    frey Keynes)
Roy Campbell (1902–1957)
  Collected Poems (1957; 2 vols.)
Austin Clarke (1896–   )
  Collected Poems (1936)
  Ancient Lights: Poems and Satires
    (1955)
W. H. Davies (1871–1940)
  Poems (1934)
Sidney Keyes (1922–1943)
  Collected Poems (1946)
Rudyard Kipling (1865–1936)
  A Choice of Kipling's Verse
    (1941; ed. T. S. Eliot)

Philip Larkin (1922–   )
  The Less Deceived (1956)
Alun Lewis (1915–1944)
  Raiders' Dawn and Other Poems
    (1942)
  Ha! Ha! Among the Trumpets
    (1945)
John Masefield (1878–   )
  Poems (1953)
Edwin Muir (1887–   )
  Collected Poems, 1921–1951
    (1952)
Kathleen Raine (1908–   )
  Collected Poems (1956)
Herbert Read (1893–   )
  Collected Poems (1953)
  *Moon's Farm, and Poems Mostly
    Elegiac* (1955)
Edward Thomas (1878–1917)
  Collected Poems (1920)

AMERICAN

Conrad Aiken (1889–   )
  Collected Poems (1953)
Elizabeth Bishop (1911–   )
  North & South (1946)
  Poems (1955)

Louise Bogan (1897–   )
  Collected Poems (1954)
Richard Eberhart (1904–   )
  Reading the Spirit (1936)
  Song and Idea (1940)
  Burr Oaks (1947)

Undercliff: Poems, 1946–1953
(1953)
Selected Poems (1951)

Robert Fitzgerald (1910–   )
The Alcestis of Euripides (1936;
with Dudley Fitts; a translation)
A Wreath for the Sea (1943)
In the Rose of Time (1956)

Vachel Lindsay (1879–1931)
Collected Poems (1923)

Edgar Lee Masters (1869–1950)
Spoon River Anthology (1915)
Domesday Book (1920)
The New Spoon River (1924)
The Fate of the Jury (1929)
Selected Poems (1925)

Edna St. Vincent Millay (1892–
1950)
Collected Poems (1956)

Carl Sandburg (1878–   )
Complete Poems (1950)

Delmore Schwartz (1913–   )
In Dreams Begin Responsibilities
(1938)
Shenandoah (1941)
Genesis (1943)

Vaudeville for a Princess (1950)

Allen Tate (1899–   )
Mr. Pope and Other Poems (1928)
Poems, 1928–1931 (1932)
The Winter Sea (1945)
Selected Poems (1937)
Poems, 1922–1947 (1948)

Robert Penn Warren (1905–   )
Thirty-Six Poems (1935)
Eleven Poems on the Same Theme
(1942)
Brother to Dragons (1953)
Promises: Poems, 1954–1956
(1957)
Selected Poems (1944)

Richard Wilbur (1921–   )
*The Beautiful Changes and
Other Poems* (1947)
Ceremony and Other Poems
(1950)
A Bestiary (1955)
The Misanthrope (1955; a trans-
lation)
Things of This World (1956)

Elinor Wylie (1885–1928)
Collected Poems (1932)
Last Poems (1943)

INDEXES

Index of Authors and Titles

Index of First Lines

A